Also by John Toland

ADOLF HITLER

BATTLE: THE STORY OF THE BULGE

THE RISING SUN

THE LAST HUNDRED DAYS

But Not In Shame

by John Toland

March, 1942. With ponderous grace the Flying Fortress touched down at Alice Springs, Australia, where the American general was met by reporters. When they asked him for a statement, he quickly scribbled a few lines on the back of a used envelope:

> "The President of the United States ordered me to break through the Japanese lines and proceed from Corregidor to Australia for the purpose, as I understand it, of organizing the American offensive against Japan, a primary object of which is the relief of the Philippines.

> *"I came through and I shall return."*

John Toland

BUT NOT IN SHAME

The Six Months After Pearl Harbor

BALLANTINE BOOKS • NEW YORK

TO TOSHIKO

Table of Contents

List of Maps

Perhaps the most controversial six months in American history started on December 7, 1941. Even now, after almost twenty years, many issues of those days are still alive and many others have remained buried because of their highly controversial nature: Why did Japan declare war on a nation as powerful as the U.S.? Did Roosevelt use Pearl Harbor as bait to lure the Japanese into war? Why was half of Mac-Arthur's air force caught on the ground at Clark Field by Japanese bombers ten hours after Pearl Harbor? Why did Singapore's vaunted defenses fall apart so abruptly? What caused the crushing Allied defeat in the Battle of Java Sea? Did Roosevelt and Marshall stab MacArthur in the back in the Philippines? What were the true facts behind the two greatest surrenders in American military history, at Bataan and Corregidor? Did the Japanese plan the murder of thousands of American and Filipino prisoners in the "Death March"? What were the mistakes that brought disaster to the Japanese at Midway?

This epochal six months also gave birth to a number of myths. Many Americans still believe Captain Colin Kelly sank a Japanese battleship, that thousands of Japanese spies infested Hawaii in 1941, that Major Jimmy Devereux radioed from Wake: SEND US MORE JAPS.

No segment of World War II was more colored by American and British politics than this period of steady, alarming defeats in the Pacific. Consequently the truth was often clouded over by polemic and political expediency. This book attempts to tell what actually happened, to record the stories —some of them untold—of America's most humiliating six months. It is based primarily on hundreds of interviews in eight countries with generals, privates, admirals, seamen, civilians. These included Admirals Kichisaburo Nomura, Raymond Spruance, Chester Nimitz and Frank Jack Fletcher; and Generals Albert Jones, Clifford Bluemel, Minoru Genda and Carlos Romulo. General Akira Nara, after years of silence, told the inside story of the first Japanese breakthrough in Bataan. Former President Sergio Osmeña disclosed at last the mystery of Philippine collaborationists. General

Bradford Chynoweth and Colonels John Horan and Jesse Traywick uncovered the details of the "strange surrenders" in the Philippines.

This book is further based on many new documents and manuscripts. Mrs. Masaharu Homma, for example, finally allowed her husband's diary and last letters to be read. Historians in many parts of the world generously contributed their knowledge. Officials of all the countries involved also helped unravel the tangled web of facts. This book could not have been written without the full cooperation of the U.S. Departments of Defense, Army, Navy and Air Force; the governments of he Republics of the Philippines and China; and Japan's official war historians.

"WITH DANGEROUS AND DRAMATIC SUDDENNESS"

On December 6, 1941, official Washington circles were waiting for the Tokyo reply to Secretary of State Cordell Hull's strong note of November 26. It could mean continued uneasy peace—or sudden war between Japan and the United States.

Tension was highest at the Japanese Embassy on Massachusetts Avenue where the following three-part message had just been received from Foreign Minister Shigenori Togo:

1. THE GOVERNMENT HAS DELIBERATED DEEPLY ON THE AMERICAN PROPOSAL OF THE 26TH OF NOVEMBER AND AS A RESULT WE HAVE DRAWN UP A MEMORANDUM FOR THE UNITED STATES CONTAINED IN MY SEPARATE MESSAGE NO. 902B.

2. THIS SEPARATE MESSAGE IS A VERY LONG ONE. I WILL SEND IT IN FOURTEEN PARTS AND I IMAGINE YOU WILL RECEIVE IT TOMORROW. HOWEVER, I AM NOT SURE. THE SITUATION IS EXTREMELY DELICATE, AND WHEN YOU RECEIVE IT I WANT YOU TO PLEASE KEEP IT SECRET FOR THE TIME BEING.

3. CONCERNING THE TIME OF PRESENTING THIS MEMORANDUM TO THE UNITED STATES, I WILL WIRE YOU IN A SEPARATE MESSAGE. HOWEVER, I WANT YOU IN THE MEANTIME TO PUT IT IN NICELY DRAFTED FORM AND MAKE EVERY PREPARATION TO PRESENT IT TO THE AMERICANS JUST AS SOON AS YOU RECEIVE INSTRUCTIONS.

The steps leading to this fateful day began in the late summer of 1940. Germany had overrun Belgium, Holland and France with ridiculous ease and apparently would soon conquer England. On the other side of the world, Japan was bogged down in her seemingly endless undeclared war on China. Only two great powers in the world were at peace, America and Russia.

The U.S. was widely split. The interventionists, led by President Franklin D. Roosevelt, were convinced their country's future and ultimate safety depended on helping the democracies crush the aggressor nations. Supporting them were the "Bundles for Britain" group and national minorities whose European relatives had suffered at the hands of Hitler and Mussolini.

Their more numerous anti-war opponents included strange bedfellows: the "America Firsters" of Charles Lindbergh, Senator Borah and the German-American Bund; the "American Peace Mobilization" of the American Communist and Labor Parties; and the traditionally isolationist Midwest which, though sympathetic to Great Britain and China, wanted no part of a shooting war.

When Roosevelt, on September 3, traded fifty old destroyers to the beleaguered British for bases, the more rabid isolationists claimed this was merely a stratagem to lead America into war through the back door. The situation worsened on September 27, when Japan formally joined the Axis. A Tripartite Pact was signed, recognizing "the leadership of Japan in the establishment of a New Order in Greater East Asia," and Hitler and Mussolini's "New Order in Europe." Each promised to help if one of the others was "attacked by a Power at present not involved in the European war or in the Chinese-Japanese conflict."

The pact, by its veiled threat of a two-ocean war, was designed to keep the U.S. neutral. It had the opposite effect. Many Americans hovering indecisively between isolationism and intervention were now forced to agree with Roosevelt that these newly united aggressors were a direct menace to the United States. By March 10, 1941, Roosevelt had gained enough new supporters to pass the Lend-Lease Act. America was at last committed to giving unlimited aid, "short of war," to the enemies of the Axis. She was to be the Arsenal of Democracy.

Little more than three months later, on June 22, Hitler shook the world, including his Axis partners, by suddenly invading Russia. This move wrecked the already greatly weakened isolationist movement in the U.S. Instantly the American Peace Mobilization, basically sympathetic to Russia, died, its followers becoming more interventionist than Roosevelt overnight.

The attack also caused a great commotion among Japan's

ruling circles. One group favored an immediate attack on Siberia, but the Army disagreed. Although most of its key moves in the preceding five years had been dominated by fear of the growing strength of Communism, General Hideki Tojo, war minister in the Konoye Cabinet, felt this was a dangerous adventure. He pressed for a drive toward Southeast Asia—the fabulous storehouse of tin, rubber and oil.

While Hitler was amazing the world with his early victories in Russia, Japan suddenly seized Indo-China on July 25, in a bloodless coup. Now there was only one great power at peace—America. And on July 26, she took a bold step up to the very brink of war when Roosevelt, against the advice of the Navy's planning chief who feared it might lead to early hostilities, froze all Japanese assets in the United States. It was an economic blitzkrieg. At one stroke, the bulk of the flow of oil, the lifeblood of battle, was shut off from Japan.

The reaction there was bitter. Japan was a dynamic country of 74,000,000 people crammed into islands whose total area was less than the size of California. Just as every dynamic country before her she felt she must either expand or deteriorate into a poverty-stricken second-class power. Why, argued her leaders, was America being so self-righteous about the China Incident when the Western world, including herself, had been setting the example of plunder in the Orient for a century?

Spurred by extremists on both sides, relations between the two countries were quickly approaching a dangerous point. The Japanese military leaders felt the negotiations for agreement being discussed in Washington by Ambassador Kichisaburo Nomura and Secretary of State Hull had less than an even chance of success. They insisted that a definite date of war with America be set. Japan's oil reserves were shrinking dangerously.

To solve this problem, an Imperial Conference was called in Tokyo on September 6. At the beginning of the session, Admiral Osami Nagano, chief of the Naval General Staff, solemnly said, "Japan is facing shortages in every field, especially in materials. In a word, Japan is becoming emaciated, while her opponent is growing stronger."

Baron Yoshimichi Hara, president of the Privy Council and a leader of Japanese conservative thought, worriedly asked the High Command to clarify the apparent subordination of diplomacy to preparations for war.

Suddenly Emperor Hirohito, who had been sitting in traditional silence, spoke. He regretted the Army and Navy hadn't made their attitude fully clear. As the others listened in shocked silence he read an ode written by his grandfather, the Emperor Meiji:

> When all the earth's oceans are one,
> Why do the waves seethe and the winds rage?

"I have always read and appreciated this poem, and kept in my heart the Emperor Meiji's spirit of peace. It has been my wish to perpetuate this spirit."

There was a long silence. Nagano rose. "I feel trepidation at the Emperor's censure of the High Command. I assure Your Majesty that the High Command places major importance upon diplomatic negotiations and will appeal to arms only at the last moment."

Then an Outline of National Policy was placed before the Conference: Japan should continue to exhaust diplomatic measures to attain her demands; but if these negotiations dragged on inconclusively, war should be declared on the U.S. and Britain. In other words, hope for peace but prepare for war before the end of 1941. The fuse was lit. Only a diplomatic miracle could snuff it out.

The talks in Washington between Nomura and Hull continued inconclusively for another month. Hull kept insisting that Japan break with the Axis and withdraw troops from China. In desperation the moderates in Japan suggested a compromise—withdrawal of troops over a period of years. The militarists were adamant. Their spokesman, General Tojo, said, "We can accept no compromise on principle. After all the sacrifices we have made in China the Army won't agree to any withdrawals. Army morale would not survive it."

Premier Hidemaro Konoye, a harried man, could no longer control the situation. On October 12, he called his key ministers to an emergency meeting at his home in Tekigaiso. "What hopes do you have of bringing war with the United States and Britain to a close once you begin it?" he asked General Tojo. America, he pointed out, was obviously superior in resources.

"There was no certainty of victory in the war with Russia in 1904," replied Tojo, a dynamic and dedicated samurai warrior. "The Premier of Japan should have enough courage to jump off the veranda of the Kiyomizu Temple!" Since this Kyoto temple stood at the edge of a cliff, he meant Prince Konoye should have the courage to take a chance.

In four days the ineffectual Konoye resigned. And on October 18 a man of decision was made the new prime minister—Hideki Tojo. The spirit of nationalism never blazed higher. The people of Japan began to believe it was their duty to build a new world based on moral principles. The damage done by Western concepts of individualism and materialism must be undone. It was, they were told over and over again, Japan's destiny to return Asia to the Asians.

Two weeks later Joseph Grew, U.S. ambassador to Japan, warned Hull of the explosive atmosphere. Because of their emotional character, he wrote, the Japanese might chance an "all-out, do-or-die attempt, actually risking national hara-kiri. . . . While national sanity dictates against such action, Japanese sanity cannot be measured by American standards of logic. . . . Action by Japan which might render unavoidable an armed conflict with the United States may come with dangerous and dramatic suddenness."

On November 26, little more than three weeks after getting this letter, Hull handed a note to Admiral Nomura and Saburo Kurusu, a diplomat recently sent to help the ambassador in the delicate negotiations. It was an answer to a note from Tokyo offering to remove troops from Indo-China if the U.S. would unfreeze Japanese assets and hand over a required quantity of oil.

Although Hull offered economic concessions that might well have eventually given Japan everything she needed for national prosperity, he insisted categorically that all troops be withdrawn from China as well as Indo-China.

After reading Hull's note, the two Japanese were dismayed. "When we report your answer to our government," said Kurusu, "it will be likely to throw up its hands." After a futile argument with the American, Kurusu said dejectedly, "Your response to our proposal can be interpreted as tantamount to meaning the end. Aren't you interested in a *modus vivendi,* a truce?"

"We have explored that," said Hull.

"Is it because other powers would not agree?" asked Kurusu. It was common knowledge in diplomatic circles that China and Great Britain were strongly advising America to take an uncompromising stand with Japan.

"I've done my best in the way of exploration," said Hull.

The interview was over. The two Japanese returned to their embassy. Nomura knew Tokyo would regard the note as an ultimatum, even though it was by no means that. It would mean the failure of his mission to America.

This was the situation on December 6, 1941, as informed

circles in Washington awaited Tokyo's answer to Hull's "ultimatum."

Early that afternoon, while most of the Japanese staff was attending a luncheon party at the Mayflower Hotel, the long-awaited message began to come in on the Tokyo-Washington circuit. Since this, like all other Japanese messages, was obviously being monitored by U.S. agents, it was in the diplomatic "Purple Code."

By 3:00 P.M. in another part of Washington, men from the Communications Security Group of the U.S. Division of Naval Intelligence were studying the same message. Theirs was the greatest secret in American military history. Four months previously a team of Army cryptanalysts, led by a retired lieutenant colonel, William F. Friedman, had broken the Purple Code.

PART 1

TIMETABLE FOR CONQUEST

1

"Climb Mt. Niitaka"

1 At the Japanese Embassy on Massachusetts Avenue, the Tokyo-to-Washington circuit was silent. Thirteen parts of the long message had come in, but the last, the fourteenth, would not arrive until the next morning, December 7. It was now late Saturday afternoon and the decoders decided to quit work although only part-way through the job of deciphering. They figured the note wouldn't be handed to Secretary Hull until Monday.

First Secretary Katsuzo Okumura was personally typing out the decoded parts. It was too secret for any stenographer. When he finished the copy on hand, he went to the basement to relax. It was a typical dead Saturday afternoon and the subterranean playroom was almost deserted. Two correspondents were playing ping-pong. One of these, Masuo Kato from Domei, laid down his paddle. He wanted to pump the first secretary about the liner, *Tatsuta Maru,* which had left Yokohama on December 2, and was due to reach Los Angeles on the fourteenth. Most of the small Japanese community expected to sail home on this ship since trouble was sure to come soon.

"I'll bet you a dollar the liner never gets here," said Okumura mysteriously.

They shook hands to seal the bet. Kato ate at a Chinese restaurant near Union Station and then decided to check in at the Domei news agency. While going up to his office in an

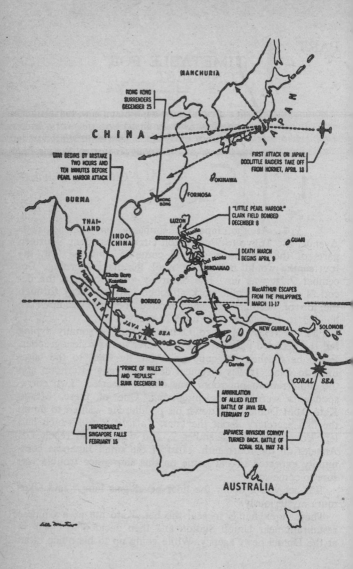

MANCHURIA

HONG KONG
SURRENDERS
DECEMBER 25

CHINA

JAPAN

FIRST ATTACK ON JAPAN.
DOOLITTLE RAIDERS TAKE OFF
FROM HORNET, APRIL 18

WAR BEGINS BY MISTAKE
TWO HOURS AND
TEN MINUTES BEFORE
PEARL HARBOR ATTACK

OKINAWA

BURMA

FORMOSA

THAILAND

HONG
KONG

"LITTLE PEARL HARBOR,"
CLARK FIELD BOMBED
DECEMBER 8

INDO-
CHINA

LUZON

Manila

GUAM

MALAY PENINSULA

Kota Baru
Kuantan

Corregidor

Bataan

DEATH MARCH
BEGINS APRIL 9

MINDANAO

BORNEO

MacARTHUR ESCAPES
FROM THE PHILIPPINES,
MARCH 11-17

SUMATRA

JAVA
SEA

JAVA

NEW GUINEA

SOLOMON
IS.

Darwin

CORAL
SEA

"PRINCE OF WALES"
AND "REPULSE"
SUNK DECEMBER 10

ANNIHILATION
OF ALLIED FLEET
BATTLE OF JAVA SEA,
FEBRUARY 27

JAPANESE INVASION CONVOY
TURNED BACK, BATTLE OF
CORAL SEA, MAY 7-8

"IMPREGNABLE"
SINGAPORE FALLS
FEBRUARY 15

AUSTRALIA

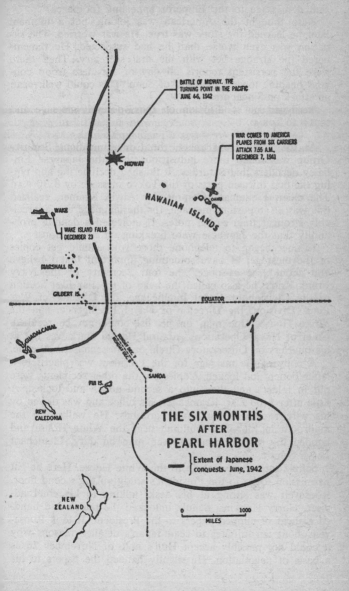

BATTLE OF MIDWAY. THE
TURNING POINT IN THE PACIFIC
JUNE 4-6, 1942

WAR COMES TO AMERICA
PLANES FROM SIX CARRIERS
ATTACK 7:55 A.M.
DECEMBER 7, 1941

MIDWAY

HAWAIIAN ISLANDS

OAHU

WAKE

WAKE ISLAND FALLS
DECEMBER 23

MARSHALL IS.

GILBERT IS.

EQUATOR

GUADALCANAL

BISMARK, DEC. 1
DOWMAP, DEC. 8

SAMOA

FIJI IS.

NEW
CALEDONIA

THE SIX MONTHS
AFTER
PEARL HARBOR

—— Extent of Japanese
conquests. June, 1942

0   1000
MILES

N

NEW
ZEALAND

elevator, an INS reporter said, "Did you know the President sent a message to the Emperor appealing for peace?"

Kato thought the American was joking, but a moment later he learned the story was true. He was worried. The situation was even worse than he had suspected. He remembered the strange bet with the first secretary. Then there were the persistent reports all day of Japanese troop convoys heading toward the Gulf of Siam. This could well mean an attack on Singapore.

He typed out a dispatch on the Roosevelt message and sent it to Tokyo.

At the Navy Department, the Communications Security Group was much more industrious than the Japanese Embassy decoders that Saturday. It finished deciphering and typing the first thirteen parts of the Tokyo message by 8:30 P.M. The chief, Lieutenant Commander Alwin Kramer, realized this was an important message, for the language was appreciably stronger than earlier notes. It indicated a definite probability that the Japanese were breaking off negotiations.

Kramer began to telephone those who should get copies of the message. "I have something important that I believe you should see at once," he told Secretary of the Navy Frank Knox; he also called the head of the Far East Section of the Division of Naval Intelligence, the Director of War Plans Division, the Director of Naval Intelligence, and the White House. One man on his list could not be reached. Chief of Naval Operations Admiral Harold Stark was not at his quarters on Observatory Circle on Massachusetts Avenue.

A copy of the message for the President was placed in a letter pouch and locked. Copies for the other recipients were put in folders and then into a second pouch and locked. A little after 9:00 P.M. Kramer left his office and was driven by his wife to the White House grounds. He walked to the mailroom in the office building near the White House and handed the smaller pouch to the man on duty, Lieutenant Lester Schulz.

Schulz took the pouch in to the White House. Here he got permission to go to the President's study on the second floor. Roosevelt was sitting at his desk, talking to his chief adviser, Harry Hopkins. Schulz unlocked the pouch and handed a sheaf of clipped papers to the President. It took Roosevelt about ten minutes to read Japan's detailed reasons why it could not possibly accept Hull's note of November 26 as a basis of negotiation. He silently handed the papers to his adviser. When Hopkins finished reading, Roosevelt said, "This means war."

While Schulz waited they talked of the deployment of Japanese forces. Roosevelt mentioned a radiogram he had sent earlier that day to Emperor Hirohito requesting the withdrawal of troops from Indo-China. A troop convoy was now heading from there to the Gulf of Siam. Where was this invasion force bound?

"Since war is undoubtedly going to come at the convenience of the Japanese," said Hopkins, "it's too bad we can't strike the first blow."

"No, we can't do that," said Roosevelt. "We are a democracy and a peaceful people." He raised his voice. "But we have a good record." Then he said he was going to call Admiral "Betty" Stark. He reached for the phone and asked to be connected with the Chief of Naval Operations. The White House operator said the Admiral could be reached at the National Theatre. Roosevelt put the phone down. "I'll call Betty later; I don't want to cause public alarm by having him paged in a theatre."

The President returned the papers to Schulz, who left the room. It was the most grievous dilemma of Roosevelt's entire career. The Japanese were about to attack British or Dutch possessions. What should—or could—be done? The British and Dutch were too weak to defend themselves. Without U.S. intervention the Japanese could carve out an empire from the Aleutian Islands to India. But the American people were in no mood for war. The Draft Bill had passed four months previously by the margin of a single vote. He remembered what he'd recently told Churchill when asked to get into the war. "If I were to ask Congress to declare war, they might argue about it for three months."

Americans, he was positive, would not go to war to save Singapore or Java or even Australia.

Admiral Stark was trying to get some relaxation after months of tension. He was watching *The Student Prince*. But it made little impression on him. Later he wouldn't even remember where he'd been on the night of December 6. His mind was still on the Far East crisis. On November 27, although he had not yet read Hull's strong note of the previous day, he was so sure Japan would strike in retaliation he had sent an unprecedented message to commanders in Hawaii and the Philippines:

THIS DISPATCH IS TO BE CONSIDERED A WAR WARNING.

NEGOTIATIONS WITH JAPAN LOOKING TOWARD STABILIZA-
TION OF CONDITIONS IN THE PACIFIC HAVE CEASED. AN
AGGRESSIVE MOVE BY JAPAN IS EXPECTED WITHIN THE
NEXT FEW DAYS. EXECUTE AN APPROPRIATE DEFENSIVE
DEPLOYMENT PREPARATORY TO CARRYING OUT THE TASKS
ASSIGNED IN WPL-46 [THE WAR PLAN].

What puzzled him, as well as his opposite number in the
Army, General George Marshall, was where the attack would
come. The troop convoy nearing the Gulf of Siam suggested
Singapore, but it could come in the Philippines or even the
Panama Canal. In Hawaii, at least, American defenses were
formidable and prepared. In fact, Stark had been so pleased
with the Joint Army-Navy Hawaiian Defense Plan for protection of the Pearl Harbor base against a surprise Japanese
air attack that he had sent it to all his district commanders
as a model.

Just before midnight, Commander Kramer, still chauf-
feured by his wife, drove up to the Arlington home of Rear
Admiral T. S. Wilkinson, Director of Naval Intelligence.
The Admiral was entertaining Captain Beardall, Roosevelt's
naval aide, and Major General Sherman Miles, Chief of Army
Intelligence. All three read the message. They agreed that it
certainly looked as though the Japanese were terminating negotiations.

Kramer, his messenger duties over, now returned the copies of the message to the safe in his office. Then he asked the
watch officer if the fourteenth part had come in. When he
was told that nothing even looking as if it might be the
fourteenth part had been intercepted as yet, the industrious
Kramer at last started for home.

It was just before 1:00 A.M., December 7. Many high of-
ficials were still awake in Washington, wondering when the
Japanese would jump, and where. Not one—Roosevelt, Hull,
Stimson, Knox, Marshall or Stark—expected it could be Pearl
Harbor.

    2   It was then almost 7:30 P.M., December 6, in
Hawaii. Here, as in Washington, there was fear of an early
war. One of the main topics of dinner conversation was
Roosevelt's unprecedented appeal to Emperor Hirohito. The
Star-Bulletin had two conflicting front-page headlines. One
read: JAP PRESS ASKS FOR WAR and the other: NEW PEACE RE-
PORT URGED IN TOKYO. Even if war came, few in the islands
had doubt of the issue. Everyone agreed with the United

States Senator who, on page ten of the same paper, was quoted as telling an AP reporter that, "The United States Navy can defeat the Japanese Navy any place, any time."

Like Marshall and Stark, the Army and Navy commanders of Hawaii were not at all worried about an air attack on Pearl Harbor. Lieutenant General Walter Short, commanding the Hawaiian Department, had received a message from Marshall similar to the war warning Stark had sent Admiral Husband E. Kimmel, commander of the Pacific Fleet. It wasn't as sharp as the Navy message but it did warn of possible "hostile action at any moment." At the same time, Short received another message, this from Army Intelligence.

JAPANESE NEGOTIATIONS HAVE COME TO PRACTICAL STALEMATE. HOSTILITIES MAY ENSUE. SUBVERSIVE ACTIVITIES MAY BE EXPECTED.

To Short this meant one thing: sabotage from Hawaii's 157,905 Japanese civilians. He reported to Washington that he was alerting the Army for sabotage. And when he got no answer, assumed he had taken all action necessary.

At the moment the general was on the *lanai* of his home at Fort Shafter holding an emergency meeting with his intelligence officer, Lieutenant Colonel Kendall Fielder, and his counterintelligence officer, Lieutenant Colonel George Bicknell. The latter had just brought the transcript of a telephone conversation monitored by the FBI from a local Japanese dentist to a Tokyo paper, *Yomiuri Shimbun*. Its editor wondered about things in general in Hawaii: planes, searchlights, weather, even the flowers. In reply to this last question the dentist-correspondent had said the hibiscus and poinsettia were in bloom.

The three officers were puzzled. Was it code? If so, why talk so openly about obvious military objects? Yet, why spend money talking about hibiscus? They had already probed the matter for almost an hour. And all this time the wives of the general and Colonel Fielder were waiting impatiently outside in a car. Short finally said nothing could be done until morning and he and Fielder joined the ladies. They would have to hurry. It was 15 miles to the Schofield Barracks Officers Club, which was putting on a special benefit show that Saturday night.

Most of the high-ranking naval officers were also spending an evening of relaxation. Vice Admiral Fairfax Leary was giving a dinner party at Honolulu's "House Without a

Key." Kimmel was there but, as usual, his chief of staff, Vice Admiral W. W. "Poco" Smith couldn't get him to relax. Kimmel was a dynamic, energetic man who was only content when working. At 9:30 P.M. Kimmel excused himself, after drinking his customary single cocktail and making the necessary small talk. He wanted to get to bed. Though there was some gossip that he and his Army counterpart, General Short, were not on speaking terms, they had a date to play golf the next morning. It would be one of the rare Sundays Kimmel didn't spend at his desk. He knew the mighty Pacific Fleet was the keystone of American defenses in the Far East. The responsibility weighed so heavily on him he had left his wife to whom he was devoted on the mainland so he could concentrate completely on work.

Both Kimmel and Short were faced with the same dilemma. Hawaii was not only an outpost but a training command. If they ordered a state of constant alert, men and material would be exhausted. Besides, the warnings from Washington hadn't specifically stated or implied that an air attack on Pearl Harbor was even a remote possibility. Influenced by this reasoning, both men decided to compromise. Kimmel was prepared for submarine attacks; Short was ready for saboteurs. But the Joint Army-Navy Hawaiian Defense Plan —the one so admired by Admiral Stark—was not in effect on the night of December 6. In fact, normal peacetime liberty had been granted to men and officers that evening.

Nothing but routine and limited air patrols were being planned for the next morning; Army and Navy anti-aircraft batteries protecting Pearl Harbor were lightly manned. Moored at this great base was the principal obstacle of any further Japanese invasion: the Pacific Fleet, 94 ships including 8 battleships and 9 cruisers. Most of the men, except the watch crews, were getting ready for bed. It was just another beautiful but uneventful tropical evening.

The only extraordinary precautions taken that night were at the Army airfields. Planes were bunched together neatly on runways so they could be protected by cordons of guards. Actually there was not the slightest danger from saboteurs. In all Hawaii there was only one Japanese Navy spy, a brusque, hot-tempered, young ensign, Takeo Yoshikawa. Except for one Nisei girl—and her help had proved worthless—the large Japanese community in the islands had refused to cooperate with him. To his surprise they considered themselves loyal Americans. It didn't make sense to him; many still worshipped at Buddhist temples and Shinto shrines and had contributed generously to the Imperial Army's relief fund.

Gossiping with American sailors had been just as fruitless. They talked a lot but said nothing. What information he got was by simple, unexciting methods. He walked almost every day through Pearl City to the end of the peninsula and scanned Battleship Row; he swam at every available beach, observing underwater obstructions and noting the tides; and most important, he sat on straw *tatami* mats with geisha girls—sometimes Shimeka, sometimes Marichyo—in the Shunchoro, a Japanese restaurant located on a hill overlooking Pearl Harbor, and drew diagrams of the ships in the big base. Once he allowed the geishas to persuade him to take them on a sightseeing air tour over Oahu. The pilot never noticed Yoshikawa—dressed in loud aloha shirt and flanked by pretty, excited girls—as he observed atmospheric conditions and took photos of military airfields.

He was getting no outside help at all. Once he had given a Nazi agent using the cover name of Karama (his real name was Bernard Kuehn) a final payment of $17,000 to signal information to Japanese submarines. But as yet the German had not transmitted a single message. All the information sent to Tokyo so far had cost only $600—the amount given Yoshikawa for expenses when he first arrived.

That night, he was working late at the Japanese Consulate in Honolulu. Here he posed as a vice-consul named Tadashi Morimura. Earlier he had radioed Tokyo in diplomatic code that there still were no barrage balloons over Pearl Harbor. Now he was at his desk writing another message in pencil: ENTERPRISE AND LEXINGTON HAVE SAILED FROM PEARL HARBOR.

He buzzed for the radio-room code clerk, gave him the message and then went for a stroll around the Consulate grounds. In the distance he could see a bright haze over Pearl Harbor. He could hear no patrol planes. Though he was restless, he started for home. He wanted to get up in time to hear the Sunday morning broadcast from Radio Tokyo. If the weather forecast, *higashi no kaze, ame* (east wind, rain), appeared both in the middle and the end of the broadcast, this meant Japanese-American relations were in danger, war was coming.

The *Tatsuta Maru,* the liner scheduled to land in Los Angeles on December 14, was supposed to be near Honolulu at that moment. But it had suddenly, and without explanation to its passengers, sharply swung off course. It was returning to Japan.

3 The lone-wolf spy in Hawaii had sent the correct information to Tokyo. Both of Kimmel's carriers were at sea. Task Force Twelve, including the *Lexington,* was delivering planes to Midway. Task Force Eight—the carrier *Enterprise,* 3 cruisers and 9 destroyers—was about 500 miles west of Hawaii. Commanded by Vice Admiral William Halsey, Jr. ("Bull" to the newspapers but "Bill" to his friends), it had delivered 12 Grumman Wildcats and their Marine fighter pilots to Wake Island three days before and was now heading for home. The *Enterprise* was a day behind schedule because of bad weather. Many of the men were griping because they'd missed Saturday night in Honolulu. Instead of enjoying themselves in port they were watching a movie about World War I, *Sergeant York.* Thought of a new war was far from most of their minds, even though Halsey had told the crew, "At any time, day or night, we must be ready for instant action."

Up in the sea cabin, Halsey was waiting for a war he knew was about to explode. Admiral Kimmel had impressed on him when he left Pearl Harbor on November 28 how important the planes were for the defense of Wake. And they had to be delivered with absolute secrecy. It was imperative that the Japanese be kept ignorant of the move.

"How far do you want me to go?" Halsey had asked.

"Goddamit," replied Kimmel, "use your common sense."

As soon as they were at sea, Halsey issued Battle Order No. 1 putting the *Enterprise* under war conditions. He ordered warheads placed on torpedoes, all planes armed with bombs or torpedoes, and pilots to sink any shipping or plane sighted.

When his operations officer, Commander William Buracker, saw this order he asked incredulously, "Admiral, did you authorize this thing?"

"Yes."

"Goddamit, sir, you can't start a private war of your own. Who's going to take the responsibility?"

"I'll take it. If anything gets in my way, we'll shoot first and argue afterwards."

After dinner that same night, Major Paul Putnam, commander of the 12 Grummans, had cornered Halsey. "I know I'm on my way to Wake, but what in the hell am I supposed to do when I get there?" He only knew that he had been ordered to fly half of Marine Fighting Squadron 211 onto the *Enterprise* and then proceed to Wake. It had to appear like a routine weekend exercise and most of his men carried only an extra pair of skivvies (shorts) and a toothbrush.

"Putnam, your instructions are to do what seems appropriate when you get to Wake. You're there under my direct and personal orders and will not report for duty to the island commander." Halsey held out his hand. "Have a pleasant cruise."

Now, 1500 miles west of the Hawaii-bound Halsey task force, Putnam and his fliers were on Wake Island. Here, because of the international date line, it was already the evening of December 7. The Marine commander had learned that his 12 planes were the only air defense of an extremely important island bastion. Yet he and his men had had only a few hours flying time in the stubby Wildcats.

Also on the island were 70 employees of Pan-American Airways, 1146 civilian construction workers, 69 Navy men, an Army Communication detail of 6, and 388 combat Marines, under Major James Devereux. In addition to the handful of planes, the island's only other defenses were 6 5-inch guns, 12 3-inch anti-aircraft guns, a few machine guns and Browning automatic rifles—and about 400 rifles.

Major Devereux had been told the mission of his Marines was merely to stand off a "minor raid." Today, for the first time in two months, he had given the men a holiday. They fished, swam and gambled. As Devereux walked to his tent to turn in he remembered the previous January when sudden overseas orders had arrived. He had told his brother, Ashton, that he guessed he was bound for "some little spitkit of an island." And when Ashton asked what would happen to him, Devereux had said, "Your guess is as good as mine—but I'll probably wind up eating fish and rice."

    4 That moment in Manila it was 5:00 P.M., December 7. It had been a hot, clear day. Here, as in the rest of the Philippines, there was a lively awareness that war was imminent. Only the time of attack was in question. Admiral Thomas Hart, commander of the Asiatic Fleet, insisted it might come any day. General Douglas MacArthur, commander of the United States Armed Forces of the Far East (USAFFE), was hoping hostilities would not start before April, 1942. By this date he had been assured that all necessary reinforcements from the United States would have arrived. MacArthur refused to be panicked, even though strange aircraft had been reported over nearby Clark Field, the main bomber base, four nights in a row.

He also discounted a warning which had come from Master Sergeant Lorenzo Alvarado, a United States secret service agent since 1917. Alvarado, fifteen days before, had attended a secret meeting of the "Legionarios Del Trabajo," an underground organization, at the Triangulo Studio on Rizal Street. Shiki Souy, the Japanese owner of the studio, told his fellow conspirators that 100 Japanese ships and many planes were then in Formosa and would soon invade the Philippines.

That night Admiral Hart was more than ever convinced that a crisis was approaching. For months the Asiatic Fleet chief had been telling his commanders that war was on the way. That was why his small fleet—1 heavy cruiser, 1 light cruiser, 13 World War I four-stack destroyers and 29 submarines—was ready for action. Ammunition was in the racks, warheads were on the torpedoes, Manila and Subic Bays were mined, and the fleet was dispersed from Manila Bay to Borneo.

The previous day Vice-Admiral Tom Phillips, commander of the British Far East Fleet, based at Singapore, had conferred in Manila with Hart and MacArthur. The three were worried about the Japanese convoy, sighted off the coast of Indo-China and then lost in fog. Was it heading for a direct attack on Malaya and Singapore or merely landing at Siam?

Although MacArthur agreed that the situation was critical, he said that by April, 1942, he would have a trained army of about 200,000 men and a powerful air force of 256 bombers and 195 pursuit planes. This great strength would assure the defensibility not only of the Philippines but the entire Southeast Pacific area.

"Doug, that is just dandy," interposed Hart. "But how defensible are we right now?" The answer to that was painfully obvious. MacArthur did have about 130,000 men in uniform, but almost 100,000 of these were poorly equipped Philippine Army divisions with only a few months training in close-order drill. Though they were enthusiastic and willing and worshipped MacArthur, they could do little but salute properly. Most had never even fired their ancient Enfield rifles. The Air Force was in worse shape. On paper MacArthur had 277 airplanes, but of these only 35 Flying Fortresses and 107 P-40s were modern combat craft.

After MacArthur left, Phillips—nicknamed Tom Thumb because he was only five feet four, an inch shorter than Napoleon—made one specific request of Hart. He wanted four U.S. destroyers to accompany his fleet on a sortie from Singapore up the east coast of Malaya as a countermove to the threatening Japanese armada. His two great ships, the battle cruiser *Repulse* and the battleship *Prince of Wales,* had only four destroyers as escort.

Hart agreed to send four of his own overage destroyers then anchored at Balikpapan. At 6:00 P.M., as everyone stood to leave, a messenger came in with a dispatch for Phillips. It was read aloud. Planes from Singapore had sighted the Japanese convoy off the Siamese coast. Course was 240 degrees.

"Admiral," said Hart to Phillips, "when did you say you were flying back to Singapore?"

"I'm taking off tomorrow morning."

"If you want to be there when the war starts, I suggest you take off right now."

The following night, December 7, the 27th Bombardment Group—1200 strong but without a single plane—was giving a party at the Manila Hotel in honor of Major General Lewis Brereton, commander of MacArthur's air force, who had arrived little more than a month before. It was a gala affair long to be remembered by those who attended as being "the best entertainment this side of Minsky's." But the guest of honor's mind was on war and his sadly inadequate air force. During the party he talked with Rear Admiral William Purnell, Hart's chief of staff. "It's only a question of days or perhaps hours until the shooting starts," said Purnell. A few minutes later Brigadier General Richard Sutherland, MacArthur's chief of staff, said the War Department believed hostilities might begin at any time.

Alarmed, Brereton went to a phone and called his own chief of staff, instructing him to put all airfields on combat alert. He was thankful heavy air reinforcements were coming. The *Pensacola* convoy, now somewhere in the South Pacific, was scheduled to arrive January 4. Its 7 transports carried 52 dive bombers as well as two regiments of artillery and large amounts of badly needed ammunition and supplies. In addition, 30 Flying Fortresses, which would almost double his bomber force, should arrive in a few days. Twelve had already taken off from California and were due to land in Hawaii at dawn.

At Clark Field, 50 air miles to the northwest, 16 Flying Fortresses were lined up ready for flight. Three others were in the hangars being camouflaged or repaired. The flat field, rimmed only by a few trees and waist-high cogon grass, was honeycombed with revetments, foxholes and slit trenches. It looked weird and unworldly in the moonlight.

In one of the nearby wooden barracks, Staff Sergeant

Frank Trammell of the 30th Bombardment Squadron was vainly trying to contact his wife, Norma, in San Bernardino, California, by ham radio. Every Sunday night for the past month he had talked with her. It was queer. The air was dead. The only thing he could raise was a city he was forbidden to talk to—Singapore.

The 220-square-mile island of Singapore was about 1600 miles to the southwest, almost the same distance and direction as a flight from New York to New Orleans. Connected to the southernmost point of Asia, the Malay Peninsula, by a causeway, it was the keystone of the Allied defense system. If it fell, not only Malaya would be lost but the entire Dutch East Indies, with its oil, tin and rubber.

That night the sky over Singapore was ablaze with the probing fingers of searchlights. Huge 15-inch guns protected the sea approaches. And in the great Naval base—built in twenty years at a cost of 60,000,000 pounds—were moored two of the most powerful war ships afloat, the *Repulse* and the *Prince of Wales*.

At every military installation there was a sense of alert excitement. The code word, "Raffles," had just been signalled throughout the Malayan Command and all ranks were standing to arms ready for immediate action. British, Australian and Indian soldiers were prepared and confident. Singapore, they felt, was an impregnable fortress.

North-northeast of Singapore about 1650 miles was Great Britain's other fortress in Southeast Asia, Hong Kong. Also an island, it was a few minutes ride by ferry from the mainland of southern China. That Sunday night the Colony of Hong Kong was practically on a war footing. Although ambassadorial telegrams from Tokyo had been extremely moderate lately, Major-General C. M. Maltby, military commander of the Colony, had alerted his 11,319 men.

By midnight, except for its patched regatta of ketches, proas, junks and sampans, the great harbor was almost barren. The previous night pages had gone through the bars and ballrooms of hotels telling all Merchant Navy seamen and officers to report to their ships immediately. Here, word of the Japanese convoy in the Gulf of Siam had meant only one thing: the balloon had gone up. But Hong Kong was ready and confident.

From Washington to Hong Kong it was apparent that Japan might strike within hours. But in many places "readiness" was only a word. Few were actually prepared for the brutal reality of war. None were aware of a detailed Japanese plan that was already developing that moment step by step.

   5 A week earlier the Imperial Conference had convened in Room 1 of the Imperial Palace in Tokyo. Present were the military and civil leaders of Japan and the Emperor himself. Everyone realized it was probably the most important meeting ever held in Japan. Out of it would come war or peace. There was a hush as Prime Minister Tojo—an intense, nervous man who every day smoked at least fifty cigarettes and drank a dozen cups of coffee—stood up.

"With the permission of the Emperor, I will take charge of the proceedings today." Everything had been done, he said, to adjust diplomatic relations with America but Hull's note of November 26 was clearly an ultimatum since it demanded withdrawal of troops from China without offering a single concession. "Submission to these demands would not only deprive Japan of her authority and forestall her efforts for the successful settlement of the China Incident, but would also jeopardize her very existence." He reviewed the situation and then concluded grimly, "Matters have now reached the point where Japan, in order to preserve her Empire, must open hostilities against the United States, Great Britain and the Netherlands."

Admiral Osami Nagano, representing the High Command, then explained the military situation. The Western powers were increasing their strength in the Far East. Soon it would be too late to strike. There was now almost no danger of an attack from Russia because of German successes. "The officers and men of the Army and Navy are in high spirits and are burning with desire to serve their Emperor and their country, even at the cost of their lives."

After optimistic reports on the nation's financial condition and food supply, Baron Yoshimichi Hara, president of the Privy Council, the supreme advisory body to the Emperor, arose. This was the voice of Japanese conservatism and his words were eagerly awaited. "The Japanese Empire can concede nothing further. If she does, the gains obtained from the Sino-Japanese war in 1894 will be completely nullified. It is to be regretted that we are compelled to fight another war after having been engaged in the China Incident for more than four years, but the conclusion of diplomatic negotiations with the United States is hopeless, in spite of everything we have done. . . .

"As there is no alternative I am compelled to give my

consent to this plan. We must have confidence in our soldiers, be convinced of victory in war and, at the same time, leave no stone unturned to maintain the nation's unity over a long period."

Tojo assured Hara the Government was ready to call off the war plans at the very last moment if America would negotiate "just terms." Then, seeing that there were no dissenting votes, the general said, "In closing, I wish to say that the Japanese Empire is now on the threshold of progress or collapse."

All present except the Emperor, who had not uttered a word, signed the documents. Later that day the papers were presented to Emperor Hirohito. For the past three days he had been convening with the "Senior Statesmen," former prime ministers, in a desperate effort to avoid war. They had assured him that if Japan bowed to America's "unrealistic and unjust" demands she would instantly become a second-rate power. And, feeling that further resistance to the advocates of war would be against the inevitable will of the people, the mild-mannered ruler reluctantly sanctioned the documents.

The next afternoon, December 2, the Imperial Navy Headquarters was told of the Emperor's decision. At 5:30 P.M. a radio message was sent to the powerful Pearl Harbor Striking Force, 32 ships including 6 carriers, already midway between Japan and Hawaii. It read: CLIMB MT. NIITAKA. It meant: Begin the War.

6   At 3:30 A.M. December 7, American minesweepers and destroyers were patrolling the entrance to Pearl Harbor, unaware that under them were five midget Japanese submarines, each manned by a crew of two. Released from their mother submarines near midnight, they were maneuvering toward the entrance to the harbor.

At 3:42 A.M. the minesweeper *Condor* was also bound for Pearl Harbor. One thousand yards from the entrance, a lookout shouted. The ship had almost run into some object apparently heading into the harbor.

The *Condor,* startled and alerted, searched for a few minutes and at 3:58 A.M. sent out a blinker signal to a nearby destroyer, the *Ward.* A suspicious object west of her sweep area had been sighted, said *Condor.* She believed it was a submarine.

Lieutenant William Outerbridge, the *Ward*'s skipper, ordered his ship to general quarters. For half an hour the old four-stacker combed a wide pattern with all topside hands on the lookout. Nothing was seen and at 4:43 A.M. everyone except those on watch went back to bed. Neither *Condor* nor *Ward* reported the incident to higher headquarters.

The anti-torpedo net across the entrance to Pearl Harbor slowly began to open at 4:47 A.M. Eleven minutes later the gate was wide open. Soon the minesweeper *Crossbill* entered. But the gate remained open. Since the *Condor* was scheduled to follow soon, those operating the net decided it was too much trouble to close it for such a short time. At 5:32 A.M. *Condor* passed through. Once more the net operators decided to keep the gate open. In forty-five minutes the tug *Keosanqua* was due to leave Pearl Harbor.

And so the mouth of Pearl Harbor was wide open for the five Japanese submarines. They were only seventy-nine feet long but each carried two full-sized torpedoes.

Thirteen minutes after the *Condor* entered Pearl Harbor, the war in the Pacific started by mistake. According to the grand plan of the Imperial High Command the first blow was to fall on Pearl Harbor at 8:00 A.M. Then Singapore, Hong Kong, the Philippines, Guam and Wake were to be bombed in succession. These were but the first steps in a master plan to conquer all Southeast Asia in six months.

The mistake was the result of overeagerness. The great Japanese convoy which had been seen entering the Gulf of Siam by the Allies two days earlier was carrying troops scheduled to conquer Singapore. A section of this convoy arrived at its destination halfway down the Malay Peninsula too soon. British defense troops on the beaches of Kota Bharu happened to spot these invasion ships and opened fire at 12:45 A.M., Singapore time, with land artillery. The war in the Pacific was on and the first shot ironically had been British.

At that moment it was 1:15 A.M., December 8, in Japan. Aboard his flagship, *Nagato,* in the Inland Sea, the commander-in-chief of the Combined Fleet, Admiral Isoroku Yamamoto, would not know for some time that the war had already started accidentally. He had been up all night waiting for word from Vice-Admiral Chuichi Nagumo, commander of the Pearl Harbor Striking Force. Nagumo's six carriers were presently about 250 miles north and slightly east of their target. In fifteen minutes, 6:00 A.M., December 7, Hawaiian time, the first wave—40 torpedo planes, 51 dive bombers, 49 high-level bombers—would start taking off. And two hours later the first bombs would be dropping on the U.S. Pacific Fleet.

Yamamoto (his first name, "Fifty-six," was the age of his father at the admiral's birth) was not waiting impatiently or nervously. A man of remarkable energy and purpose, his face showed no emotion. Unlike others in his own head-quarters and in Tokyo, he was not worried about the Pearl Harbor attack. He had planned it carefully and prepared it efficiently. If Nagumo followed his instructions, he was sure the attack could not fail.

It was ironic that his strategy was being used for he had strongly opposed a war with the United States and Britain, feeling Japan would have no chance of victory. Overruled, he had then devoted his time to proving he was wrong. After study, he concluded that Japan's only chance was to cripple the Pacific Fleet with a single blow. This would checkmate America's main strength in the Pacific and, he hoped, dampen her fighting spirit.

There had been sharp opposition to Yamamoto's plan from his own subordinates as well as the Naval Staff. Not until October 20, when Yamamoto had threatened to resign, was the Pearl Harbor attack finally approved.

Despite his optimism, he still hoped there would be a last-minute cancellation of the Climb Mt. Niitaka order. "Admiral Nomura is a very capable man," he had recently told friends. "Perhaps he will save the United States-Japan situation." But as time ran out that evening, he realized this was now a forlorn hope.

In Tokyo, American Ambassador Joseph C. Grew was just presenting Roosevelt's personal plea to the Emperor to Foreign Minister Shigenori Togo. It had been held up more than ten hours by the Tokyo Central Telegram Office by order of an officer of the General Staff.

Grew asked Togo to arrange an Imperial audience in spite of the late hour. Togo agreed, and read the message. It recalled the long friendship between Japan and America, suggesting that if Japan would withdraw from Indo-China, no other country would invade that area.

Though this was by no means a new proposal, Togo felt the Emperor should see it. If a last-minute peace were to be arranged, there was no time to lose. Late that afternoon he had sent off the fourteenth and final part of the long reply to Hull's "ultimatum." With it he had also sent Nomura instructions to deliver the entire memorandum at exactly 1:00 P.M., December 7, Washington time, thirty minutes before the Hawaiian raid. The Third Hague Convention had prescribed no minimum time which should elapse between declaration of war and attack and to Togo's legalistic mind this half-hour warning would prevent the United States from later accusing Japan of a "sneak attack."

Togo telephoned Marquis Koichi Kido, lord keeper of the privy seal. An immediate audience with the Emperor was granted, but first a translation of the telegram had to be made.

7 In Washington it was then Sunday morning, December 7. Lieutenant Commander Kramer, though up late the night before delivering messages, was at his office in the Navy Department shortly after 7:30 A.M. He learned the anxiously awaited fourteenth part of the Tokyo message had finally come in at 4:00 A.M. and was almost decoded. In a few minutes Kramer had the message. It was short but its last paragraph was ominous.

> THE JAPANESE GOVERNMENT REGRETS TO HAVE TO NOTIFY HEREBY THE AMERICAN GOVERNMENT THAT IN VIEW OF THE ATTITUDE OF THE AMERICAN GOVERNMENT IT CANNOT BUT CONSIDER THAT IT IS IMPOSSIBLE TO REACH AN AGREEMENT THROUGH FURTHER NEGOTIATIONS.

The entire fourteen parts were assembled, put in folders and once more Kramer began making his delivery rounds.

General Marshall was just then eating breakfast at his home in Virginia. Although copies of the same thirteen-part message delivered to Roosevelt and the Navy officials the previous evening had been automatically routed to the Army, the chief of staff knew nothing about the vital memorandum. It was odd because in addition to other Army officers even Colonel Bedell Smith, secretary of the General Staff, had received it Saturday night.

At any rate, Marshall, ignorant of a message that had meant war to the President, finished reading the papers and then about 8:30 A.M. began his usual Sunday horseback ride. He headed at a lively gait toward the government experimental farm, the site of the future Pentagon Building.

Across the Potomac River, Kramer was still delivering the full fourteen-part message. By 10:20 A.M., his rounds completed, he was back in his own office. Another decoded

Japanese message was waiting for him, this of an even more alarming nature. It was a note from Foreign Minister Togo to Nomura marked "Urgent—Very Important."

> WILL THE AMBASSADOR PLEASE SUBMIT TO THE UNITED STATES GOVERNMENT (IF POSSIBLE TO THE SECRETARY OF STATE) OUR REPLY TO THE UNITED STATES AT 1:00 P.M. ON THE 7TH, YOUR TIME.

While it was being put in folders, Kramer hastily made a time circle. He wanted to get a picture of how the one o'clock time tied in with the movement of the big Japanese convoy in the Gulf of Siam. It would be, he learned, 1:30 P.M. December 8 in Kota Bharu; not a particularly significant time of day to start an attack. He then figured the time in Hawaii. There it would be 7:30 A.M. Since he had spent two years at Pearl Harbor he knew this was the normal time for the piping of the crew to Sunday breakfast—a very quiet time indeed.

He hurried down the corridors of the sprawling Navy Building and by 10:30 A.M. reached Admiral Stark's office. Stark, just arrived from a long, leisurely walk around the grounds and greenhouses of his quarters, was busy reading the fourteen-part message. While waiting in the outer office for the Admiral to finish, Kramer chatted with his own chief, Commander Arthur McCollum, head of the Far East Section. Kramer pointed out the possible significance of the one o'clock time with reference to Malaya and Hawaii.

At last Stark finished the long memorandum and read the "one o'clock" note. It was suggested he send an alert to Navy commanders. Stark vetoed the idea. He felt his "war warning" of November 27 was enough to keep everyone on his toes.

Out on northwest Massachusetts Avenue at the Japanese Embassy, the officials in charge of incoming telegrams, adapting themselves to leisurely American Sundays, had reported late and Admiral Nomura was just then reading Togo's instructions to deliver the memorandum at 1:00 P.M. Nomura immediately telephoned the office of Cordell Hull. He asked for an interview at 1:00 P.M.

The secretary of state had a luncheon appointment.

Nomura asked to see the undersecretary of state. There was a pause. Since Ambassador Nomura insisted it was a matter of the utmost importance, Mr. Hull would see him at 1:00 P.M.

As soon as Nomura hung up, he asked to see the rest of

the fourteen-part message. He had only read the first few
sections before leaving the Embassy the day before. To his
dismay he learned that the decoders had quit work early on
Saturday and would need two or three hours to finish.
Nomura was frantic. It was almost 11:00 A.M.

George Marshall, finally alerted by his office that an important message had come in, was just then hurrying from
Virginia to the War Department Building. By a few minutes
after 11:00 A.M. he was reading the fourteen-part message.
Some sections he read twice. Finally he reached the end.
Underneath was the "one o'clock" note. Instantly he was
alarmed. This was much more critical and significant. He
was very much taken aback because of the time he had spent
on the preceding lengthy message.

He immediately telephoned Admiral Stark. They discussed the possible significance of the "one o'clock" note.
"What do you think about sending the information concerning the time of presentation to the Pacific commanders?"
suggested Marshall.

"We've sent them so much already, I hesitate to send any
more. A new one will be merely confusing."

Marshall hung up. In spite of Stark's opinion, he still
thought a warning to the Pacific was necessary. He wrote out
in longhand on a ruled sheet:

Japanese are presenting at 1 P.M. Eastern Standard Time today
what amounts to an ultimatum. Also they are under orders to
destroy their code machine immediately. Just what significance
the hour set may have we do not know but be on alert accordingly.

His phone rang. It was Stark. His voice was concerned.
"George, there might be some peculiar significance in the
Japanese ambassador calling on Hull at 1:00 P.M. I'll go
along with you in sending that information to the Pacific."
Stark then offered the Navy's transmission facilities.

"No thanks, Betty, I feel I can get it through quickly
enough."

"George, will you include instructions to your people to
inform their Naval opposites?"

Marshall agreed, adding a sentence to that effect on the
message. He marked it "First Priority Secret," and then ordered it rushed to the message center for transmission to San
Francisco, the Panama Canal, the Philippines and Hawaii.
Worried about the time factor, he sent an officer several
times to find how long it would take to encipher and send

the message by radio. The final answer was reassuring—within thirty minutes. Marshall didn't even consider using the direct scrambler telephone. Since this was an ordinary commercial line, and easily tapped, the Japanese might possibly deduct that their Purple Code had been broken.

The handwritten warning was rushed to the message center. Soon it was encoded and by a few minutes after noon San Francisco, the Panama Canal and the Philippines were warned. But Hawaii could not be raised. There were still two other direct radio communications to Hawaii available; those of the Navy and FBI. The message center signal officer, failing to realize how precious every minute was, sent it by Western Union. It wasn't even marked urgent.

8 Five days previously Captain Eddie Layton, Kimmel's radio intelligence officer, had reported he had no information on Japanese Carrier Divisions 1 and 2. They had mysteriously disappeared from Hitokappu Bay a week before and hadn't been sighted since.

Kimmel's face was stern but there was a twinkle in his eye when he said, "Do you mean to say that they could be rounding Diamond Head this minute and you wouldn't know?"

"I hope they would be sighted by now, sir."

But even by 6:30 A.M. Sunday, December 7, Nagumo's Pearl Harbor Striking Force was still unsighted. And the first wave of attackers had been airborne half an hour on their approximately two-hour trip to Hawaii.

Outside the mouth of the great naval base, Lieutenant William Outerbridge, the young skipper of the destroyer *Ward*, had just been roused from his bunk by his gunnery officer, Lieutenant Oscar Goepner. Wearing glasses and a Japanese kimono, Outerbridge peered off the port bow in the murky light of dawn at the target ship *Antares* which was towing a raft into Pearl Harbor. Behind the raft was a strange object.

"We've been watching it, sir," said Goepner excitedly, "and we think it's moving."

It looked like a conning tower to Outerbridge, and it apparently was following the *Antares* into the harbor. "Go to general quarters," he shouted. At that moment the *Antares* blinkered a confirming message. A small sub was 1500 yards off her starboard quarter!

The midget submarine was seen also by Ensign William Turner, pilot of a passing PBY Catalina flying boat, but in the dim light of dawn he thought she was an American vessel in distress. Seeing the *Ward* speed toward the submarine he decided to help the "rescuers" and dropped two smoke bombs.

The *Ward*, now only 100 yards from the submarine, began firing. At point-blank range, No. 1 gun fired and missed. A moment later No. 3 gun fired, hitting the conning tower. The midget began to sink. While the gunners were still cheering, Outerbridge shouted, "Drop depth charges!" The destroyer's whistle blasted four times and four depth charges rolled off the stern.

When Ensign Turner in the PBY saw the *Ward* attack, he decided he'd made a mistake and dropped several bombs. Then he wondered if he'd been right in the first place. What if he had sunk an American sub?

Some on the *Ward* also began to wonder if they had just blasted an American boat, but Outerbridge was sure he'd done the right thing. At 6:51 A.M. he radioed the Fourteenth Naval District:

> WE HAVE DROPPED DEPTH CHARGES ON SUB OPERATING
> IN DEFENSIVE AREA.

A moment later he decided this message wasn't strong enough. He was almost positive he'd sunk the midget. And so at 6:53 A.M. he sent a second message:

> WE HAVE ATTACKED FIRED UPON AND DROPPED DEPTH
> CHARGES UPON SUBMARINE OPERATING IN DEFENSIVE SEA
> AREA.

A few minutes later there was another alarm aboard the *Ward*. A white sampan was sighted in the forbidden waters. Outerbridge gave chase and as the *Ward* approached, the skipper of the sampan, a Japanese fisherman, waved a white flag.

Outerbridge immediately radioed:

> WE HAVE INTERCEPTED A SAMPAN. WE ARE ESCORTING
> THIS SAMPAN INTO HONOLULU. PLEASE INFORM COAST
> GUARD TO SEND CUTTER TO RELIEVE US OF SAMPAN.

Because of delay in decoding by a yeoman, Outerbridge's second message about attacking the submarine didn't reach Captain John Earle, chief of staff of the Fourteenth Naval District, until 7:12 A.M.

It took Earle three minutes to reach the commandant, Admiral C. C. Bloch. After passing through so many hands the tone of Outerbridge's message did not appear so urgent.

"What do you know about it?" asked Bloch.

Earle was dubious. "We get so many of these false sightings. We can't go off half-cocked."

"I agree," said Bloch. In the past few months there had already been nearly a dozen such sub warnings, all false. "Ask this to be verified."

A moment later any alarm at Fourteenth Naval District headquarters was allayed when Outerbridge's report of the sampan arrived. If the *Ward* had actually attacked a sub, everyone agreed, she never would have left her post to proceed to Honolulu.

At this same moment another warning of a different nature was being reported by telephone to the Army Aircraft Warning Service. At the Opana outpost on the northernmost tip of Oahu, Private George E. Elliott, Jr. of the 515th Signal Aircraft Warning Service had just seen a large blip on his radar unit. He was not supposed to be watching the radar since it was customarily turned off at 7:00 A.M., but Elliott, a recent transfer from the Air Corps, wanted more experience and had been given permission by his platoon leader to operate beyond the scheduled period so that Private Joseph Lockard, his partner, could instruct him in the operation of the oscilloscope.

When the blip had appeared at about 7:06 A.M. Lockard shoved the novice aside and began operating the radar. It was the largest group he had ever seen on the scope. It looked like two main pulses. He began to check the machine, certain there was something wrong with the equipment, but soon he too decided it was a large flight of planes.

By now Elliott had already located the blip on the plotting board: 137 miles to the north, 3 degrees east. He excitedly suggested they telephone the reading to the Information Center at Fort Shafter. Lockard disagreed. Their problem, he said, was over at 7:00 A.M.

Elliott persisted, arguing that the Information Center might be able to make some sense out of their reading. Finally Lockard relented and let his assistant make the call.

"There's a large number of planes coming in from the north, three degrees east!" reported Elliott.

The switchboard operator at the Information Center, Private Joseph McDonald, dutifully wrote down the data. But he told Elliott no one was around and *he* didn't know what to do.

"Well, get someone who does know and let him take care of it," persisted Elliott and hung up.

McDonald finally spotted an officer at the plotting table, Lieutenant Kermit Tyler. The operator handed the message to Tyler, then asked, "Do you think we should do something about it, sir?"

Tyler, a pilot on duty here only for the training, wasn't excited. He figured the blip was either the big flight of Flying Fortresses coming in from the mainland or planes from a Navy carrier.

McDonald returned to the phone and called Opana. Lockard answered. By now he was as excited as Elliott. The blips were bigger and their distance from Oahu was less than 90 miles. Lieutenant Tyler now came to the phone. He listened to Lockard but was still convinced the oncoming planes were friendly. "Don't worry about it," he said and hung up.

This skepticism quieted Lockard's momentary alarm. When he started to shut down the unit and go off the air, Elliott protested. The novice wanted more practice. At 7:30 A.M. he and Lockard watched the flight approach to within 47 miles. Nine minutes later the distance had shrunk to 22 miles. Then it suddenly faded out, lost in the blacked-out area caused by nearby hills. The two men shut down the station and went to breakfast.

By now the 183 planes of the first wave of attackers from the Pearl Harbor Striking Force were already racing down the northwestern coast of Oahu. A minute later, at 7:40 A.M., Commander Mitsuo Fuchida, the flight leader, fired his signal pistol once. Dive bombers, horizontal bombers and torpedo planes quickly orbited into attack position.

Ironically, they were coming because an American naval officer, Commander Matthew Perry, had forced his way into Tokyo Bay with a squadron of warships in 1853. For 250 years previously no Japanese had been allowed to travel abroad, no foreigners were admitted to Japan. Perry's warships, loaded with commercial samples, forcibly opened the doors of feudalistic Japan, whose warriors still used bows and arrows and wore armor, to the wonders of civilization. Now eighty-eight years later, they were returning Perry's visit with vastly improved samples of the products of civilization.

9 In Tokyo, Foreign Minister Togo was talking to the dynamic premier, General Tojo, about the Roosevelt message which he was about to take to the Emperor. After discussing the reply that should be sent by Emperor Hirohito, Togo said jokingly, "It's a pity to run around disturbing people in the middle of the night."

"It's a good thing the telegram arrived late," said General Tojo cryptically. "If it had come a day or two earlier we would have had more of a to-do."

Togo hurried to the Royal Palace. He read the contents of the telegram to Marquis Kido, the keeper of the privy seal.

"That's no use, is it?" replied Kido. "What's Tojo's opinion?"

"The same as yours."

Togo was then received by the Emperor. The foreign minister read the telegram, explaining it was quite similar to a former proposal, and presented the draft of the reply he and Tojo had written.

The Emperor approved the answer: a polite refusal. At exactly 3:15 A.M. Togo withdrew from the Emperor's presence, deeply moved by his countenance. On it he had read "a noble feeling of brotherhood with all peoples."

Guided by a court official, Togo solemnly passed down the long corridors of the Palace. Emerging at the Sakashita Gate he looked up at the bright stars. The Palace plaza was dead silent. As he drove away the only noise in sleeping Tokyo was the crunching of gravel under his car. In a few minutes, he thought, one of the most momentous days in the history of the world would begin. He was convinced that Japan was taking the only possible course.

1 Banks of cumulus clouds collected around the peaks of the mountain ranges east and west of Pearl Harbor on Sunday morning. But over the great naval base, lying in the valley between, were only a few scattered clouds. Visibility was good and a wind of 10 knots blew in from the north.

At 7:45 A.M. several civilian pilots were lazily circling over the area. There wasn't a single military ship visible. Eighteen planes approaching from the carrier *Enterprise* were scheduled to land at Ford Island within the hour.

The only Army Air Corps planes aloft in the vicinity were the 12 Flying Fortresses from California earmarked for MacArthur. They were due to land at Hickham Field, several miles south of Ford Island, in about an hour. But of the Oahu-based Army planes, not one was on patrol. Still on four-hour notice, they were all tightly bunched together wing tip to wing tip for security against saboteurs at Hickham, Bellows and Wheeler Fields. So were the Marine planes at Ewa.

Of all the military planes in Hawaii, only 7 Navy PBY's were on patrol. And these were many miles to the southwest. Anti-aircraft defense was almost as lax. The Pacific Fleet in the harbor had about a quarter of its 780 anti-aircraft guns manned. Of the Army's 31 anti-aircraft batteries, only 4 were in position, and these had no ready ammunition. It had been returned to depots after practice since it was "apt to disintegrate and get dusty."

About 25 miles to the northwest Japanese pilots in the leading attack planes were marvelling at the peaceful green scene below them. The entire island seemed to be lazing luxuriantly in the early sun. Not even a trace of smoke was coming up from the motionless mass of ships in Pearl Harbor.

At 7:49 A.M. Commander Fuchida from his high-level bomber gave the attack signal in Morse code, "TO . . . TO . . . TO." Four minutes later the great naval base was spread out below him like a huge relief map. It looked exactly as he had imagined. Still no fighters were climbing up to challenge; nor was there a single mushroom explosion of anti-aircraft fire. It was unbelievable. They had achieved complete surprise.

Even before a single bomb dropped he now radioed: "TORA . . . TORA . . . TORA" (Tiger). The repeated word was heard by Admiral Nagumo. It was also heard directly on board the *Nagato,* at Combined Fleet Headquarters in Japan. When the message was brought to Yamamoto he said nothing, his face betrayed no emotion. The other officers spontaneously cheered when the laconic message was read aloud. The *Nagato* was engulfed in excitement. The message decoded meant: "We have succeeded in surprise attack."

Still no bomb had fallen. Except for the roar of approaching planes all was quiet in the Honolulu area. At the RCA office, Tadao Fuchikami, one of the messengers, was checking over a handful of cables he was to deliver. One was addressed simply to "Commanding General" and was obviously for General Short at Fort Shafter. This was the same message Marshall had written so excitedly in pencil almost two hours previously, but since there was nothing on the envelope such as *Secret* or *First Priority* or even *Rush,* Fuchikami decided to make other calls first.

At that same moment, near the center of the island of Oahu, Japanese fighters and bombers began to dive on the Army's Wheeler Field, adjacent to Schofield Barracks.

Second Lieutenant Robert Overstreet, of the 696th Aviation Ordnance Company, was sleeping in the two-story wooden BOQ. He was awakened by a terrific noise. At first he thought it was an earthquake. "Looks like Jap planes," he heard someone shout. "Hell, no," said someone else. "It's just a Navy maneuver."

Overstreet's door opened and an old friend, Lieutenant Robert Skalwold, looked in. His face was white, his lips trembling. "I think Japs are attacking."

Overstreet looked out the window, saw planes circling overhead. They seemed to be olive drab. One dove on the barracks, coming so close he could see the pilot and a rear gunner. On the fuselage and wing tips were flaming red suns. He finished dressing as he ran out of the barracks and headed for his organization. Soon he came onto a group of fighter pilots.

"We've got to get down to the line and tag some of those bastards," shouted one, Lieutenant Harry Brown. Another pilot pointed to the burning hangars and the ramp. There the closely grouped planes were already ablaze.

"Let's go to Haliewa," said Brown. This was an auxiliary field on the north coast where a few P-40's and P-36's were kept. Brown and several other pilots piled into his new Ford convertible and left. Lieutenants George Welch and Kenneth Taylor followed in the latter's car.

Hundreds were milling around in shocked confusion as bombs fell and buildings erupted. Overstreet weaved his way through the mob toward the permanent quarters area. On the Circle he saw Brigadier General Howard Davidson, the fighter commandant, and Colonel William Flood, the base commander, standing by their front doors in pajamas, staring at the sky, their faces aghast.

"Where's our Navy?" said Flood. "Where're our fighters?"

"General," shouted Overstreet, "we'd better get out of here. Those planes have tail-gunners." He ran toward the ordnance hangar. To his horror it was in flames. Inside were a million rounds of machine-gun ammunition ticketed for Midway Island. Suddenly the hangar began to explode, like an endless row of huge firecrackers.

Fifteen miles to the south, just below Pearl Harbor, Jesse Gaines and Ted Conway, aircraft mechanics at Hickham Field, were walking toward the flight line. They'd gotten up early that morning because they knew B-17's were due from the States and they had never seen a Flying Fortress.

At 7:55 A.M. a V-formation of planes suddenly appeared from the west. As they began to peel off, Conway said, "We're going to have an air show."

Gaines noticed something fall from the first plane. He guessed in alarm that it was a wheel.

"Wheel, hell, they're Japs!" cried Conway.

As Gaines said, "You're crazy," a bomb exploded among the neatly packed planes on the field. The two men began to run toward the big three-storied barracks, "Hickham Hotel." Gaines saw some gas drums and dove behind them for protection. Fighters were now diving in a strafing attack, their machine guns spitting orange flames. Gaines felt himself being kicked in the rear.

"Don't you know better than that," shouted an old sergeant. "Those damn drums are full!" Gaines scrambled to his feet and headed away from the ramp. He looked up and saw bombs falling. All seemed to be heading for him. He ran in terror first one way, then another.

Two miles to the north, right in the middle of Pearl Harbor, the first bomb was falling on the naval air station at Ford Island. Ordnanceman Third Class Donald Briggs was sitting in a PBY. He thought a plane from the *Enterprise* had spun in and crashed. Then the sky seemed to cave in as a dozen more explosions followed.

The Japanese plan was simple but efficient. First, to prevent an air counterattack, the airfields were being systematically wiped out. In the first few minutes the Navy bases, Kaneohe and Ford Island; the Army bases, Wheeler, Bellows and Hickham; and the lone Marine base, Ewa, were all but crippled.

A moment after the first bomb fell, the Pearl Harbor signal tower alerted Kimmel's headquarters by phone. Three minutes later, at 7:58 A.M., the message heard around the world was broadcast by Rear Admiral Patrick Bellinger from Ford Island:

AIR RAID, PEARL HARBOR—THIS IS NO DRILL.

Closely on its heels, at 8:00 A.M. Kimmel's headquarters radioed Washington, Admiral Hart in the Philippines and all forces at sea: AIR RAID ON PEARL HARBOR. THIS IS NO DRILL. Even as the messages were going out, torpedo planes were diving on the main target, Battleship Row.

Admiral C. C. Bloch was shaving at his quarters in the Navy Yard. He thought workmen were blasting in the nearby stone quarry. When the explosions continued he told his wife, "I'm going outside and see what that noise is." He ran out the front door. Overhead he saw a plane in flames. He went back into the house. "The Japanese are bombing us. I've got to get to the office. Don't stay down here."

At the naval housing unit adjacent to Hickham Field, First Class Metalsmith Lawrence Chappell was in bed. A plane roared overhead.

"What are those planes?" asked his wife, starting toward the window. "It's too late for the Bomber Patrol."

"Probably stragglers."

"The Rising Sun! The Rising Sun! JAPANESE!" cried Mrs. Chappell.

"You're foolish, go back to bed." Another plane roared over and Chappell went to the window. A torpedo plane swept by, so close he could see the pilot turning around, unconcerned. He hurriedly dressed and ran outside. Now he heard anti-aircraft fire and saw flames and billows of black smoke rising from Pearl Harbor.

Kimmel was watching the torpedo attack from the hill at Makalapa near his quarters. Short was standing on the *lanai* of his home near Fort Shafter watching the billows of smoke in the west and wondering what was going on at Pearl Harbor.

The smoke was rising from Battleship Row, on the east side of Ford Island where seven battleships, the heart of the

Pacific Fleet, were moored. They were not protected from aerial torpedoes by nets because of Pearl Harbor's 40-foot depth. This matter had been discussed many times by Kimmel and Stark. Even the British had been consulted. Everyone agreed a minimum depth of 75 feet was necessary for torpedoes.

This unanimous conclusion was surprising since the British themselves had made a successful plane attack on the Italian fleet at Taranto the previous year with specially rigged torpedoes. The Japanese bombers diving on Battleship Row were proving clever as the British. They were dropping torpedoes with ingeniously constructed wooden fins, specially designed for shallow water.

Not far from Battleship Row, Yeoman C. O. Lines of the oil tanker *Ramapo* was in the crew's quarters. Boatswain's Mate Graff rushed down the ladder. "The Japs are bombing Pearl Harbor!" he yelled.

The men in the room looked at him as if he were crazy.

"No fooling," he said.

Someone gave a Bronx cheer.

"No crap. Get your asses up on deck!"

Lines hurried topside to the fantail. He thought Graff was ribbing as usual. Then he heard a dull explosion and saw a plane dive toward the battleship *California*.

She was the last of the seven big vessels in Battleship Row. Two torpedoes hit her almost simultaneously. The ship took an 8-degree list and began to settle. Her fractured fuel tanks began to flood an entire lower deck. Bombs now fell and half a dozen fires flared. In minutes oil gushing from the ruptured ship burst into flame. She was surrounded by a wall of fire. The word was passed: Abandon ship.

Ahead, in tandem formation, were the *Maryland* and *Oklahoma*. A torpedo couldn't hit the *Maryland* because she was berthed inboard, next to Ford Island, and was protected by her mate. But the outboard ship, the *Oklahoma*, was hit by four torpedoes within a minute. As she listed to port, Commander Jesse Kenworthy, senior officer aboard, ordered the ship abandoned over the starboard side. He calmly walked up the ship's side over the blistered ledge and then over the bottom. Soon the ship settled, its starboard propeller out of the water. Below more than 400 men were trapped in the rapidly filling compartments.

Next in Battleship Row came another pair, the *Tennessee* and *West Virginia*. Like the *Maryland*, the *Tennessee* was inboard and safe from torpedo attack. On the *West Virginia*'s battle conning tower, Lieutenant Commander T. T. Beattie, the ship's navigator, heard Captain Mervyn Bennion groan.

"I've been wounded," said the skipper, doubling up. A fragment, probably from an armor-piercing bomb that had just hit the nearby *Tennessee,* had torn into his stomach and part of his intestines were protruding. The captain sank to the deck. Beattie loosened his collar and sent a messenger for a pharmacist's mate. But the captain knew he was dying and only wanted to know how his ship was being fought. Some fires swept toward the bridge. There was no escape except by swinging hand over hand along a fire hose.

Next in line came the *Arizona.* The first torpedo planes struck at the *Arizona* and missed. A moment later high-level bombers attacked. Five bombs hit. One of these dropped through the forecastle into the second deck, starting a fire. About 1600 pounds of blackpowder, the most dangerous of all explosives, were stored here against regulations. Suddenly the blackpowder exploded, igniting hundreds of tons of smokeless powder in the forward magazines.

To those on nearby ships, the *Arizona* seemed to leap out of the water amidst a tremendous blast of fire and debris. The great 32,600-ton ship apparently broke in two and then quickly settled. Sheets of flame and clouds of black smoke swirled around the *Arizona.* It didn't seem possible that a soul could have survived.

Ahead of the *Arizona* was the leading ship in Battleship Row, the *Nevada.* She was down several feet by the head from a torpedo in her port bow and a bomb in the quarterdeck.

On the other side of Ford Island, torpedo bombers were diving on the thirty-three-year-old battleship, *Utah.* Now a target ship, her decks had been stripped and covered with timber and from above she looked like a carrier. Dive bombers were swarming all over her. The first torpedo hit at 8:01. Four minutes later the *Utah* was listing to port at 40 degrees. As fighter planes swept down to strafe the tilting deck, the word was given to abandon ship. At 8:12 the tired old ship flopped over, keel sticking out of the water. There was a momentary quiet and men in a recently dug trench on Ford Island heard a faint knocking inside the ship. People in the ship's bottom were still alive.

Even by 8:10 A.M. only one ship in the entire harbor was under way. This was the destroyer *Helm* and she was trying to escape. At 27 knots she raced through the channel toward the mouth of the harbor.

Here, the anti-torpedo net, opened hours earlier for the

Condor, was still unclosed. A Japanese midget submarine, its gyro-compass out of order, was trying to stab its way blindly into this opening and raid Pearl Harbor. The commander, Ensign Kazuo Sakamaki, surfaced to get his bearings. Through the periscope he saw columns of black smoke. He excitedly called to his aide, Second Class Petty Officer Kiyoshi Inagaki, "The air raid! Wonderful! Look at that smoke. Enemy ships burning. We must do our best too, and we will."

At 8:15 A.M. he sighted the *Helm* racing out of the harbor. It was so close he could see the white uniforms of the sailors aboard. Guessing correctly it was only a destroyer, he didn't fire. His two torpedoes were marked for bigger game, battleships. He quickly submerged and again blindly aimed at the mouth of the harbor. He hit a reef, backed away, tried again. This time he ran up on the reef and his conning tower stuck out of the water.

At 8:18 A.M. he heard a terrific explosion and figured the destroyer had seen him. The little boat shook violently. Something hit Sakamaki's head and he briefly lost consciousness. When he came to, the tiny inner chamber was filled with white smoke. He felt dizzy, sick. He reversed the motor to back off from the reef but the boat didn't budge. There was only one solution. He wormed his way on his stomach up the narrow passage to the bow and began the painful job of transferring 11-pound ballast weights to the stern. Finally to his relief he felt the submarine move.

On the surface, the *Helm* was still firing at the bobbing midget with no success. Suddenly its target slid off the coral, vanished. SMALL JAP SUB TRYING TO PENETRATE CHANNEL, radioed the destroyer.

While this new alarm was being signaled from ship to ship, another midget was slowly rising to the surface just west of Ford Island and preparing for attack. She had slipped through the open mouth of Pearl Harbor earlier that morning and hidden on the bottom.

A moment later, at 8:30 A.M. the *Breese* spotted its conning tower. Several ships quickly opened fire. The midget launched her two torpedoes. One detonated against a dock, the other against the shore. Then the destroyer *Monaghan* slammed into the submarine. As the midget sank, depth charges from the destroyer finished the job.

By now action from the sky had slacked off momentarily. Admiral "Poco" Smith, Kimmel's chief of staff, who had been shaving in his apartment near the Royal Hawaiian Hotel when he learned about the raid, now drove up to the submarine base. Outside Kimmel's office he saw a group of Marines shooting rifles into the empty sky.

Inside Fleet headquarters, Kimmel was calm. He was talking to Vice Admiral William Pye, commander of Battle Force. Pye, too, was calm, though covered with oil. He had just escaped from his flagship, the *California*. Smith, after some persuasion, convinced Pye and Kimmel to get in different rooms so one bomb wouldn't kill both of them.

A few minutes later, a little after 8:40 A.M. the sky above Pearl Harbor was again dark with raiders. This was Nagumo's second wave; 80 dive bombers, 54 high-level bombers and 36 fighters. This time they came from the south and east hitting Battleship Row and Drydock No. 1, where the *Pennsylvania*, the eighth battleship, was berthed. Soon 18 dive bombers from the southeast joined the attack on Battleship Row.

A principal target was the *Nevada*, moving slowly past the blazing *Arizona*. Her gun crews were shielding their ammunition from the intense heat with their own bodies. In a few minutes the *Nevada*, already suffering from one torpedo hit, drew up to the toppled *Oklahoma*. Several men stood up on the sides of that ship and cheered as the *Nevada* headed for open water.

But the attackers were finding the range. In minutes six bombs hit. The bridge and forestructure of the battleship burst into flames. The ship turned to port and, with the help of two tugs, was beached not far from the *Pennsylvania*'s drydock.

The 12 Flying Fortresses from California began to arrive during this attack. The first squadron of six, under Captain Ted Landon, bewildered by the heavy traffic over Oahu, headed uncertainly for Hickham Field. Four landed safely and one was shot in half by ground troops as it touched down. The sixth plane turned north and crash-landed at Bellows.

As the second squadron of six approached Waikiki Beach, Captain Richard Carmichael, the squadron commander, was pointing out the sights to Captain Jim Twaddell. When Carmichael saw planes ahead, he figured it was some Navy maneuver. Then he saw flames leaping from Hickham Field and knew it was an attack. He called the tower, asking permission to land.

"Land from west to east," said Major Gordon Blake. "Use caution. The field is under attack."

As Carmichael lowered his wheels violent anti-aircraft fire broke out from ships in Pearl Harbor. He quickly turned north toward Wheeler. This field, too, was under heavy attack. Hangars and barracks were burning as dive bombers strafed the line.

Carmichael flew around the Koola Mountain Range. Only half an hour's fuel was left and he had to find a home quickly. He started for Bellows Field, keeping near the coast line. But Kaneohe Naval Air Station was also under attack. Suddenly he remembered Haliewa, a sod field for P-40's. He went north of the mountains and in a few minutes touched down on the short grassy fighter field. It was only 1200 feet long and by the time the big Flying Fortress skidded to a stop he had used every foot of it. All 6 of his planes landed safely: 2 at Haliewa, 1 at Kanuka Golf Course and 3 at Hickham.

On the Hickham flight line, Second Lieutenant William Welch, and other eager young pilots of the 11th Bombardment Squadron, were squabbling to see who would fly the one bomber still intact. A bomb landed 50 yards away, knocking them all flat.

"Let's go across the field," suggested an old master sergeant. Welch, eager to do anything, followed him. As they reached the parking area, three Zeros skimmed by at tree level, their machine guns spitting. Bullets sprayed over their heads into a group of pilots just standing and looking up curiously. Welch turned and fired his .45 pistol at the last plane. It was his only shot of the day.

Just then several Flying Fortresses from the States began to land. Welch ran out to disperse them. Two sprucely dressed captains stepped out of the first plane, looking shocked. "Get your ammo, load up and get ready to go," said Welch.

The captains, too surprised to move, told Welch they were in no shape for battle. All their guns were packed in cosmolene and would take hours to clean.

At Wheeler there was the same feeling of shock. The men were still groggy from the first attack when the second hit. Lieutenant Overstreet was arguing with a sergeant from the Base Ordnance Office. Overstreet wanted rifles and pistols.

"I doubt if I'm authorized to give you any without a hand receipt," said the reluctant sergeant as bombs exploded nearby.

"Hell, man, this is war," said Overstreet angrily. He got the guns.

At Ford Island Field there was also frustration. Not a single Navy fighter had gotten into the air. By now all the planes were destroyed or inoperable. There was nothing to do. Six pilots, including Ensign Elbert Cain, were hiding behind palm trees and shooting at the invaders with their pistols.

Only about 30 Army Air Force fighters managed to get into the air that morning and these could do little to hinder the rain of bombs and torpedoes. Two pilots, Lieutenants Kenneth Taylor and George Welch, were credited with seven of the 11 Japanese planes shot down.

By 10:00 A.M. the skies above the smoke-bound harbor were suddenly empty. The second attack was over. The stink of burning oil was overwhelming. Battleship Row was a shambles. The *Arizona,* the *Oklahoma* and the *California* were sunk at their berths. The *West Virginia,* hopelessly ablaze, was sinking. The *Nevada* was aground. The other three battleships—the *Maryland, Tennessee,* and drydocked *Pennsylvania*—were all damaged.

In nearby Honolulu, Takeo Yoshikawa, the lone Japanese Navy spy, was eating breakfast when windows rattled and several pictures dropped to the floor. Then he heard great explosions coming from Pearl Harbor. He ran outside in his slippers and saw Consul General Nagao Kita standing in front of his official residence. The two looked at each other but couldn't say a word. Other consular officials poured out into the courtyard, dazed and unaware of what was actually going on.

Kita and the spy went inside and tuned in Radio Tokyo. They heard "east wind, rain," repeated twice. War with America! They hurried to the consul general's office and feverishly burned codebooks and secret instructions. By the time the police arrived at 8:30 A.M. everything except a half-finished sketch of Pearl Harbor had been destroyed.

Then the FBI arrived; Yoshikawa knew it was the end of the war for him. He whispered to himself, "Good-bye to the days of my youth—forever." But he had accomplished his mission. The smoke boiling up from Pearl Harbor was in great part due to the information he had gathered for $600.

There was no panic in Honolulu even though explosions had hit many parts of the city. None of these were Japanese bombs, but strays from American guns. Even so, many people had no idea what was going on a few miles away. The first radio report came just as the second attack started, but when it announced that, "A sporadic air attack has been made on Oahu," many listeners thought "sporadic" meant a mock attack.

Others in the city lived out the day as any ordinary Sunday. At the height of the attack Hawaiian girls in costume appeared as usual at the Pan American dock, arms loaded with leis to bid Aloha to departing Clipper passengers. They had to be told it was the end of traditional ceremony for a long, long time. They turned away bewildered and sad.

     2 Kimmel's "This Is No Drill" broadcast was picked up by Mare Island Navy Yard in San Francisco and instantly relayed to Washington.

Secretary of the Navy Frank Knox was in his office in the Navy Department on Constitution Avenue. It was long past noon and he was getting hungry. He was about to order lunch when Admiral Stark burst in with the message from Kimmel.

"My God," said Knox, "this can't be true! This must mean the Philippines."

Stark assured him grimly it did mean Pearl Harbor. Knox picked up the phone connected directly with the White House. It was 1:47 P.M. He asked for the President. In a moment Roosevelt, lunching in the Oval Room with Harry Hopkins, answered. Knox read the dispatch.

Roosevelt couldn't believe it. Nor could Hopkins. Surely Japan would never attack Honolulu. Roosevelt talked at some length of his efforts to keep America out of war, then said soberly, "If this report is true, it takes the matter entirely out of my hands."

At 2:05 P.M. Roosevelt called Hull, advising the secretary of state to receive Nomura and Kurusu but not to mention that he already had the news of Pearl Harbor. He should be formal, cool, and bow them out.

Then Roosevelt called Stimson. "Have you heard the news?" he excitedly asked the secretary of war.

"Well, I've heard the telegram which came in about the Japanese advances in the Gulf of Siam."

"Oh, no, I don't mean that. They have attacked Hawaii! They are now bombing Pearl Harbor!"

A little later Roosevelt saw Dr. Hu Shih, the Chinese ambassador, and suggested a telegram be sent to Chungking requesting that there be no outward signs of joy because Pearl Harbor had suddenly made America a potent ally.

Back at the Navy Department, Stark, after getting the President's permission, was already sending a message to all commanders in the Pacific area and Panama:

EXECUTE UNRESTRICTED AIR AND SUBMARINE WAR-
FARE AGAINST JAPAN.

A few doors away, Knox was talking on the telephone to Admiral Bloch at Pearl Harbor. The navy secretary was amazed at Bloch's coolness as he described the damage which he could see through the window. It was a great disaster, Bloch said, but it could have been greater. "The *Oklahoma's* badly hit. Also the *Arizona*. But the *Pennsylvania* and *Tennessee* are only superficially damaged and we can raise the *California* without too much trouble. Fortunately there's no damage to the Navy Yard and oil reserves."

Knox hung up, hurried to the White House to pass on the information. There the President had just called a special meeting of the Cabinet to work out the war address Roosevelt would deliver the next day to Congress.

Just an hour after the first bomb fell on Hawaii, Ambassador Nomura and Special Envoy Saburo Kurusu were waiting in the outer office of Cordell Hull at the old-fashioned Department of State Building. Twenty minutes earlier, at 2:00 P.M. the two men had arrived with the fourteen-point message which was supposed to have been delivered at 1:00 P.M. Maddening delays in decoding and typing had caused the hour's tardiness.

Nomura, who had lost his right eye in the bombing of a parade at Shanghai in 1932, was embarrassed. Not only was he late, but the hastily typed message contained several minor typographical errors. First Secretary Okumura had wanted to do a fresh draft but the impatient Nomura had snatched it away from him. In fact the admiral still hadn't had time to read the note carefully. But it was apparent from a cursory glance that the talks with Hull had reached a dead end.

At 2:21 P.M. Nomura and Kurusu were finally ushered into Hull's office. "I was instructed to hand this reply to you at 1:00 P.M.," said the admiral apologetically, holding out the note.

Hull's face was set, stern. "Why should it be handed to me at 1:00 P.M.?"

"I do *not* know why," confessed Nomura, puzzled that his friend should be so upset just because he and Kurusu had been an hour late.

The secretary of state, without explaining the reason for his open anger, seized the note abruptly, scarcely glanced at it and said bitterly, "I have never uttered one word of untruth during the last nine months. I have never seen a document so crowded with falsehoods and distortions!"

The two Japanese statesmen, bewildered by Hull's antagonism, left the building. When Nomura reached the Embassy, Okumura said, "Our planes have bombed Pearl Harbor!" Now the admiral understood.

It was only then that the American public learned of the attack. At 2:26 P.M. WOR interrupted its broadcast of the Giant-Dodger football game with the first news flash. No war announcement was made at the Polo Grounds itself where Brooklyn was just kicking off after scoring the game's first touchdown in the second quarter against the already crowned champions of the Eastern Division. But a little later, when Colonel William J. Donovan was paged by Washington over the P.A. system, there was an ominous buzz.

Much of America heard the news a moment before the 3:00 P.M. CBS broadcast of the New York Philharmonic concert. In Washington Admiral Chester Nimitz, chief of the Bureau of Navigation, was just sitting down to enjoy the Artur Rodzinski concert when the flash came. He jumped out of his chair and soon was on his way to the Navy Building with his assistant, Captain Shafroth.

A few blocks away Masuo Kato, correspondent for Domei, was in a taxi heading for a funeral chapel to attend services for Colonel Kenkichi Shijo, the assistant military attaché who had died of pneumonia.

"God damn Japan," said the driver when the flash came over the cab radio. "We'll lick the hell out of those bastards now."

Most Americans were caught completely unprepared. There were no scenes of excitement or panic, but strangers on the streets began to look at each other with a new awareness. Personal problems were overshadowed by national catastrophe. The bitter wrangles between the interventionists and the America Firsters suddenly had no meaning. With almost no exceptions 130,000,000 Americans instantly accepted total war.

3   In England it was already Sunday evening. At his country residence, Chequers, Prime Minister Winston Churchill was tuning in the nine o'clock news on the portable radio given him by Harry Hopkins. He still knew nothing about Pearl Harbor. In fact, he was ignorant of the much earlier attack on Malaya. A BBC announcer calmly told of fighting on the Russian front, in Libya and then mentioned an attack on Hawaii by the Japanese.

Averell Harriman and United States Ambassador John Winant, Churchill's house guests, sat up straight, shocked.

"It's quite true," said the butler, Sawyer. "We heard it ourselves outside. The Japanese have attacked the Americans."

There was silence. Then Churchill strode to his office. He picked up the phone and asked to speak to President Roosevelt. Winant, assuming the prime minister was going to declare war on Japan, as he had recently promised "within the moment," said, "Good God, you can't declare war on a radio announcement!"

"What shall I do?"

"I will call up the President and ask him what the facts are."

"And I shall talk to him too."

A moment later Winant was conversing with Roosevelt. "I have a friend who wants to talk to you," said Winant cryptically. "You will know who it is as soon as you hear his voice."

Churchill picked up the phone. "Mr. President, what's this about Japan?"

"It's quite true," said Roosevelt. "They have attacked us at Pearl Harbor. We are all in the same boat."

"This actually simplifies things. God be with you." Churchill couldn't help feeling the greatest joy, with the United States now at his side. Britain had won after all. The Commonwealth of Nations and the Empire would live! He recalled Edward Grey telling him thirty years previously that the United States was like a gigantic boiler. "Once the fire is lighted under it, there is no limit to the power it can generate."

Saturated with emotion, he went to bed and slept soundly.

4 The rising sun was just lighting up Tokyo. At Imperial Navy Headquarters there were waves of excitement as details of Pearl Harbor came in directly from planes returning to their carriers. Even to the most conservative it was obvious the Pacific Fleet had been crushed. It was also obvious that Nagumo's force, already on the way back to Japan, would escape scot free. The Americans were searching to the south, in the wrong direction. Yamamoto's brilliant, controversial scheme had succeeded beyond all expectations. With the main instrument of Allied power in the Pacific paralyzed, the conquest of Southeast Asia could now continue.

The next step was to crush enemy air power in the Philippines.

5 Almost four hours after the first bomb fell on Pearl Harbor, Tadao Fuchikami, the RCA messenger, passed through the gates of Fort Shafter on his Indian Scout motorcycle. He had been delayed, quite understandably, by the attacks. The message from Marshall warning Short to be on the alert was finally delivered. Since no one at Shafter was particularly interested in advice from Washington at the moment, it wasn't decoded and delivered to General Short until a moment before 3:00 P.M.

When the general read it, he threw it disgustedly in the wastebasket. It was seven hours late.

Because of an almost incredible series of errors, mischances and coincidences the Pacific Fleet—the main deterrent to Japan's conquest of the Southwest Pacific—was crushed. Eighteen ships had been sunk or badly damaged; 188 planes destroyed and 159 damaged; 2403 Americans killed.

The cost had been minuscule. The Japanese lost 29 planes and 5 midget submarines. Fifty-five airmen had died and 9 submariners. One, Ensign Kazuo Sakamaki, was captured.

The reasons for the disaster would be debated bitterly for years. Stripped of politics, they were simple. The American high command had never dreamed the Japanese could even mount an independent carrier striking force. They also never imagined the Japanese would be "stupid enough" to attack Pearl Harbor.

In a deeper sense, every American would have to accept a share of the blame. Like many other great military disasters, it was caused by a national weakness of character. Americans had refused in the large to face the facts of twentieth-century world politics and economy until the festering war exploded.

Now the American people were presented with an even more important test. How would they react, after this sudden catastrophe, to the prospect of a long, expensive war?

1   As the last raider wheeled and left the wreckage of Pearl Harbor, other Japanese planes were hitting Singapore. An hour and a half later the Philippines and Guam were lightly bombed. Then Hong Kong's airfield was attacked, its tiny air force wiped out.

Two hours after this air raid, the strategic atoll of Wake, surprisingly, was still untouched. At a few minutes before noon, in the radio trailer of the small Army communications detail, Sergeant James Rex was busy relaying messages from the Philippines to the States, since direct contact had been lost. All morning, he had been trying to pass on news of Pearl Harbor to operators in Australia and New Guinea, but they kept telling him to stop kidding and he'd finally given up.

At the Pan-American base on Peale, the tiny island just off the northwest tip of the main island, the Clipper had just been emptied of passengers and mail. At dawn it had taken off for Guam but returned when the skipper, John H. Hamilton, learned of war. Hamilton was almost ready to take his ship on a voluntary patrol. He was talking by phone to Major Paul Putnam, the commander of Marine Fighting Squadron 211, who was five miles away in a tent at the edge of the airstrip on the main island.

Putnam hung up the phone, stepped out of the tent and looked across the bald, narrow 3000-foot-long strip. Eight planes were scattered at 50-yard intervals. Six other planes were being warmed up, two to escort the Clipper and four to relieve the patrol then in the air. Even though there had been a constant air watch since dawn Putnam was worried. Other equipment had arrived recently, such as a garbage truck, but they still had no listening device, no radar.

At 11:58 A.M. Putnam happened to look to the south where a low-lying rain squall was sweeping in. He saw planes only 1500 feet up, gliding noiselessly, eerily out of the squall.

"Take cover—bombers," he shouted. Most of the men were

paralyzed a few seconds as they stared at the 34 medium bombers. Others reacted instantly and ran toward their foxholes. There was no foxhole near Putnam, but 100 yards away was the head. Before the first fragmentation bomb fell he was running. In high school he had once raced 100 yards in 10.2 seconds. Today he knew he would break 10 seconds. Out of the corner of his eye he saw bombs falling, about 12 from each plane. Still short of the head he dove when he heard machine guns sputter. He slid on his belly into the open latrine, head first, his legs still dangling in the air. His hands and nose were covered with filth but he was glad to be there.

In five minutes it was all over. Most of the raiders disappeared but ten turned and raked the Pan-American station. The hotel was blasted, several buildings completely destroyed, fuel tanks set afire. Ten employees, all Guamanians, were killed.

The airfield on Wake was an inferno. Seven of the parked planes and the two 12,500-gallon aviation gasoline tanks were blazing. Parts of bodies were scattered; the wounded moaned. Putnam, himself grazed by a bullet in the back and dazed by concussion, refused first-aid treatment as he tried to bring organization from chaos. His air force was crippled. Half of his men were killed or wounded and there were only four undamaged planes left to protect the island.

At Peale, workers feverishly patched the many bullet holes in the Clipper. The passengers, all unwounded, were loaded. Then, after throwing off two Guamanian stowaways, as many white employees as possible boarded. At 1:00 P.M. the big plane took off, heading for Midway.

On the island of Kwajalein, about 650 miles south, the main body of the Wake Invasion Force was almost ready to leave. Tokyo hadn't given Rear Admiral Sadamichi Kajioka, the over-all commander, a definite deadline for conquest. It was too simple a job. As the last of the Japanese invaders were climbing aboard, word came from returning bombers that all but four planes on Wake had been destroyed. Kajioka's mission now seemed ridiculously easy. Wake should be taken in two days.

2 Earlier that morning, Major General Lewis Brereton, commander of MacArthur's Far East Air Force, reported to No. 1 Victoria Street in the Walled City section of Manila. It was almost 5:00 A.M., December 8, two and one-half hours after the first bomb had fallen on Hawaii. Unable

to see MacArthur, then in conference with Admiral Hart, h
was talking with General Sutherland, so often the buffe
between the commanding general and his subordinates.

"I'd like to mount all the B-17's at Clark Field for mission
to Formosa," said Brereton. He wanted his Flying Fortresse
to leave immediately after daylight and bomb Takao Harbor
in southern Formosa, about 600 miles to the north.

Sutherland told him to go ahead and make preparation:
but warned him to make no final commitment until approva
by MacArthur was granted. Brereton left. There was nothin
now for him to do but wait, since he had already alerte
his headquarters at Nielson Field to prepare the Flyin
Fortresses for the mission to Formosa. For Brereton, eage
to hit the Japanese before they hit him, the next hour crawle
with painful slowness.

A few minutes later, dawn and the Japanese reached th
Philippines simultaneously. On Mindanao, the southernmo
of the major islands, Japanese Navy dive bombers swept i
from an island to the east, Palau, and attacked the seaplan
tender, *William Preston,* and two PBY's in Davao Harbo
The ship evaded the bombs but the two planes were sun
and the first American in the Philippines, Ensign Rober
Tills, was killed. At about the same moment Army Zero
from Formosa hit the radio station in Aparri, a good-size
town on the north coast of Brereton's own island, Luzon
the northernmost of the major islands.

But the Far East Air Force chief knew nothing about thes
attacks so close to his own two main bomber bases—Clar
Field in central Luzon and Del Monte Field in norther
Mindanao—as he impatiently returned to No. 1 Victori
Street at 7:15 A.M. Brereton hurried into Sutherland's office
Across the hall, Colonel William Morse, one of MacArthur'
staff officers, could hear the two men talking through ope
doors.

"I want to go up and bomb Takao," Brereton said insist
ently.

"I'll ask the general," said Sutherland. Morse saw the chie
of staff walk into MacArthur's office and return a momen
later. "The general says no. Don't make the first overt act.'

Morse then heard Brereton protest that bombing Pear
Harbor was certainly an overt act. Sutherland was unmoved
Besides he felt that Brereton knew very little about th
targets on Formosa since there had been almost no recon
naissance. Such a raid on Formosa would just be a wil
stab. Brereton's role for the present, he said, was defense

Half an hour later Brereton reached his headquarters

Nielson Field. On the southern outskirts of Manila, it was on a barren plain, protected by no natural cover. The hangar roof, painted in bold black and yellow squares, was an inviting target.

His staff was waiting eagerly. Captain Allison Ind, the intelligence officer, had assembled target folders on Formosa and although he had no maps indicating the best approaches and bomb release lines, the information was as good as it would be for a long time to come.

Brereton, face pale, entered his office. "What's your decision about bombing Formosa?" he asked the staff.

They had been arguing about the bombing ever since dawn but had now agreed the B-17 Flying Fortress at Clark Field should set out immediately for Formosa.

"No," said Brereton, his jaw hardening. "We can't attack till we're fired on." He explained that Sutherland had ordered him to prepare the B-17's but to take no offensive action. The staff officers were incredulous. If they didn't strike now, they probably wouldn't get a second chance.

The problem was much more complex than the airmen realized. Although the Philippines were an American possession, they were a Commonwealth and, in preparation for the full freedom which had been planned for three years hence, had their own elected government.

MacArthur, also unaware of the two minor air raids on the islands, was positive the Philippines would soon be attacked but many Filipino authorities had high hopes the Japanese would consider them an independent nation and spare them. If he made a wrong move now, MacArthur knew his whole delicately constructed plan of local self-defense might collapse. He also remembered Marshall's recent orders: "If hostilities cannot be avoided, the United States desires that Japan commit the first overt act."

As Brereton was ordering several planes to Formosa on photo-reconnaissance in case approval from MacArthur came through, he was called to the phone. It was Major General Henry "Hap" Arnold, commanding general of the Army Air Forces in Washington. Arnold warned him how everyone had been "caught napping" at Pearl Harbor. Every precaution should be taken in the Philippines. He didn't want Brereton's air force destroyed the same way.

In western Formosa, Japanese Navy officers of the 11th Air Fleet were just as disgusted and disappointed as the American fliers. Heavy fog surrounded their fields. They were to have taken off before dawn for strikes at the American fighter

bases—Nielson, Nichols and Iba—and the main target, Clar
Field. As the hours passed, worry grew that the Clark
based Flying Fortresses would suddenly appear and wipe ou
their own planes, gassed and lined up neatly on the runway

East of the Navy fields the fog over the Japanese Arm
bases had lifted at dawn. One flight had already bombe
Aparri. Other flights were nearing their targets: Baguio, th
former summer capital of the Philippines about 85 air mile
north of Clark, and Tuguegarao, 50 air miles south of Aparr
But the 11th Air Fleet men were not at all cheered by th
better weather of their Army brothers. They knew the Arm
was bombing merely tactical targets. The fate of the entir
Philippines campaign depended on the success of their ow
mission: quick destruction of the main body of MacArthur
fighters and bombers. If the weather didn't clear soon, a
might be lost.

Even at 9:00 that morning most Filipino villages were sti
completely unaware that war had come to their countr
Hundreds of barrio fiestas were starting all over the island
for today was the Feast of the Immaculate Conception an
—except for the Moslem-worshipping Moros of Mindana
the Igorots and Negritos of Luzon and other tribes u
touched by civilization—most Filipinos had adopted the r
ligion of their first conquerors, the Spaniards.

But in Manila, almost every one of its 600,000 peopl
had heard the news by breakfast because of the newspape
extras and Don Bell's frequent news broadcasts over KMZI
Even these reports didn't completely convince many Amer
cans. Although everyone had been sure war was comin
very few were mentally prepared to accept it. Many remem
bered the panic caused by Orson Welles' broadcast on th
invasion from Mars.

In the city's suburbs at Nielson Field, the Air Warnin
Room was receiving reports of bombers heading for Lingaye
Gulf. These were the Japanese Army bombers bound fc
Baguio but everyone at Nielson thought their target wa
Clark Field. The B-17 base was warned and soon all but on
of the Flying Fortresses took to the air bombless, in fear c
being caught on the ground. At the same time 18 P-40
from Clark and 18 from Nichols Field, on the outskir
of Manila, headed for Lingayen Gulf to intercept the invader

Back at Nielson scores of reports were pouring in: enem
battleships sighted off the northern coast of Luzon; thre
Japanese flying boats seen over the tiny islands north c
Luzon. As messages piled up, all civilian secretaries wer
abruptly ordered evacuated in case of a raid.

At the height of the ensuing confusion, at 9:25 A.M., two even more startling reports came in. Luzon itself had been bombed at Baguio and Tuguegarao. Now there could be no argument about an "overt act." Brereton picked up the phone and told Sutherland about the attacks. "If Clark Field is attacked, we won't be able to operate on it." He again begged for permission to bomb Formosa. His face fell and he hung up. Turning to Lieutenant Colonel Eugene Eubank, commander of the B-17's, he shook his head. Permission not granted. Eubank started back for Clark Field at 10:10 A.M.

Four minutes later a call came from No. 1 Victoria Street. Offensive air action against Formosa was authorized. But it seemed too late to hit Takao Harbor as planned. Brereton's staff hastily plotted new missions.

In Formosa activity was just as frenzied at 10:10 A.M. The fog had cleared. On the Japanese Navy fields 196 planes were warming up for take-off. Suddenly sirens all over the island screamed. American planes were reported approaching Formosa. Gas masks were hurriedly passed out. The horde of medium bombers and Zero fighters hastily took to the air on two separate missions. Fifty-three bombers and 53 fighters were to wipe out the fighter field at Iba; 54 bombers and 36 fighters were to hit the main target, Clark Field.

Just as the great armada was leaving Formosa the approaching planes which had alerted the entire island were spotted. Fighters left the Navy formation and sped to the attack. Just in time red suns were seen on the "Americans'" wing tips. They were Japanese Army bombers returning from the Baguio and Tuguegarao missions.

In the Philippines the big Flying Fortresses milling aimlessly around Mt. Arayat in fear of being caught on the ground by these same enemy Army bombers were now getting permission to return to Clark Field. The alert was over; false alarm. As soon as they landed and lined up neatly, the P-40's flying their cover came in for gas and lunch. By 11:00 A.M. the terrific tension of the morning slackened. Calm had returned to Clark Field.

Forty miles west of Clark Field, across the rugged Zambales Mountains, and on the South China Sea, was Iba, a village consisting of little but nipa huts. Next to it was a single grass landing strip, bordered on its west side by a sandy beach. After Nichols it was the most important fighter field in the Philippines. In addition to its 18 combat-ready P-40's, it had the only working radar in MacArthur's command.

The Iba pilots were dog-tired. Since 2:00 A.M. they'd been

chasing phantoms seen on the screen in the half-buried radar shack. Now they were sitting in their planes, smoking cigars, waiting for the next alert. Some were kidding the squadron commander, Lieutenant Henry Thorne. They felt he should think up a memorable fighting phrase for that first day of war. Someone suggested, "Damn the torpedoes and take to the hills."

At 11:27 A.M. the radar screen was again alive. A big formation was coming in across the China Sea. Thorne ordered his men to start their motors. The chase was on once more. Three minutes later Iba was telling Air Warning at Nielson Field that a large formation was presumably heading for Manila. Immediately 18 fighters from nearby Nichols were sent to patrol Bataan and Manila Bay.

In Manila air raid sirens began to wail, but there was still no panic on the streets. Alarms, by now, were coming to suburban Nielson by telephone and telegraph from towns all along the northwest coast of Luzon. Some spoke of 27 planes, apparently fighters, others of 54 heavy bombers. The plotters tried to make sense of the tangled information. Apparently one big group was heading for Manila and several for Clark Field.

The base of the Flying Fortresses was still calm. No sirens screeched. At Fort Stotsenberg, a mile away, cavalrymen were eating lunch. So were mechanics and air crews at Clark.

At 11:45 A.M. Colonel Alexander Campbell, the aircraft warning officer at Nielson, sent a teletype to Clark. But the message was not getting through. Radio was then tried. Still Clark could not be raised. Evidently the operator was having lunch. Colonel Campbell finally got a faint telephone connection with Clark. A junior officer assured Campbell he would pass on the news to the base commander or operations officer immediately.

It was 11:56 A.M. While sirens shrieked and all except key personnel were trying to find cover on barren Nielson Field, Brereton was telephoning Sutherland. The new bombing missions had been drawn up. The Flying Fortresses at Clark would hit known fields in southern Formosa at dusk; the other 14 B-17's, now 550 miles to the south at the Del Monte pineapple plantation in Mindanao, would fly up to Clark, arriving after dark, and prepare for raids on Formosa the next dawn. Sutherland approved.

By 12:10 P.M. all fighter pilots on Luzon were either in the air or waiting for orders to intercept the oncoming attackers. All that is, but the fighters in the Clark Field area. Forty minutes earlier, the 18 P-35's at Del Carmen, 14 miles south of the bomber base, had been ordered to fly cover over Clark but the message never arrived. And at Clark itself the junior officer who had talked with Colonel Campbell had not yet passed on the warning.

Even the alerted pursuit planes were becoming hopelessly tangled because of poor communications and confused orders. Twelve of Iba's 18 planes were still circling above their own field. But six planes of B Flight, losing radio communication, had sped to Manila looking for the Japanese. Suddenly their radios cleared up. They heard, "Tallyho!" Then a voice shouted, "Bandits over Clark!" The six P-40's streaked, full-throttle, to the north.

The 12 fighters hovering over Nichols heard the same call. As they headed for Clark, the squadron commander, Lieutenant William Dyess, radioed Nielson. Brereton's headquarters told Dyess to come back and patrol Manila Bay.

By now the six planes of Iba's errant B Flight were in sight of Clark. All was peaceful. Another false alarm. They turned west, heading for home.

It was now 12:25 P.M. and not a pursuit plane was flying cover over the parked Flying Fortresses at Clark. At that moment 27 new-type "Betty" bombers, with flaming red suns on their wings, roared over Tarlac, only 20 miles to the north. They were heading directly for Clark. An excited Filipino plane observer ran to the telegraph office to make his report.

At Clark Field many of the ground crew were walking unconcernedly from the mess halls to the flight line. Ordnance men were loading bombs on the big, unpainted Flying Fortresses. Pilots of the 18 P-40B's, under Lieutenant Joe Moore, were sitting in their planes at the edge of the field near their empty fuel drum revetments. Many of the men were still eating. At the 30th Squadron mess hall mechanics and Flying Fortress crewmen were listening to Don Bell broadcasting the news.

"There is an unconfirmed report," said Bell, "that they're bombing Clark Field."

Since the only noise was the usual clatter of talk, dishes, knives and forks, Bell's words were greeted with derision and laughter. Many of the men still refused to believe the Pearl Harbor reports, thinking it was probably just some harebrained general's idea of putting everyone on the alert.

The first of the two flights of Japanese bombers were then within sight of Clark. In fact their crews had spotted the mass of B-17's, shining in the bright sun, from Tarlac.

Their prey was ridiculously obvious, sitting out in the great, unprotected central Luzon plain. As an extra guidepost, Mt. Arayat, 15 miles east of the field, stuck up like a huge traffic marker. No one could miss this 3867-foot lonely peak standing in the middle of miles of plain, its cone dented, according to native lore, when Noah's ark landed.

Now, the neat outlines of Fort Stotsenberg became distinct to the bomber pilots with its white buildings, lines of acacia and mango trees and the big polo field. A mile east stretched Clark Field. Not a single protecting pursuit plane was above it. At first the Japanese pilots couldn't believe what they saw: rows and rows of parked P-40's and Flying Fortresses. It was incredible luck. Almost ten hours after Pearl Harbor every plane based at Clark was a helpless, sitting target.

The second flight of 27 old-type "Nell" bombers swung in behind the leading Betties. Suddenly 36 Zero fighters were hovering above the bombers like shepherds. Everything was working with precision. It was 12:35 P.M.

George Setzer, who had the taxi concession at Fort Stotsenberg, was just driving out the gate. Hearing a growing roar, he stopped the car. He and his daughter, Stella, got out. They saw a mass of silver planes coming from the northwest.

"It's about time they came to help us," he said joyfully.

On the perimeter of the airfield, New Mexican National Guardsmen of the 200th Coast Artillery were having lunch or loafing around their 37-mm. and 3-inch anti-aircraft guns. They, too, thought the approaching bombers were friendly. At the cry, "Here comes the Navy," Sergeant Dwaine Davis, of Carlsbad, grabbed the movie camera bought from company funds and began taking pictures.

"Why are they dropping tin foil?" asked someone.

"That's not tin foil and those are goddam Japs!"

Just then there was a sound as of rushing freight trains.

At the west end of the field, a crew chief of the 20th Pursuit Squadron was standing in front of the operations tent. He looked up. "Good God Almighty," he shouted. "Yonder they come!"

Hearing this, Lieutenant Joe Moore, the squadron commander, raced for his P-40. Followed by six others, he quickly taxied into position. He shot into the air, swung wide and started a maximum power climb. Two others got into the air, but the last four planes were hit by bombs.

Corporal Douglas Logan, a B-17 gunner and cameraman, was at Headquarters Building watching Major Birrell Walsh conduct the briefing for the photographic mission over Formosa at a blackboard. Just left of Logan stood Colonel Eubank, the bomber commander. Logan saw him look absently out the window at the sky and turn away. The corporal looked out and saw men running frantically on the field.

Eubank, realizing what he had seen, jumped back to the window, then yelled, "Take cover, men! Here they come!"

As everyone headed for the rear door a stick of bombs exploded. The last to reach the door was Logan. Suddenly the floor pitched. Logan flopped. As he rolled toward a corner he instinctively put his hands over his face.

The air raid siren was now wailing. Someone shouted to get out of the hangars. Men began to saunter out. Above they saw planes in a great V. It was such a beautiful formation, they were thrilled—until they realized bombs were falling on the P-40's and B-17's at the far end of the field. They dove for the trenches, recently built by the base commander, Lieutenant Colonel Lester Maitland, and till now chidingly referred to as "Maitland's Folly."

At the west end of the runway, Corporal Durwood Brooks, a combat radio operator, was sprawled on his bunk when he heard the first bombs fall. He sprang up and ran into the latrine. Then he wheeled and ran outside toward a row of slit trenches. They were filled with white-clad cooks. He looked up and saw three V's, forming one great V. It was so perfect it was beautiful. He watched in fascination until a bomb hit 100 yards away. He was shocked. Someone was trying to kill him. He ran to the library and hid behind a heavy wooden piling. Every time a bomb hit he seemed to rise a foot in the air.

Except for the bombs dropped on the pursuit planes about to take off, the raiders were concentrating on hangars, shops and buildings. Anti-aircraftmen of the New Mexico National Guard were shooting 37-mm. and 3-inch guns at the passing formations. It was the first time most of the men had fired live ammunition. Much of their training in the United States had been with broomsticks and boxes or wooden models. And even if their bursts were exploding far below the targets, it was satisfying and somehow exhilarating to shoot finally in earnest.

At Fort Stotsenberg, cavalrymen were standing under mango trees with their horses. They were proud of their mounts. Not one had panicked even though the ground shook from reverberations and flak from Clark Field clattered down on all sides.

Major General Jonathan "Skinny" Wainwright was watching the bombing from outside his headquarters. His houseboy ran to him, eyes big with terror. He was wearing the general's steel helmet. "Mother of God, General, what shall I do?"

"Go get me a bottle of beer," yelled the general above the din. A moment later his aide, Captain Tom Dooley, drove up.

"Tom, you damn fool," shouted Wainwright angrily. "You didn't drive past Clark during this bombing, did you?"

"You sent me orders to report as fast as I could."

Wainwright walked into his headquarters and wrote Dooley an order for a Silver Star.

Abruptly the bombing of Clark stopped. Corporal Brooks dazedly walked toward the flight line. The idea of war was new and terrifying. Bodies and parts of bodies were lying all over. In a slit trench he saw two Filipino pin boys. They were good friends, killed by someone who hadn't even seen them. Brooks couldn't figure it out. Then he saw another friend, a Polish boy of nineteen. By some freak he was blown up like a balloon by an explosive bullet and to Brooks looked almost transparent.

Others staggered from the trenches. In the sudden silence the groans of the wounded could be heard. Many of the buildings were burning. The big oil dump blazed, sending dark rolls of smoke across the field.

As Colonel Eubank started a hurried inspection of the Group, the two B-17's being painted were taxied unharmed out of their burning hangar. Eubank learned only a few of the Flying Fortresses parked on the field were damaged. His bombers had been saved by a miracle.

Lieutenant Joe Moore was now about 20,000 feet above Clark in his P-40 with Lieutenant Randall Keator on his tail. Trailing half a mile behind and 3000 feet below was Lieutenant Edwin Gilmore, the third of the pursuit pilots to take off successfully from Clark. Nine Zeros suddenly swooped down on Gilmore. Moore and Keator jumped the Japanese. Almost instantly Keator shot down a Zero. It was the first American kill over the Philippines. A moment later, Moore found a Japanese in his sights. As Moore pulled the trigger, he wondered how it would feel to shoot live ammunition. Up until now it had been forbidden because of its scarcity. A Zero blew up in his face. He dove on another target. There was a second explosion.

Pilots of the 34th Pursuit Squadron in Dell Carmen, 14 miles to the south, saw smoke rising from Clark Field. Without orders they took off in their worn P-35's. Before they reached Clark several Zeros confidently attacked the much larger

American group. Easily out-maneuvering the outdated 35's, the Japanese drove them off.

At 12:40 P.M. the 12 P-40's of Flights A and C were still circling over their field at Iba, looking anxiously for raiders. Suddenly over their radios they heard a hysterical voice shouting, "All pursuits to Clark Field! All pursuits to Clark! Enemy bombers overhead!" Then they heard the crash of bombs in their headsets. They raced to the east.

Standing near the strip at Iba, Second Lieutenant Glenn Cave watched the P-40's disappear. A moment later at 12:44 P.M. another pilot said, "Look at that pretty formation of B-17's."

Cave looked to the west. He counted 52 planes in perfect formation at 13,000 feet. "You're crazy," he said, "there aren't that many B-17's in the Philippines." Black objects started wobbling from the planes. The two pilots dove into one of the few foxholes on the beach. Cave landed first, the other man on top of him. As bombs exploded and the earth shook he was glad he was the man on the bottom.

At that moment the six Iba planes of B Flight which had flown to Manila and returned when they heard the mysterious false alarm from Clark were innocently approaching their home field for landing. The control tower frantically called the incoming planes, warning of the bombers high overhead, but the radios of the P-40's were jammed.

As the first plane touched down, Second Lieutenant Andy Krieger, pilot of the plane flying cover for the other five, saw the field explode in a great blinding flash. Krieger climbed away so fast he had to level off at 10,000 feet to let his engine cool. Looking down he saw what looked like a squadron of P-35's circling the field. They were crazy to try and land on that bombed-out strip. Then he saw they had big red spots on the wings—Japanese! He dove into their circle, and shot at the plane ahead. When tracers suddenly zipped past him, he turned and saw three Zeros on his tail.

On the field below, Cave also thought the planes swooping down were P-35's. Red lights on the wings were blinking. Cave was puzzled. Suddenly bullets spattered in the sand. He finally realized he was being strafed. He heard a deep rumble. Another flight of bombers was making its run. This time the other man got to the bottom of the foxhole first. Cave looked at his legs sticking up and wondered if they'd be hit.

Halfway to Clark, the other Iba pursuit planes heard Lieutenant Krieger call, "All 3rd Pursuit to Iba." Half of the 12 planes turned back. But Lieutenant Fred Roberts and five other Iba pursuit pilots flew headlong into the Zero fighters preparing to dive onto Clark Field. Almost out of gas, three Americans were quickly shot down. To Roberts' amazement the Japanese planes were faster, more maneuverable and climbed at a terrifying rate. How could these possibly be Japanese? He and other pilots had been told there was no such thing as a good Japanese fighter plane.

He didn't know, of course, that exact data on these Zeros had been sent to the War Department by the brilliant, unorthodox Claire Chennault in the fall of 1940. The chief of the Flying Tigers had also revealed how the heavier P-40 could master the faster Zero, but this information, which could have saved the lives of bewildered American pilots dying that moment, had been filed and forgotten. Chennault was not at all popular with Air Corps commanders.

Holes appeared in Roberts' wings. Suddenly a cable at his feet was shot out. He felt a sting in his leg, then numbness. The needle of his gas gauge wobbled near empty. He pulled sharply to the west, heading for Iba.

As he crossed the Zambales Mountains smoke was rising from his home field. Tiny objects, obviously Japanese strafers, were diving and circling, but he had to come in. As he approached the field he tried to lower his wheels. Something was wrong. As he swung in behind a two-place Japanese fighter, the man in its rear began blinking a red light at him. Roberts loosed a burst and turned out to sea. With only ten gallons of fuel, he decided to beach his plane. He headed toward the water at 120 miles an hour, then realized he'd misjudged the distance. He was too high. He quickly nosed down, crashing into the surf 50 yards from shore.

He swam to the beach. The barracks was burning. So were other buildings, and a gas truck. He heard a pig squeal and looked toward what had been the village of Iba. All the nipa shacks were blazing; palm trees were mowed down; carts were tipped over; horses lay dead, feet in the air. Children screamed in terror. Filipinos were moaning, "Help me, Joe."

The strip was a mass of craters. Several P-40's were crackling. The radar shack was a shambles, its operators killed. The control tower was riddled with bullets, its crew of four dead.

Disaster had struck suddenly. Iba was completely destroyed and most of the survivors were in a state of shock. The coolest man was not a combat pilot but the young flight surgeon, Lieutenant Frank Richardson. Taking charge, he commandeered a bus, quickly loaded the wounded and headed for Manila.

Back at Clark, as the survivors stared unbelieving at the wreckage, there was a cry, "Here come the strafers!"

The Zeros which had been circling far above the bombers were diving. Their main targets were the big Flying Fortresses and P-40's parked on the field. Soon they were joined by 44 of the 53 Zeros from Iba, now looking for new targets. One by one the parked Fortresses exploded with great roars as tracers ignited their gas tanks.

"Get in the woods," shouted an officer to men in the big ditch near the main hangar. Several dozen men scrambled out of the deep straight ditch and headed for the nearby woods as three Zeros swept over, riddling the area.

A score of white-coated Chinese dashed out of Charlie Corn's PX restaurant. A Zero swooped and the ground was instantly white with their bodies. Nearby, Corporal Brooks was looking helplessly for quick shelter. He threw himself at a shallow ditch, digging frantically with hands and feet as two Zeros dove at him, their bullets squealing past. He ran to a deeper ditch and jumped onto a master sergeant.

"Excuse me," he said.

"Never mind," said the sergeant. "That's just one more it has to go through to get at me."

In a nearby trench an antique water-cooled .30-caliber machine gun was spitting bullets at the strafers. A youthful mechanic was pumping it to keep it cool. After the first wave passed, the young man still kept pumping frantically as if in a trance.

A truck swung by, blood dripping out of the sides. It was filled with wounded heading for the Fort Stotsenberg Hospital. Other wounded were walking dazedly, eyes blank.

The Zeros now had little opposition except from the machine guns of the 200th Field Artillery, and the 192nd and 184th Tank Battalions. When the water-cooled barrels of the artillerymen's old Brownings burned out, the gunners grabbed rifles and shot at the swooping Zeros.

As suddenly as it started the attack was over. Great black clouds of smoke covered the field. All the parked P-40's and 30 medium bombers and observation planes were burning. All but three of the Flying Fortresses were completely destroyed. In one raid the Japanese Navy airmen had knocked out half of MacArthur's Far East Air Force. Too late America had learned what the lessons of war in Europe should have taught: a heavy bomber force without adequate fighter protection, air warning and anti-aircraft guns is helpless, useless.

The returning Japanese planes were checking in. Not a bomber had been lost and only 7 fighters were missing. The claimed results were so fantastic—25 planes shot down and 71 destroyed or severely damaged on the ground—that conservative officers at Formosa were dubious. Yet as claim piled on claim it was obvious that, even allowing for the natural optimism of all fliers, complete surprise had been achieved. It was a second Pearl Harbor.

At Imperial Navy Headquarters in Tokyo the news was received with another enthusiastic demonstration. In half a day, two of the three most powerful deterrents to complete success in Southeast Asia had been cancelled: the Pacific Fleet and MacArthur's air force. The third was British Admiral "Tom Thumb" Phillips' powerful striking force. According to the last reconnaissance report the battleship *Prince of Wales* and the battle cruiser *Repulse* were still in Singapore harbor —too shallow for their conventional aerial torpedoes and well protected by anti-aircraft batteries.

If only the two big ships could be lured into the open sea.

4

1 It was dusk, December 7, in Pearl Harbor. Smoke still rose from the shattered fleet. The stink of spilled oil, burning and death was thick and nauseating. It was drizzling.

Hawaii was in a state of shock. The seventy-one-year-old governor, Joseph E. Poindexter, after a soothing telephone talk with Roosevelt, had been persuaded to declare martial law a few hours earlier. There were wild rumors from all sides. Eight Jap transports were seen rounding Barbers Point. Gliders and paratroopers had dropped at Kaneohe. Other paratroopers were coming down in sugar cane fields southwest of Ford Island, still others in the Manao Valley. At 11:46 A.M. the Navy reported: ENEMY TROOPS LANDING ON NORTH SHORE. BLUE COVERALLS, RED EMBLEMS.

Fifth Columnists, saboteurs and spies were reported everywhere: driving taxis, waiting on tables, tending gardens, selling groceries. They had cut arrows in cane fields and ringed Oahu with sampans to direct the Japanese raiders to their targets; they had driven milk trucks down airstrips, methodically knocking off the tails of parked American planes; they had poisoned reservoirs and caused other damage and mischief. Takeo Yoshikawa, now in the hands of the FBI, would have been amused.

The Navy was in a state of alert. A new grim joke was going around. "On this day even the chiefs worked."

At the Navy Yard, Admiral Bloch was having more than his share of alarms. A telegram from the Office of Naval Intelligence in Washington warned him of a Japanese-operated radio in the basement of the Marine Barracks. Nothing was found but the usual mops, brooms and supplies. Then Bloch discovered that some public-spirited but misinformed person had put up signs on the yard hydrants: DON'T USE THIS WATER, POISONED!

With darkness it was unsafe to be abroad. Every moving object was a potential target for wide-awake riflemen. At Wheeler Field, someone heard a pilot, obviously referring to the fuel in his plane's tank, mention gas. In minutes the gas alarm was spread. At Hickham Field, barracksless men were sleeping on cots under the sky. Suddenly a guard saw a mysterious dark shape sneaking toward him. It was a friend returning from the latrine. But the guard fired several rounds. Instantly there was wild confusion and shouts of, "Japs landing! Bombing! Attack coming!" Anti-aircraft guns burst out on all sides in a fantastic Fourth of July display. Every man with machine gun, rifle or pistol shot into the air. Falling flak and bullets sent more to the hospital.

At 7:30 P.M. Lieutenant Fritz Hebel was calling Ford Island tower. His flight of six planes from the carrier *Enterprise* was just off Diamond Head, and he requested landing instructions. They were returning from a fruitless search to the southwest for Nagumo's carriers.

"Break formation with landing lights on," was the answer.

As six planes skimmed over the sand of Waikiki Beach, the pilots could see spots of light all over the island in spite of the new blackout rule. Pearl Harbor itself was dark except for ghostly red glows from still-smoldering ships. The planes roared along Battleship Row, passing through great clouds of smoke. The pilots relaxed. It had been a rough day and they were glad it was over.

They formed in a neat right echelon at 100 feet, their red and green wingtip lights on as instructed. As Hebel dropped his wheels, a single string of tracers shot up from the Navy Yard. Then a second.

Hebel saw Herb Menge's plane explode. He banked to the right, but he too was hit. He headed in a crash dive for Aeia. Eric Allen was already parachuting through a hail of fire, toward the oil-covered water.

The other three pilots flicked out their lights. Gayle Herman dove for the Ford Island runway. He just made it, his plane peppered with eighteen holes. The other two pulled up wheels and scooted for the sea. One, Jimmy Daniels, waited for the firing to stop and then came back with lights out, low and fast, to land safely. The second, Dave Flynn, parachuted into a cane field at Barbers Point.

The anti-aircraft score was almost perfect. Of six planes, four were destroyed and one damaged. This time Pearl Harbor had not been caught napping.

Soon the area was again comparatively quiet. The only lights came from fires on the *Tennessee* and a few other burning ships. There were also flares from the overturned *Oklahoma* where men with acetylene torches were frantically trying to cut a hole in the hull and rescue ten suffocating comrades inside.

Other trapped men were inside the *West Virginia*, lying flat on her keel at the bottom of the harbor. A huge pocket of air, sealed inside the ship when she sank, was keeping alive some of the 66 still aboard. The survivors were tapping on the sides of the ship to attract attention. But no one heard them.

2 In Manila it was then only late afternoon. At his headquarters MacArthur was reading a radiogram from Marshall. It assured him he had "the complete confidence of the War Department," and promised he could expect "every possible assistance within our power." It was reassuring after months of squabble for more men and material.

Ironically, at almost that very moment the *Pensacola* convoy bound for Manila with planes and men was being diverted to the Fiji Islands. Four other big troopships bound for Manila, the *President Johnson, Bliss, Etolin* and *President Garfield,* had already been ordered back to San Francisco.

MacArthur had not yet been informed of these moves nor was he aware of a secret British-American military agreement that had been reached long before Pearl Harbor, which recognized Hitler as the chief threat to the democracies and specified that the bulk of all supplies and men must go to Europe. The main strategy in the Far East, it had been agreed, would be defensive. It was a logical plan, unanimously approved by both high commands.

Just after dusk the aircraft tender *Langley*, the light cruiser *Boise* and two oilers eased out of Manila Bay. Admiral Hart had ordered his striking force south where it would be safe from bombing. The following noon those on the *Langley* bridge saw a silver object overhead. It looked like a twin-engined plane diving through the moving clouds.

"It has all the appearance of an unfriendly aircraft," said the officer of the deck. "Tell all guns to stand by for a dive."

Chief Petty Officer Gus Peluso, the captain's talker, instantly broadcast the alarm. Anti-aircraft fire burst out from every 3-inch gun on the ship. The *Boise* joined in. After half an hour a message by portable tube blinker came to the *Langley* from the navigator of the oiler *Trinity*: "Your convoy is shooting at a fixed position millions of miles away—the star, Venus."

By nightfall of December 8, except for submarines, two

destroyers being repaired at Cavite, and a few supply repair ships, the Navy had left the defense of the Philippines to MacArthur's ground and air forces.

At Iba there was no longer a fighter base. The pockmarked strip was useless. The burned-out barracks and buildings were completely deserted. Part of the 3rd Pursuit was hurrying south along the highway to Manila. Part was tramping in terror across the Zambales Mountains. According to rumor, the Japanese were landing on the coast near Iba. One pilot recalled the motto jokingly suggested that morning: "Damn the torpedoes and take to the hills." Now it wasn't funny.

There was the same feeling of near-panic at Clark Field. Most of the men were hiding out in the cogon grass, fearful of a new bombing. Some were miles away in the hills. There were constant rumors of parachuters and saboteurs. Many slept that night next to their guns, gas masks clamped to their faces. On the flight line, Colonel Eubank, who reminded some of Will Rogers, climbed up on a tractor. "Gentlemen," he said to those who grouped around him, "we're just like a good bird dog that's been shot too close to on its first time out."

Eubank's words had a strangely calming effect. Word passed that the old man was still full of fight. The sense of shock that made many worry more about their footlockers than war itself began to leave Clark Field.

In Manila, MacArthur was assessing his forces. Soon he would have no navy, probably no air force, but he still had his ground forces—and Marshall's promise of every possible assistance.

3 In the United States, people were reading their Monday morning papers. Most Americans were completely stunned by the greatest military disaster in U.S. history. For the most part, Washington officials were in as great a state of shock as the man in the street. The smashing of the Pacific Fleet and the destruction of the heart of MacArthur's air force had altered in a single day the entire concept of war in the Pacific. The most immediate fear of the War Department was another Japanese carrier attack—this time on the locks of the Panama Canal or on aircraft factories on the California coast, or a new attack on Pearl Harbor and its still undamaged Navy Yard.

As the truth of the first losses began spreading around official Washington, a wave of hysteria swept over many of the most eminent government officials. One even telephoned the White House, shouting that the West Coast was no longer defensible and demanding that battle lines be established in the Rocky Mountains.

The public response in general was quite different. It was a war born in shame. But the humiliating defeats acted as a spur to the people. Telegrams and letters flooded the White House pledging full aid and cooperation. Yamamoto had made a colossal blunder. Instead of striking fear into American hearts, the crippling of the Pacific Fleet had insulted the people, filling them with fury and fight. They would never forget Pearl Harbor.

A little after noon, senators walked down the long corridor of the Capitol, through the rotunda. They entered the House chamber behind Majority Leader Barkley of Kentucky and Minority Leader McNary of Oregon. Then came the justices of the Supreme Court in black robes, sitting to the left of the rostrum. Also down front were Stark and Marshall. In the packed gallery was Mrs. Roosevelt. Near her at the President's request was the widow of another war president, Woodrow Wilson.

At 12:28 P.M. the Cabinet entered. A moment later, Speaker Sam Rayburn rapped his gavel for silence and said, "The President of the United States!"

There was great applause as Roosevelt slowly entered on the arm of his eldest son, James, who was wearing the uniform of a Marine captain. After a brief prayer by the chaplain, the President opened a black loose-leaf notebook and in the hush began to read: "Yesterday, December 7, 1941 —a date which will live in infamy—the United States of America was suddenly and deliberately attacked by naval and air forces of the Empire of Japan."

Tension rose as Roosevelt scornfully described the attack on Pearl Harbor even as peace talks were going on. It built as he recited tersely the other points of attack. "Japan has, therefore, undertaken a surprise offensive extending throughout the Pacific area. The facts of yesterday and today speak for themselves. The people of the United States have already formed their opinions and well understood the implications to the very life and safety of our nation.

"As commander-in-chief of the Army and Navy, I have directed that all measures be taken for our defense, that always will our whole nation remember the character of the onslaught against us."

There was a sudden cheer as the mass tension was suddenly released. Roosevelt looked up from the notebook, smiled and waved his hand in acknowledgment. By now everyone was standing, applauding loudly.

The speech, often interrupted by applause, continued for several minutes. Finally he said, "With confidence in the armed forces, with the unbounding determination of our people, we will gain the inevitable triumph. So help us God.

"I ask that the Congress declare that since the unprovoked and dastardly attack by Japan on Sunday, December 7, 1941, a state of war has existed between the United States and the Japanese Empire."

The room was filled with applause, whistles, shouts and rebel yells. Roosevelt closed the notebook, lifted his arm in greeting. Then he took the arm of his son and, with the great room still in an uproar, left the dais.

For the first time as President, Roosevelt had spoken what was in every American's heart. People of all political convictions and beliefs were today welded into one great angry voice. Partisan politics, for the moment at least, were forgotten. America was at total war.

It was already Monday evening in Italy. Foreign Minister Count Galeazzo Ciano was called to the phone. It was Joachim von Ribbentrop. The German minister was overjoyed about the Japanese attack. He was so happy that Ciano, himself very dubious of its long-range advantages, became infected with the German's enthusiasm. That is, until Ciano put down the phone and began to worry again.

Most Japanese were then eating breakfast, for it was early morning, December 9, in Japan. By now the average Japanese had recovered from the shock of realizing his country was at war with America and Great Britain. Four years of the China Incident had prepared him to accept the idea of total war. Restrictive measures had been applied so subtly, so gradually, that he accepted as necessary and almost normal what would have seemed impossible four years before. Great Britain and America were obviously to blame for the desperate situation. They had plundered the Orient and now selfishly refused to allow Japan even the oil necessary to run her ships.

The Japanese citizen had been trained since childhood to accept authority and to devote his life to service to the living god, Emperor Hirohito. And he and his sons were imbued with Japanese *seishin*, spirit, making them fanatics in battle.

The first full day of war, with its amazing and sweeping victories, had brought all Japan together. Even the most conservative accepted war with calmness and quiet determination. Even the most liberal were still Japanese and though many had done their best to avoid war, they now realized it was impossible to shape the future course of events. Some reformers even believed that war would help bring about their long-sought domestic dream: equality. As in America, all conflicting groups instantly became united. Japan was fighting a holy war of righteousness and self-defense. Every Japanese was ready for total sacrifice.

4 The citizens of Singapore first learned of the war in the Pacific when they were awakened by the crash of bombs at 4:00 A.M., December 8, just two hours after the Pearl Harbor attack. Though the Fighter Control Operations Room got a report of unidentified aircraft 140 miles from Singapore half an hour earlier, no one answered its repeated telephone calls to the Civil Air Raid Headquarters.

Consequently the lights of the city guided the pleasantly surprised invaders to their target. In fact the lights stayed brightly lit during the entire raid since the man with the keys of the master switch could not be found.

Although 63 were killed and 133 injured and not a single Japanese plane was downed, there was no sense of real alarm in Singapore. The great majority were soothed by the Order of the Day issued later that morning by Air Chief Marshal Sir Robert Brooke-Popham, commander-in-chief in the Far East.

We are ready. We have had plenty of warning and our preparations are made and tested. . . . We are confident. Our defences are strong and our weapons efficient. . . . What of the enemy? We see before us a Japan drained for years by the exhausting claims of her wanton onslaught on China. . . . Confidence, resolution, enterprise and devotion to the cause must and will inspire every one of us in the fighting services, while from the civilian population, Malay, Chinese, Indian, or Burmese, we expect that patience, endurance and serenity which is the great virtue of the East and which will go far to assist the fighting men to gain final and complete victory.

A few, like Yates McDaniel, the American representative of Associated Press, were not at all reassured by Sir Robert's words. McDaniel knew the Brewster Buffalo fighter planes protecting Singapore were slow and cumbersome. He knew there wasn't a single tank in Malaya; that almost every one of the great fixed guns of Singapore was pointing to the sea, useless in case of a land attack down the peninsula; that the troops in Malaya had no jungle training; and that the native groups had been excluded from any participation in the defense of their homes.

On the morning of that first day of war, about the same time Japanese fliers were ending their devastating attack on Clark Field, the telephone in the newsman's room at the Cathay Building rang. It was McDaniel's good friend, Vice-Admiral Sir Geoffrey Layton.

"We're sending out two capital ships under Tom Thumb Phillips," he said. By the tone of his voice McDaniel knew Layton strongly disapproved. "Would you like to go along?"

"How long will they be out?"

"Five or six days." He explained that Phillips was determined to sail north, up the east coast of Malaya, and attack the great invasion convoy which was still landing Japanese troops at two points. These troops, obviously, were going to drive south down the peninsula and assault the island of Singapore by the back door.

McDaniel was tempted. It sounded like a good show, but since he was the only AP man in town and big news was liable to break at Singapore, he refused.

Cecil Brown of CBS was eating his dessert, ice cream, in the dining room of the famed Raffles Hotel when he was called to the phone.

"Do you want to go on a four-day assignment?" asked Major C. R. Fisher, in charge of facilities for correspondents.

"What is it?"

"I can't tell you what it is, or where we are going, but I must have an immediate yes or no and you must leave at once."

Brown hesitated a moment, then said, "All right, I'll take it."

By this time McDaniel was talking face to face with Layton. The newsman's guess had been right. Layton was very upset by Phillips' decision to sortie out of the relatively safe harbor with little or no air cover and attack an unknown force with the *Prince of Wales*, the *Repulse* and four destroyers.

Layton said he had objected strenuously but, even though he was senior to Phillips, he didn't have the authority to override him. When McDaniel left he was uneasy. Layton was an old China Station hand who had spent many years in these waters and was a keen student of Japanese capabilities. The newsman had met and admired Phillips, obviously a brilliant man of great decision and courage. He had been struck by the strangely heroic figure of the little admiral standing on a box so he could look over the bridge. But this was his first major sea command. McDaniel remembered the black cat of the *Prince of Wales* sitting in President Roosevelt's lap at the signing of the Atlantic Charter. It gave him a feeling of foreboding.

Just before sailing, Phillips asked Air Vice-Marshal C. W. Pulford what air cover the fleet could get on its sortie. Pulford, a former Navy man, was eager to cooperate but his airfields in north Malaya were already reportedly knocked out. He promised to give Phillips air reconnaissance the next day, December 9. But he doubted if he could spare any planes at all on December 10.

Phillips then boarded the *Prince of Wales*. Captain L. H. Bell, captain of the fleet, noticed the admiral's uneasiness.

"I'm not sure," said Phillips, "that Pulford realizes the importance I attach to fighter cover over Singora on the tenth. I'm therefore going to send him a letter stressing this point again and asking him to let me know as soon as possible what he can do for certain."

The admiral wrote the letter. He handed it to Bell who gave it to a messenger on the jetty. As Bell stepped back on board the *Prince of Wales'* securing wires were cast off. The sun was setting as the fleet steamed out of Singapore. The *Prince of Wales* led, followed by the *Repulse* and the destroyers. As they passed Changi Signal Station at the east end of Singapore Island, Phillips was handed a radiogram from Pulford:

REGRET FIGHTER PROTECTION IMPOSSIBLE.

Phillips shrugged his shoulders. "Well," he told his staff, "we must get on without it." After the blaze of publicity about the two great ships since their arrival in Singapore, it would have been unthinkable, he felt, to do nothing now. The two big ships and their escorting destroyers continued on their northern course.

Hidden by rain and clouds, the *Prince of Wales* and the *Repulse* were halfway to their goal by noon the next day, December 9. They would be ready to attack the Japanese convoy the following morning. Cecil Brown, the CBS correspondent, was talking to Captain William Tennant, skipper of the *Repulse*. Brown was not at all happy about being on the *Repulse* instead of the flagship. "We can't even mention that the *Repulse* is out here," he said.

"That's nothing," said Tennant, laughing. "The *Repulse*

hasn't been mentioned for as long as I remember." In two and a half years of war the ship had never been in action and its men were keen for something to happen.

At 1:45 P.M. the Japanese submarine I-56 sighted the two warships and their destroyer escort speeding north. The commander excitedly radioed the news. But the reception was bad. The submarine's radioman couldn't make himself understood. He tried again and again.

In Saigon, Rear Admiral Sadaichi Matsunaga, of the 22nd Air Flotilla, was just starting a special staff conference. Two "Babos," reconnaissance planes, had falsely reported sighting the *Prince of Wales* and the *Repulse* in Singapore harbor. The problem was how to attack. Pilots were alerted and told to study the depth of the harbor and the best directional approach.

At 3:00 P.M. another message was handed to Matsunaga. It was from the I-56. Two men-of-war and four destroyers were sailing north at 14 knots near Procondor Island. Which report was right? After discussion the staff agreed the submarine report was more logical. Torpedo planes were ordered to prepare for attack.

At the bases of Matsunaga's two air groups, while torpedoes were being hastily loaded and unpinned, excited Army officers drove up. Somehow the word had mysteriously spread that the Navy had tracked down the two great British ships. Each plane took off amidst cheers of enthusiasm and hope.

On the *Repulse* a notice was posted just as Cecil Brown came to the wardroom for tea at 3:30 P.M. "All officers and ratings from dawn tomorrow are to be at action stations and are to wear clothing to resist burns from flashes of exploding bombs and shells."

Then a message came from Admiral Phillips:

> WE HAVE MADE A WIDE CIRCUIT TO AVOID AIR RECONNAISSANCE AND HOPE TO SURPRISE THE ENEMY SHORTLY AFTER SUNRISE TOMORROW, WEDNESDAY. WE MAY HAVE THE LUCK TO TRY OUR METAL AGAINST SOME JAPANESE CRUISERS OR SOME DESTROYERS IN THE GULF OF SIAM. WE ARE SURE TO GET SOME USEFUL PRACTICE WITH HIGH-ANGLE ARMAMENT, BUT WHATEVER WE MEET I WANT TO FINISH QUICKLY AND SO GET WELL CLEAR TO THE EASTWARD BEFORE THE JAPANESE CAN MASS TOO FORMIDABLE A SCALE OF AIR ATTACKS AGAINST US. SO, SHOOT TO SINK.

Quiet excitement spread over the *Repulse*. At last the ship was to see some action. After a dinner of hot soup, cold beef, ham, meat pie, pineapple and coffee, a group of officers in the wardroom mulled over Japanese capabilities.

"The Japs are bloody fools," said one. "All these pin-pricks at widely separated points is stupid strategy."

"The Japs can't fly," said another. "They can't see at night and they're not well trained."

"They have good ships," said a third. "But they can't shoot."

"You British are extraordinary," said Brown at last. "You always underestimate the enemy. You did it time and again, in Norway and France, in Greece, in Crete."

The officers were shocked at such open criticism. "We're not overconfident," one told Brown. "We just don't think the enemy is much good. They couldn't beat China in five years and now look what they are doing out here, jumping all over the map instead of meeting at one or two places. They cannot be very smart to be doing that."

Then at 9:05 P.M. Captain Tennant's voice came over the loudspeaker of the wardroom. He announced the fleet had been detected by three enemy aircraft and Admiral Phillips was sure the Japanese convoy at Singora would now scatter.

"I know that you all share with us the disappointment in not engaging the enemy at this time," said Tennant regretfully, "but I am sure you will agree with the commander-in-chief's judgment. We are, therefore, going back to Singapore."

The officers groaned in disappointment and bitterness. Brown hurried to a sailor's mess to get their reactions. Men were sitting around long tables, some with tears in their eyes.

"How do you fellows feel about this?" asked the newsman.

"This always happens to the *Repulse*," said one.

"We're just an unlucky ship," said another.

The three planes which had just forced Phillips to turn back were not Japanese, but Allied. They either did not see the British Fleet or neglected to report it.

Back in Saigon it was midnight and Rear Admiral Matsunaga was getting discouraged. None of the scores of planes he'd sent to find and attack the *Prince of Wales* had seen anything but Japanese ships. The first report must have been true. The big British battleships were probably safely tied up at Singapore. He decided to recall the planes.

On the *Prince of Wales*, Admiral Phillips was handed a

message from his chief of staff, Admiral Sir Arthur Palliser, still in Singapore. It read:

ENEMY REPORTED LANDING AT KUANTAN.

This was a point on the east coast of Malaya midway between Kota Bharu and Singapore. It wouldn't be too far off the track on the return home. Earlier in the evening Palliser had reported that the airport at Kota Bharu had finally fallen. This made Kuantan even more important. It had to be defended.

At 12:52 A.M., December 10, the *Prince of Wales* altered its course and speeded west at 25 knots toward Kuantan, where in fact not a single invader was landing. The Japanese submarine I-58 was heading for the same general area. Their paths slowly converged. Little more than an hour later, at 2:10 A.M., the I-58 spotted the two big British ships at "Fumoro 45," naval code for the position 140 miles off Kuantan. Excitedly the commander maneuvered his submarine till the *Repulse* was in his sights. Two torpedoes were fired. Then four more. All missed.

The big battle cruiser, unaware of her narrow escape, slipped by.

" It Was Such a Beautiful Ship"

1 Action on the third day of war started at Guam Island. This American possession, about midway between Wake and Manila, was almost within sight of the Japanese mandated island of Tinian. In spite of this strategic position Congress had thought it a waste of money to build fortifications or even dredge a harbor.

Consequently Navy Captain George McMillin, governor of the island, commanded only a token force. His 430 Marines and Navy men and 180 native Insular Guards were armed with 13 World War I Lewis machine guns, 15 BAR's and 170 Springfield rifles.

At 2:00 A.M. on December 10, Seaman Second Class Juan Perez of the Insular Guards was on beach patrol at Tamuning, several miles east of the capital, Agaña. He and his three mates could see great ominous shadows on the water. Then they heard splashing as landing boats approached. Perez loosed a burst from his Browning automatic rifle at the first boat. Then he ran down the road toward Agaña. He had to warn Captain McMillin that the invasion had started.

The boats nearing shore contained 400 Japanese Marines. Landing at three other points on the island were three battalions of Colonel Masao Kususe's 144th Regiment. In all, 5400 men from 9 transports—escorted by 4 destroyers, 1 seaplane tender and 1 mine layer—were about to storm an unfortified island.

At 4:30 A.M. Perez, now manning the Palace grounds at Agaña with 100 other guards and Marines, saw a figure steal across the Plaza. He fired. A large group of figures ran for cover. A fierce fire fight broke out.

As first daylight came, a bugle blew retreat. Perez and the other defenders ran back into the Palace.

"Fight for your lives!" shouted someone. Perez put down his empty BAR and grabbed a rifle.

At 5:35 A.M. an auto horn blasted three times. American fire ceased.

As Commander D. T. Giles walked out of the Palace, Perez

sneaked out the back and crawled toward the swamps. In front of the Palace, Commander Hiromu Hayashi was assuring Giles in sign language that the civil rights of the natives would be respected and prisoners treated according to the laws of war.

These were laws of war new to Americans. As soon as Captain McMillin came out to surrender, Japanese soldiers tore off his outer clothing, leaving him clad only in shorts. The Battle of Guam was over. Seventeen Americans and Guamanians were dead. One Japanese was killed.

2 By dawn of that same day, two convoys lay off Luzon, the main island of the Philippines; one at Aparri on the north coast and one at Vigan on the northwest coast. About 400 of the Tanaka Detachment of 2000 men began to transfer from transports to landing craft. The detachment's mission was to set up a flying field near Aparri. It was a miracle, thought Colonel Toru Tanaka. Since leaving Formosa three days before, he had been constantly expecting an enemy air attack. So far not a shot had been fired at them.

In Aparri a young American reserve officer, Lieutenant Alvin C. Hadley, was watching this formidable array of ships off shore. To defend the town he had about 200 untrained Filipinos. The 400 Japanese approaching the docks looked like an army to Hadley. He ran to the telegraph office, wired regimental headquarters that 10,000 Japanese were landing. The answer soon came back: Attack immediately and drive them into the sea.

Young Hadley did the sensible thing. He packed up his half-dozen worn machine guns, and by sign language and pidgin English, managed to convey to his men, who spoke half a dozen different dialects, that they were to withdraw south.

At Vigan the Kanno Detachment, also 2000 men, and also detailed to set up an advance airfield, didn't have even young Hadley to deal with. There wasn't a defender in town. Only the heavy seas battled the Japanese. But Lieutenant Grant Mahony, flying a P-40 on a lonely night reconnaissance, spotted this cluster of ships at 5:13 A.M. and radioed back the alarm. Forty-seven minutes later, five Flying Fortresses, recently flown up from Del Monte, left Clark Field. It was the first U.S. bombing mission of the war and the pilots were eager. Major Cecil Combs led his squadron up the middle of Luzon, then turned west, coming over Vigan at 12,000 feet. Transports sprouted white wake. Farther out to sea the decks of several Japanese light cruisers seemed ablaze with ack-ack fire.

"Christ almighty, there they are," shouted someone excitedly.

The squadron roared over, dropping bombs. It turned and made a second run. Now P-40's darted out from land and dove on the transports. They dropped fragmentation bombs and sprayed the landing barges with machine bullets.

Finally worn-out P-35's from Del Carmen arrived, their hungry pilots groggy from lack of sleep. Sixteen had started but, because of engine failure, only seven had made it. As the cruisers and destroyers covering the landing moved inshore to defend, the seven old planes, led by Lieutenant Sam Marrett, made a series of low runs. Several barges were sunk and three transports set afire. Marrett, nicknamed "The Rat" because of his pointed nose and small face, continued to rake the largest transport with his machine guns. He wouldn't leave it alone, going back time after time. He dove again, guns blazing at mast level. Suddenly the transport blew up, tearing off the wing of Marrett's plane.

In spite of the spirited American air attack the bulk of the Kanno Detachment landed near Vigan by noon. At that same time wave after wave of Japanese medium bombers from Formosa began passing overhead, southward-bound.

Twenty minutes later, whistles began to blast in the suburbs of Manila, 210 miles to the south, at Nielson Field. Men ran through the corridors of Brereton's headquarters shouting, "All out! All out! Air raid!"

Captain Allison Ind, the intelligence officer, was getting his first sleep in two days at his desk. "They're coming fast," shouted his assistant, Lieutenant Lou Bell. "And they're headed straight for this layout."

Ind was instantly wide awake. "Serious, Lou?"

"This looks like it! There's a big formation of mixed stuff coming down from the north. They may smack Clark on the way, but the guess is that they keep rolling right down. We're going to catch it this time."

It was a good guess. The medium bombers from Formosa were approaching in three separate attack groups. Twenty-seven Betties were scheduled to strike at the fighter base at Nichols; 27 Betties at Del Carmen; and 27 Nells at the Cavite Naval Base. Flying cover slightly ahead of these bombers and now only about 40 miles north of Manila were 73 Zeros.

Just before 1:00 P.M. the twenty-seven Betties bound for Nichols roared over Manila. A moment later their bombs fell on the barracks, offices and warehouses of the airfield. Within minutes Zero fighters dove, strafing the grounded planes. The American fighter pilots already aloft on patrol fought hard but could not stem the invaders. Almost every American was shot down or crashed for lack of gas.

Captain Robert Taylor, chaplain of the 31st Infantry (U.S.), watched the attack from Isaac Peral Street. At the first sound of bombs falling on Nichols Field there was a sense of crowd panic. Then above the noises of sirens, horns, and clatter of ponies drawing *calesas,* the church bells of Manila started ringing. Taylor noticed the soothing effect on the people. It seemed to him the bells were saying, "Be calm. Have faith. Use good sense. God is the same in hours of battle as in peace." It made him suddenly realize it was his job to minister to men in time of battle and keep their spirits high.

About 10 miles to the northeast, Captain Jesus Villamor was in the officers' mess at Zablan Field when he heard the distant clanging of Manila's church bells. The commander of the 6th Pursuit Squadron of the Philippine Air Corps ran toward the hangars, followed by his pilots. He could see about six Zero fighters swoop down. Their bullets tore into trainers lined up on the parking apron.

Villamor clambered into his plane. Two men laboriously wound the engine and it finally caught. Without warm-up, Villamor taxied the antiquated P-26 fighter down the field. It was practically a museum piece, with nonretractable landing gear. As he took off, he saw a Zero close in from behind. For the first time he realized how awful it was to be a flier. He was alone and scared. Knowing he had only seconds of grace, he suddenly dipped down in the valley at the edge of the field. The Zero followed. Villamor hedgehopped recklessly, then climbed steeply to the right. Though the Zero was still on his tail, Villamor's confidence had returned. He knew he was a hot pilot and with a few tight turns could get behind the Zero.

At an altitude of only 500 feet, he made the tightest turn of his career. The Japanese followed easily. Again and again Villamor turned, but he couldn't shake the Zero. He knew it was hopeless. Only something unexpected and unorthodox would save him.

He suddenly dove under a row of high-tension wires. Evidently assuming the P-26 was crashing, the Japanese climbed, looking for another victim. Villamor was safe—for the moment.

By now the second group of 27 bombers was sweeping toward Manila. These had abandoned their run on Del Carmen because preceding Zero fighters had almost totally destroyed that field's remaining P-35's in strafing attacks. These Betties were now heading for their secondary target, the shipping in Manila Bay.

U.S. High Commissioner Francis Sayre watched them approach from his terrace on Dewey Boulevard. It looked as if his last hour had come. But abruptly the planes turned west and began unloading on merchant ships in the harbor.

Ten miles across the Bay, the siren sounded at Cavite Naval Base. From the control tower, Cecil Browne, supervisor of tugs, barges and ferryboats, had seen the third group of bombers, the 27 Nells. They were coming in across Corregidor Island in a great V. As he was calling Operations, Browne saw the planes pass almost overhead and continue east without dropping a bomb. Then they abruptly turned and started back. At 1:10 P.M. their bombs began to fall on Cavite. The nine 3-inch anti-aircraft guns from the naval base opened fire but their bursts were far below the high-flying Nells.

Bombs exploded near the pier, missing the ammunition dump but hitting the lumberyard, powerhouse, dispensary, Commandancia and torpedo storage. Browne and the two others in the forty-foot tower were so stunned they didn't move during the bombing. He saw 27 more bombers approach. These were the Betties which had just bombed the shipping in Manila Bay. Suddenly Browne realized he was surrounded by glass. "What the hell are we doing here?" he shouted. The three men hurried to the ground and hid under the dock.

Thousands in Manila watched the destruction of Cavite in horror and fascination. From atop the Marsman Building in the Walled City, Admiral Hart, in spite of warnings from his staff, was a grim witness. Carl Mydans of *Life* and Mel Jacoby of *Time* watched from the shore of Manila Bay. Mydans, peering through glasses, was amazed at the precision of the Japanese. Not a single bomb seemed to be wasted. The bombing in the Russo-Finnish war, he told Jacoby, was never as effective as this.

Back at Cavite, Lieutenant Malcolm Champlin—the aide of Rear Admiral Francis Rockwell, commandant of the Sixteenth Naval District—was racing in his car to the scene of action.

As Lieutenant Champlin approached the bridge leading to the Navy Yard, cars poured out, loaded with wounded. A truck just ahead of Champlin swerved to avoid hitting a group of running Filipinos and collided with a truck coming from the yard. Champlin jumped out of his car. The two

Filipino truck drivers were shouting at each other, waving arms.

"Shut up," shouted Champlin. Seeing bumpers were hopelessly locked, he ordered the wounded in the first truck transferred to private cars. He himself jumped into the back of the truck and helped pass out the wounded. The last man was covered with blood, one eye missing. As Champlin gently carried him to a car, the Filipino opened his good eye. Seeing Champlin's officer insignia he tried to smile. "Thank you, sir. Thank you, sir," he mumbled. He gurgled and suddenly slumped. He was dead.

As Champlin ran into the yard, fires were raging. Cars moved slowly to avoid the many bodies in the streets. He hurried to the small shelter near the Commandancia. There he saw Rockwell, hatless, blood over his shirt, carrying wounded.

The powerhouse was demolished, eliminating the fire-fighting system. Rockwell telephoned to Manila for all engines capable of pumping water from the sea wall and dock. The admiral's face was tense as he told Champlin they had to stop fires before they reached the ammunition dump. Abruptly the wind shifted and the flames rose to new heights. Champlin looked around him. The most important shops were ashes and twisted beams. And close to 500 men were dead.

The Filipino fighter commander, Jesus Villamor, was about 4000 feet above Zablan Field when he saw 27 Betties make a second devastating attack on Cavite and then turn leisurely and head north for home.

He climbed to his ceiling and just as the bombers were closing in he dove head-on at the leading plane. He loosed a short burst with his two puny .30-caliber guns. To his amazement, smoke spilled out of the bomber and it spun out of formation.

Three other equally daring Filipino fighter pilots were right behind Villamor. One, Lieutenant Jose Gozar, tried three times to ram his plane into a bomber, but his P-26 was too slow. Except for the plane shot down by Villamor all the raiders escaped.

The fires at the naval base were still raging late that afternoon. Lieutenant Champlin and a pickup crew of volunteers were pulling cases of gas masks from a burning loft. They saved 700, escaping just as the building collapsed.

Champlin thanked the men.

"I'm up for summary court-martial," said one. "Will you testify for me?"

Champlin assured him he would.

Then the rest of the crew piped up, "Will you do that for all of us?" They had all been released from the brig during the bombing.

The yard was a shambles. The submarine *Sealion* had received a direct hit at its mooring and more than 200 torpedoes had been destroyed. By now Admiral Hart had assessed the damage and made up his mind. Manila was untenable as a naval base. He ordered 2 destroyers, 3 gunboats, 2 submarine tenders and 2 mine sweepers south. Almost nothing was left of the Asiatic Fleet in the Philippines except submarines.

As darkness came, rumors swept Manila. The Philippines were being abandoned by the Americans; Japanese paratroopers were landing all over; saboteurs were ready to strike at the water system; spies were sending up rockets to guide bombers.

The rash of paratrooper reports had started that morning. By now Fort McKinley was being combed for Japanese; airmen and cavalrymen were roving the slopes of Mt. Arayat. Terror spread with every hour. Not a Japanese paratrooper had landed. The parachutists had been American fliers escaping from their burning planes.

      3 By far the most important action on this third day of war was taking place 1500 miles southwest of Manila, just off the Malay Peninsula. By midmorning, the 10 search planes and 96 bombers of Rear Admiral Matsunaga's 22nd Air Flotilla, alerted before dawn by the submarine I-58, were still searching in vain for the *Prince of Wales*.

The two ships were almost 100 miles west of the nearest Japanese planes, lying off Kuantan. The destroyer *Express*, sent to investigate that harbor, was signalling Admiral Phillips by lamp, "All's as quiet as a wet Sunday afternoon." The report of a Japanese landing had been a false alarm.

Before returning to Singapore, Phillips decided to investigate a suspicious-looking tug and 4 barges sighted at dawn. The 2 big ships—escorted by the destroyers *Express*, *Electra* and *Vampire*—headed toward the tug at 9:00 A.M. The fourth destroyer, *Tenedos*, had been sent home the night before because of low fuel.

By this time the 96 Japanese bombers and 10 search planes had about given up all hopes of finding the British. In fact, the search planes were on their way home. Then at 10:15 A.M., just as they were about to radio the bombers to return to their bases, one sighted 2 large battleships and 3 destroyers through the clouds. Excitedly, the word was radioed back to Saigon.

At 10:30 A.M., radio contact was finally made with the 27 Betty torpedo planes of the Kanoya Group and the new position of the British ships given. The Betties changed course, levelling off at 10,000 feet. Lieutenant Haruki Iki, leader of the 3rd Division of this group, forgot his exhaustion and hunger immediately. He was eager for action. He'd trained his nine-plane division so well they had been given the title of Champions of the Navy by the Combined Fleet. At 10:50 A.M. Iki saw what looked like a British Walrus observation plane through the clouds. The enemy fleet must be near!

It wasn't until then that Lieutenant Sadao Takai, leader of the 2nd Division of the Genzan Group, received a code message from Matsunaga pinpointing the British ships 70 nautical miles southeast of Kuantan. Takai radioed his own planes and headed north-northwest toward the enemy. The 1st Division, though it did not get the message, saw Takai's nine torpedo planes change course and followed. The 3rd Division had long since gone home, its nine bombs having ignominiously missed the *Tenedos* earlier that morning as it was heading for Singapore.

Clouds began to fill the skies but patches of sea appeared occasionally. Every man strained to have the honor of being the first to see the enemy. Takai was so nervous his hands shook. He had a strange impulse to urinate. He remembered what Captain Kosei Maeda, the commander, had told them that morning just before take-off: "Calm down and put your strength in your abdomen."

The British Fleet was also getting ready for battle. The Japanese search planes had been seen and Admiral Phillips had ordered first degree of High Angle readiness. Excitement was building on the *Prince of Wales,* the *Repulse* and the three destroyers. Action was coming at last.

On the *Repulse* CBS correspondent Brown was taking pictures of a gun crew playing cards. As the ship zigzagged he snapped the *Prince of Wales* half a mile ahead. Then at 11:07 A.M. he heard the loudspeaker announce, "Enemy aircraft approaching. Action stations!"

He looked to the south. Nine planes in single file were coming in at about 12,000 feet. Rooted to the port side of the flag deck as if hypnotized, he watched the falling bombs get larger. Suddenly 10 yards away a great geyser shot out of the

sea, drenching Brown and his camera. As he instinctively
hunched there was a dull thud and the ship shuddered.

"Fire on the boat deck! Fire below!" blared the loudspeaker.

Gunner T. J. Cain of the destroyer *Electra* had been watching these bombers with little apprehension, even though their
formation was amazingly precise. In his long experience high-
level bombing was usually more frightening than dangerous.
Even with the much higher-rated Germans it hadn't proved
very effective against moving ships.

Then he saw bombs dropping. The pattern was impressive,
horrifying. A series of bursts seemed to envelop the 794-
foot-long battle cruiser. There was a great cloud of smoke
and the *Repulse* disappeared behind a giant wall of water. The
men on the destroyer watched, shocked into silence. Suddenly the big ship reappeared, black smoke belching from her
deck. The men on *Electra* cheered spontaneously.

The battle cruiser's lamp blinked, "One hit . . . some damage . . . but under control. Fighting efficiency unimpaired."
As the message was translated the men of *Electra* cheered
again.

Iki saw the bombing from about seven miles' distance. His
throat was dry. As his nine planes went into single file, he
saw three Betties of his group's 1st Division and two from
the 2nd dive on the *Prince of Wales* and launch torpedoes.
The other 13 planes were heading for the *Repulse* so Iki
decided to attack the *Prince of Wales*. He swept down, veins
pounding with excitement. Five miles from the target he saw
a terrific explosion in the rear of the ship. Then the front of
the *Prince of Wales* erupted. Two direct hits. Thinking quickly, Iki pulled up and turned north. No use killing a cripple.
He was going after the *Repulse*.

The *Prince of Wales*, listing 13 degrees to port, was already weaving uncertainly at 15 knots. Both port shafts
were out of action and her steering gear wouldn't work.

The two divisions of Genzan Group now approached the
battle area. Lieutenant Takai heard the group commander
say, "Form assault formation." Then, "Go in!" The 1st Division swept forward ahead of Takai and started a gradual
dive. Takai followed. It was standard practice for the 1st Division to hit the largest vessel; he was supposed to take the
next largest.

To his amazement there were no enemy fighters even
though they couldn't be much more than 125 miles from
Singapore. Anti-aircraft fire seemed to engulf the 1st Division
but there was none near him. Through binoculars he studied

a large ship giving off a narrow plume of white smoke, moving straight, flanked by three destroyers. It was the *Repulse,* but to Takai it looked exactly like the battleship *Kongo.* His blood ran cold as he saw the 1st Division approach. Were they attacking their own ship? Takai called the observer who answered shakily, "It looks like our *Kongo* to me, too."

Takai was now at 1700 feet, the position ideal, but he still couldn't make up his mind. Finally he got a close look. It was definitely *not* the *Kongo.* He turned into the clouds to confuse the enemy and changed course. Suddenly he darted out of the clouds. He was a mile and a half from his target.

On the *Repulse* a bugle blew. Over the loudspeaker came a roar, "Stand by for barrage!"

Every gun on the battle cruiser blasted as Takai's nine torpedo bombers swept in.

"Look at those yellow bastards come," said someone next to Brown. The newsman could do nothing but look. He saw paint blisters on the guns as big as tennis balls. The gunners' faces were eager, excited, streaked with sweat. He saw torpedoes drop one by one. The big ship dodged each one with heavy grace. The attack was abruptly over.

"Plucky blokes, those Japs," said the man next to the correspondent. "That was as beautiful an attack as ever I expect to see."

To Brown's surprise the men seemed ecstatically happy, with no hate for the enemy. On the bridge Captain William Tennant had just sighted "not under control" balls hoisted from the *Prince of Wales.* He asked the flagship what damage she had suffered but Phillips did not answer. He signalled the admiral, "We have dodged 19 torpedoes thus far, thanks to Providence." He added that all damage from the bomb hit was under control. The *Repulse* was fit for action. But he still got no answer from the listing *Prince of Wales.* He wondered if Phillips had told Singapore of the attack. To be on the safe side he radioed home:

ENEMY AIRCRAFT BOMBING.

The message from Tennant was received in Singapore at 12:04 P.M. It was the first word they had received of the fleet since a message early that morning saying Phillips would be home sooner than expected. Six Brewster Buffalo fighters were sent to the rescue at 12:15 P.M.

Three minutes later Captain Tennant asked Phillips if his wireless was out of order. Getting no answer, he reduced the *Repulse*'s speed to 20 knots and moved closer to the flagship to see if he could be of any assistance. Just then nine more torpedo planes headed toward the *Repulse*. Six of these abruptly turned left and headed for the *Prince of Wales,* but the other three dove straight at the *Repulse*. Tennant started to swing his ship to starboard. One torpedo dropped, heading for the *Repulse*. Tennant helplessly watched it for a minute and a half. If he turned he would be hit by at least two other torpedoes. It struck amidships. "Order all possible men to starboard," he said as the battle cruiser listed to port.

Even with this hit the *Repulse* was still in no serious trouble. It could maneuver at 25 knots. But another much more powerful attack was already developing. Lieutenant Iki's nine torpedo planes were nearing the battle cruiser. Iki dropped quickly to 1300 feet, below the clouds. Pompom bursts blossomed on all sides. He had an impulse to pull up but he knew he had to get in much closer. Now he was skimming 125 feet above the water. Ahead was a wall of fire from the *Repulse*. He had to get through it. Nineteen hundred feet from the ship he yanked his release. He had it broadside!

Holes appeared in his wings. He pulled sharply to the left. As he did the ship turned to starboard and momentarily the two were parallel. Below he saw sailors in what appeared to be raincoats lying down on the deck. He saw faces looking up as his crew peppered them with machine guns. There was an orange blaze as the plane behind Iki, piloted by Chief Petty Officer Toshimitsu Momoi, burst into flame. The third plane, Petty Officer First Class Yoshikazu Taue's, exploded and pinwheeled into the ocean. Iki saw two quick explosions on the bow of the *Repulse*. Of his first three planes, two had made direct hits. As he climbed 3200 feet to wait for his six remaining planes, he saw another torpedo hit.

The men on the *Electra* saw the torpedo drop from Iki's plane and skim toward the *Repulse*. It exploded near her bows, shooting a great column of water above her upper deck. Before the water fell another huge spout rose a few yards astern. The big ship veered crazily, like a blind man staggering helplessly.

When Iki's torpedo hit near the gunroom the rudder jammed. The *Repulse* was out of control. Captain Tennant, on the bridge, knew his ship could not survive. Then three more torpedoes—two on the port side, one on the starboard —smashed home.

The decision to cease all work below is a hard one for a ship's captain to make, but Tennant didn't hesitate. To save the men in the hold he ordered everyone to come on deck. Carley floats were cast loose.

In a minute the ship listed 30 degrees to port as men poured onto the deck wearing their life belts. Tennant looked over the starboard side of the bridge and saw about 250 men filing up from below in an orderly manner. His men, long eager for battle, were responding as he had known they would. "Prepare to abandon ship," he said over the loudspeaker in a cool voice. He told the men how well they had fought the ship, paused and said, "God be with you."

On the flag deck, Brown was amazed by the lack of panic. It was incredible. Then one young sailor tried to shove to the head of the line.

"Now, now," quietly scolded an equally young sub-lieutenant, "we are all going the same way, too." The young sailor stopped pushing.

It was 12:32 P.M. The big ship hesitated as if deciding whether to roll over completely or not. Ahead, almost hidden in smoke, Brown could see the *Prince of Wales* settling. She belched steam and water and seemed to lie helpless in the water.

Men were jumping off the tilting *Repulse*. Brown saw an eighteen-year-old Australian, Midshipman Peter Gillis, dive 170 feet from the control tower at the top of the mainmast. Another dove from another tower but crumpled as he hit the side of the ship. A third dove straight down the smokestack. A dozen Royal Marines leaped from the deck near the stern and were quickly sucked into a propeller.

Many men scrambling up from the hold were trapped by the rising water. A group of 42 climbed up frantically inside the dummy smokestack but their way to freedom was barred by a wire screen. They were caged.

The ship was listing 70 degrees as Captain Tennant told his staff, "Well, gentlemen, you had better get out of it now."

When one asked if he was coming too he said, "Off you go now. There's not much time."

They pleaded when he would not leave his ship. Several pushed him through the doorway onto the deck. He struggled to stay aboard but officers and men seized him, forcing him to leave the bridge.

At 12:33 P.M. the ship rolled over. Brown was hanging indecisively to the hull of the ship. He watched someone slide past him and then dive gracefully into the sea. Brown stood up and jumped, his camera swinging from his neck. As soon as he hit the warm oily water he automatically looked at his watch. It was 12:35 P.M. Eyes burning from oil, he saw the bow of the *Repulse* sticking up like a church steeple, its underplates a gruesome red.

Five thousand feet above, Iki couldn't believe what he saw. The great ship was pointing straight at him. Then it dove out of sight. It was not possible. "Banzai, Banzai!" he screamed, throwing up his hands. The bomber, with no hands on the wheel, dipped.

Iki's crew of seven were screaming as wildly as he was. He ordered wine passed. They all drank a toast. Below he saw hundreds of dots in the water. Two destroyers were darting about picking them up.

Brown was struggling in the oily water, his only support a small table. "I've got to remember all this," he said to himself. Then he thought, "What the hell's the use? I will never be able to report this story." Almost exhausted, he drifted to a Carley float, but it was so full he didn't even try to get aboard. A young Marine, Morris Graney, pulled the half-drowned correspondent aboard. "My Lord," said the Marine, "do you still have your camera?"

"Yes."

"Let's all sing," suggested Graney. He and a few others sang, "When Irish Eyes Are Smiling." Then Iki's planes roared overhead. "They're coming over to machine-gun us," someone shouted.

"Dive under the water!"

Brown knew if he dove he'd never come up again. He just watched. But the planes ignored them, flying on north. Many in the water thought the Japanese were merely out of bullets. It had never occurred to Iki, who had plenty of ammunition, to dive and strafe the survivors. The British had fought gallantly, in the tradition of Bushido. War was still new, chivalrous. Both sides would soon learn an enemy spared today might kill tomorrow.

It was 12:41 P.M. The *Prince of Wales,* already hit by five torpedoes and settling badly, was barely steaming forward. Nine high-level bombers approached. The ship's remaining five .25-inch guns and pompoms sent up a heavy barrage but the planes came on. At 12:44 P.M. bombs wobbled down. Four straddled the ship but one hit the catapult deck.

The 35,000-ton battleship staggered. The destroyer *Express* darted alongside the starboard side of the quarter-deck. Captain Leach ordered all wounded disembarked. Then he told those not required to fight the ship to board the destroyer.

Admiral Phillips, on the bridge, was still determined to

save the flagship. "Tell the *Express* to signal Singapore for tugs to tow us home."

But the *Prince of Wales* had received her death blow. A few minutes later the great ship began to founder. Her beams were almost awash. Leach ordered all hands to abandon ship, while he and Phillips stood together on the bridge waving to their departing men.

"Good-bye," called Leach. "Thank you. Good luck. God bless you."

At 1:19 P.M. the *Prince of Wales* heeled over quickly to port and the little admiral and Captain Leach disappeared. A minute later the famous battleship sank from sight, almost dragging with it the *Express*, still faithfully standing by her side.

At that moment the six lumbering Buffaloes from Singapore arrived. Not a Japanese plane was in sight. Flight Lieutenant T. A. Vigors looked down, shocked. He swung low over the hundreds of men struggling in the water. Men waved and held up their thumbs. Vigors had seen disaster and courage at Dunkirk and in London night raids but he never encountered such an indomitable spirit. He came so low he could see the faces of the survivors. Any minute they might drown or be strafed, yet they waved and joked as if they were holiday-makers at Brighton.

The men of the *Electra* were accustomed to tragedy. They had seen the *Bismarck* sink the *Hood*. The little destroyer was again senior ship in a force struck by major disaster. Commander May quickly passed the news to Singapore. But why, he asked himself as he saw the Buffaloes overhead, hadn't Admiral Phillips called for air cover earlier?

Perhaps the admiral thought such a request couldn't be met, for he had been told that fighter cover would not be given off Singora. Phillips also knew that all the northern airports had become untenable because of the Japanese advances down the Malay peninsula. Friends of Phillips guessed he might not have wanted to give away his position by breaking radio silence. The admiral had been noted for his extreme sensitivity to this danger. In any case, the answer would remain a mystery. All the senior officers on the bridge of the *Prince of Wales* went down with Phillips and Leach.

Lieutenant Iki was now approaching his home base near Saigon. His excitement was marred as he thought of his two good friends, Momoi and Taue. Although he was reasonably sure his own torpedo had hit the *Repulse*, he reported that the first two hits had been made by Momoi and Taue. It was the least he could do for them.

When the division landed, excited pilots and mechanics crowded around each plane. Iki and the others were dragged out and thrown up in the air. Then the group commander, Captain Naoshiro Fujiyoshi, his face beaming with happiness, embraced Iki. He had told his men, just before they took off, "Let us meet each other at the Yasukuni Shrine in Tokyo. Let us fight to the death." His fliers had vowed to fight so as to leave no regrets. They had done so.

A few minutes later one of Iki's pilots came to him. "As we dove for the attack," he confessed, "I didn't want to launch my torpedo. It was such a beautiful ship, such a beautiful ship."

In Singapore the *Express, Vampire* and *Electra* were unloading the 2081 saved from the two ships. Eight hundred and forty would not come back. Already a fantastic rumor was sweeping the city—1000 Japanese planes from carriers had suddenly appeared, completely destroying the *Prince of Wales* and the *Repulse.*

The news of the loss shocked the colony. At one stroke the fleet was gone. Most naval authorities were sure the ships had been sunk by carrier-based planes. Some, still doubting Japanese capabilities, claimed the *Tirpitz,* brother ship of the *Bismarck,* had helped.

Air Vice-Marshal Pulford was shaken by the news. Many of his boyhood friends had gone down with the two ships. When he saw Captain Tennant he said, "My God, I hope you don't blame me for this! I had no idea where you were."

At the request of the over-all commander in the Far East, Duff Cooper—Churchill's special representative—made a radio broadcast that evening to the people of Singapore. He pointed out that the loss of the *Prince of Wales* and the *Repulse* must not lead to despondency but merely to a determination to fight all the harder and so avenge the loss.

The words meant little to the people in Singapore. The unsinkable had been sunk. Were the island's defenses really "impregnable" as the authorities boasted?

Tokyo was just as shocked by the news. To old Navy men it was impossible. Great battleships under way simply couldn't be sunk by planes. Younger Navy airmen were exultant. Their theory was now a fact. And only four planes had been lost.

In England it was only the morning of December 10. Winston Churchill was in bed, opening his dispatch boxes before rising. The phone rang. It was the first sea lord, Sir Dudley Pound. "Prime Minister, I have to report to you . . ." Pound coughed and gulped ". . . that the *Prince of Wales* and *Repulse* have both been sunk by the Japanese—we think by aircraft."

"Are you sure it's true?" Churchill was astounded. This was the most direct shock of the war.

The next dawn Lieutenant Iki flew over the graves of the *Repulse* and *Prince of Wales*. As he passed the sunken hulls of the two ships he dropped bouquets of flowers.

6   *The Death Watches*

1   On December 11, at 1:50 A.M., 11 Japanese ships cautiously approached the subtropical atoll of Wake, America's lonely mid-Pacific outpost. They drew within 8000 yards, then stopped. This was the Wake Island Invasion Force—the light cruiser *Yubari*, 6 destroyers, 2 patrol craft, 2 transports and a landing party of 560 infantry-trained sailors. They had come from the Japanese-mandated Marshall Islands to the south. Each patrol craft began lowering a single landing boat holding 80 armed men. Though the wind was brisk, they were safely launched. Now boats were carefully lowered from the two transports, but they banged dangerously against the steep sides of the old-fashioned ships and were quickly hauled back aboard. Word of this difficulty was flashed to the flagship, *Yubari*, and the over-all commander, Rear Admiral Sadamichi Kajioka, postponed the landing until after sunrise.

A little before 3:00 A.M. the *Yubari* and 4 destroyers began to move toward the island. According to the latest intelligence report, the daily bombings of Wake had crippled at least half of the coastal guns and completely wiped out the air force. Kajioka was determined to bombard the remaining guns to rubble. There was still no sign of life ashore. The enemy, the admiral assumed, was asleep as usual.

But the Americans were well aware of the enemy off their southern shore. Major James Devereux was watching from the beach through night glasses. The problem of defending Wake was complicated by its peculiar geography. The visible top of an inactive underwater volcano, it is an atoll shaped like a V with the open end to the northwest. Each arm is about five miles long. Narrow channels cut off the tips of each arm so that there are actually three islands. The tiny island that is the end of the right arm is called Peale; the one at the end of the left arm, the southern side, is Wilkes. The main island is Wake. The land area of all three is only two and a half square miles, about that of New York City's Central Park.

Devereux was faced with an almost bald defense position. The atoll's highest point was 21 feet and except for some dwarf trees and shrubbery there was no cover. He could use only four of his six 5-inch guns to defend the arm of the atoll now about to be invaded and all of these had been damaged partially by the bombings. Neither the two guns of Lieutenant Clarence Barninger at the apex of the V-shaped atoll, Peacock Point, nor the two of Lieutenant J. A. McAlister, on tiny Wilkes Island, had range finders.

As Devereux walked back to his dugout command post, which was about a mile inland of Peacock Point, he worked out his plan of defense. He telephoned McAlister and Barninger: "Don't fire until I give the word." Then he called Major Putnam of Marine Fighting Squadron 211 who was at the narrow airstrip. This was about 400 yards south of Devereux and ran east-west for a little more than a mile along the southern arm of the atoll. "How many planes do you have in commission?" asked the soft-spoken Devereux.

"Four."

"Don't take off until I open fire. I'm trying to draw them in, and the planes would give the show away."

"Okay. Good luck."

Just as the first faint daylight appeared, the *Yubari* headed directly for the apex of the atoll. When it was about 7000 yards off Peacock Point, it swung to the west closely followed by the 4 destroyers. All 5 ships opened fire about 5:30 A.M.

When *Yubari* reached Wilkes, the end of the atoll's left arm, she reversed, coming in a few hundred yards closer, and continued the bombardment of the southern shore. At Peacock Point she again reversed and moved in to 6000 yards. When there still was no answering fire, Kajioka was convinced the Wake guns were harmless.

On Wake, Devereux's phone was clamoring. Barninger and McAlister kept begging for permission to fire. "Under no circumstances fire until I give the word," he told his talker, Corporal Robert Brown.

"Hold your fire till the major gives the word," Brown relayed to the gunners.

"What does that little bastard want us to do?" one answered. "Let 'em run over us without even spitting back?"

But the major still refused to give the word as the Japanese moved closer with each pass. At 6:10 A.M., the invaders were only 4500 yards from Barninger's guns on Peacock Point.

"Commence firing," ordered Devereux.

There was a roar from Barninger's battery. The first salvo went over. The *Yubari*, stunned by the close miss, zigzagged out to sea. The next salvo from Barninger straddled the cruiser.

Destroyers darted wildly, trying to lay a smoke screen to protect the flagship. The two guns from Wilkes opened fire on the destroyer *Hayate*. After the third salvo a great cloud of smoke covered the ship. When the smoke cleared there was no sign of the *Hayate*.

McAlister's gunners yelled and cheered.

"Knock it off, you bastards," shouted Sergeant Henry Bedell. "Get back on the guns. What d'ya think this is, a ball game?"

By 6:15 A.M., Putnam and three other Marine pilots were 15,000 feet above Wake, waiting for an expected attack by carrier planes.

"Well, it looks as if there are no Nips in the air," said Putnam on the two-way radio. "Let's go down and join the party."

Putnam's Wildcat broke through the overcast. Anti-aircraft fire burst all around but he kept coming. At 3500 feet he began a steep dive. At 1500 feet his two 100-pound fragmentation bombs, slung under the plane with homemade lugs, dropped. They missed a destroyer by 200 yards.

Putnam dove on another destroyer. The crew had neglected to take down the glass from the bridge. Sun glistened as Putnam came head-on at bridge level. He got all four guns on the glass. The shattered splinters made a rainbow. Bombs and ammunition gone, Putnam headed back to reload.

Kajioka's force was wildly zigzagging trying to avoid the shells and bombs. A Wildcat swept down on the *Yubari*, its machine guns raking the bridge and narrowly missing Kajioka himself. The admiral ordered withdrawal. The flotilla turned south, but Fighting Squadron 211 followed.

At 7:37 A.M. Putnam, now on his fourth flight, saw a

destroyer, the *Kisaragi*, lagging behind the main body. He hesitated, wondering if he should go after the cripple or follow the cruiser. Just as he decided to make a pass at the destroyer, the *Kisaragi* suddenly became a ball of fire. Moments later, at 7:42 A.M., Putnam could see no wreckage below. Just empty, sparkling ocean. Although some thought he had sunk the ship, Putnam guessed a bomb dropped earlier by Captain Henry "Baron" Elrod had started a fire that finally reached the magazines.

The first battle for Wake was over. The southern horizon was clean of ships. Back at Devereux's command post all was quiet. Reports of casualties came in: three men slightly wounded by shrapnel. Devereux was puzzled. Why hadn't the Japanese brought air cover? Why hadn't they bombarded thoroughly before moving in? Why hadn't they sent assault troops ashore in landing craft?

"It's been quite a day, Major, hasn't it?" said Corporal Brown to Devereux.

The little major nodded absently. He was already thinking of the next attack.

2　There was excitement that same morning in Manila. Rumors of a great battle at Lingayen Gulf the previous night raced through the city: the main Japanese landing had at last come but the 21st Division (Philippine Army) had sunk most of the invasion vessels; the bay was filled with floating bodies and the beaches strewn with Japanese dead.

When *Life* photographer Carl Mydans heard that the wild battle was still raging, he drove quickly to the battleground. Arriving at Lingayen Bay near noon he found no bodies on the beaches, no sign of battle. Except for Filipino soldiers resting beside their weapons, the great expanse of sand was empty.

"Looking for bodies?" asked an American major, smiling.

"Well, that's what headquarters reported," said Mydans. "I heard there was a big battle here."

The major explained that several dark shapes had been seen approaching the mouth of the Agno River the previous midnight. A battery of the 21st Field Artillery opened fire. A moment later Lingayen Gulf was ablaze as every gun in the area, from 155-mm. guns to pistols, opened fire.

The cause of "The Battle of Lingayen Gulf" was a small Japanese motorboat on a reconnaissance mission. Not hit, it reported that the main landing, actually not scheduled for eleven more days, should be made 30 or 40 miles farther north, where there were almost no beach defenses.

Two days later MacArthur received heartening news from Washington. At General Marshall's instigation, the *Pensacola* convoy, originally bound for Manila and then turned back to Hawaii, was again being rerouted. Its desperately needed guns, planes and men were headed once more to the Philippines, this time by way of Brisbane, Australia.

MacArthur, delighted at the change in atmosphere in Washington, immediately conferred with Admiral Hart. It was not a happy conference. The two men had been in conflict ever since MacArthur took command of the U.S. Army forces in the Far East the previous July. Their differences of opinion were sharpened by the sudden disasters of the past week. The admiral threw cold water on MacArthur's plan to bring the *Pensacola* convoy up from Australia. The Japanese, he surmised, would throw a complete blockade around the Philippines before the convoy could leave Brisbane. Hart gave MacArthur the impression that the islands were doomed.

Nothing could have incensed the general more. Upset by what he considered defeatism, he wired Marshall:

IF THE WESTERN PACIFIC IS TO BE SAVED IT WILL HAVE
TO BE SAVED HERE AND NOW.

No American knew the temper and ultimate capabilities of the Filipinos better than MacArthur. His father, General Arthur MacArthur, had been the first military governor of the Philippines. The son had served ten years in the islands, as a lieutenant, a brigadier general, commanding general of the Philippines Department and as military advisor to President Quezon.

MacArthur was a highly controversial figure. Though Filipinos, almost to a man, regarded him as the greatest man alive, most of those who served under him had widely divergent opinions. Close associates, like Colonel Hugh Casey, his engineer, claimed MacArthur had a photographic mind that worked with the precision of a calculating machine; most men on the staff felt he was the outstanding military leader of his day. Detractors—and most of these had little personal contact with the general—insisted he was an egomaniac surrounded by an inferior staff whose main purpose was to build a legend around their chief; they ridiculed MacArthur's specially designed marshal's cap, his carefully combed but thinning hair, the clenched corncob pipe and the jutting jaw.

MacArthur told Marshall that as soon as the Filipinos discovered the U.S. had abandoned hope, the entire structure would collapse around him. "The Philippine theatre of operations," he radioed, "is the locus of victory or defeat." He begged Washington to review its entire strategy and send him immediately air power to delay the Japanese advance. Saving the Philippines, he argued, would justify "the diversion here of the entire output of air and other resources."

The next day, December 14, tension in the Philippines increased. A reported Japanese landing at Legaspi on the southern end of Luzon was confirmed. But MacArthur guessed correctly that this, like the previous landings on the northern end of the island, at Aparri and Vigan, was a minor probing. Again he held back, waiting for the main landing that was bound to come soon. "The basic principle of handling troops," he told reporters, "is to hold them intact until the enemy has committed himself in force."

Many in Manila thought this main landing had already come, for the papers were still headlining eyewitness stories of the great conflict at Lingayen Gulf. The "battle" was even confirmed by Major LeGrande Diller, MacArthur's press chief. He gave reporters a release stating that an enemy landing had been attempted in the Lingayen area but was repulsed by a Philippine Army division.

While other reporters were wiring their papers and magazines of the great victory, Carl Mydans buttonholed Diller. "Pic," he protested, "I've just been to Lingayen and there's no battle there."

Diller pointed to the communiqué he had just read aloud. "It says so here."

This, thought Mydans, was a startling indication of how poorly the war was being covered. He alone of all the reporters had gone to the scene of action. The others had stayed in town, satisfied to pass on press handouts. It wasn't the correspondents' fault primarily. There was no organization and little pressure from back home to get out and see what was really going on.

The Japanese were already laughing at a communiqué of December 12 claiming that Captain Colin P. Kelly, Jr., had put the battleship *Haruna* out of commission during the landings at Aparri. On the day she was supposed to have been sunk, December 10, the *Haruna* was 1500 miles away in the Gulf of Siam. There hadn't been a battleship near the Philippines. In fact nothing had been sunk or even heavily damaged near Aparri that day.

The Kelly story was already a news sensation, its facts

becoming distorted with every telling. The most popular version, the one many Americans would retain through the years, was that Kelly won the Medal of Honor by diving his plane into the smokestack of the *Haruna,* becoming the first suicide pilot of the war.

The facts were far different. On the morning of December 10, a Japanese carrier was reported operating just north of Aparri. Two Flying Fortresses were sent from Clark Field to attack. One, piloted by Kelly, flew north and as it approached Aparri at 20,000 feet, its occupants continued north almost to Formosa but no carrier was sighted. It was almost noon when Kelly turned back toward the Philippines.

When the B-17 approached Aparri, still at 20,000 feet, the crew saw a "big ship" just off the coast and was sure it was a battleship of the *Haruna* class. The Americans were puzzled when the ship took no evasive action, only continuing its course up the coast. It didn't even fire its antiaircraft guns at the Flying Fortress.

Since there wasn't a warship of any size in the entire Aparri area, it was probably a large transport, which explains why it didn't evade or fire ack-ack. Corporal Meyer Levin, the bombardier, using the touted Norden bombsight, began his run ten minutes from the target. The three 600-pound bombs were dropped in train. All those in the plane except Kelly looked from the windows, following the course of the bombs. They saw the first hit some fifty yards short. The second was a near miss alongside. The third appeared to go down the ship's smokestack. Smoke poured from the ship's stern. Though Kelly circled twice, the smoke became so thick, it was impossible to see the exact damage, but almost everyone aboard the B-17 was confident the ship had been sunk.

The plane, its crew in a celebrating mood, now sped south toward its home base, Clark Field. The rugged mountains of North Luzon were crossed and Kelly began to lower the big bomber. As Second Lieutenant Joe M. Bean, the navigator, leaned forward to check the altimeter, there was a burst of fire and his instrument panel suddenly shattered. The ship was under attack by a Zero fighter piloted by Saburo Sakai. The first round from Sakai's cannon had also wounded PFC Robert E. Altman and beheaded the radio operator, Staff Sergeant William J. Delahanty, who was manning the left waist gun.

A moment later the left-wing gas tanks, which were not self-sealing, broke into flames. Sakai fired another burst with his cannon. This severed the B-17's elevator cables and the big plane headed into a steep dive.

Flames spread rapidly and Kelly ordered his men to bail out. The bottom emergency hatch was pried partway open by Bean and Levin. The bombardier was the first man out. Then Sergeant James E. Halkyard, PFC Altman, PFC Willard L. Money, Bean and Second Lieutenant Donald D. Robins, the copilot, jumped. The ship suddenly blew up. A moment later it crashed on a dirt road about two miles west of Mt. Arayat, almost hitting a group of men from the 26th Cavalry led by Major (now Lieutenant General) Thomas J. H. Trapnell, trying to catch some reported Japanese paratroopers. Close by was the body of Colin Kelly. His chute was unopened. He had sacrificed his life so his crew could live.

By now Brereton's headquarters at Nielson Field was getting fragmentary reports of Kelly's bombing mission off Aparri. A heavily armored battleship had been badly hit and probably sunk. Captain Allison Ind excitedly raced to his office and opened a copy of *Jane's Fighting Ships*. While he was studying it the phone rang. It was Colonel Francis Brady, Brereton's chief of staff.

"It's either the *Haruna* or her sister!" said Brady. "At least she must be one of that class."

Ind compared notes. He too was positive the victim had been of the *Haruna* class. The news swept headquarters. Everyone was wildly exultant. At last American air power had asserted itself. The news was passed on to MacArthur's headquarters. Later the six survivors were closely questioned and a detailed report submitted to Brereton stating that Kelly's bombs had opened the seams of the battleship "more on the starboard than the port side" and forced it to be beached. There was no doubt. A Japanese battleship had been wrecked.

When MacArthur read this report he accepted it at face value and issued the December 12 communiqué: "One spectacular instance was the feat of Captain Colin P. Kelly, Jr., of Madison, Florida, who successfully attacked the battleship *Haruna*, putting that ship out of commission."

America now had its first great hero of World War II, for the story of the Irish pilot and Jewish bombardier was a copywriter's dream. Kelly's heroic action certainly deserved the posthumous D.S.C. he was awarded. But the fanfare was bad for the morale of other American air units whose pilots had accomplished more that same day over the Philippines —and without a line of public acclaim. Major Emmett "Rosie" O'Donnell, Jr., and Lieutenants G. R. Montgomery and George Schaetzel all had more fruitful bombing missions and Lieutenant Sam "The Rat" Marrett's daring attack at Vigan in his outmoded P-35 was already a legend among American airmen.

On the morning of December 14, the story of "The Battle of Lingayen Gulf" broke in newspapers all over the United States. The New York Sunday *Times* banner headline read: JAPANESE FORCES WIPED OUT IN WESTERN LUZON. Lingayen Gulf, reported the *Times,* had been retaken from the Japanese in a great victory.

The United Press stated there had been a fierce three-day fight at Lingayen Beach. One hundred and fifty-four enemy boats had been blasted by the defenders. Not a one had reached shore.

While American readers were being bolstered that Sunday by the paper victory in the Philippines, a recently promoted brigadier general, Dwight D. Eisenhower, was reporting to General Marshall in Washington. Two days previously Eisenhower had been chief of staff to the commanding general of the Third Army. He had no idea what his new assignment in Washington was going to be.

Marshall outlined the situation in the Western Pacific. Then he abruptly asked, "What should be our general line of action?"

Eisenhower had spent four years in the Philippines as MacArthur's senior military assistant and he realized the problem was almost unlimited in its complexity. For the next few days he concentrated on Marshall's question. The facts as outlined were depressing. The Pacific Fleet didn't dare sail to the Philippines. Major reinforcements could be sent only when the Navy was rehabilitated. There was only one solution: set up Australia as a base for offensive operations.

Eisenhower reported back to the chief of staff on December 17. "General," he said, "it will be a long time before major reinforcements can go to the Philippines, longer than the garrison can hold out with any driblet assistance, if the enemy commits major forces to their reduction. But we must do everything for them that is humanly possible. The people of China, of the Philippines, of the Dutch East Indies will be watching us. They may excuse failure but they will not excuse abandonment. Their trust and friendship are important to us. Our base must be Australia. . . . We must take great risks and spend any amount of money required."

"I agree with you," said Marshall simply and then added, "Do your best to save them."

The previous day, Admiral Chester Nimitz, chief of the Bureau of Navigation, had entered the office of Secretary of

Navy Knox. Nimitz had no idea why he'd been summoned
Like other Navy officers he had been stunned by Pearl Harbo
but since then he had been so busy alleviating the troubles o
survivors that he hadn't had much time to study the desperat
situation in the Pacific.

Knox, who had just returned from a personal inspec
tion of Pearl Harbor, explained that Kimmel and his staff had
understandably, been badly shaken by the attack. So shaken
that their recent estimate of the situation completely revised
the strategy of a Pacific war. "The loss of battleships," they
wrote, "commits us to the strategic defensive until our forces
can be built up."

A new commander must be sent to Hawaii, said Knox, one
who could dispel the gloom and sense of fear that permeated
Pearl Harbor and inspire a bold offensive.

Nimitz agreed. Defensive tactics never won a war.

"How soon can you get ready to travel?" asked Knox
"You're going to take command of the Pacific Fleet."

Nimitz was startled. It had never occurred to him that he
would be the one to relieve Kimmel. There were twenty-
eight flag officers senior to him. "Sir," he said, "first I'l
have to get someone to relieve me. I want Rear Admiral
Randall Jacobs."

"You can't have him; FDR doesn't like him."

"I have to have him."

"Get him."

Nimitz said Jacobs was presently at sea but he would send
for him. As Nimitz walked out of Knox's office, he was surprised to see Admiral Jacobs in the corridor.

"Randall, where did you come from? You're just the
person we're looking for. From now on you're chief of the
Bureau of Navigation."

3 On the morning of December 13 the last Indian,
Scotch and Canadian troops on the mainland of China had
been evacuated across the narrow bay to the island of Hong
Kong. The arrival of these defeated soldiers caused a near
panic for few had realized how desperate the military position
actually was. Life had been going on normally with shops
open, buses running on schedule and night clubs filled to
capacity.

Later that morning, at nine o'clock, a launch bearing a
white flag of truce put off from Kowloon, the mainland city
just across the bay. It docked at Hong Kong's Victoria Pier
and a Japanese officer, Lieutenant Colonel Tokuchi Tada,

stepped out. He had a letter addressed to His Excellency the governor, from the commander of the Hong Kong Assault Force, Lieutenant General Takashi Sakai, advising the governor to surrender. This was, wrote Sakai, a humanitarian measure, taken to spare the lives of innocent noncombatants. If refused, severe artillery fire and aerial bombardment would follow.

Governor Young politely but categorically refused the offer. The siege of Hong Kong—a rocky, mountainous island only half again larger than Manhattan—was on.

The facts of the sudden fall of the vaunted defense line on the mainland—its name, ironically, was Gin-drinkers Line —were now common knowledge. The key point in the line, the Shingmun Redoubt, had been captured by a few Japanese wearing sneakers. They had merely crept up a mountain to the concrete redoubt, where the defenders were locked inside in apparent safety, and dropped hand grenades down the vents.

On December 14 the island's 10,000 troops were heartened by a message from Winston Churchill addressed to Governor Young and the "Defenders of Hong Kong."

> WE ARE ALL WATCHING DAY BY DAY AND HOUR BY HOUR YOUR STUBBORN DEFENSE OF THE PORT AND FORTRESS OF HONG KONG. YOU GUARD A LINK BETWEEN THE FAR EAST AND EUROPE LONG FAMOUS IN WORLD CIVILIZATION. WE ARE SURE THAT THE DEFENSE OF HONG KONG AGAINST BARBAROUS AND UNPROVOKED ATTACK WILL ADD A GLORIOUS PAGE TO BRITISH ANNALS.
>
> ALL OUR HEARTS ARE WITH YOU IN YOUR ORDEAL. EVERY DAY OF YOUR RESISTANCE BRINGS NEARER OUR CERTAIN FINAL VICTORY.

The following day morale rose sharply when the Colony's single-sheet newspaper issued a bulletin announcing that the 7th Chinese Army was only 30 miles from the border and would soon relieve Hong Kong.

That night a number of Japanese put off from Kowloon in junks, small rafts and rubber boats. But the British were ready. Four boats were sunk and the landing thwarted.

Three days of almost intolerable tension followed. Then at dusk of December 18, the "death watch" ended as Japanese big guns began a heavy bombardment of the northeast coast of the island. Soon hundreds of launches and rubber boats quietly pushed off from the mainland. They came in three main groups, each a regiment of Major General Tadayo-shi Sano's veteran 28th Division.

Overcast skies and frequent showers hid the invading armada of small boats. As they neared the northeastern coast of Hong Kong, shells from the mainland hit oil tanks near North Point. Great black billows of smoke covered the water front, almost blinding the defenders.

In minutes the coastline between North Point and Lyemun—the area closest to the mainland—was alive with Japanese. The landing was so confusing and the fighting so deadly silent that few defenders realized Hong Kong had been invaded. In an hour most of the hill at Lyemun was in Japanese hands, yet 100 yards away the sentry at No. 2 Gun at Lyemun Fort reported, "Nothing unusual has occurred."

At 10:00 P.M. the men of the fort heard someone shout, "We Japanese have captured Saiwan Hill. It is useless to resist."

By dawn the situation was desperate. General Maltby, realizing the entire eastern half of the island was now in danger of being cut off, ordered the men who manned the great artillery pieces on D'Aguilar Peak to destroy their guns and retreat to Stanley Peninsula. Near panic hit the troops as they blew up their guns and then dashed down the narrow unprotected cliffside road toward Stanley. They left behind all their ammunition, chocolate, extra clothing, Christmas puddings and gin.

At 11:30 A.M. Governor Young visited Maltby in his underground headquarters, Battle Box. Shaken by the wild reports of sweeping Japanese victories, he told Maltby that no matter how bad the military outlook might be, the battle must be fought to the end. Every day gained was a direct help to the Empire war effort.

By noon the next day the Japanese had taken half of Hong Kong Island, penetrating to Repulse Bay on the southern side. Even so, General Sakai was disappointed. He had assumed that once landings had been made, the British would surrender. Instead the defenders, in spite of heavy losses, were fighting tenaciously for every foot they gave up.

Maltby was still hopeful of aid from China. The previous day the Chinese had wirelessed that 60,000 troops were at the frontier, ready to attack. Maltby passed on this encouraging news to every unit. "All ranks," he said, "must therefore hold their positions at all costs and look forward to only a few more days of strain."

But at 4:00 P.M. the military attaché in Chungking wired

that the main Chinese attack could not start before January 1. Even the most optimistic at Battle Box now knew Hong Kong was doomed. The end would come any hour.

4 Early that same morning, December 20, it looked as if the "death watch" in the Philippines was also approaching its end. At 2:00 A.M., MacArthur's headquarters had received a report that a large convoy of 80 transports had been sighted by a submarine 40 miles north of Lingayen Gulf.

Later that morning MacArthur learned more bad news. Before dawn 5000 assault troops in 14 Japanese transports, escorted by a cruiser squadron and the carrier *Ryujo,* had approached Davao in southern Mindanao. A single Filipino machine gun squad of the 101st Division held up the storming of Davao until it was knocked out by a Japanese shell. By 3:00 P.M. the city and airfield were occupied. Before dark half of the assault troops were already being organized for the next step, the capture of nearby Jolo Island. Since Japanese troops were already in North Borneo, the capture of strategic Jolo would fulfill Admiral Hart's gloomy prediction: MacArthur would be completely cut off from Australia.

The next day, the submarine *Stingray* saw the great Japanese convoy approaching Lingayen Gulf. When MacArthur received this report he knew this was the main invasion. He rushed tanks to the north and ordered Brereton to collect every bomber in the area for a morning strike at Lingayen. The beach defenders were warned to expect heavy landings momentarily.

Although the Americans were forewarned, they were fooled. They had expected the Japanese to land near the mouth of the Agno River where the bulk of the artillery was emplaced. The 85 transports of the vast armada were planning to land about 40 miles up the coast where there were almost no defenses. At 1:00 A.M., December 22, the convoy was only a mile or two off the beaches of northern Lingayen Gulf.

The transports carried the main body of the Philippine invasion force, the 14th Army of Lieutenant General Masaharu Homma. The general, a heavy-set man almost six feet tall, was leader of the pro-British-American minority in the Army and was an open enemy of the German-trained General Tojo.

Homma had spent eight years with the British, including service in France in 1918 with the B.E.F. After the fall of

Nanking he had publicly stated that "unless peace is achieved immediately it will be disastrous." Later when the Koiso Cabinet was formed he begged General Koiso to stop the war. The enmity between Tojo and Homma reached its climax when General Muto asked Homma what he thought of Tojo as a possible minister of war. Homma had objected strenuously. Now Tojo was not only head of the Army but Japan's prime minister.

Few of Homma's men knew where they were. Five days before they had been secretly loaded at Formosa and the Pescadores amidst confusion and uncertainty. Only a few officers knew they were going to the Philippines and these were given only the vaguest instructions.

Homma had been warned by the Imperial General Headquarters to expect bombings. As the days passed and the convoy neared its goal without being attacked neither Homma nor his staff could believe their luck. Where was the United States air force, where the Navy?

At 1:10 A.M., the pilot ship dropped anchor. Too late the skipper discovered he had been fooled by the darkness and was eight miles south of his intended goal. By this time the long line of transports behind had also begun to weigh anchor in a 15-mile line to the north. Now every landing craft would have to travel an extra eight miles to its designated beach.

At 2:00 A.M., the first of the 43,110 men of the 14th Army started going over the sides of the lead transport. Homma nervously waited for beach batteries to open up, but the only noise was the banging of landing craft against the sides of the transports. The high seas almost swamped the first boats, tossing them about like chips.

It wasn't until 4:30 A.M. that two battalions of infantry and one battalion of mountain artillery were loaded and ready to assault the beaches. Forty-seven minutes later the first boat hit the beach just below Agoo. It couldn't report because its radio, like every other radio coming ashore, had been ruined by the salt water. Already General Homma was out of communication with his men.

Many of the landing craft, tossed high on the beach by the roaring breakers, were overturned. Some hit the beaches so hard they were out of commission for the rest of the day. The landing schedule was soon such a shambles that Homma ordered the heavy artillery and other heavy units to wait for calmer weather.

Fortunately for Homma not a single rifle shot welcomed the first invaders at Agoo. Not a single plane appeared overhead to drop a bomb. In spite of this incredible luck, he was consumed with worry. What if a pack of submarines was suddenly loosed among his 85 transports?

Five American submarines were now roaming the Lingayen waters. At 6:00 A.M. the S-38, an old-type submarine, raised its periscope and found it was surrounded by dozens of Japanese transports. They looked to the skipper, Lieutenant Wreford "Moon" Chapple, like cars in a parking lot.

Admiral Hart had warned submarine commanders at the outbreak of the war not to be foolhardy. "We have no idea what Japanese anti-sub capabilities are now. It will be a long war with plenty of glory for all." But Chapple, formerly a champion boxer at Annapolis, decided this was no time for caution. He slipped past escorting destroyers and carefully lined up four targets. The first torpedo missed. So did the next three. Assuming he'd misjudged the draft of the transports, Chapple ordered the submarine to submerge for a reload. He didn't know that all Mark 10 torpedoes ran four feet deeper than set and some were not even detonating on contact. Due to pre-war economy the submarine commanders had never been allowed to test-fire these torpedoes. At 7:58 A.M., though now chased by destroyers, Chapple moved in close to another transport. He fired two torpedoes. Thirty seconds later the submarine rocked from an explosion. He had hit the *Hayo Maru*. In minutes the 5445-ton transport disappeared. Only one other Japanese ship had been sunk by American submarines since Pearl Harbor.

The few planes left in Brereton's air force did even less damage. Not a bomber could respond to his call for a morning strike. Most were in Australia. A few were now bombing Davao in southern Mindanao, which was already in Japanese hands. Several P-40 fighters strafed the transports for a few minutes but soon the sky was full of Zeros. In the brief attack, Lieutenant "Buzz" Wagner, who had become America's first ace of World War II a few days previously, was knocked out of action when a shell hit his wind screen putting a glass splinter in his eye.

By mid-morning Homma's first wave landed. The only opposition along the entire 15-mile beach area came at the north end, near Bauang. Here, a Filipino battalion of the 11th Division fought well, holding off the invaders with several machine guns. But despite heavy casualties the Japanese pushed ashore, drove off the Filipinos and headed north to meet the 4000 men who had landed in northern Luzon on December 10 and were now moving south down the coast.

At 11:00 A.M. contact was made. The beachhead was consolidated.

In Manila, General MacArthur was anxiously awaiting news from Lingayen Gulf. The next few hours were the critical ones. His desperate need was air and naval support. He radioed Marshall asking for any inkling of the strategic plans for the Pacific Fleet, suggesting that carriers could bring fighter planes within radius of the Philippines:

CAN I EXPECT ANYTHING ALONG THAT LINE?

Marshall replied that the Navy insisted it was impossible. As for planes, he would have to rely on those in the *Pensacola* convoy, just then docking at Brisbane.

By 5:00 P.M. Homma, still on an anchored transport, could see heavy surf and high seas raising havoc all along the beaches. The infantry and half the tanks had been landed, but as yet they had almost no artillery support. For all he knew the men ashore could be walking into a trap. Even so, he decided to adhere to the original plan. He ordered them to advance south down Route 3, the paved highway which ran along the beach.

Boldness, as usual in battle, paid off. By dark the Japanese had pushed south five miles, easily routing Filipinos of the 11th Division and a platoon of light tanks. Now they headed due east up a hill. At the top of the rise were less than 500 experienced Philippine Scouts of the elite 26th Cavalry.

At 8:00 P.M. the tankers supporting the Scouts claimed they had orders to fall back. This unit, Company C, 192d Tank Battalion, began to retreat east down the hill toward the town of Rosario. A moment after they left, Japanese tanks came out of the darkness from the opposite direction. The mounted Scouts, thinking they were also American, let them pass through their lines. Suddenly the tanks began to fire into the mass of horses, mules and men.

Riderless horses, mules and men raced down the steep slippery highway in panic. Major Thomas Trapnell tried to stop the chaotic rout but it was impossible. He ran to the bottom of the hill and set fire to a wooden bridge. For several hours, at least, the Japanese advance was halted.

5   At 10:30 P.M. on that same night, Major Devereux was standing on top of his Wake command post, a half-buried concrete igloo. He was watching strange flashes in the sky far to the northwest. At first he thought they were signals but when they increased in number and intensity, he decided a naval battle must be going on.

Men all over the three islets that made up the Wake atoll were watching and arguing. Most guessed it was Task Force 14, the relief force that was coming to bring reinforcements and evacuate the 1200 civilians. Though everyone was exhausted from the almost daily bombings since the first invasion attempt, though Devereux's firepower had been bombed into half its effectiveness, the flashing lights kindled hope and enthusiasm. Help was coming.

The lights came from Japanese ships. A special unit, including 2 carriers, had been detached from Admiral Nagumo's returning Pearl Harbor Striking Force to support the second invasion of Wake. Planes from these carriers had shot down the last of Putnam's Wildcats earlier that day.

At that moment Wake was almost completely ringed by Japanese warships. Ten miles to the south 9 blacked-out ships were slowly approaching the lee side of the atoll. Admiral Kajioka was determined to regain face lost when he had been forced to turn back from Wake on December 10. About 150 miles to the east, also in support of Kajioka, was a third Japanese force: 4 heavy cruisers, 2 light cruisers and 2 destroyers.

The American relief force so eagerly awaited by the men of Wake was still some 500 miles east of Wake. On his flagship, the carrier *Saratoga*, Admiral Frank Jack Fletcher, commander of Task Force 14, was just finishing one of the most frustrating and exasperating days of his long career. A Medal of Honor winner at Vera Cruz in 1914 and destroyer commander in World War I, Fletcher was known throughout the fleet as a man who could be both genial and salty. Today he was salty. Because of rough seas he had been able to refuel only four destroyers since morning. Several tow lines had parted in the long cross swell. Seven fuel lines had broken.

More important, Vice Admiral William Pye, who was taking Kimmel's place as fleet commander until Nimitz's arrival in Pearl Harbor, couldn't seem to make up his mind. First Pye had sent word to proceed to within 200 miles of Wake and launch planes to search out and attack the enemy. This order was countermanded and the seaplane tender *Tangier* was sent ahead to evacuate Wake's personnel. Then that order too had been countermanded. Fletcher wondered what was going on. Fleet Headquarters knew a lot more than he did. Perhaps the great force that had laid waste to Pearl Harbor was closing in to attack him. Looking out from the admiral's sea cabin he could see almost nothing that dark night—nothing but a threatening enemy sea.

The two and a half square miles of Wake's coral rubble were in the minds of most Americans that day. With little else to be thankful for in the vast Pacific battlefield, the island had become a symbol of United States resistance. Here a handful of Marines were showing the Japanese how Americans could fight. Here were men who, when asked what they needed, had answered, "Send us more Japs."

When the men of Wake heard a news commentator from America eloquently embellish the story of this heroic remark, they jeered. Devereux swore he hadn't sent the message; nor had Commander Winfield Scott Cunningham, the island commander. No one on that bleak pile of rubble would ever have sent such a message. The general feeling was: send our share of Japs somewhere else.

The famous words were not, as many later thought, the brain child of some public relations officer. They were sent; but only as nonsensical padding in a coded report. The sender never thought any intelligent decoder would possibly take it at face value.

At 11:00 P.M. a rain squall swept past and the flashes in the northwest grew dim, then faded completely. As Devereux climbed down from the top of his igloo, the roar of the surf sounded like artillery. He hurried into his command post, lay down on his cot and was almost immediately asleep.

By now Kajioka's invasion fleet was only five miles to the south. First came three destroyers, then the light cruiser *Yubari,* with Admiral Kajioka aboard. At 11:30 P.M. Patrol Craft 32 and 33 slid past the *Yubari* and slowly headed for Wake. These were old destroyers, rebuilt into troop transports. They were to be purposely grounded as close to shore as possible. Aboard, assault sailors were given last-minute instructions.

An hour later, at 12:30 A.M., December 23, the first of Kajioka's 830 assault troops, in PC 32, neared a reef almost in the middle of the southern arm of the atoll's V.

"Shore ahead," shouted the ship's commander. The men dropped to the deck. There was a loud crunching sound as the transport piled up on the reef. Only one landing boat could be lowered from the grounded ship because of the turbulent surf. Eighty men piled in. At 12:40 A.M. it beached at Peacock Point, the apex of the V. The men slowly crept across the coral beach. To their amazement not a shot greeted them.

Ten minutes later the other transport, PC 33, crashed onto

the reef not far to the left of PC 32. From it two landing boats were lowered but no one could board them because of the crashing waves.

By now a destroyer two miles southwest of Wake was also lowering two boats, each carrying 80 invaders. These 160 men were to storm Wilkes, the tiny island at the extreme end of the atoll's southern arm, but halfway to the shore one of these boats lost its bearings and drifted to its right toward the main island of Wake.

It was now almost 1:00 A.M. and the defenders still were unaware that the second invasion was under way.

1   At Devereux's igloo command post, Corporal Robert Brown was sleepily listening to the air raid warning phone. This was a network kept open for simultaneous communication among all positions on the atoll. Just before 1:00 A.M., December 23, Brown sat up, startled. He shook the sleeping Devereux. "The enemy are reported on Toki Point, sir," he said excitedly.

Devereux was instantly wide-awake. Toki was the extreme point of the atoll's right arm, the end of Peale Island. "Any confirmation?" he asked.

"No, sir."

Devereux now phoned Lieutenant Woodrow Kessler at Toki Point. "Any boats beached?"

"Negative," answered the commander of Toki's two 5-inch guns.

Devereux thought any landing on Toki would be just a feint. The main landing would probably come from the opposite direction, the south, since it was the lee side. This was where he'd placed his heaviest defenses. Even so the four-and-a-half-mile-long stretch was held by only about 200 Marine, Navy and civilian infantrymen. The rest of Devereux's entire defense force, about 250 Marines and 100 volunteers, were manning anti-aircraft and coastal guns. It was not a reassuring prospect.

Of the 200 infantrymen defending the atoll's southern arm only 70 were located on Wilkes. At 1:15 A.M. Gunner Clarence McKinstry, commander of the 3-inch battery on the tiny island, thought he heard something off shore. McKinstry was a big man—six foot three, weighing 260 pounds—and wore a long red beard and bristling mustache. He told his men to pipe down. He listened again. In spite of the booming surf he heard a motor turning over. He called the over-all commander of Wilkes, Captain H. M. "Cutie" Platt, an easygoing man from South Carolina.

"Are you sure it's a motor, Mac?" asked Platt. McKinstry was sure. "Then fire."

At 1:20 A.M. McKinstry's .50-caliber machine guns fired. Tracer bullets lit up a boat coming into the beach. Two volunteers, Sergeant Bedell and PFC William Buehler, ran across the rough, coral-strewn beach. As the craft grated in the sand, the two men lobbed grenades among its occupants.

A mile north of Peacock Point, the apex of the atoll's V, Devereux was getting a dozen reports at his igloo command post as Japanese began scrambling ashore at four places on the main island.

By now the 5-inch guns couldn't be lowered enough to shoot at the grounded landing craft. But a mile west of Peacock Point there was an unmanned 3-inch anti-aircraft gun on the dunes just above the beach. Lieutenant R. N. Hanna, commander of the machine guns at the airstrip, volunteered to man this gun. Corporal Ralph Holewinski and three civilians followed him as he ran south a quarter of a mile through the rough underbrush toward the beach.

Japanese sailors were beginning to wade ashore from the two grounded ex-destroyers by the time Hanna and his crew reached the gun. There were no sights and Hanna had to peer through the bore to line up one of these ships. The first shot hit the bridge of PC 33. Flames shot up, momentarily lighting the area.

Less than a mile northeast of Hanna, at the airstrip, Major Putnam was talking on the phone to Devereux. The commander of Fighting Squadron 211 was ordered to form a protective infantry line between Hanna's gun and the beach. As Putnam's 11 officers and 11 men started from the airstrip, 22 civilians who had been helping repair the Wildcats fell in.

These were part of the few hundred construction workers who, with their supervisor, Dan Teters, had volunteered for any job since the first bombing. The majority of civilians had done little but sit in tunnels or hide in the brush, only coming out at night to scavenge for food.

"If you're captured in combat your chances are mighty poor," Putnam told the 22 workers. "You can't go with us."

John P. Sorenson, leader of this group of civilians, pushed forward. Although twenty years older than Putnam he was bigger and more rugged. "Major," he said, "do you think you're really big enough to make us stay behind?"

"I'm proud of you," said Putnam. "I'd be glad to have you as Marines. But take off. Join the other civilians." As Putnam and his men zigzagged through the brush toward Hanna's gun, Sorenson and his men followed, loaded with extra ammunition. The wind and surf were so loud, Putnam could hear nothing else as he placed his men in a skirmish line in front of Hanna's gun and then along the dunes a hundred yards toward Peacock Point. He sat at the angle of his line and waited tensely. Where were the Japanese?

Eighty enemy sailors were a mile to his left near Peacock Point. Still unseen, they were creeping north toward Devereux's command post. They wondered where the Americans were. Not a shot had yet been fired at them.

The main body, however, was concentrated on a mile-long stretch of beach just to Putnam's right. Here were the remaining 550 Japanese sailors from the two grounded landing craft and the 80 who had planned to land on Wilkes but drifted to the east.

Devereux, guessing this would be the main landing point, walked over to Lieutenant Arthur Poindexter, who was standing by with two truckloads of men—20 Marines and 14 civilians—on the main road. These 34 men comprised Devereux's entire mobile force.

"Take your people and set up between Camp One and the west end of the airstrip, Art," ordered Devereux. Camp One was about three miles west of Peacock Point just short of the narrow channel between the main island and Wilkes.

The two trucks rushed west, skirting the airstrip, as fast as they could move in the dark. Young Poindexter stopped his trucks at the western end of the airfield about half a mile to Putnam's right and set up two .30-caliber machine guns on each side of the road. He put the rest of his men in a skirmish line facing southeast.

Although a few Japanese mortar shells were falling, Poindexter couldn't determine where they were coming from. He told his men to hold fire until they had a definite target. He felt rising excitement for he was one of those rare individuals who liked to fight.

Suddenly firing broke out to Poindexter's right along the shore south of the water tower near Camp One. Leaving Sergeant T. Q. Wade in charge of the line, Poindexter jumped into a truck and hurried farther west. The four machine guns on the beach near the water tower were manned by inexperienced sailors. He figured someone had opened fire at a shadow and everyone had joined in.

"Hold up," he called to the nearest gunner. Then Poindexter saw there were real targets. Two large landing craft, apparently barges, had run aground a few hundred yards up the beach. The first was the boat which had drifted east from Wilkes. The second was PC 33, one of the remodeled transports.

By this time, probably, both were empty, but Poindexter had no way of knowing this. He told the gunners to fire again. Tracers splattered against the ships and then ricocheted off. Only grenades would be effective. He quickly selected Boatswain's Mate First Class Barnes, Mess Sergeant Gerald Carr and a civilian, Raymond R. Rutledge, an officer in World War I.

"Cap," Poindexter told the civilian, "take Carr and get one barge. We'll get the other."

The four men, each armed with six grenades, ran from the brush to the water's edge. They pitched their grenades at the grounded vessels. All fell short. They ran back to cover. Poindexter ordered the four machine guns to open fire again. After a few bursts he told the gunners to suspend fire.

"Let's try again and get closer this time," he said. Rearmed with grenades he ran to the beach. The other three followed. Several veteran Marines watching couldn't make up their minds about Poindexter. They figured he was either "crazy as a bedbug or the bravest guy alive."

This time Poindexter and Barnes waded into the water. After 10 yards they reached a coral reef and lobbed grenades into the first landing craft.

Suddenly the area was brilliantly lit by a spotlight from the right, and Poindexter could see that no one was coming over the sides of either vessel. In fact, he couldn't see a single Japanese anywhere. As he and Barnes scampered back to the machine gun nests, the light abruptly went off.

The illumination had come from an American spotlight on Wilkes Island and only hit the two grounded craft near Poindexter by chance. Captain Platt had ordered it turned on his own beach, in front of McKinstry's 3-inch guns.

The light was shot out by the Wilkes Island invaders in less than a minute. But in that time McKinstry and his men saw a landing craft beached right in front of them. Japanese with fixed bayonets poured over the sides. These 80 men were the only ones to reach Wilkes of the 160 scheduled for landing.

McKinstry didn't have riflemen to stop the attackers. "Cut the fuses at zero," he shouted. He looked through the barrel of a 3-inch gun and fired point-blank. The attackers fell back but then started flanking McKinstry from both sides. As grenades began to fall in his position, McKinstry decided to withdraw and set up a new skirmish line. He told his men to remove the firing locks from the big guns and follow him. He headed east, toward the main island of Wake, through the rough underbrush. The beach here was empty. There was nothing to do but wait.

It was now 2:30 A.M. A moment after the searchlight on Wilkes was shot out, Devereux had lost communications with that isle. He knew little more about the real situation on Wake itself. At Peacock Point, Barninger reported machine-gun fire sweeping his position from a distance but he had no targets for his 5-inch guns. Then there was silence.

Poindexter near Camp One reported he was being flanked. Then silence. There was no word from Putnam.

Devereux ordered his executive, Major George Potter, to set up a last-ditch defense line 100 yards south of the igloo command post. Potter scraped together thirty clerks and communications men and dug them in across the road leading to the airfield.

About four miles to the North, near the channel separating Peale and the main island, Commander Cunningham was sending a message to Admiral Pye:

ENEMY APPARENTLY LANDING.

Then he sent a message to the submarine *Triton* to attack enemy ships south of Wake.

At 3:19 A.M. Cunningham got an answer. It came from Pye.

NO FRIENDLY VESSELS IN YOUR VICINITY NOR WILL BE WITHIN THE NEXT 24 HOURS.

By 4:00 A.M. rain was lashing the three islands. The fighting had become completely confused. No one, Japanese or American, knew exactly what was going on. Poindexter and the defenders of Camp One were cut off. Mortar shells were falling all along the line he had set up at the edge of the airstrip. Several civilians had been killed, half a dozen Marines wounded.

"They're all over, on all sides," Sergeant Wade whispered to him. Poindexter ordered the men to withdraw west toward Camp One and the Wake-Wilkes channel by sections.

When Peale Island reported all quiet, Devereux ordered all their available men to hurry south by truck to back up Potter's defense line. Just then a terrified civilian staggered in. One of Poindexter's men, he had seen Japanese bayonet-

ng the machine-gun crews at the edge of the airstrip.
"They're killing 'em all!" he cried hysterically.

Devereux looked at his watch. It would soon be dawn. He
wondered if the men from Peale would arrive in time.
Corporal Brown, monitoring the air raid warning network,
said, "I've got something, sir." Someone was whispering over
and over into a phone, "There are Japanese in the bushes."

Someone else on the network suddenly broke in, "For
Christ's sake, where are you?"

"There are Japanese in the bushes. Definitely. They are
definitely Japanese." Suddenly there was a burst of sound,
then silence.

"I guess they got him," Brown said.

At 5:00 A.M. Cunningham, after hearing a report on the
general situation from Devereux, sent another message to
Pearl Harbor:

ENEMY ON ISLAND—ISSUE IN DOUBT.

2   At Pearl Harbor Admiral Pye was conferring
with Rear Admiral M. F. Draemel and Captain C. H. Mc-
Morris. After much discussion all three concluded it was too
late to evacuate or relieve Wake. The question now was:
Should Fletcher be allowed to push west with Task Force 14
and engage the enemy assault force?

A little later the answer to this question was radioed to the
Saratoga. When Admiral Fletcher read Pye's order he said,
"We're called back to Pearl Harbor."

There was open dismay and indignation on the bridge.
Several staff officers urged Fletcher to disobey. When he
refused, the talk became so bitter that Rear Admiral Aubrey
Fitch, who sympathized with the malcontents, left the bridge.
Marine fliers in the ready room cursed upon learning the news;
some wept.

Fletcher ignored the comments. He wasn't running a popu-
larity contest. He was as eager to go in as the others—but
the only time to disobey orders was when you knew more
than headquarters. He didn't know a damn thing. Apparently Pye did know something.

Pye had been governed not by special information but by
overcaution, a common trait in Hawaii since the Pearl
Harbor disaster. If Fletcher had been allowed to continue
west he would easily have caught Kajioka's invasion fleet
lying off Wake. Unprotected by carrier aircraft these ships
would have been sitting ducks for the *Saratoga* planes.

At the Officers' Club in Pearl Harbor there was bitter talk about the recall of Task Force 14. It wasn't helped when Tokyo Rose jibed, "Where, oh where, is the United States Navy?"

Pye was radioing an explanation to Admiral Stark:

> THE USE OF OFFENSIVE ACTION TO RELIEVE WAKE HAD BEEN MY INTENTION AND DESIRE. BUT WHEN THE ENEMY HAD ONCE LANDED ON THE ISLAND, THE GENERAL STRATEGIC SITUATION TOOK PRECEDENCE AND THE CONSERVATION OF OUR NAVAL FORCES BECAME THE FIRST CONSIDERATION. I ORDERED THE RETIREMENT WITH EXTREME REGRET.

3   Putnam was on his stomach under a bush. His muscles were stiff from the long, tense wait. So far he hadn't seen anything. Suddenly at first light of day two silhouettes loomed over him. He emptied his pistol. One Japanese fell sideways, another forward, his helmet colliding with Putnam's. The American hauled the two Japanese toward his position. Both were dead. Now firing broke out to the right. It was a wild, hand-to-hand melee. His thin line slowly fell back toward the gun they were protecting. More Japanese jumped out of the bushes. Putnam saw the civilian Sorenson leap up to meet them, throwing rocks until he was cut down. Then Captain Hank "Baron" Elrod, Putnam's hottest pilot and a wildman in the air, jumped up shouting, "Kill the sons of bitches!" He raked the invaders with his tommy gun. The attack was stopped momentarily.

The Japanese re-formed and pressed forward again. Putnam told his men to fall back all the way to the 3-inch gun. He and four others made it. There they found Lieutenant Hanna and two men. As mortar shells began to fall, they all hid under the gun's perforated steel platform. A bullet creased Putnam's cheek and went through his neck. He didn't realize he'd been hit, only wondered why he was suddenly so sleepy. He passed out. A moment later he came to, cursed violently and passed out again.

At 6:00 A.M. Kessler called Devereux from Toki Point on Peale. He said he could see three destroyers closing in on Wilkes. They were within range. Devereux told him to fire, then called Cunningham, informing him Jap flags had been seen all over Wilkes. The island had evidently fallen, and there was still no word from Putnam or Poindexter on the southern part of the main island. Japanese were already firing on Potter's defense line near the igloo and were less than 300 yards away.

At 7:30 A.M. Devereux again called the island commander. "It looks to me," he told Cunningham, "as though the Japs have secured Wilkes, Camp One, the channel, the airstrip and probably Peacock Point. That's the best I can judge the picture on the dope I've got."

There was a pause and then came the reply, "Well, I guess we'd better give it to them."

Devereux hadn't thought of surrender. "Isn't any help coming?"

Not even submarines were coming.

"Let me see if there isn't something I can do down here," said Devereux. He asked for more riflemen, but Cunningham had only the five Army communicators.

Devereux, too, decided the situation was hopeless. To hold out any longer would only be a waste of lives. He said tightly, "I'll pass the word."

By now most of the Japanese on Wilkes were concentrated at McKinstry's 3-inch guns. Gunner McKinstry was trying to retake this position and had already started back west with his men. Several hundred yards from the guns he met Lieutenant McAlister. Combining their thirty men they began to move toward the entrenched Japanese. But the advance was soon stopped by three invaders hiding behind a large rock.

"Clean out behind that big rock," ordered McAlister. As the big red-bearded McKinstry started forward, the lieutenant said, "No, detail a man for the job."

"I've got 'em, Gunner," said Corporal Halstead, a small, agile young man. Halstead quickly, quietly ran up the rock. He emptied his Springfield into the three surprised Japanese crouching below him. Without a word, he waved for his comrades to follow. When they saw the three dead bodies behind the rock, their spirits rose.

McAlister and McKinstry decided to split the attack. The lieutenant took his small detail down the beach. McKinstry formed a skirmish line with his twenty-five men and pushed straight forward through the brush. The gunner led the way throwing grenades as fast as he could and shouting in a bull voice to the others to keep their flanks up. Two civilians kept feeding grenades to the big man as he plowed forward. Seeing a supposedly dead Japanese suddenly rise and try to bayonet one of his men in the back, McKinstry shouted a warning. The "dead" man was shot. "Be sure the dead ones are dead," he yelled.

Captain Platt, with two machine-gun crews and eight riflemen, was attacking the 3-inch gun position from the opposite side. But McAlister and McKinstry didn't know this. By now McKinstry's right flank had run into a machine-gun nest. "Get going," he bellowed when he saw his men pinned down. "Move on! You don't want to stay here and die of old age." The right flank moved up.

Now McKinstry could see a group of Japanese in his old ammunition hole. He threw a grenade. A fire blazed and then ammunition exploded. The gunner rushed forward, Halstead at his side. There was a wild burst of fire from the 3-inch battery emplacement. Halstead dropped dead at McKinstry's feet.

Corporal Lee started around the first gun. A "dead" Japanese suddenly leaped to his feet. Lee and the Japanese lunged at each other with bayonets. Both missed, pulled back and lunged again. This time both found the mark, both were dead.

McKinstry lobbed a grenade into the emplacement. There was an explosion. After a momentary silence, McKinstry saw a figure rise on the other side of the battery. It was Captain Platt, the irrepressible South Carolinian, grinning as usual. "Mac," he called out, "that ugly voice of yours sounded like an angel's when you came through."

As the three American forces met at the battery position, five Japanese escaped in the brush. The rest were dead.

"Bring back one alive, Mac," shouted Platt to McKinstry, who was already starting after the escapees. Suddenly dive bombers from the two Japanese carriers northwest of Wake swept down on Wilkes. Platt's men hugged the almost bare ground. It was 7:40 A.M. At the 3-inch position, one of McKinstry's men climbed up to pull down a Japanese flag. "Leave it there a minute," shouted someone.

Just across the channel, on the main island, Poindexter was still holding the Camp One area at 8:00 A.M. His line of thirty-four riflemen and ten machine guns was in a semicircle facing seaward and to the southeast. Like Platt, he too had long since lost contact with Devereux but the young lieutenant was feeling hopeful about the situation. His line had held so well the Japanese were only probing occasionally. He decided it was time to counterattack east toward Peacock Point. He called a runner, telling him to go back and round up every able-bodied man at Camp One who had a weapon.

A few minutes later the runner dove into the shelter at

Camp One. It was crammed with a searchlight section, a few truck drivers, supply men and the gun-shed crew. "The lieutenant says for everyone with a rifle to move up to the line on the other side of the water tower," shouted the runner. No one moved.

Suddenly a small eighteen-year-old with glasses, a clerk named Fish, jumped up and yelled, "What are we sitting on our asses here for?" He grabbed his rifle and charged out of the shelter; the others lumbered dazedly after him.

At 8:30 A.M. Poindexter turned and saw young Fish scampering toward him across the coral. He was followed by some twenty other reinforcements. Poindexter took a quick count. He had about fifty-five armed men. More than enough. He quickly formed a platoon of three squads. "All right," he said after issuing orders for the attack, "let's move out." He squirmed forward through the thick brush.

Outside Devereux's igloo, Gunner John Hamas was shouting to cease fire. "We're surrendering! Major's orders."

Devereux, thin-faced, haggard, appeared in the doorway of his command post. "It's not my order, God damn it!"

He was called to the phone. The line to Barninger's battery on Peacock Point had finally been repaired. Barninger reported he was ready for attack.

"Cease firing," said Devereux. "Destroy all weapons. The island is being surrendered."

The order was passed along Potter's line and to the gun positions not yet overrun. Men took bolts from their rifles and threw them away. Blankets were crammed into muzzles and guns fired. Cables were cut, directors and height-finders shot with pistols. Weapons destroyed, the men now brought out the little food they had been hoarding. They sat and ate and waited for the Japanese.

Sergeant Bernard Ketner came into Devereux's command post. Seeing the major sitting dejectedly before the phone, he held out his hand. "Don't worry, Major," he said. "You fought a good fight and did all you could."

They shook hands.

Devereux told his phone man to call the hospital, located in another concrete igloo, about 400 yards toward the Japanese. Dr. Kahn was to raise a white flag and surrender to an officer. But the hospital didn't answer.

"Rig a white flag you can carry," said Devereux. "We'll have to go down there."

Sergeant Donald Malleck tied a white rag on a swab handle. Then he and Devereux started down the road. Near the hospital igloo a Japanese rifleman slowly rose and cautiously came forward. Devereux was brought to the steel door of the hospital.

"Well, we are surrendering," said Devereux to an officer wearing a sword.

The Japanese offered the major a cigarette and told him he had attended the San Francisco Fair in 1939. Both heard an excited shout. A United States truck had been stopped on the road. Commander Cunningham, dressed in formal blue uniform, came forward.

"Who Number One?" asked the Japanese officer.

Devereux pointed to Cunningham. "While you arrange the formal surrender," he told the island commander, "I'll go around the island with Malleck to be sure that everybody gets the word to surrender."

At 9:30 A.M. the surrender party reached Hanna's gun. Devereux pushed through the crowds of Japanese surrounding the gun and climbed onto a revetment. "This is Major Devereux," he shouted. "The island has been surrendered." When no one answered, Devereux called again. A few men staggered out. Of the thirteen defending the gun, only Captain Tharin was not wounded.

Putnam was awakened. Weak from loss of blood and still unaware he'd been wounded, he looked up at Devereux, his face a red smear. "Jimmy, I'm sorry. Poor Hank is dead." Elrod had been killed as he was throwing a grenade. Putnam staggered to his feet. He was relieved his men didn't have to shoot any more. He didn't yet know that 80 per cent of his squadron were casualties; that half of his twenty-two civilians were dead.

Devereux, Malleck and their Japanese guards began moving slowly west toward Camp One and the tip of the main island. Firing could be heard ahead and they progressed cautiously.

At 11:00 A.M. Poindexter was advancing east toward the surrender party. He was elated. Although his attack had been held up on the left flank for an hour, he had finally regained all the ground lost the night before. The Japanese were falling back slowly but steadily and he figured he should join up with the Marines at Peacock Point by nightfall. Then he saw a small group walking toward him down the road with a white flag.

He assumed the Japanese were surrendering. "Cover me," he told his riflemen. He cautiously moved out to the center of the road. He was a fearsome sight as he approached

Devereux's surrender party. His face was smeared with black ointment as medication for flashburns. He wore a pistol belt with a .45 in the holster. The breast pockets of his khaki shirt bulged with grenades and he carried a Springfield at the ready.

As he neared the group he grinned in triumph. Then he heard one of them shout, "Drop your rifle."

Poindexter was startled. Finally he recognized Devereux, who was not much taller than the Japanese. He dropped his rifle and moved forward automatically. When Devereux kept shouting, he dropped his pistol belt. He approached Devereux with a look of complete consternation on his face.

As he dejectedly took the grenades out of his pockets the Japanese, apparently thinking he was about to commit suicide, scattered in alarm. He dropped the grenades with safety levers intact on the road.

"Have your men stand up and leave their weapons on the deck," said Devereux.

As soon as Poindexter's men did as commanded, the Japanese who had been fighting them all morning jumped up. Yelling "Banzai!" they dashed forward with fixed bayonets. The Japanese surrender officer stepped in front of the Americans and stopped the charge.

The surrender party continued west toward Camp One. An American flag was still flying from the water tower. Japanese, cheering, ran forward. One started up the tower.

"Hold it," shouted Devereux to his Marines as they glared at the climbing Japanese. "Keep your heads, all of you."

On the other side of the tower at Camp One, Sergeant Dave Rush saw the Japanese taking down the flag. He drew a perfect bead with his machine gun. As he was about to fire he saw Devereux. He pushed the gun into the pit, pulled out the firing pin and threw it in the ocean.

Others at Camp One still couldn't see the surrendering party. A plane suddenly roared down. Sergeant John Cemeris, near the channel between Wake and Wilkes, opened up with his .30-caliber machine gun. Black smoke shot out of the plane. It was fine marksmanship but Poindexter and Devereux were afraid it might touch off a massacre. They hurried forward. "Stand up," called Poindexter. "Put your hands over your head."

Across the channel on Wilkes Island Platt's men had now cleaned out the few surviving Japanese. Three had been captured. At noon a destroyer moved within 2000 yards.

Behind were several other ships. Platt ordered McAlister to fire with his 5-inch guns, but word came back that all pieces had been knocked out by the carrier dive bombers.

Watchers reported that a number of small Japanese boats were moving in toward the channel. Platt ordered everyone to advance to the east and repel them. The little force was halfway to the channel when a rifleman shouted, "Someone's coming down the road."

McKinstry ordered his men to hide behind rocks near the beach. He saw a white flag, and thought it must be a trick. Then he heard someone shout, "This is Major Devereux. The island has been surrendered. Don't try any monkey business."

McKinstry was unable to believe it until he saw Devereux and Poindexter. Dazed, he stripped his pistol and threw away the parts.

Prisoners were being rounded up all over the three islands. Devereux was taken back to the Japanese headquarters located near Hanna's gun. He felt weary and dead inside. He was full of despair. Just then prisoners in skivvies were marched by. They looked filthy, exhausted and hopeless. Their leader, Technical Sergeant E. F. Hassig, a barrel-chested man with a bushy mustache, turned and glared at the men. "Snap outa this stuff. Goddam it, you're Marines!"

The men's heads came up. They marched proudly in perfect cadence, past their commander.

Near the channel Gunner McKinstry was under guard. Afraid that one of the three Japanese survivors of Wilkes would recognize his long red beard, he was looking for something with which to cut it off. Finally he found a butcher knife and began hacking.

Poindexter was a few hundred yards away, looking through the brush for wounded Americans. A Japanese lieutenant, using a Samurai sword as a cane, was accompanying him. They came upon a Japanese officer, shot in the face. The Japanese lieutenant pulled a small flag from his pocket. He put it over the dead man's chest, tucking one end under the belt and the top corners under the shoulder straps.

The two enemy lieutenants and two United States Marines carried the dead officer down a path. Poindexter saw a can of pears on the ground. He reached down and picked it up.

The body was tossed on a truck. Poindexter sat beside the corpse and began to eat the pears. The Japanese lieutenant jumped up on the truck and joined Poindexter. When they had finished the pears, the Japanese pulled out a round tin of cigarettes. He gave a handful to the American.

Later that afternoon, Admiral Kajioka, wearing whites, medals and dress sword, came ashore to take formal possession of Wake. It was renamed Bird Island.

1   About the time Devereux was walking toward the Japanese with a white flag, a plane landed at Washington, D.C. Here it was only late afternoon of December 22. A short, stocky man, easily recognizable by his bowler hat and big cigar, stepped out of the plane and walked briskly to a waiting limousine. He shook the strong hand of the smiling man in the back seat. Churchill had arrived for the conference known as "Arcadia."

Roosevelt and his guest were driven to the White House. Here Mrs. Roosevelt installed the prime minister in the big bedroom across the hall from Harry Hopkins' room. The next few days the three men would detour the mounds of Christmas presents in the hallway to visit each other's rooms at all hours, while they plotted the ultimate destruction of the Axis and discussed the immediate fate of the Southwest Pacific.

Churchill was one of the few men the President thought worth listening to; Roosevelt was one of the few men the prime minister let talk at any length. During this conference their intimacy was so great, Hopkins told friends, that once Roosevelt was wheeled into Churchill's room as the prime minister came from the shower stark naked. When Roosevelt apologized and started to leave, Churchill said, "The Prime Minister of Great Britain has nothing to conceal from the President of the United States."

It was evident by midnight of the first evening that Arcadia would be a harmonious success—even though Churchill later denied Hopkins' story. "I never received the President," he said, "without at least a bath towel wrapped around me."

2   In the Philippines, as at Wake, it was already December 23. That dawn the remnant of Brereton's air force had finally attacked the great Japanese convoy in Lingayen

Gulf. Four Flying Fortresses dropped their 100-pound bombs and headed south for Australia.

General Homma was given an anxious moment but little damage had been done. His ground troops were having just as little trouble. The main force had finally rebuilt the bridge burned by Major Trapnell and pushed down to Rosario. By noon they had advanced another three miles to an important junction, the southern terminus of the 20-mile mountain road leading down from the old summer capital, Baguio. Thus all MacArthur's troops to the northeast—the men of Baguio's Camp John Hay and a regiment of the 71st Division —were cut off.

Lieutenant Colonel John Horan, commander of Camp John Hay, had been keeping MacArthur informed by radio of Homma's progress. The previous day, Horan had asked permission to retreat south down this winding, precipitous road from Baguio to the junction but MacArthur's headquarters, thinking he was "unduly perturbed," notified him to stay until ordered out. Still waiting for word to retreat, he was peeved and anxious. Since a subordinate had destroyed the radio and code book, he had to send an ambiguous message to MacArthur in the clear:

> MY RIGHT HAND IN A VISE, MY NOSE IN AN INVERTED
> FUNNEL, . . . MY REAR WIDE OPEN, MY SOUTH PAW OPEN.
> REQUEST ORDERS.

He figured some intelligence officer would figure it meant he was cut off in Baguio and could escape only to the north or east.

Early in the afternoon Homma's men attacked the Filipinos holding the main highway four miles south of the Baguio junction. These troops, the two remaining regiments of the 71st Division, had had only ten weeks of training. Few had learned how to shoot their outdated Enfield rifles. The great majority could only drill and salute.

The inevitable happened. Like their untrained brothers of the 11th Division, they broke and fled to the rear leaving their artillery unprotected.

When Wainwright learned of the rout, he realized the situation was critical. Further defense of the Lingayen beaches, he phoned MacArthur, was impractical and he requested permission to withdraw behind the Agno River. This, the first formidable natural obstacle, was about 45 miles south of the first landing point on Lingayen Gulf and only 90 air miles above the final goal, Manila. From here he could counterattack—if MacArthur would give him the well-trained Philippine Division.

In Manila, MacArthur was dismayed by the collapse of the two green divisions. Yet it was not surprising. They were fighting an experienced, tank-equipped enemy, with rifles and old-fashioned, water-cooled machine guns that easily jammed.

With no air force or navy, MacArthur had to abandon his cherished strategy of holding the enemy at the beaches. He was now forced to consider War Plan Orange-3. This was the plan formulated by his predecessors in the Philippines, and its primary mission was the defense of Manila Bay. If enemy landings on Luzon could not be prevented, and pressure became too great, the defenders would slowly withdraw to the Bataan Peninsula. Here a last-ditch defense could be made for about six months. By then, it was hoped, the Navy could send in supplies and reinforcements. MacArthur had shelved WPO-3 upon assuming command of the Philippines. It was, he felt, a defeatist move that might well lose him the support of Filipinos. Now he had no other choice. He called in his staff. "Put WPO-3 into effect," he ordered.

In spite of the quick advance of Homma and the collapse of the 11th and 71st Divisions, there was still no panic among the other Philippine units.

The 21st Division, which had been defending the lower part of Lingayen Gulf, was retreating south in good order, with morale unimpaired. Outside of their midnight "battle" with the single Japanese reconnaissance boat on December 10, they had yet to meet the enemy.

Third Lieutenant Antonio Aquino, the elder son of the speaker of the Philippine Assembly and recently admitted to the bar, had been sent to Manila to commandeer eight trucks for this division's retreat. He had sent back the trucks and returned the previous night to his family's great sugar plantation near Tarlac, about 30 miles south of Wainwright's Agno River line, so he could speak to the workers.

"Attorney," their apprehensive, puzzled spokesman had said, "what are we fighting for? Why do not America protect us?"

Despite the sweltering heat, Aquino was nattily dressed in olive drab woolens, tailored hunting coat and steel helmet. He told the tenants that America was going to send help but Filipinos would have to do most of the fighting in the meantime. "We are fighting with America because we believe in the American way of life."

He told them the Japanese were advancing from the north. They should evacuate to the mountains with their families. "Wait for me if we lose this war. I shall escape and we shall be guerrillas like the time Grandfather hid in Mt. Arayat." This was General Aquino who had fought against the Americans with Aguinaldo. "We shall not give up the fight. America will come back and we shall not lose faith with her. Are we all agreed?"

The tenants cheered. They no longer had doubts.

The next day, about the time MacArthur ordered WPO-3 in effect, everyone had left the vast plantation. Aquino went out to the fields and set fire to the standing sugar cane and rice. He got into his brand-new yellow convertible and with his "man Friday," Eladio, beside him, set off to rejoin his division. After a mile he stopped and looked back at the roaring fire and the rising columns of black smoke. He hoped his father would approve his "scorched earth" tactics.

In spite of his words to the tenants, Tony Aquino secretly believed, as almost everyone else in the Philippines believed, that the war would be over in two weeks or a month at the most. By that time convoys filled with soldiers, planes and guns from San Francisco would arrive. He had plenty of supplies in the back of his car to last until then: a case of Scotch, a complete kitchen, hunting equipment, a radio, a portable table and chairs, a large bag of ping-pong balls, a tuxedo complete with shoes and studs, and, in case of emergency, $1000 in pocket money.

That night, Wainwright was in his tent on the bank of the Agno River planning a counterattack. It was based on the hopeful assumption that MacArthur would lend him the elite Philippine Division, for of his 28,000 men only 3000 were trained.

The phone rang. It was USAFFE, MacArthur's headquarters. Perhaps he was getting his old division.

"WPO-3 is in effect," said Colonel Constant Irwin.

Wainwright couldn't talk. He knew this meant MacArthur had abandoned his pet theory of stopping the Japanese at the beaches. It also meant that the situation was desperate.

"You understand?" said Irwin when Wainwright didn't answer.

"Yes, Pete," said the other quietly, "I understand." Like many other senior officers he had always felt WPO-3 was the only practical defense of the Philippines. But fifteen precious days had already been lost. Was it too late? It was up to him, he realized, to stem the Japanese tide until the rest of MacArthur's troops could escape into Bataan.

The following morning, MacArthur learned that what he had feared most had happened. During the previous night 24 Japanese transports had landed in Lamon Bay, 60 air miles southeast of Manila. He was now caught in a giant pincers. Not a single big gun and less than two infantry battalions protected this east coast. Before mid-morning 9500 Japanese of the 16th Division were pushing toward Manila in three columns. At 10:00 A.M. Major General George Parker got orders from MacArthur to slowly withdraw the two divisions of his South Luzon Force to Bataan. The battle in the south was over before it started.

At 11:00 A.M. MacArthur's staff was called to a conference at No. 1 Victoria Street. General Sutherland informed them headquarters was being moved to Corregidor Island that evening. Men were to take field equipment and one suitcase or bedroll.

Nearby in the Marsman Building, Admiral Hart was telling Admiral Rockwell that he had decided to move his headquarters south to Borneo so he could be with the operating fleet. Rockwell would take over supreme command of the remaining naval forces.

As the sixty-four-year-old admiral was telling Rockwell to destroy all fuel, Diesel oil and aviation gas stored in Manila, planes roared overhead. Bombs began to fall in the Walled City. One hit the Marsman Building but Hart continued the conference. Subs, he said, should operate from Manila Bay as long as possible. Another bomb hit. Captain Dessez should blow up everything at Sangley Point and the Cavite Navy Yard. As a third bomb rocked the building, he told Rockwell to turn over the 4th Marines to MacArthur.

The port area was in flames, a chaotic shambles. Huge craters pockmarked the streets; streetcars were flung into buildings, the tracks behind curling up fantastically. Clouds of dust from pulverized cement and stone mixed with black billows of smoke to hang a pall over the entire Pasig River section.

A new Packard pulled into the Walled City, then was stopped by the jumbled streets. Its occupant, General Brereton, walked into No. 1 Victoria Street, wondering why MacArthur had sent for him. The air chief had argued a few days before that he and his staff be sent south. There was nothing they could do in the Philippines without planes. USAFFE headquarters was alive with activity as Brereton was taken into MacArthur's office. The general, obviously distraught, was terse. He told Brereton to take his headquarters south. When Brereton now offered to remain personally and serve MacArthur in any capacity, the general said, "No, Lewis, you go on south. You can do me more good with the bombers you have left and those you should be receiving soon than you can here."

Brereton rose.

"I hope," said MacArthur, "that you will tell the people outside what we have done and protect my reputation as a fighter."

"General," said Brereton, shaking his hand, "your reputation will never need any protection."

At Malacañan Palace, President Manuel Quezon was talking to his executive secretary, Jorge Vargas, Vice-President Sergio Osmeña, and José Laurel. Quezon's voice was choked. He, Osmeña and a few other officials were about to leave for Corregidor. The president, wearing a United States uniform and helmet, made them all promise never to reveal what he was about to say. Then he said to Laurel and Vargas, "You two will stay here and deal with the Japanese."

Laurel protested that people would think he was a collaborator. Quezon agreed but insisted it was Laurel's duty.

Laurel burst into tears. He begged to be taken to Corregidor.

"Someone has to protect the people from the Japanese," said Quezon.

Laurel at last sadly agreed. He knew that to his dying day only those in this room would know the truth. Perhaps the truth would never be revealed and he would go down in history as a traitor.

A few minutes later Quezon's limousine left the Palace grounds, heading for Manila Bay. Bombs were still falling on the port area as it passed the Walled City.

Quezon, his wife Aurora, his daughters Maria Aurora and Zeneida, and his son, Manuel, Jr., stepped onto the pier next to the Manila Hotel. While servants carried family belongings, including a parrot, from a truck, Quezon never stopped talking to those who quickly gathered on the dock. Always a flamboyant speaker, he was never more eloquent. He hated to leave, he shouted, but it was his duty as president.

Calling out farewells, he walked slowly with Vargas toward the float. The two shook hands emotionally. Quezon knew he was dying of tuberculosis. Already his body was skeletal, his face emaciated. There was so much to do for the Philippines before he died. He stepped into his private speedboat. With a roar it headed into the bay.

Ashore, correspondent Arch Gunnison of *Collier's* asked Vargas, "Well, what's next?"

"I wish I knew. But whatever it is, it looks like it's going to be for a long time." As he watched Quezon's speedboat approach the inter-island steamer *Mayon,* he added a little bitterly, "Well, some of us have to stay. I've got more to do now than I know how."

By this time, the streets of Manila were crowded with Army trucks and commandeered squat, fat-bellied Pambusco buses filled with soldiers and supplies. Traffic crept impatiently in the hot sun. Everything was going north—to Bataan.

Military installations in the Manila area were in a state of wild confusion as personnel hastily loaded into trucks, cars and buses. At Air Headquarters, recently transplanted to Fort McKinley, General Brereton was telling his staff of their retreat to Australia. The move was to be kept secret even from other headquarters officers. The big problem was how to get there. There wasn't a Flying Fortress in the Philippines. The Navy was telephoned. Brereton could have four seats on a PBY leaving for Java that night. The general picked three men to accompany him and the four hurried out to pack. The others, slated to follow soon in a transport, also left to pack.

Air Headquarters soon became utterly disorganized. No one knew what was going on. Brereton had disappeared, so had his personal officer. Colonel George couldn't be found. No one knew, in fact, who was in command.

Nielson Field was just as chaotic. It was the wildest and most fantastic day in the history of the 27th Bombardment Group. Early that afternoon they had been told to move to Bataan. The only explanation from Air Headquarters was that Manila was to be declared an open city to save it from further bombing. The greatest haste was urged. When Fort McKinley was called back for further instructions there was no answer. Air Force Headquarters, apparently, had just quit work and disappeared.

The 17th Pursuit Squadron at Nichols Field, presently commanded by Second Lieutenant David Obert, was to be at the Manila docks by 6:00 P.M. By midafternoon Obert knew he'd never make the deadline so he decided to send the men ahead with whatever they had already packed. He hurried to McKinley to get approval. There, to his dismay, he too found Headquarters had evaporated. People were scurrying around excitedly burning papers and collecting personal equipment. It looked to him as if all the units were on their own.

At Zablan Field, the eighteen remaining planes of the Philippine Army Air Corps were being burned. It was a crushing blow to the Filipino pilots but the orders had come from some excited officer at Air Headquarters. Their planes destroyed, they began to set fire to hangars and barracks.

One hundred air miles to the north, Homma's advance troops were smashing at Binalonan, about ten miles above Wainwright's main line of defense on the Agno River. For the first time they had been stopped. Since 5:00 A.M. only 450 men, the tired remnants of the 26th Cavalry, had held off heavy attacks on the town.

By 3:00 P.M. the cavalrymen's situation was desperate. Japanese tanks were rolling toward their roadblock and they had no anti-tank guns. Captain Barker, commander of Troop B, called his platoon leaders together and asked for volunteers to knock out the oncoming tanks. Only one, Private Soria, raised his hand. As the rest of Troop B fell back to prepared foxholes, Soria hid in the ditch with grenades and three Coca-Cola bottles filled with gasoline.

As the first tank rumbled by, Soria leaped on the rear. He tapped on the hatch with his pistol hoping the turret would open. Instead the turret gun swung around, sweeping Soria into the road. The tank backed off and its 37-mm. gun roared. Machine-gun bullets raked the ditch. Soria, grazed in the shoulder by the big gun, jumped out of the ditch and ran to the rear. The tank hesitated and then, apparently scared off by Soria, retreated.

Word came from Wainwright to pull back; the cavalrymen had held the Japanese long enough for the Agno River line to be manned. The troopers ran from their foxholes to their horses. Trotting five minutes, then walking five minutes, they headed for the Agno River.

A rout had been saved by a few Coke bottles and the 26th Cavalry. Wainwright, an old cavalryman himself and perhaps a bit prejudiced, reported it had been "a true cavalry delaying action, fit to make a man's heart sing." It also proved what MacArthur had always insisted: the Filipino if well trained made an excellent, courageous soldier.

In Manila, Major Carlos Romulo, MacArthur's press and radio chief, sat at his desk watching his commander in the adjoining room. He saw the general answer a phone. Some field commander obviously was reporting directly. MacArthur hung up and began pacing the floor, hands clasped behind him, head slightly bowed, his hawklike face lined with bitterness. Abruptly he stopped pacing and put on the gold-braided cap of field marshal of the Philippine Army. He glanced quickly at his flags, the beautiful oriental art objects col-

lected over the years, the V-for-Victory poster, then strode
into Romulo's room. It was exactly 6:00 P.M.

Quietly he told the ex-newspaperman that he was going to
the island of Corregidor to direct the Battle of Bataan. Romulo
was to remain in the rear echelon. "It's more important than
ever," said the general, "that I be kept in touch with the
press while I'm in the field." He held out his hand. "I'll be
back, Carlos."

MacArthur and most of his staff headed for the docks and
boarded the *Don Esteban*. It was beginning to get dark when
the steamer started across the bay toward Corregidor, less
than 30 miles away. The moon was shining and the men
of USAFFE headquarters sat in their shirt sleeves on the
decks talking in hushed tones as they watched flames rise
from Cavite's oil dump. It was a strange Christmas Eve for
Americans used to cold and snow.

Colonel William Morse was watching his chief. MacArthur
sat, head in hands.

The dark streets of Manila were jammed with creeping
civilian cars. Occasionally there would be a shout of "Ilao
(Lights)," then a rifle report as a shaded headlight, approved
by the city's blackout committee, was shot out. Already innocent pedestrians and drivers had been killed by trigger-
happy volunteer local guards, many recruited from the no-
torious, gangster-ridden Tondo slums.

On the east coast of Bataan, the first evacuées from Manila
were already setting up Hospital No. 1 at Limay. Second
Lieutenant Hattie Brantley had been told she was coming to
a 1000-bed hospital, completely equipped. She had mentally
pictured beautiful buildings, surrounded by flowers. She
had found thirty long nipa (palm) buildings, completely
empty and covered with dust. Medical supplies in a nearby
tin warehouse were wrapped in 1918 newspapers. Some of
the cots crumbled to pieces when they were unfolded. Now the
nurses were being issued new clothing. Lieutenant Brantley
was given a size 42 pair of coveralls and heavy GI shoes.
Then the fifty nurses were led into their quarters, a one-
story wooden shack. There were six cots.

"Do we sleep on the floor?" asked someone tiredly.

Dark Christmas

1   Christmas was a night of hell in Hong Kong. The Japanese held three-fourths of the mountainous island's 32 square miles. The British forces were split in two. In the south, 2500 were jammed into Stanley Peninsula. The main force, about 5000, held the populous northwest corner, including the capital of Victoria. With no air or sea power and few anti-aircraft guns or mortars, defense lines everywhere were crumbling. Ammunition was running low and with most of the reservoirs captured there was only water for another day or two.

The defenders were exhausted. The three mainland battalions had been fighting, withdrawing and fighting for two weeks with almost no rest. The other three battalions and the Hong Kong Volunteer Defence Corps had been fighting three days without pause for sleep or food. Up until now morale had been high, though losses were heavy, but there were increasing murmurs of despair among the rank and file. Why postpone the inevitable by sacrificing their lives for a few hours of possession?

On the mainland the resistance had been disappointing. The stand on the barren, rugged mountain mass that was Hong Kong Island had been stubborn. Much of the credit belonged to the 1759 men of the citizen volunteers. At first disdainfully called "playboy soldiers" by the regulars, this conglomerate mixture of local British, Eurasians, Chinese and Portuguese had fought as bravely and well as any of the other troops. In fact some regular officers felt the citizen soldiers' determined defense of their home city had put steel into the better trained men.

Even the Japanese had been amazed by the gallant defense of Hong Kong Island. To them the desperate fight made no sense.

Churchill's message asking for a last-ditch stand made sense to Governor Young and General Maltby. Every day, every hour, they knew, was vital to the Empire war effort, but even they realized by midnight of Christmas Eve that the end was near. The Japanese held the power station and there were no fresh vegetables or meat. The 1,750,000 civilians of Victoria were beginning to suffer severely. With only a driblet of brackish water to drink, none could be spared for washing. Water closets were stopped up and the most luxurious hotels stank.

In the south, most of the men cut off at narrow Stanley Peninsula were dug in near the fort, on the high ground at land's end. Only a few men held the first defense line which ran through Stanley Village where the isthmus was barely 700 feet wide. And by 1:00 A.M., Christmas morning, these had been driven back to the second line, the low ridge beyond St. Stephen's College.

This put the main building of the college, presently an emergency hospital, between two fires. At dawn Private T. J. Cruz, a Portuguese volunteer stretcher-bearer, was looking out a downstairs window. To his horror he saw Japanese, bayonets at the ready, creeping toward the "hospital."

"What'll we do?" he asked his officer, a second lieutenant.

"Every man for himself!"

Cruz and the other stretcher-bearers grabbed their rifles as the attackers outside began shrieking "Banzai!"

"No," shouted someone, "throw away your rifles. Depend on the Red Cross armbands!"

The sixty-five wounded patients in the main room, which was lit only by a hurricane lamp, stared in horror, some ducking under their blankets as the shouts grew louder. Private J. Jones (this is not his real name) had been brought by coincidence that afternoon to the hospital where his young wife was a nurse. She now shoved him under his bed and crawled next to him.

Cruz and the other stretcher-bearers ran up to the second floor as the front door burst open. Dirty, unshaven, wild-eyed soldiers stampeded through the doorway. To Cruz they looked like Formosans or Koreans and they acted drunk. Peering down in terror, he saw them run into the main room and with savage shouts begin bayoneting the men in the beds. These Japanese had seen rifles and tommy guns stacked in the anteroom and could have thought those in bed were unwounded soldiers trying to hide.

Just then Lieutenant Colonel G. D. R. Black, a prominent Hong Kong doctor and head of the hospital, came from a rear room holding up a white sheet. Behind was his assistant, Captain Whitney.

"Look, you can't do that," cried Black. Followed by Whitney, he ran forward to block the doorway. The two men were shot, then stabbed many times. The attackers continued frenziedly up and down the rows of beds bayoneting the wounded. As they headed for adjoining classrooms containing another thirty patients, Japanese officers ran in and stopped the massacre.

Upstairs Cruz and five others were hiding in a classroom. They could hear the piteous screams of the stabbed, the triumphant yells of the bayoneters. Then there were footsteps. A foot crashed against their door; the glass shattered. A man holding a tommy gun burst in shouting. Cruz came forward, hands up. The others in the room followed. The Japanese hit Cruz with the butt of his gun and motioned him to enter the next room. When forty survivors were crowded into the small room, the door was slammed. Outside the sound of battle continued.

Two hours later the Japanese combat troops returned to the emergency hospital. They broke into a small room where four Chinese and seven British nurses were confined. The Chinese girls, all wearing the St. John's ambulance badge, were dragged to another room. They were raped over and over and thrown into another room. Next the three youngest British nurses, including the wife of Private Jones, were taken out of their room. They, too, were raped many times.

Private Cruz and the others heard the screams of the women. Then their door was opened. "You were stupid; you should have surrendered," said a Japanese in English. "You will be slowly killed four at a time," he added and closed the door. A few minutes later agonized cries came from the next room. Cruz wondered when their turn would come.

The main British force defending the capital, Victoria, was also being overwhelmed. Japanese were breaking into buildings in the suburbs. At 9:00 A.M. Major C. M. Manners, a retired officer, and a civilian, A. L. Shields, were escorted from the Japanese lines under a white flag. They told General Maltby of the incredible number of Japanese guns they had seen. In their opinion it was useless to continue the struggle. The Japanese, they said, promised not to fire for three hours while the British made up their minds. Maltby called a special defense meeting.

Though the situation was hopeless and Japanese were even in some of the air raid tunnels, it was decided to continue fighting. At noon, the three-hour truce was over; Japanese artillery resumed fire. By 3:15 P.M. Maltby knew he'd reached the end. He advised Governor Young that no further useful military resistance was possible, then ordered his commanders to surrender.

Rumor of the surrender spread through the city. There was a sense of immense relief in spite of the humiliation of defeat. The useless slaughter had stopped. At the Gloucester Hotel someone suggested that all the liquor in the many luxury hotels in the neighborhood should be destroyed. Thousands of bottles were dumped down the bathroom drains. Since these were clogged, champagne, gin, bourbon and Scotch began running down staircases. But many of the bottles were consumed. It was a last, glorious, desperate binge.

Below the fort, at St. Stephen's College, Private Cruz was still waiting in the emergency hospital with his forty captured comrades. Though they had heard cries of agony about every half-hour from the next room—now called "the torture room"—none of them had yet been taken. They knew their luck couldn't hold much longer. When the door opened at 5:30 P.M. Cruz felt it was his last moment. A Japanese officer came in and said, "You boys are very lucky. Hong Kong has surrendered. Now we will no longer have to kill you."

The prisoners were told to clean out the next room. Cruz almost retched when he looked inside. The seven British and Chinese nurses who had been raped were gone but blood covered the floor like a thick claret carpet. Mattresses and cushions were soaked red. Cruz splashed through the blood and picked up a cushion. It was soggy and heavy. The prisoners stacked the mattresses and cushions in the yard. Bodies—some with ears cut off, all bayoneted—were carried on stretchers from the building to the yard. The pile of mattresses was ignited. Three bodies were flung on top of the flames. It would take many more fires for at least seventy inside the hospital had been slaughtered. The flames cast fantastic shadows as more bodies were heaped on the pyre.

This was the end of Christmas on Hong Kong Island.

December 26, Boxing Day, was a bitter one for the British. Lieutenant Bill Stoker of the 2nd Scottish Company, still uncaptured, had heard rumors of rapings at St. Stephen's College. Late that morning with two volunteers he drove into Stanley Peninsula. The Japanese paid no attention to him as he entered the emergency hospital. He found the four older British nurses exhausted and near hysteria. As he boldly escorted them past the guards, Private Jones called out from a group of captured soldiers, asking if

Stoker had seen his wife. Stoker and his men looked but none of the seven missing British and Chinese nurses could be found.

A Japanese officer, Captain Kawai, pitying the frantic Private Jones, volunteered to help. He went outside. A moment later he called Jones. The British citizen-soldier ran outside, saw a pile covered with a coat belonging to his wife. Private Jones hesitantly pulled back the coat. Underneath were three dead women. One was his wife. He collapsed.

In Aberdeen Harbor, famous for its elaborate floating restaurants, every junk, proa and sampan was flying a Japanese flag. In Victoria, Japanese troops were making a formal triumphant entry as planes roared overhead, leaving a fluttering trail of pamphlets proclaiming the Co-Prosperity Sphere of East Asia. Thousands of Chinese lined the streets waving Rising Sun flags. To the Japanese it was a "never-to-be-forgotten ceremony." European onlookers also would never forget it. The lead car, carrying a smiling Japanese general, had recently belonged to a Dutchman. A bright sticker on the windshield read:

HOLLAND SHALL RISE AGAIN.

2 It had also been a dark Christmas in the Philippines. On the morning of December 25 MacArthur was reviewing the deteriorating military situation at his new headquarters on Corregidor. This was an island in the shape of a polliwog that sat in the mouth of Manila Bay, not 30 miles from the city, and easily visible on any clear day.

Whoever held Corregidor controlled Manila Bay, for it stuck in its throat like a bone. To MacArthur it had an even more important value. Less than two and a half miles to the north was Bataan, the mountainous peninsula which was to become the main battlefield of the Philippines.

Corregidor, aptly nicknamed The Rock, was perfectly designed by nature for defense. The body of the polliwog was 519 feet high and covered with foliage. Here, dug in rock and well camouflaged, were the fort's main big guns. The middle of the island, where the tail began, was almost at sea level. Then after a few hundred yards, there rose another hump of solid rock, Malinta Hill. Through it had been bored a great tunnel with many laterals, so ingeniously constructed that ten thousand could live in its dank catacombs indefinitely without fear of bomb or shell. This was Malinta Tunnel.

MacArthur and his family lived in a small cottage half a mile beyond the eastern mouth of the tunnel, further out on the polliwog tail. On Christmas morning he sat in this cottage confronted by apparent instant disaster. Without air or sea support his basic plan for aggressive defense of the Philippines had collapsed and he had been forced to the humiliating strategy of holding out on Bataan until help arrived.

The chances of successful withdrawal to the peninsula seemed hopeless to many that morning. One effective bombing would cripple the mass movement. Manila Bay was dotted with slow-moving barges, pleasure steamers, launches and tugs shuttling men, munitions and food to Corregidor and Bataan. Highway 3 leading north out of Manila was jammed with trucks, 155's on their carriages, naval guns on trucks, buses, cars, cartelas and oxcarts. One bomb on the Calumpit Bridge over the wide, unfordable Pampanga River, 30 miles north of Manila, would cripple the entire withdrawal plan.

Ten miles beyond this bridge the line of vehicles turned left at the busy town of San Fernando, sugar center of the Philippines, and until recently overhung with the nauseatingly sweet smell of burning sugar cane. Here was a chaotic traffic snarl, for almost as many trucks and buses were pouring in from the north. This southbound traffic was the van of Wainwright's main body, fleeing to Bataan while the covering force delayed the onrushing men of Homma. Many of these Filipino troops had no transportation and were marching barefoot, their outsize GI shoes tied to rifle barrels. They trudged along the hot unshaded roads in blue denims and pith helmets.

The road from San Fernando westward to Bataan was so narrow that traffic had backed up into town by 11:30 A.M. Ambulances, tank trailers and guns were parked on every side street, on the sidewalks and even the fields near the railroad station and cockfight arena. Those trapped in the town kept looking nervously into the clear sky. One dive-bomb attack would not only destroy hundreds of vehicles but tie up this key junction for days.

The same fear haunted men for the next 42 miles on the narrow stretch of road to Orion, halfway down the east coast of Bataan. It was lightly tarred but the crust had been crumbled by the first heavy vehicles in the line. Dust rose from San Fernando to Orion scribbling swirling plumes in the sky. Climbing hundreds of feet, this great spoor was visible for many miles, a luring target.

Just before noon the rumble of many motors could be

heard to the north. As it grew louder, some vehicles stopped and men scrambled into sugar fields or rice paddies; some vehicles kept going, racing madly to avoid the attackers. In San Fernando there was nothing to do but hide under the flimsy buildings and nipa shacks or in ditches.

Soon a large formation of Japanese planes flew above the crowded town. Not a bomb dropped. Not a plane peeled off for attack. The attackers flew serenely south, oblivious of the panic below. They passed Calumpit Bridge without dropping a bomb and continued over jammed Highway 3 all the way to the city. At noon they were over Manila. Finally their bombs fell, hitting the port area and the Walled City, evacuated by MacArthur only the day before. Then the fliers headed back for Formosa, reporting that their objectives had been hit, mission accomplished.

While the smoke was still rising from the wreckage in the port area, the great exodus was already in motion again. But there was no sense of relief. Other raiders must be getting ready to dive or make their bomb runs. The long winding target from Manila to Bataan was too obvious to miss.

PFC John Connor, leading a convoy of twenty trucks loaded with C rations, felt a sense of shame as he drove north past crowds of staring Filipinos. Some would smile, hold up fingers in a V for Victory sign and shout, "Hello, Joe." Most just stared. They seemed to say, "You're running off and leaving us."

By dusk the Japanese still hadn't bombed the road to Bataan. In the north Wainwright had successfully drawn behind the Agno River, the second defense line of WPO-3, and a formidable natural barrier about 90 air miles above Manila.

But in the south, three columns of Japanese were steadily moving northwest from Lamon Bay and were only 55 air miles from the capital. Early that morning the 1st Infantry Regiment, which had been holding back the column nearest Manila with a stiff defense, suddenly withdrew by mistake when orders were confused. Brigadier General Albert Jones, the new commander of the South Luzon Force, was eating his Christmas dinner when a motorcyclist drove up to his command post. The messenger said the 1st Infantry was coming back over the mountain.

Jones, an energetic officer of Welsh descent, angrily jumped into his staff car and headed for the front. MacArthur had chosen Jones to command in the south because of his well-known aggressive spirit and his firm belief that the Japanese could be whipped. Jones ran into the retreating troops near Luisiana. When the senior American instructor of the 1st Infantry stepped forward, Jones said, "Just what the hell do you mean pulling back?"

"I was ordered to pull back by the commander of the South Luzon Force, sir."

"Well, I'm the new commander of the South Luzon Force and you turn your people around in a hurry." As an example Jones told his own driver to head down the road toward the enemy. He figured there wasn't enough time to persuade an advance guard to precede him. He knew he'd eventually meet the Japanese but that would take care of itself. By now it was dusk. At a bend in the narrow dirt road lined with bamboo and cocoanut trees, Jones came to a half-track astride the road. Written in chalk on its side was *Miss Oregon*.

The Americans in the half-track aimed their automatic weapons at the general's car. As they were about to shoot, Jones asked them who they thought they were aiming at.

"We thought you were Japs," apologized the sergeant in charge of the half-track.

"Where are the Japs?"

The sergeant pointed east. "Down the road about three kilometers."

"I'm going ahead and reconnoiter," said Jones. He waved the half-track to precede the staff car. The sergeant jumped into the half-track as it went down the dark road. After passing three kilometer posts it squealed to a stop.

Jones saw figures jumping out from behind cocoanut trees.

"Halt," shouted the sergeant from the half-track. The figures didn't answer. "Halt!"

There was a roar as a concealed Japanese gun at the bend of the road ahead hit the radiator of the half-track. Then machine-gun fire opened up from the right side of the road. Jones ran from the staff car, trying to get into the half-track, but machine-gun bullets had found the mark and were bouncing off the sides. The general dove into the left-hand ditch. As he landed in the mud, his driver flopped on top of him. Machine-gun fire chattered from the left side of the road, 25 yards away.

The men in the half-track were firing back with their machine gun and Jones wondered how they could live in the hail of fire. It looked as though a stream of bullets were passing through their bodies. Jones heard a terrific crack over his head. He thought he'd been hit. A bullet had struck his driver's pistol, knocking it out of his hand. Abruptly there was silence.

"Let's get the hell out of here," said Jones. His driver quickly turned the staff car around. Jones and the men from the half-track jumped into the car and it speeded up the road to the rear, lights on. Shots came from both sides of the road.

"Kill the lights," said Jones.

The lights went off but it was too dark to drive. "Put them on again," said Jones, "and drive like hell."

After a few miles they met 1st Infantry troops returning to battle. Jones ordered them to fight a delaying action until forced to withdraw. They needed no urging to keep moving forward. They were more afraid of the angry general than of the Japanese.

At 4:00 A.M., the next day, December 26, Admiral Rockwell's barge silently left the dock at the middle of Corregidor, where the polliwog's tail began. Manned by an American coxswain and a Filipino crew of three, its sole passenger was a lieutenant junior grade, Malcolm Champlin. Six months ago he had been an FBI agent in Baltimore. Called back to service in the Navy, he had protested strenuously, but by now he was reconciled to his fate. As Admiral Rockwell's aide, his work was varied and interesting. This morning, for example, he was to steal back to Manila, which might fall at any minute, and give Captain Morsell instructions to blow up the vast oil dumps in the city. Morsell was to locate the American, British, Dutch and French owners of the oil and persuade them by diplomacy if possible to destroy their own property. Rockwell impressed on him the vital importance of the mission. It was still dark as the admiral's barge swung into the channel between Corregidor and Bataan. Then it turned right toward Manila and soon approached the mine sweeper guarding the channel.

"Boat, ahoy," called someone from the sweeper. When the admiral's barge swung in close, Champlin could see three large black hulks behind the sweeper. "Can you lead these ships through the mine fields?" shouted the sweeper captain from the wing of his bridge.

"No," promptly answered Champlin. He had been through the field only once months before when the *President Harrison* brought him to Manila. Besides he had his own mission to worry about.

"Well, you can spot the buoys, can't you? These ships have Army on them and can't stay here during daylight. They'll be sunk by Jap planes. I want you to take them through to Bataan if you possibly can."

Since the sweeper captain outranked him, Champlin said, "Aye, aye, sir. Tell the leading ship to follow me and to stay well behind. I'll find the buoys but I don't want the heavy ships to follow too closely in my wake."

The captain thanked Champlin, gave him a compass bearing, and left. As the young lieutenant led the way through the mines he couldn't help thinking of the steamboat *Corregidor,* blown up two weeks earlier almost at this very spot with the loss of many lives. He glanced behind and saw the first ship, its rail lined with troops. Instead of staying well behind, the three ships were closing in fast, as if eager to get the suspense over.

Finally a Filipino in the bow of the barge spotted a little spray. Champlin guessed it was the buoy marking the end of the mine field. He changed course and passed clear of the spray on the open channel side. He was right. The barge and three ships slipped safely between the last buoys. Champlin waved to the soldiers on the decks and headed back through the mine field toward Manila.

The city was confused with rumors. Some said the Japanese were at the outskirts. Others said they were hundreds of miles away. Champlin borrowed a car and hurried to Captain Morsell's office. It was abandoned. Everyone had gone to Bataan. He hurried through crowded lines of vehicles heading north toward the Marsman Building. Hart's headquarters was also deserted. The admiral had left early that morning on the submarine *Shark* for parts unknown. The others were on their way to Corregidor or Bataan. Finally Champlin found one officer, Commander R. L. Dennison. "Do you have any instructions about the oil supplies and their destruction?" asked Champlin.

Dennison knew nothing about oil. He was destroying radios and making a last checkup of the building. Champlin realized he had inherited the mission, but he had no idea what to do. Where were the oil executives? And if he found them how could he persuade them to destroy their own property?

Early that afternoon at the Army-Navy Club, Champlin finally learned that the man who controlled most of the oil in Manila was a Mr. Rock of the Standard Oil Company who was probably near by at the University Club. Champlin hustled along Dewey Boulevard for half a block. He found Rock at the University Club and the oil man promptly agreed to help.

"How much oil is there in Manila?" asked Champlin. He was informed there were enough petroleum products in the

Pandacan area to operate the Asiatic Fleet for two years. "Admiral Rockwell told me Manila is going to be made an open city some time today. You and your workmen have got to help me destroy this petroleum before the Japs come."

"You might burn down the whole city." Rock explained that burning oil might flow into the Pasig River and set fire to every dock, ship and warehouse. The only solution would be to bleed oil off into the ground before igniting it, but 100 policemen would have to cordon the area. Sparks from a hobnail boot or a dropped cigarette could set off everything prematurely.

"We'll get every fire engine and policeman in Manila to help us," Champlin promised.

Rock agreed to burn his petroleum products, then added, "You may have trouble with the French and British oil companies."

The two men called a meeting of the oil executives involved. All but the British representatives soon arrived and Rock explained the problem. Next Champlin told the oil men how important this was to the Allied war effort. They were not enthusiastic. After an hour's futile discussion, Rock picked up a telephone. "Gather forty workmen," he told his foreman. "Destroy all Standard Oil products in Manila beginning with alcolate."

Rock's example tipped the scales. When the other oil men had completed similar telephone calls, Champlin arranged to have eight fire engines and 100 policemen report to the Pandacan area. While he and Rock relaxed with a round of Scotch whisky, the oil man warned him there would probably be trouble with the two British executives controlling the Shell Oil holdings.

Champlin recalled the recent report that Kowloon oil, not set afire by the British during the battle for Hong Kong, was now being used by Japanese tanks rolling steadily down the Malay Peninsula toward Singapore. "In that case," he suggested, "why don't you instruct your foremen to be ready to destroy the Shell holdings at a single word from you?"

Rock called his foreman and made arrangements. A few minutes later the two British oil men, carrying tennis rackets and wearing long shorts, strolled into the University Club. Champlin explained that Japanese advance parties were probably nearing the Pandacan area.

"We are mere agents," said one, a Mr. Crawford. "We would have to obtain permission from our principals in Singapore before destroying their property."

"This is also a British war," said Champlin. "We can presume your principals would give an affirmative answer."

The British weren't so sure. The argument went on. Finally Champlin said, "Would you rather see this oil in the hands of the Japanese than violate your instructions as agents?"

"Yes," replied Crawford. "We cannot violate our instructions."

Champlin nodded to Rock, who picked up a phone. "Go ahead as planned," Rock told his foreman, and put down the phone.

Champlin brought the British oil men drinks. Suddenly there was a distant, hollow explosion. "Gentlemen," said Champlin when the British finished their drinks, "your oil is now in flames."

Pillars of smoke climbed as more explosions followed. Great tongues of flame from the Pandacan area lit up the early evening darkness. Electric lights began to pop on all over Manila. Don Bell, official news commentator for the Civilian Emergency Administration, was announcing over KZRH that to save the city from destruction MacArthur had just declared Manila an open city. The blackout was over.

But the confusion continued all through the night as self-appointed air raid wardens shot out windows showing light. No one knew exactly what was going on. The mood in the oppressive, muggy heat was bizarre and frightening. With the black swirls of smoke clouding the skies, the distant explosions from Cavite, and the occasional hollow booms of self-destruction from Fort McKinley and Nielson Field, it seemed to some as if the end of the world was coming. Yet many night clubs were open. This might be the last hour of freedom.

The hastily organized exodus to Bataan had become a nightmare. Since few military police controlled the traffic, terror and selfishness caused many wrecks and tie-ups.

On Bataan, hundreds of men and vehicles checked in every hour. Many had no idea where their units were. There were few road signs or markers. The Filipinos in the barrios and villages that suddenly became dumping grounds for thousands stared in wonder as incredible numbers of trucks, cars and guns roared past, coating their bamboo houses with thick layers of dust.

According to WPO-3, the civilians on Bataan were to be evacuated. None had been. Moreover, thousands of terrified civilian refugees in the path of Homma's 14th Army were streaming toward Bataan in oxcarts, cartelas and old cars. No one stopped these people as they flooded from the north into the future battleground. The plan also specified defense positions were to be dug by 20,000 civilian laborers, under direction of Army engineers. The trenches and fortifications were still only on paper.

But food was the biggest problem. WPO-3 called for a food supply of six months. The quartermaster, Brigadier General Charles Drake, since getting his orders on the morning of December 24, had now stocked the island of Corregidor with enough food for 10,000 men for six months. Except for 3000 tons of canned meat and fish already stored on the peninsula, little else was in Bataan. More food was on its way by water, rail and highway, but how many more days would the road to Bataan be open? How many hours?

According to MacArthur's plan, Wainwright would delay Homma's main attack, holding the key town of San Fernando until January 8. This would give the men already on Bataan time to dig defenses and Jones time to retreat with his South Luzon Force up through Manila and into Bataan.

But before midnight the Japanese had broken across the Agno River in a dozen places. The last formidable natural fortification between Homma and San Fernando was breached. It was now obvious that Wainwright's poorly trained, poorly equipped and exhausted troops could not possibly hold until the eighth. Or even the seventh or sixth. In fact, front-line commanders were wondering if they could hold until the first.

3   On Christmas morning a flying boat approached Hawaii from the northeast. In it was Admiral Chester Nimitz, the man chosen to relieve Kimmel. He was a trim-looking man with hair turning white and piercing light blue eyes. He wasn't too happy about the assignment, preferring a sea command. Down below he could see, even in the rain, hundreds of boats in the great harbor. As soon as the big four-engine plane touched the surface, a launch pulled alongside. Nimitz got in and shook hands with Rear Admiral Patrick Bellinger.

"What are those boats doing?" asked Nimitz as they slowly pushed through the oily muck that still covered the harbor.

"They're full of drowned sailors and Marines," explained Bellinger.

Nimitz soon found what he had feared—too much pessimism. Morale, since the recall of the Wake Island Relief

Force, was at rock bottom. He learned from the fleet surgeon that the shock of the December 7 attack had literally turned some commanders' hair white. In fact the staff generally had become so jittery, the surgeon had been forced to feed some of them sedatives.

Nimitz, who had brought with him only a flag secretary, called together his inherited staff. "There will be no changes," he said in his gentle, courteous manner. "I have complete confidence in you men. We've taken a terrific wallop but I have no doubts as to the ultimate outcome." Later he told Kimmel, the man he had relieved, "You have my sympathy. The same thing could have happened to anybody."

In his Academy classbook, Nimitz had been described as a man "of cheerful and confident tomorrows." From this first day his calm air of serenity and trust was infectious. The complete rehabilitation of spirit at Pearl Harbor, however, would take much longer. It would be several months before the Pacific Fleet would be ready to strike back in force at the Japanese.

On that Christmas morning, all tapping from the sunken battleship *West Virginia* had stopped. The last three survivors, clad in blues and jerseys, now lay lifeless on the lower shelf of storeroom A-111. Nearby was a calendar with an X marked on every day from December 7 through the twenty-third.

PART 3

BATTLE FOR BATAAN

10

Roads to Bataan

1 At 4:00 P.M., December 30, a few men sat on a wooden platform in a clearing outside Malinta Tunnel. As the audience of 150 watched solemnly, Virginia Bewley played "Hail to the Chief" on a hand organ. This bizarre ceremony was the second inaugural of President Manuel Quezon and Vice-President Sergio Osmeña. Chief Justice José Abad Santos administered the oaths. Then Quezon, his gray hair long and tangled, began to speak. Although now confined to a wheel chair, he spoke as a young man, his eyes bright with their old fire. The reason for this youthful enthusiasm was evident when Quezon read aloud a message he had recently received from President Roosevelt. "News of your gallant struggle against the Japanese aggressors has elicited the profound admiration of every American. . . . I give to the people of the Philippines my solemn pledge that their freedom will be redeemed and their independence established and protected. The entire resources in men and materials of the United States stand behind that pledge."

Francis Sayre, United States high commissioner, then spoke. And finally MacArthur stood up, looking to some spectators like a tired hawk. The day before he had narrowly missed death when bombs levelled his headquarters. As a bomb crashed through his bungalow, MacArthur had been standing on a hill counting the 72 raiders. His Philippine orderly, Sergeant Domingo, took off his own helmet and put it over MacArthur's unprotected head. The general pushed the helmet away. Domingo stubbornly pushed it back just as a piece of shrapnel hit it, nicking the sergeant's hand.

The close brush with death had acted as a tonic to MacArthur and today he, too, had been encouraged by the Roosevelt message. Perhaps, after all the delays and excuses, substantial help was really coming. His quiet, slow voice was a dramatic contrast to Quezon's high-pitched excitement and his audience had to strain to hear.

"The thunder of death and destruction, dropped from the skies, can be heard in the distance. Our ears almost catch the roar of battle as our soldiers close on the firing line. The horizon is blackened by the smoke of destructive fire. The air reverberates to the roar of exploding bombs.

"Such is the bed of birth of this new government, of this new nation. For 400 years the Philippines have struggled upward toward self-government. Just at the end of its tuitionary period, just on the threshold of independence, came the great hour of decision. There was no hesitation, no vacillation, no moment of doubt. The whole country followed its great leader in choosing the side of freedom against the side of slavery.

"We have just inaugurated him, we have just thereby confirmed his momentous decision. Hand in hand with the United States and the other free nations of the world, this basic and fundamental issue will be fought through to victory. Come what may, ultimate triumph will be its reward."

The brave new hopes on Corregidor were not reflected on the roads to Bataan. Though the first few days of bumper-to-bumper traffic had ended, the highways were still busy with convoys and single vehicles fleeing into the peninsula ahead of the invaders, their occupants frantically eyeing every plane that approached. But Calumpit Bridge still stood. San Fernando, the key escape town, was still intact.

The Japanese had completely misunderstood the mass migration to Bataan. General Homma and his staff thought it was a frantic, disorganized flight of unimportant elements of the Philippine Army. Only Homma's chief of staff, Major General Masami Maeda, disagreed with this theory. A student of the Spanish-American War, he had predicted since October that MacArthur would pull his main forces to Bataan. But the Imperial General Staff, the Southern Army leaders and the rest of Homma's staff insisted Manila was the key to the campaign. Once the capital was taken the Philippine campaign would be over, although MacArthur would probably hold out on Corregidor and the end of Bataan for a few weeks.

And so that day the Japanese main forces kept driving at Manila from north and south, paying little attention to the lines of vehicles disappearing into the jungles of Bataan. The relationship of the peninsula to Corregidor, lying little more than two miles from its tip, was ignored.

In French Indo-China at Nahtrang, Admiral Nobutake Kondo, commander of the Second Fleet and the staff of General Count Hisaichi Terauchi, commander of the Southern Army, were holding a conference to decide the future of the Southeast Asia campaign.

Homma's rapid march toward Manila and Yamashita's steady drive down the Malay Peninsula toward Singapore had exceeded all expectations. Why not invade Java a month ahead of schedule? This would mean complete occupation of all Southeast Asia while the Allies were still off balance.

Everyone agreed. The first step would be the early transfer of the 48th Division from Homma to the Java invasion force. It was obvious this crack unit was no longer needed in the Philippines.

Late that night Brigadier General Jones was returning from the South Luzon front to his rear echelon headquarters at Fort McKinley near Manila. He was tired but in a good mood. The day had been spent in setting up an ambush about 40 miles south of Manila. His men were in position on a ridge and would soon catch the approaching Japanese completely by surprise.

As Jones approached Fort McKinley he noticed lines of cars heading north. His headquarters troops were apparently being evacuated. Angrily he hurried into his command post. It was almost deserted. Here to his consternation he learned that orders had been changed without his knowledge. South Luzon Force was to retreat immediately to Bataan. MacArthur wanted all troops immediately available sent to Plaridel, a little town north of Manila, to try and stop the main Japanese forces which were heading straight for Manila. Jones was to hold Plaridel with these few troops until the rest of his men swung in behind him and escaped into Bataan.

Jones realized something very bad must have happened in Wainwright's North Luzon area. The withdrawal to Bataan was a week ahead of schedule. Jones now followed his troops that had gone ahead, driving north out of Manila on High-

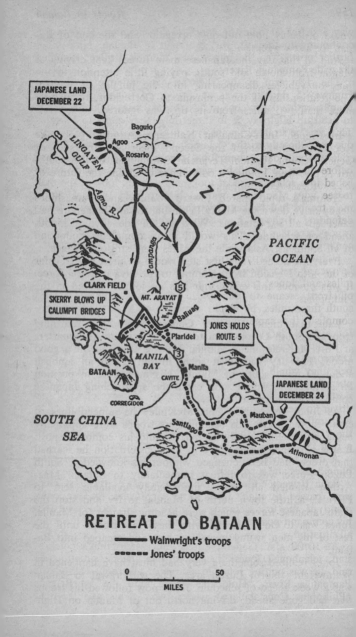

JAPANESE LAND
DECEMBER 22

Baguio

Agoo

Rosario

LINGAYEN
GULF

Agno R.

L U Z O N

Pampanga R.

PACIFIC
OCEAN

CLARK FIELD

MT. ARAYAT

SKERRY BLOWS UP
CALUMPIT BRIDGES

Baliuag

Plaridel

JONES HOLDS
ROUTE 5

MANILA
BAY

Manila

BATAAN

CAVITE

CORREGIDOR

JAPANESE LAND
DECEMBER 24

SOUTH CHINA
SEA

Santiago

Mauban

Atimonan

RETREAT TO BATAAN

—— Wainwright's troops
------ Jones' troops

0   50

MILES

way 3. After 21 miles he came to a Y junction. Highway 3, continuing to the left, was the road to Bataan. Nine miles farther north was the important Calumpit Bridge, spanning the wide Pampanga River.

The right arm of the Y junction, going due north, was Highway 5. Homma was coming down this single road to Manila with 90 per cent of his troops. Jones told his driver to head up Highway 5. In three miles they came to Plaridel. This was a strategic point, for a good road ran six miles due west directly to the Calumpit Bridge on Highway 3.

It was still dark when Jones reached this little town. Just before dawn he found his new command post already established in a schoolhouse. It took only a quick look at the map to see why MacArthur wanted him to hold Plaridel. Homma's troops had broken through the two Philippine divisions defending Highway 5. A strong Japanese infantry-tank advance force was already only 20 miles north of the town and coming fast.

Homma had two alternatives once he reached Plaridel. If he turned west, he would reach the Calumpit Bridge in six miles and Jones' remaining men in the south would be cut off from escape to Bataan. If Homma continued straight south three miles, he would come to the Y junction and accomplish the same purpose. The answer was simple to Jones: hold Plaridel.

To help Jones defend it were the retreating 71st and 91st Divisions of Wainwright's North Luzon Force. How much help they would be, he didn't know. By daybreak Jones had put a battalion of his own 51st Division astride the road just north of Plaridel. Then he got into his staff car and told his driver to head farther north. He wanted to reconnoiter. In four miles he ran into exhausted, terrified stragglers from the 91st and 71st Divisions. It looked like the beginnings of a rout. Something had to be done to stop them.

A mile farther north he came to Baliuag, a town of rambling houses and nipa huts.

Soon Brigadier General Luther Stevens, of the 91st Division, passed through. Jones ordered Stevens to take command of the first delaying position so he could return to his command post at Plaridel and devote himself to the overall situation.

At 10:00 A.M. General Sutherland, MacArthur's chief of staff, telephoned Jones. Because of the chaotic situation, he said, he was putting Jones in charge of all troops east of the Pampanga River. "Hold the bridge until the 1st Brigade (Philippine Constabulary) passes over." This was the rear guard of Jones' own South Luzon Force. "Remember, all troops will have to be west of the Pampanga River by 0600, January 1. That's when the bridge will be blown."

By now Homma's advance infantry-tank force had reached Baliuag, only five miles north of Jones' command post, and were organizing an all-out assault, spearheaded by tanks. Though he didn't know it, complete disaster threatened Jones because of a strange confusion in command. Unfortunately Wainwright had not yet been told that his two divisions, the 71st and 91st, had been transferred to Jones. Thinking he still commanded these troops, Wainwright ordered them to retreat immediately to Bataan.

And so at 2:00 P.M., just as the Japanese advance infantry-tank detachment was deploying its forces for an attack on Baliuag, the defenders of the town began pulling out in buses and speeding toward the Calumpit Bridge and safety. A few minutes later General Wainwright walked into Jones' schoolhouse command post at Plaridel. "Take up positions for a close-in, perimeter defense of the Calumpit Bridge," he ordered.

"No, sir," said Jones. This would mean abandoning Plaridel and writing off all his troops coming up from the south. "My orders are to defend the bridge until all my people come through. If I fell back to the river I wouldn't have enough space to slow down the Japs."

"I'm giving you a direct order," said Wainwright angrily.

Jones, shorter than the angular Wainwright, looked up at him defiantly. It was an unpleasant situation. Wainwright had two stars, he had only one. "I've been ordered by Sutherland to take command of all troops below the Pampanga River."

Wainwright was astounded.

"I'm not going to withdraw," said Jones.

One of Jones' staff officers rushed in breathlessly, excitedly. "The 71st Division has pulled out of Baliuag!" he said.

Just then General Stevens walked in.

"Stop them!" Jones angrily told Stevens to put the 71st in position between the Japanese and the Calumpit Bridge. Then, as Wainwright left, still upset by the mix-up in command, Jones ran to his staff car. He soon discovered the 71st had already passed through Plaridel and was halfway to Calumpit Bridge. He ordered his driver to follow, but after several miles he realized the chase was hopeless and returned in disgust to the schoolhouse.

Word from Baliuag was alarming. By now Japanese tanks were massing in the east part of town. Jones ordered ten tanks of Company C, 192nd Tank Battalion, to rush north and hit the Japanese before they could launch their own attack. He told Lieutenant Colonel David Babcock to support the American tanks with half a dozen 75-mm. self-propelled guns.

At 5:00 P.M. after a barrage by Lieutenant Colonel Halstead Fowler's 71st Field Artillery, the only unit which had stayed in Baliuag, 10 tanks commanded by Lieutenant William Gentry moved into the town. As dusk fell American tanks crashed through the nipa huts, tumbling them over and scattering Japanese infantry. American and Japanese tanks mixed in a wild free-for-all in Baliuag's narrow streets, firing at point-blank range. After a brief, savage fight 8 Japanese tanks were knocked out. Gentry pulled back. Now Babcock's 75's opened fire, leveling what remained of the town and completely disrupting the Japanese infantry-tank force.

Tanks, derided up until now by many infantry officers who knew little of their capabilities or limitations, had paid for themselves that day. They had given Jones the few extra hours he needed. Now there was nothing to do but wait and hope. He went outside the schoolhouse and lay on flagstones near a fountain. The moon was bright, the evening fragrant with the exotic scent of frangipani. He could hear the distant rumble and rattle of trucks and buses coming from the south and heading toward Calumpit. Was there enough time for his rear guard to reach the bridge?

2 As hundreds of vehicles rolled into Bataan that New Year's Eve, the *Mayon*, the same interisland steamer Quezon rode to Corregidor, was being loaded at the southern end of the peninsula. Six hundred and fifty men of the 19th Bombardment Group were bound south for the island of Mindanao. They were to rebuild and defend the airfields at the Del Monte pineapple plantation.

As the steamer left Mariveles Harbor, the airmen's commander, Major Emmett "Rosie" O'Donnell, thought caustically of the brief disappointing fight made by the air force. No real money had been spent on Clark Field. It was merely a sod field with run-down hangars and little else. The B-17 had no tail gun and was helpless in a rear attack. When war broke out there were no supplies, no radar, no housing. There were too many sunshiners in the service. Hundreds had taken off in panic after the first bombing. The withdrawal to Bataan had been an unholy mess, a bad, humiliating memory. Now they were probably headed for some other damn foul-up.

The rock silhouette of Corregidor soon became clearly etched in the moonlight as the *Mayon* headed south. Then it passed a launch pulling a barge slowly toward Mariveles, the port at the tip end of Bataan.

On the barge were Lieutenant Colonel Allen Stowell and fifteen men. They were laying a submarine cable of 100 circuits from Corregidor to Bataan. MacArthur had given Stowell a month to do the job. So far the Japanese hadn't discovered what he was doing.

At 1:00 A.M., New Year's Day, Jones rose from his flagstone bed in Plaridel and drove west across the six-mile connecting road to Highway 3 and the Calumpit Bridge. The last elements of the 51st Division were just crossing the bridge. Only his rear guard, left on the other side of Manila to hold off any attack from the south, was missing. When they arrived his entire South Luzon Force would have escaped.

An hour later the ten tanks of Lieutenant Gentry, which had scored such a brilliant victory at Baliuag, slowly crossed the long bridge. Soon Jones heard a low rumble from the south. The noise increased and in a few minutes trucks and buses approached the long, three-span bridge. Jones, standing at the north end of the bridge, anxiously watched them draw near. It was his rear guard, the Constabulary Brigade of Brigadier General Simeon de Jesus. Every one of his units had been safely pulled out of South Luzon. Now he could call in his last troops, the small covering force holding Plaridel.

Standing near Jones was General Wainwright. He too felt great relief to watch the last of the troops from South Luzon pass by. He walked up to his engineer, Colonel Harry Skerry, and asked if everything was ready for the bridge's demolition.

Skerry was prepared but MacArthur's engineer, Colonel Hugh "Pat" Casey, had ordered him to hold off the demolitions until 5:00 A.M. to permit the last elements from the south to clear. There was still a platoon of engineers under Major N. L. Manzano and other demolition groups destroying bridges and key facilities between Manila and Calumpit.

Casey himself was still at MacArthur's old headquarters in No. 1 Victoria Street, Manila. He was at the phone, talking to one of the several hundred civilian mining engineers he had recently commissioned. The man was south of Manila with a few assistants.

"Calumpit's going to be blown pretty soon," said Casey. "You won't be able to make it in time over the road. Better come up here to Manila and try to get a boat to Corregidor or Bataan before the Nips get here."

Casey looked at his watch. It was almost 3:00 A.M. He decided to make a last quick tour of the city and then proceed to Corregidor before it was too late. Casey and his driver left the deserted headquarters building and started slowly through the rubble of the Walled City. Manila was shrouded by great black columns of smoke. The Pandacan area was ablaze. A few hours earlier his men had set off charges on each of the big oil tanks that had survived the fire set by Navy Lieutenant Champlin a few days earlier. The flames still roared so loudly that conversation within a few hundred yards was impossible. Pylons of smoke were also rising from Nichols Field, Fort McKinley and the entire port area. And across the bay the remaining facilities of Cavite Naval Base blazed.

There was nothing else Casey could do. He and his driver stepped into a launch and headed into Manila Bay. On all sides were smoke and flame. His engineers had done a thorough job. He was satisfied. Not far away, lights from the Manila Hotel twinkled and the nostalgic, distant music of a dance band could be heard.

Thirty miles to the north, the last Constabulary truck of Jones' rear guard was just then clearing the Calumpit Bridge. Jones telephoned his chief of staff. "Get over to Plaridel," he said. "Withdraw the covering force immediately."

This order came none too soon. As the covering force, commanded by Lieutenant Colonel Loren Stewart, pulled out of Plaridel in their trucks, rifle fire came from the north. Homma's advance force broke into the town just in time to see Stewart's trucks disappear west on the road to Calumpit Bridge. At 5:00 A.M. the last of these trucks crossed the bridge and passed a small group of officers—four generals and a colonel.

"Are all your units safely across?" asked Wainwright. Stevens, Jones and Brigadier General James Weaver, provisional tank group commander, all replied in the affirmative.

"All right, Skerry," said Wainwright, turning to his engineer. "Blow it."

Skerry asked for a delay. Major Manzano's demolition

crew still hadn't arrived and no large explosions to the south had been heard.

"All right," said Wainwright. "Wait an hour."

Skerry made a last-minute check of the four tons of dynamite on the highway bridge. Then he checked the three tons of explosives on the railway bridge which ran parallel 50 yards to the west.

At 5:45 A.M. Wainwright extended the time of demolition to 6:15. He and Jones, both groggy from lack of sleep, went to a commercial truck overturned in the ditch and got a bottle of champagne. They toasted the New Year and the successful withdrawal of Jones' troops.

Dawn was now beginning to break. Scattered rifle fire could be heard coming from Plaridel. Every minute it grew louder. "The situation is getting serious," Wainwright told the other generals. He adjusted his field glasses. In the dim light he saw a Japanese patrol advancing and turned to his engineer. It was almost 6:15 A.M.

"Skerry," he said regretfully, "we cannot wait any longer. Blow it now."

Skerry walked to the demolition group tensely standing at the abutment. "Blow the highway bridge," he told Lieutenant Derrick. "Then the railroad bridge."

Everyone took cover. At exactly 6:15 A.M. there was a terrific rolling roar. Then a second. The sky lit up as debris from the two parallel bridges rained down. Wainwright and the demolition crew went back to the riverbank. In the swirling waters of the wide, deep, unfordable Pampanga River they saw tangled, curled masses of metal. Wainwright's flank was now safe, but he sighed. "It's too bad we had to destroy such costly and important structures."

Jones was on his way to Bataan, his South Luzon Force already dissolved. He was again only a division commander. He drove through San Fernando marveling that such a key junction was still undestroyed. Then he headed due west toward Bataan. Soon he caught up to the tail end of his 51st Division. It was moving slowly, painfully, held up by the line of traffic ahead, which wound all the way to the middle of Bataan.

All morning light bombers of the Japanese 5th Air Group crossed and recrossed the crowded highway, sometimes high, sometimes low, but still none bombed or strafed the retreating troops. Near noon, several planes appeared over Jones. They circled, obviously preparing for attack. The line of vehicles kept crawling forward. There was no other place to go; nothing to do but march and pray. Bombs fell but all exploded in cane fields and rice paddies. It was a miracle, thought Jones, as the planes turned and disappeared.

  3 In Manila stores were boarded up. Thousands were moving out to the hills and villages with cars and carts piled high with possessions. Thousands were moving back into the city after a few days in the country. Many just sat on their heels, waiting stoically for the conquerors.

Homma's troops were converging on the city from two directions. Those from the south were still about 40 miles away because Casey's dynamiters had destroyed so many highway and railroad bridges. In fact, the commander of this force, Lieutenant General Susumu Morioka, had been walking all day just like the infantrymen and was hot and frustrated.

The main body, under Homma himself, was making better progress from the north. With Jones' covering force at Plaridel withdrawn, there was nothing to stop the drive straight down to Manila, but when they were 17 miles from their goal, Homma halted his men. He wanted them to spruce up and reorganize before entering the city. The general knew that soldiers filthy from combat might pillage. Those in clean uniforms were more likely to parade in orderly fashion.

Near Manila's dock area, Arch Gunnison of *Collier's* and Carl Mydans of *Life* were watching citizens looting stores and warehouses. Everything from automobiles to unexposed moving picture film was being carted away in an orderly, systematic, good-natured mass operation involving about 40,-000 civilians.

Gunnison noticed a man sitting by a pile of straw hats that completely encircled him. "You've got a lot of hats there," he said.

"You like them, seer?" The man smiled. "You like, you take."

When Gunnison protested the man said, "You take, seer. Plenty hats. Plenty for you. Plenty for me. Plenty for everyone. I can get plenty more. You take these." He started to leave.

"You'd better not go away," warned Gunnison. "Someone is likely to take these hats."

"This is my pile. No one will touch." He pointed to other piles that dotted the streets. One simply did not steal another person's loot.

When Mydans returned to his hotel his wife, Shelley, showed him a cable from *Life*. It requested:

. . . ANOTHER FIRST-PERSON EYEWITNESS STORY BUT THIS
WEEK WE PREFER AMERICANS ON THE OFFENSIVE.

Shelley showed him her answer:

BITTERLY REGRET YOUR REQUEST UNAVAILABLE HERE.

About 150 air miles to the south the *Mayon* was hiding in
a cove of the island of Mindoro. At dark it would continue its dangerous trip down to Mindanao. The 650 men
of the 19th Bombardment Group were loafing, gambling and
griping. All were wondering where they were going and why.

"They're sending us to Frisco," someone told Sergeant
James Holcomb. "To make us into chaplains."

About noon a four-engine flying boat roared by. It circled,
as if to attack.

"One of our seaplanes thinks we're Japs," cried someone.

Sergeant Frank Trammell looked up and saw a red sun
on the fuselage. "Meatball!" he yelled.

An excited young lieutenant ran along the deck shouting,
"Don't jump in the water if we're bombed. The concussion
will kill you."

The flying boat lazily circled, coming lower and lower. A
bomb dropped, missing the ship by 50 yards. The excited lieutenant, forgetting what he had told the others, jumped into
the water. A dozen men followed. Corporal Durward Brooks,
wearing a helmet, thought his head was going to be jerked
off when he hit the water. His pistol, canteen and ammunition belt dragged him down. He unbuckled his belt
and took off his shoes and finally popped to the surface.

The second bomb fell short. The third hit the railing,
bounced into the water and exploded harmlessly. Major Rosie
O'Donnell watched the lone bomber make a leisurely dry-run
overhead, then turn back toward the ship. He grabbed a mattress and put it over him. Another copied his and shouted
as the bomber approached, "Drop it, you Jap son of a bitch."

Five more bombs fell, narrowly missing the ship. The captain of the *Mayon,* a Spaniard, shouted, "Release oil. Make
them think we're hit." A minute later black smoke poured
from the stack and oil spilled into the water. The bomber
circled once more and, completely fooled, disappeared.

On Corregidor, MacArthur was reading a radiogram from
Marshall suggesting that President Quezon come to the United
States and set up a government in exile. MacArthur quickly
drafted a reply. Evacuation of Quezon was too hazardous.
Besides, he warned, his departure "would be followed by

the collapse of will to fight by the Filipinos." He pointed out
that most of his army were Filipinos. "In view of their
effort the United States must move strongly to their support
or withdraw in shame from the Orient."

At 8:00 P.M. he asked Quezon to come to his cottage near
the mouth of Malinta Tunnel. He showed Quezon the radiogram from Marshall and his own reply. Then he asked the
president if he was going to the United States.

"I'll have to consult my War Cabinet first," said Quezon. He
immediately called a meeting and read the telegram from
Washington. The vote was unanimous to evacuate Quezon
from the Philippines.

"But wouldn't my departure dishearten the Philippine
Army?"

Vice-President Osmeña and the others thought it would
have the opposite effect. In America Quezon could get more
help. But when the president told them what MacArthur's
reply was going to be they urged Quezon to refuse to go.
MacArthur knew best.

The president, not sure what should be done, now wrote a
letter to MacArthur. "I am willing to do what the government
of the United States may think will be more helpful for the
prosecution of the war."

But he was troubled and his growing doubts were inflamed
by his sickness. Roosevelt's message offering the full resources of the United States had thrilled him but when was
that help coming? Could he ask his soldiers to keep fighting
against hopeless odds unless definite commitments were
made?

Across the bay, only 30 miles away, the Japanese were at
the gates of Manila.

Great clouds of smoke covered the city. Flames still soared
from the Pandacan oil fields. Fort McKinley, Nichols and
Nielson Fields and Cavite were still burning amidst occasional
explosions. Manila, a beautiful city a few weeks before, was
filthy with the ashes and soot of destruction.

At 5:45 that afternoon, Major General Koichi Abe led three
battalions of his 48th Division into the city from the north
while General Morioka, who had borrowed a car from Japanese civilians, led the way in from the south. Japanese freed
from internment cheered wildly as Morioka and Abe passed.
The lines of Filipinos only stared stolidly, sullenly.

From their rooms in the Bayview Hotel, Carl and Shelley
Mydans and Arch and Marjorie Gunnison watched two companies of Japanese sailors and a company of infantry form

ragged lines on the lawn in front of High Commissioner Sayre's residence, just across the street. The American flag was lowered from a flagpole. Three small cannon fired as the flag fluttered to the ground. A sailor unhooked it, stepped on it and fastened in its place the emblem of the Rising Sun. As the Japanese flag slowly rose, the band played the *Kimigayo*, the national anthem.

11 *Action at Abucay*

1 On January 1, the Calumpit Bridge was the focal point of the American retreat into Bataan. Four days later action centered on another bridge. This, the Layac Bridge, was the only entrance to Bataan and was situated at the neck of the peninsula.

At 10:00 P.M., January 5, there were still more than 8000 Americans and Filipinos north of the bridge, waiting to escape into Bataan. On their heels, Japanese were pressing from two sides—from the east along the main highway from San Fernando, from the north on a dirt road from Clark Field.

The greatest danger lay in the north. Holding off the Japanese on this dirt road was the 21st Division of Brigadier General Mateo Capinpin. Capinpin was now standing at Layac with his chief adviser, Colonel Ray O'Day. Both were worriedly watching a confused mass of trucks, guns, tanks and exhausted marching men from the 11th Division pour over the narrow bridge. Until these men passed, Capinpin's division, stretched out to the north on the dirt road for several miles, was at the mercy of Japanese planes or artillery—or, worse still, a sudden infantry-tank attack.

Wainwright and his engineer, Colonel Skerry, now arrived at the bridge. A few minutes later, at 10:30 P.M., the last man and last vehicle of the 11th Division crossed.

There was a short pause. Then Capinpin's impatient division surged into Bataan as if they were entering the promised land. To O'Day it was a painful and tragic sight. His exhausted troops trudged along toting ridiculously large loads of equipment and personal effects. Many teams of two carried bundles of clothing, ammunition belts, helmets, even chickens on bamboo poles.

As they slowly dragged by, General Capinpin excitedly hurried up and down the columns kicking and driving the men to go faster. O'Day was amused: Matty was actually the kindest commander in the world.

Wainwright joined the two. "How many men have you shot today, Matty?" he joked.

By 1:00 A.M. all the foot troops and tanks from the north had crossed. Now word was sent for the platoon of tanks on the east road, the last covering force, to withdraw. O'Day reported to Wainwright. He held up his right hand and said, "To the best of my knowledge and belief all units of the 21st Division and tanks have cleared the junction." Then O'Day and Capinpin walked across the bridge.

Wainwright and Skerry followed.

A minute later the tank commander of the covering force reported to Colonel Skerry. He too raised his right hand and swore all his tanks had crossed. Suddenly there was a rumble in the darkness. A United States tank surged from the gloom and rattled across the bridge.

Wainwright turned to Skerry. "Blow it," he ordered. Skerry signaled to Captain A. P. Chanco. At 2:00 A.M. there was a roar. The road to Bataan was severed. Wainwright shook his engineer's hand.

Several miles south of the blown bridge, General Capinpin and O'Day were overtaking their toiling, trudging infantrymen. Capinpin, still worried and anxious, ran out of his staff car and again began cursing the men.

"They've had a hard march for almost twenty-four hours, Matty," pointed out O'Day.

The general got back in the car and as it passed the troops he now leaned out and solicitously called, "The trucks will come back for you! You'll get your truck!"

General Homma still had no suspicion that MacArthur had fooled him, escaping with the great bulk of his Luzon forces into Bataan. Even so, he was very disturbed. Higher headquarters, assuming the fall of Manila meant the virtual end of the Philippine campaign, had ordered Homma to ship at once the heart of his army, the 48th Division, to Java. The general knew the mopping-up operations would be difficult and the loss of his best division would place an extremely heavy burden on his remaining troops.

The Japanese chasing MacArthur into Bataan came from the about-to-be-relieved 48th Division. Their job was about to be inherited by the 65th "Summer" Brigade. Its commander, Lieutenant General Akira Nara, was surprised when he was told his 7500 troops were to go into combat. The brigade, mostly older men, was almost totally unprepared and unequipped for front-line fighting. It had been sent to the Philippines merely as an occupation force.

Nara, a well-known tactician and administrator, had been picked originally to command these garrison soldiers because of his many years in the United States. A graduate of the Fort Benning Infantry School, he had also been a classmate of President Coolidge's son at Amherst College.

On the night Layac Bridge was demolished, Nara—a stocky, middle-aged man—was walking to battle. He was about 10 miles behind the Japanese troops he was supposed to relieve.

Behind him, stretching halfway back to Lingayen Gulf, were his footworn, forlorn troops already delayed for days by Colonel Skerry's engineers, who had left 184 destroyed bridges behind them. Unused to marching in the tropical heat, many were sick. Colonel Takeo Imai, commander of the 141st Infantry Regiment, was having trouble keeping his unconditioned men on the move.

The tropical evening was beautiful. The air was fragrant with the heavy sweetness of tropical flowers. Every so often Imai would pass bushes clustered with fireflies. They reminded him of Christmas trees. Suddenly he wondered what was delaying his troops up ahead and sent a runner forward. His men were bogged down in a stream. They had put their heavy equipment and supplies in carts drawn by sturdy Filipino carabao, usually so gentle that children often slept on their broad, armored backs. All had gone well for several miles. Then the water buffaloes, smelling the stream, had waded in, relentlessly dragging the carts with them.

Under harrowing conditions MacArthur had brought his troops safely into Bataan without losing a single major unit. Wainwright, in his difficult delaying fight, had lost 12,000 men but most of these were desertions. Jones had lost 1000.

Now MacArthur had 15,000 Americans and 65,000 Filipinos in Bataan. Ten thousand were professional soldiers of the elite Philippine Division. The rest was a conglomerate ill-equipped group almost totally untrained. With this force he was supposed to hold out for six months.

His greatest asset was the rugged terrain of Bataan. As it was largely covered with mountains and thick jungles, defense positions could be hidden from air observation. The peninsula, 15 miles wide and 30 miles long, was almost completely occupied by two great extinct volcanoes, one in the north, one in the south. There were only two roads. The main highway from Layac Bridge, the gate to Bataan, led down the flat, swampy east coast, around the tip and two-thirds of the way back up the other side of the peninsula;

a cobblestone road cut across Bataan like a belt through the valley between the two volcanoes.

MacArthur had already ordered 5000 men to fight a delaying action a few miles below the Layac Bridge so the battle lines could be completed and manned. The main battle position, where the first real stand would be made, was about 10 miles south of Layac. It ran from Manila Bay across the northern volcano. The mouth of this volcano, dead for eons, had been eroded by time into four jagged peaks. The eastern and highest peak was rugged, precipitous Mt. Natib.

The inexperience of his troops didn't worry MacArthur as much as the serious shortage of food and clothing. In eight days his quartermaster, Brigadier General Charles Drake, had sent numerous launches, tugs and over 300 bargeloads of supplies from Manila to Bataan. In the last three days of December 200 American, British and Allied civilians, in response to a radio plea, had helped Colonel Frederick Ward load last-minute supplies on the docks of Manila in spite of bombings and rumors of approaching Japanese patrols.

Relatively few supplies had come by highway. The shortage of trucks was only partially to blame. Because of red tape, stupidity and sheer panic, much food and clothing were being abandoned at Forts McKinley, Stotsenberg and other depots. The commander of the Tarlac Depot, Lieutenant Colonel Charles Lawrence, was forbidden to take 2000 cases of canned food and much clothing belonging to Japanese firms. MacArthur's headquarters said he had no right to commandeer personal property and threatened him with court-martial. But the greatest loss was at the Government Rice Central at Cabanatuan. Because of Commonwealth regulations forbidding rice to be transported from one province to another, 10,000,000 pounds of rice—enough to last the Filipinos on Bataan for six months—were left in the warehouses.

That night MacArthur checked the food inventory just prepared by General Drake. There were only enough unbalanced field rations for 100,000 men for thirty days. Desperate measures had to be taken. He ordered everyone on Corregidor and Bataan to be placed on half-rations.

By the morning of January 9 MacArthur's men were in position. Morale was high. The men of Bataan were tired of running. They wanted to stand and fight. MacArthur split the Main Battle Position in two, assigning the left, the western half, to Wainwright. His men, badly battered from their chaotic retreat from Lingayen, were in no condition for immediate combat.

The first Japanese attack, obviously, would come on the

other side of Bataan, down the east coast road from the Layac Bridge. This eastern half was turned over to Major General George Parker and 25,000 men. Though Parker had reached Bataan on Christmas Eve, his defense positions were only partially constructed. His problems were varied. The east coast of Bataan was flat and swampy, with fish ponds and rice paddies extending inland for about two miles. Then came gradually rising hills covered with cane fields and patches of bamboo for another five miles. At this point rugged Mt. Natib, scarred by innumerable ravines and covered with huge trees and dense jungle growth, began to rise dramatically.

Parker's left flank ended here for he felt it was not only impossible to defend Mt. Natib but unnecessary. No military force could possibly come over that matted mass of precipitous crags, ravines and cliffs.

General Jones' 51st Division held this difficult left flank. One regiment extended up the slopes of Natib trailing off into scattered foxholes; to the right his other front-line regiment ran just in front of Abucay Hacienda, a small cluster of nipa shacks housing sugar-cane workers.

The middle of Parker's line, along the steep banks of the gorge above the Balantay River, was held by the untried 41st Division commanded by a Philippine general, Vincente Lim, a West Pointer and part-Chinese. Parker's extreme right flank, rice paddies and fish ponds bisected by the coastal highway, was given to a regiment of the elite Philippine Scouts, the 57th Infantry. Parker wanted his best troops here, the most obvious point of attack.

This was the Abucay Line. The Filipinos were anxious to show MacArthur that they deserved his faith and that the routs of the 91st, 71st and 21st Divisions on the hectic retreat from Lingayen Gulf hadn't been a fair test of the Filipino soldier.

Their American instructors, many now disgusted and frustrated with their charges, were not as sanguine. Here on the Abucay Line retreat would be difficult. It was fight or die.

A few miles to the north, General Nara's 7500 men had relieved the veterans of the 48th Division and were getting ready to launch an attack on the Abucay Line. Less than half of Nara's overage soldiers had rifles; all were exhausted from the long march to Bataan. But what worried the general most was his almost complete ignorance of the enemy's whereabouts. To guide him he had only a road map and several 1/200,000 scale maps. The 14th Army had given him no plan of attack. His instructions were merely to pursue the enemy in column down the highway.

For six years he had been a professor at the War College, teaching his pupils never to attack without accurate maps and proper preparations. A member of Homma's staff had assured Nara, however, that the job of capturing Bataan would be simple. Intelligence estimated there were at most 25,000 disorganized troops on the peninsula. These men would retreat almost immediately to Mariveles at the tip end, make a brief stand here and then withdraw to Corregidor Island.

Although Nara protested, asking for time to make a survey, he was ordered to attack immediately. He hastily made plans. In addition to his own troops he had inherited two artillery regiments and the 9th Infantry Regiment of the 16th Division. He was delighted to get the 9th for it was commanded by an old and trusted friend, Colonel Susumu Takechi, an extremely aggressive and capable officer.

Nara's plan was simple; it had to be, with only a day for organization. Since the enemy was apparently weak, he ordered his own 141st Infantry, commanded by Colonel Takeo Imai, to attack straight down the coastal highway. Keeping his third infantry regiment in reserve, he told his friend, Takechi, to head inland with the 9th Infantry to the west, toward the slopes of Mt. Natib and circle behind the American positions, finally joining Imai at the highway.

At 3:00 P.M. there was a roar of Japanese artillery that seemed to Nara to shake the northern part of Bataan. When the hour-long barrage lifted, Imai headed down the highway and Takechi struck off into the wild jungle. Suddenly, to Nara's dismay, there was an even greater roar as tons of explosives from Parker's artillery fell on the highway in front of Imai. It was immediately obvious that the intelligence reports about American weakness were not accurate. What he still didn't realize was that Homma's intelligence officers had mistakenly placed the American defenders too far north. Nara's men wouldn't reach the Abucay Line for another three miles.

That night Wainwright and Parker both got a message from Corregidor. They were to assemble all general officers to receive an important visitor the next morning. At dawn a PT boat dashed from Corregidor to Mariveles. MacArthur and his chief of staff, General Sutherland, stepped out. They drove up the east coast road to Parker's headquarters where MacArthur gave an inspiring talk, promising planes and heavy reinforcements soon. Then he drove across the middle of Bataan on the winding 15-mile cobblestone Pilar-Bagac Road to inspect Wainwright's positions.

MacArthur's Ford stopped in front of I Corps headquarters. The general walked up to Wainwright. "Jonathan," he said cordially, "I'm glad to see you back from the north. The execution of your withdrawal and of your mission in covering the withdrawal of the South Luzon Force was as fine as anything in history."

Wainwright wondered if he deserved that much praise, but said nothing.

"Where are your 155-mm. guns?" asked MacArthur.

Wainwright suggested they walk over and see them.

"I don't want to *see* them," replied MacArthur characteristically, "I want to *hear* them."

Sutherland told Wainwright he was worried by what he'd seen that day. There was a gap of more than five miles between the two corps. Mt. Natib was completely undefended. Wainwright did not agree. The terrain, he argued, was too difficult for major attack.

By the morning of January 11, Nara realized the defenders hadn't retreated and that Imai's regiment was only now running into the American Main Line of Resistance. To escape the heavy bombardment Parker's artillery was laying on the coastal highway, Imai shunted most of his regiment into the fields to the west. He ordered one battalion to hide in a tall cane field near the highway and launch an attack late that night.

The defenders of the highway, the well-trained Philippine Scouts of the 57th Infantry Regiment, felt secure. Out front were heavy barbed-wire entanglements; fields of fire had been cut through brush and bamboo clumps. They were in perfect position to stop anything—infantry or tank—coming down the road, but they had completely neglected the large sugar cane field just west of the road. It hadn't occurred to anyone to cut it down.

At 11:00 that night Japanese artillery fire began to fall on the left flank of the Philippine Scouts. Then rifle fire, surprisingly, came from the cane field. The front-line troops called for an artillery concentration, but as soon as American shells began to fall, a mass of dim figures leaped from the cane in the moonlight.

Yelling *"Banzai!"* the first attackers threw themselves against the barbed wire in front of the Philippine Scout positions. Comrades, using them as stepladders, leaped over the wire like acrobats and then charged at the main line. Now they stopped yelling and the defenders in foxholes could only hear Japanese officers and noncoms calling orders.

Tracers seemed to come from every direction as infiltrating Japanese worked behind the Scout positions. Officers waving samurai swords led the attackers forward. Wave after wave of screaming Japanese flung themselves through the withering fire. The Scouts wavered, then broke.

Major Pete Wood, the executive officer of the battalion holding this sector, hurried to the rear to bring up his reserve company. He was an amiable, easy-going man but he thrived on combat. In a few minutes he reached the reserve company and told its commander, Captain Ernest Brown, to prepare his people for an attack.

The eager Wood called together Brown's noncoms and personally formed the reserve company in a skirmish line. As he started leading the men forward he noticed Brown sitting in a rice paddy smoking a cigarette. "What the hell are you doing?" he said.

"You're giving all the orders," said Brown. "You take charge."

Wood grinned good-naturedly and called back the noncoms. "Disregard what I said. Captain Brown will take over."

Brown jumped to his feet. "Follow me!" he said, and ran as fast as he could across the open field in the gray sickly light of early dawn. Sporadic rifle fire came from the cane field. As Brown jumped over the first string of Scout barbed wire, he heard a rip. His canteen belt and holster were hanging on the wire. He grabbed the pistol, noticing dirt dancing around in the dust a few inches away. He leaped into one of the deserted Scout foxholes. He looked back and saw Wood, with drawn pistol, stalking a Japanese rifleman behind a truck. Wood dashed forward and fired point-blank at the Japanese. He missed and the Japanese ran around the truck, Wood chasing. During the second round trip Wood began to laugh. Brown started to laugh too. It was like a Mack Sennett comedy, until the third trip around the truck when a Filipino shot the Japanese.

In the full light of morning Brown could see about 250 dead Japanese in the field, but there were still Japanese infiltrators in the battalion position. While Brown was leading a mop-up party, he heard a cry for help. A badly wounded Japanese was holding his hands out entreatingly. Brown told his men to give any wounded enemy first aid. After the Japanese was bandaged, a presumably dead Japanese lying nearby grabbed a rifle and fired. A Philippine Scout dropped dead. It was an experience Brown would never forget. He decided that mercy could not be shown to a wounded Japanese, nor respect for their dead. They had to be bayoneted.

Second Lieutenant Alexander Nininger, Jr., a recent graduate of West Point, now came over to help Brown mop up. Recklessly he ran from foxhole to foxhole, wiping out dug-in Japanese with grenades. Finally a burst from a machine gun cut him down. Locating its position, he staggered forward. Just as he hurled a grenade, a burst of fire caught him in the face. He dropped dead—and became the first to win the Medal of Honor on a World War II battlefield. Even as he died he had killed the machine-gun crew, completely clearing the area in front of the cane field.

Colonel Imai, about a mile and a half to the rear, had heard the fierce attack and counterattack. Now he was getting reports of the action. His battalion commander was dead and so were two-thirds of the attacking force. It had been a disaster.

At this moment he got a phone call from Nara. "Move to the west," said the general. "I want you to become the brigade right flank. I'm bringing up the reserve regiment to take your place on the left flank."

This unusual order was caused by the mysterious disappearance of Nara's entire right flank. Colonel Takechi's regiment had vanished in the heavy jungle of Mt. Natib. Nara didn't report this to Homma. Nor did he record it in his war diary or the brigade report. Takechi had been a classmate at the Academy and Nara wanted to protect his friend's reputation.

By dark that night, Imai had shuttled his regiment to the west and filled in the hole left vacant by Takechi's strange disappearance. He began to probe for a weak spot in the west flank of the Abucay Line. He couldn't make a frontal attack since he was down to about 500 men and half of these were not infantry and had no rifles. He would have to slip through a hole in the American lines and attack from the rear. At midnight groups of Japanese infiltrated through the Abucay Line near the junction of Jones' 51st Division and Lim's 41st Division. They had orders from Imai to make hit-and-run terror attacks, giving the impression of great numbers.

Before dawn Lim's division, to the right of Jones', was hit by one of these Imai attacks. Lim's left flank bent back. Seeing this withdrawal, the adjoining right flank of Jones'

division also pulled back. No one knew what was happenin
in the deep ravines and heavy jungle. Terror spread lik
fire. Isolated Imai groups behind Jones' men began to pic
off the defenders from the flanks and rear. Rumors tha
great masses of Japanese were on all sides spread from fox
hole to foxhole.

2   That same day, January 13, a sudden dangerou
rift threatened to split Fil-American relations. On Corregido
Quezon was writing a radiogram to Roosevelt. Almost tw
weeks had passed since Roosevelt's pledge to help the Philip
pines, yet not a new plane had arrived, not a new compan
of infantrymen. In blunt terms Quezon asked Roosevelt t
direct the full force of American strength against the Japa
nese without delay. Still burning with indignation, he wrot
an explanatory note to MacArthur:

This war is not of our making. . . . We decided to fight b
your side and we have done the best we could and we are sti
doing as much as could be expected from us under the circum
stances. But how long are we going to be left alone? Has it a
ready been decided in Washington that the Philippine front is o
no importance as far as the final result of the war is concerne
and that, therefore, no help can be expected here in the immed
ate future, or at least before the power of resistance is exhaust
ed? If so, I want to know, because I have my own responsibilit
to my countrymen. . . .
I want to decide in my own mind whether there is justificatio
for allowing all these men to be killed when for the final out
come of the war the shedding of their blood may be wholly un
necessary. It seems that Washington does not fully realize ou
situation nor the feelings which the apparent neglect of our safe
ty and welfare have engendered in the hearts of the peopl
here. . . .

MacArthur was deeply disturbed by Quezon's abrupt change
of heart but he felt that the Filipino was justified. Washing
ton kept complaining of the difficulty of sending things up
through the blockade the Japanese had thrown between the
Philippines and Australia. MacArthur felt it was a pape
blockade. A good determined push by a naval task force
could break through and save the islands. The trouble, he
believed, was that the Navy had been terrorized by Pear
Harbor.

And so MacArthur forwarded Quezon's message. He hoped
it would stir them up in Washington.

On the Abucay Line, Jones was in a dangerous position
by January 15. His 51st Division was quickly becoming
demoralized by the incessant behind-the-lines attacks of Colonel Imai.

Jones' best regiment, shot up on the retreat to Bataan, was
in reserve. The two regiments on the line were green, and in
Jones' opinion the outpost position was untenable. Jones now
reported to Parker that his troops were perceptibly weakened and that unless he got reinforcements, he might have to
withdraw his outpost.

Parker, in turn, asked MacArthur for reinforcements and
as a result the remaining two regiments of the experienced
Philippine Division were ordered to rush to the troubled spot,
the west flank of the Abucay Line. Encouraged by this help,
Parker decided to regain the ground lost by Jones, ordering
him to counterattack the next morning at dawn. To Jones
this was a ridiculous order. In the blunt language he used
alike with subordinates and superiors, he told Parker his
division had been seriously weakened from continuous combat losses the past month. Such a counterattack would be
extremely hazardous. "Moreover," he added, "the present position is being held only with great difficulty."

In spite of this vigorous protest, Parker insisted. He was
sending up a battalion to help Jones. It should arrive at
4:00 A.M. Angrily Jones prepared his exhausted and demoralized troops for attack. If Corps people came up to the
front once in a while, he thought, they'd see what the real
situation was.

All along the Abucay Line that night company commanders
were reading a message from MacArthur designed to whip up
the flagging spirits of the tired defenders, even though the
commander-in-chief himself had doubts of Washington's intentions:

Help is on the way from the United States. Thousands of
troops and hundreds of planes are being dispatched. . . . No further retreat is possible. We have more troops in Bataan than the
Japanese have thrown against us; our supplies are ample; a determined defense will defeat the enemy's attack. . . .
I call upon every soldier in Bataan to fight in his assigned position, resisting every attack. This is the only road to salvation.
If we fight, we will win; if we retreat, we will be destroyed.

Some of the men, mainly American noncoms, openly
jeered. Ample supplies? They were already on half-rations.
Their grenades were no good, only one in four or five ex-

ploding. Their old Stokes mortars were more dangerous t
them than the enemy. Six out of seven rounds failed t
detonate on landing; and too often the ill-fitting shells burs
the barrels.

But to the great majority, the Filipinos, MacArthur's word
were a bright hope and inspiration. The Filipinos were de
termined to prove they were men of courage, worthy to figh
under the American flag.

3   About 150 miles north of the Abucay Line, i
the mountains above Baguio, the old summer capital, Lieu
tenant Colonel John Horan, former commander of Fort Joh
Hay, was walking toward Mankayan, home of the Surja
Gold Mine and the Lepanto Copper Mines. On Christma
he had led his 184 officers and men from cut-off Baguio in :
march up and down precipitous trails. Now he was trying t
organize a guerrilla army of Igorots, a proud, fierce trib
whose warriors still wore G-strings. Two weeks previously
he had made his decision to stay in the mountains and figh
rather than try and break south to Bataan. Calling together al
his officers, he told them he was going back into the moun
tains and conduct guerrilla warfare. It had been the hardes
decision of his life but he felt that after taking salary fo
over twenty-five years, he owed it to the Army.

"You have my authority," he said, "to go on your ow
and try to get through the enemy into Bataan. Or you ca
return with me into the mountains."

Several elected to leave but 184 officers and men staye
with Horan. Now on the morning of January 16 he wa
holding a meeting with the miners of Mankayan.

"I want you to help me organize a guerrilla regiment o
Igorots," he said. "We will blow up bridges, roads and over
hanging cliffs. We'll create avalanches over road fills o
hillsides, ambush troop and supply columns and destroy
warehouses and supply dumps."

Every man volunteered. Horan enrolled them into the 31s
Infantry and promised to recommend them all for commis
sions as soon as he could make radio contact with Mac
Arthur. After the meeting, Horan headed back towar
Baguio to look for a miner named Walter Cushing, alread
a legend in the mountains for his daring raids on Japanes
columns. Cushing would make a good assistant.

On dawn of the same day Jones started his counterattack
even though the promised reinforcements had failed to ar

·ive. Heavy resistance was met but one of his regiments pressed forward so aggressively that the Japanese fell back. Before noon this regiment had pushed ahead of units on both sides.

Colonel Imai, realizing the Americans had formed a salient more dangerous to themselves than to him, quickly attacked the east side of the bulge. Just then, purely by chance, Colonel Takechi and his "lost" regiment burst out of the jungled slopes of Mt. Natib and found themselves on the other side of the Jones bulge. Takechi also attacked.

Jones' salient, assaulted from opposite sides, wavered, then began to crumble. By noon, when increased firing was heard near the rear, it completely collapsed. The green troops scattered in terror leaving a two-mile-wide hole in the Abucay Line.

Part of Takechi's troops, still vague about their position, now began assaulting the western flank of Imai's regiment, but Takechi soon discovered he was fighting friends. He hurried to General Nara's field headquarters to make a personal report. The colonel—uniform in tatters, his face lined with fatigue and hunger—explained how he had become hopelessly lost in the jungles of Mt. Natib. Nara listened silently, sympathetically, then said, "I'm putting you in reserve."

"*Hai*, General," said Takechi. He saluted crisply and left.

Nara was greatly relieved. Now with Takechi in reserve and his rear protected, Nara could attack with confidence. He gave orders for increased artillery fire.

But Takechi was not heading north into reserve as ordered. Without pausing for supplies or rest, he was already leading his weary regiment back to the south. This time he was determined to take his men over Mt. Natib or die trying. To be ordered into reserve meant a great loss of face, and Takechi had mistakenly thought Nara had done this to punish him for getting lost.

Jones, as usual, was far up front. He didn't know that back at Division command post his staff had become alarmed by reports and ordered the regiment on the left to fall back before it was surrounded. By mid-afternoon that regiment had pulled out of its position and was hurrying to the southwest across the rugged slopes of Mt. Natib. The entire west flank of the Abucay Line had disappeared.

Only at dusk did Jones finally learn his division had evaporated. At a key junction of the Guitol Trail about two miles behind the Abucay Line, he grabbed terrorized men fleeing from the front and put them astride the strategic trail; but almost as fast as he would put them in place, they would sneak farther to the rear.

At dark Jones had only 100 men dug in. It was all that remained of his 51st Division; the smallest division in the world, he thought sardonically. And these 100 had to hold the entire left flank of the Abucay Line. From his new command post in a muddy, slimy hole just off the trail he telephoned Parker's headquarters far in the rear. After a long wait he reached the commander of II Corps. "As far as I'm concerned," said Jones disgustedly, "I'm through." He hung up. Obviously he'd be busted and relieved of command, but until then he'd keep fighting.

Now he telephoned his aide, Lieutenant Pete Perkins, commanding the 100-man division. Perkins had no infantry training.

"They're infiltrating," said Perkins.

Jones, muffling the bell of the field telephone with toilet paper to prevent Japanese patrols from hearing its ring, advised Perkins how to handle each development. Finally he lay in the mud, telephone to his ear, and tried to rest.

The last three miles on the western end of the Abucay Line had dissolved. Except for Jones' 100 men on the trail, nothing was left to stop the Japanese, but at last luck was with the Fil-Americans. Colonel Imai, wary of being cut off himself, had turned his attack back toward Lim's division. And Colonel Takechi was circling far west of the Abucay Line, in a quixotic dash to regain honor.

By midnight Lim's 41st Division was punch drunk, but the unseasoned Filipinos hung on in spite of casualties already exceeding 1200.

In the inky darkness, the two crack regiments of the Philippine Division were moving forward as fast as possible to plug up the giant hole. "Come on," an ex-football star, Captain Jack Ellis, of the 31st Infantry (U.S.), the only all-American regiment in the Philippines, told those retreating, "now you're going in with the big team."

But the other regiment, the Philippine Scouts of the 45th Infantry, was lost. They had no moon, no stars, no sign, and often no distinct trail to guide them. Their column stopped. Not far to the north Captain Louis Besbeck could hear the fast firing of artillery and see splashes of light in the blackness. Groups of Filipinos drifted past from the north, eyes shocked, yelling, "The Japs are coming!"

Besbeck stopped one who was wearing the single star of a brigadier general and asked for road directions. "It was awful," answered the general dazedly, obviously suffering from battle shock. "They just faded away."

Besbeck repeated the question.

"It was awful. They just faded away." Other figures came out of the darkness from the north. The general, still babbling, followed.

About a mile to the left, another one-star general, Jones, was trying to get some sleep for the first time in three nights. He was deathly tired. The six men at his muddy command post were holding one another's ankles, ready to alert each other if a Japanese patrol appeared. For the past hour his aide, Captain André Soriano, had kept pulling Jones' ankle. Each warning had been a false alarm. Again Soriano yanked Jones' ankle.

"Damn it, André," said the general, "if you wake me up again, you'll have something to really worry about."

A moment passed. Again came the jerk of warning. Jones leapt to his feet. "Are there any Japanese sons of bitches out there?" he shouted. "If there are, let's get it over with." He yanked out his pistol and fired several times. "Now they know damn well where we are, and we can get some sleep." He flopped down and went to sleep instantly.

1 Until now, midnight of January 16, very little had happened on the west side of Bataan, from Mt. Natib to the South China Sea. The reason was obvious. There wasn't a single road leading down into Bataan on this coast. Here the mountainous jungle continued all the way to the South China Sea.

But Wainwright's vacation was coming to an end. Five thousand Japanese were quickly closing in on his front-line positions by boat and trail. They had already reached the American front line at Moron, a town about a third of the way down the west coast. By late afternoon of January 17, Wainwright was pushed out of Moron and retreated to a ridge several miles behind the town.

The next morning the Japanese commander, Major General Naoki Kimura, arrived in Moron. When he learned that Wainwright's defense line extended only five miles inland from the sea to the western slopes of the great volcano, he decided to send a battalion of about 700 men around Wainwright's right flank and cut off the Americans from the rear. Lieutenant Colonel Hiroshi Nakanishi, well known for his aggressive spirit, was selected as leader. By dawn of January 21, Nakanishi had secretly circled around Wainwright's line. Then he turned sharply west and at 10:00 A.M. reached the west coast highway which ran from Moron to the tip end of Bataan. In one brilliant stroke he had cut off Wainwright's 5000 front-line troops.

When word reached Wainwright at I Corps Headquarters that there was a Japanese roadblock between him and his front line, he quickly gathered the men available, only twenty, and drove north. After several miles of mountainous road the Wainwright party came to Nakanishi's roadblock. Here the general found a platoon of Filipinos, and led them, and his own twenty men, in a futile two-hour attack. While standing against a high bank on the east side of the road, his orderly, Sergeant Hubert Carroll, suddenly grabbed the seat of Wainwright's pants and yanked him down.

"God damn it, General," said Carroll in his Texas drawl, get down or you'll get your damn head shot off." Just then here was a burst of rifle fire and two men standing next to he crouching general fell dead.

Meanwhile a company under First Lieutenant Beverly kardon had been sent back from the front and was hitting Nakanishi from the north, but the well-dug-in Japanese threw ack this attack too, determined to die rather than be dis-odged.

2 That same night, January 21, Nara's constant ttacks on the other side of Bataan had brought the de-enders of the Abucay Line to the edge of their endurance. he two experienced regiments of the Philippine Division —sent in to plug up the vanished left flank—had become ogged down in the dense vegetation and rugged cre-asses. The past five days they had attacked aggressively and ercely but were learning that tying down a flank on a rough, nknown piece of terrain was impossible. Many units had had o food or water for several days nor could they evacuate heir wounded.

To their right, General Lim's 41st Division was also groggy rom constant fighting, hunger and exhaustion. When artil-ery wasn't falling, planes were strafing and bombing, or mai's infantrymen were making slashing flank attacks. And o heighten the terror, the Japanese kept shooting firecrackers nto the rear. When these exploded the cry would often go p, "We're surrounded!"

That night General Lim and his staff could hear small arms nd machine-gun fire from their 41st Division command ost. They conferred in whispers. "It looks bad," said Colo-el Malcolm Fortier, the division instructor. All reserves had een committed.

A little later Captain Rigoberto Atienza, one of Lim's staff, eard the Filipino telephone operator mumbling in his sleep, My guardian angel is with MacArthur." No one paid any ttention to the muttering. Suddenly the operator sprang up, houting, "You Americans, why are you standing back there? Vhy do we keep on defending? Are you afraid to attack? 'll lead the attack. My guardian angel is with MacArthur!"

Waving a pistol, he ran into the woods. A little later the perator came back, his eyes wild. "Why didn't you follow?" e screamed angrily. "If you are afraid to lead, I'll lead. 'ou cowards! That's why we're losing this war."

Atienza and several others tried to soothe the man. They told him he was tired and should rest.

"I am not tired. But these goddam Americans are cowards and we're fighting for them."

"Shut up," said the assistant operations officer, "or I'll slap you down."

"Sir, I do not quarrel with you. But these Americans are no good."

A big figure came out of the shadows and said in a deep voice, "I'm a full-blooded American. You want to quarrel with me? Or will you shut up?"

The operator swung wildly at the American, then jumped at Colonel Fortier, who was listening to the telephone in the dugout. The Filipino officers grabbed the operator and dragged him away.

"Goddam American cowards," he screamed, struggling to break loose. Suddenly he slumped as if slugged and fell.

General Nara, who had been friendly with General Lim when both attended the Fort Benning Infantry School, was just as worried as the Filipino commander. Takechi and his regiment, instead of going to the rear in reserve, had again mysteriously disappeared on the jungled slopes of Mt. Natib. As before, Nara kept this information to himself.

Nara was being constantly needled by Homma's staff. Why hadn't he broken through and annihilated the enemy? Nara knew he could never battle his way directly down the coastal highway. The Philippine Scouts of the 57th Infantry had taught him that costly lesson. The only possibility for quick success was to launch an all-out attack against the disintegrating west flank of the Abucay Line. He hated to ask Colonel Imai to do this. The 141st Infantry had already lost most of its company officers and was groggy from constant attack.

"You are to drive the enemy southeastward," he told Imai, "and annihilate them." The attack would start the next day, January 22, at noon.

MacArthur's chief of staff, General Sutherland, happened to be in Bataan on the twenty-second when Nara's all-out attack began. He had come to get "a clear picture of the situation." When he returned to Corregidor that evening, he told MacArthur the situation was so alarming that an immediate withdrawal should be made to a defense line behind the cobblestone road cutting across Bataan.

After hearing the details, MacArthur agreed. Parker and Wainwright were telephoned. Starting at darkness the next day, January 23, a general retreat would begin to the next line, the last line.

That same evening a United States Navy motor torpedo boat was cruising up the west coast of Bataan on a routine mission. The torpedo squadron commander, Lieutenant John D. Bulkeley, wore two pistols at his side; he had a long, ragged beard; his eyes were bloodshot and red-rimmed from nightly missions and lack of sleep. Bulkeley noticed a dim light low in the water.

The torpedo boat, PT 34, headed toward the light. Soon Bulkeley could make out a queer-shaped vessel. From it came strange blinking dot-and-dash signals but Bulkeley told the men not to fire. These were American waters. They were 10 miles below Wainwright's front lines.

"Boat ahoy," he called through his megaphone.

A stream of tracers spat out from the other boat as it headed for the American-held shore. Now Bulkeley could see it was a landing barge, armored on bow and stern, packed with Japanese. As the four .50-caliber machine guns of PT 34 showered the barge, it twisted and turned to keep Bulkeley from coming broadside. Bulkeley attacked head on, machine guns blazing. The barge began to sink and finally disappeared. Then American shore guns began to blast at Bulkeley.

"Half the time those dumb bastards don't know friend from foe," he told Ensign R. G. Kelly, the torpedo boat commander. A shell landed only 200 yards away and PT 34 pulled out, continuing up the coast on its mission. Before long Bulkeley met and attacked another invasion barge. He jumped aboard and before the barge sank, captured single-handed three Japanese and a dispatch case of secret documents.

Bulkeley didn't know there were many other Japanese barges heading for shore. Nine hundred men, led by Lieutenant Colonel Nariyoshi Tsunehiro, were about to land here, far behind Wainwright's lines. If they could reach the coastal road, about two miles inland, I Corps would be cut off from the main supply line to the rear.

Bulkeley's solo assault upset Tsunehiro's plans by splitting the flotilla of barges in two sections. Tsunehiro and the larger group of 600, confused by treacherous tides and poor maps, landed five miles south of their goal. The smaller group of 300 was even more confused, drifting almost to the end of Bataan.

Early the next morning, Tsunehiro's group found themselves

on a narrow beach about halfway between the tip of Bataan and Wainwright's front lines. This was Quinauan Point. They heard movements and whispers on the cliff above but not a shot was fired. They climbed a precipitous path and plunged into a jungle of huge trees and dense underbrush.

American airmen of the 34th Pursuit Squadron, positioned on the cliff, had heard the Japanese. They were so startled they abandoned their machine guns without firing a shot and crept to the rear. About an hour later, at 2:30 A.M., the alarm reached Brigadier General Clyde Selleck. It was his difficult job to protect the rugged western coast line from Wainwright's rear to the tip of the peninsula with a conglomerate and poorly armed force of Filipinos and U.S. pilots, mechanics, sailors and marines. Most had no training and few had even fired a rifle.

Selleck ordered a battalion of the Philippine Constabulary to drive the Japanese back into the sea, but by the time the former policemen reached the area, Tsunehiro was hidden in the dense jungle of Quinauan Point.

Farther south, near the tip of Bataan, the smaller group of 300 was sighted at daylight by a naval lookout. Soon American blue jackets attacked the invaders, now on the slopes of the small mountain overlooking the harbor town of Mariveles. With their whites dyed a sickly mustard color, the Americans plunged toward the Japanese, crashing through the underbrush, smoking and talking loudly.

The Japanese were confused and shaken. They thought a new type of suicide squad, purposely dressed in brightly colored uniforms, was attacking and hurriedly pulled back into the thick woods.

It was now late afternoon of January 23. Nara's day-old, all-out attack on the Abucay Line was apparently making little headway. Not realizing that Imai's constant, terrorizing attacks already had the defenders on the verge of collapse, General Nara, ordinarily a calm man, was in a rage. Imai, according to front-line reports, was going nowhere and there was still no word from Takechi. Figuring rightly that his friend, against direct orders, must again be trying to cross Mt. Natib, Nara requested planes to drop bundles of food at various points.

None of this food reached Takechi. This time he had successfully crossed the slopes of the forbidding mountain; but again because of poor maps he had failed to cut east at the Salian River as originally ordered by Nara. Instead, he had continued on several miles to the next river, the Abo

Abo. Here at last he turned sharply to the east and headed for the coastal highway. Unknown to him this was the road that was vital to the great American withdrawal starting that dusk. If Takechi could reach it in time, the men of the Abucay Line would be cut off.

The Japanese in Nara's all-out frontal assault were as exhausted as the Fil-Americans on the other side of the Abucay Line. At a forward battalion outpost, Second Lieutenant Hisamichi Kano of the Propaganda Corps was preparing his small group for a trip far forward to broadcast appeals to surrender with a small portable public address set. Kano, who had gone to school for seven years in England, New York and New Jersey, would talk a little, then play Philippine folk songs.

The battalion commander, a nervous man of forty, urged Kano not to go out that night. Following every Kano broadcast, a heavy barrage had saturated the area. Now, for the first time in days it was peaceful and the commander wanted to keep it that way. The phone rang. "Yes, sir," he said, "I'll send out patrols to find out what's going on." He hung up. Instead of forming patrols, he said, "Tell the boys to fire a few rounds on the light machine guns." A minute later there was a short chatter, then silence. "The enemy must have withdrawn," he remarked with relief. Of his company officers, only two who had started the battle were alive. Half his staff were dead.

The phone rang again. "No, sir," lied the commander. "My patrols haven't come back yet." Then he turned to his officers. "They want us to start pursuit in an hour. We'll wait until daybreak."

Kano, who had heard only stories of fanatic Japanese courage in battle, was shocked. In spite of objections from the timid commander, he went forward with his four-man team as soon as darkness fell. After passing the last outpost, the propagandists crept even farther into the black jungle that was no man's land and set up their equipment.

"You are outflanked," said Kano, his voice booming toward the Abucay Line. "The Japanese Army is driving down the main highway. A regiment has smashed through your left flank and is surrounding you. If you want to save your lives, surrender immediately or make a beeline for the south."

For the first time there was no answering fire. Kano played a sentimental Philippine record and then led the way back to the rear. Near the battalion command post he heard a burst of fire only a few yards behind him.

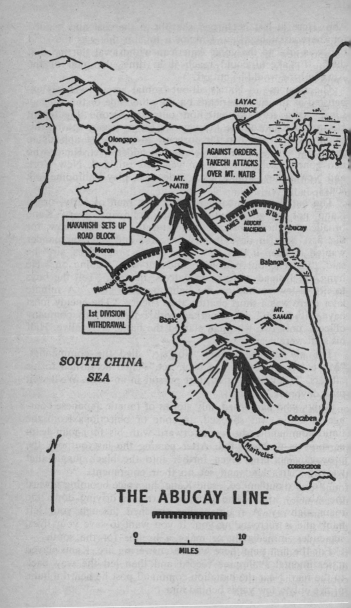

LAYAC
BRIDGE

Olongapo

MT.
NATIB

AGAINST ORDERS,
TAKECHI ATTACKS
OVER MT. NATIB

IMAI

NAKANISHI SETS UP
ROAD BLOCK

JONES LIM

ABUCAY
HACIENDA

57th

Abucay

Moron

Balanga

Mauban

1st DIVISION
WITHDRAWAL

Bagac

MT.
SAMAT

SOUTH CHINA
SEA

Cabcaben

N

Mariveles

CORREGIDOR

THE ABUCAY LINE

0   10

MILES

"It's the speaker, Lieutenant," said one of his men cheer-
fully. "The Americans just filled it full of holes."

Kano knew his men had shot it up themselves but he said
nothing. There was no replacement for the speaker. They
would all have to return to Manila.

Kano had drawn no artillery fire that night because the
first phase of the great Fil-American withdrawal had just
begun. All service and artillery troops were heading south
toward their new positions. The front-line troops also with-
held their fire. They didn't want to incite any trouble. The
next night, January 24, their own evacuation would begin.

In Malinta Tunnel, MacArthur was writing a radiogram
to Marshall. With about 35 per cent of his entire force lost,
he was retiring to a line behind the Pilar-Bagac Highway
running across the middle of the peninsula.

> I HAVE PERSONALLY SELECTED AND PREPARED THIS PO-
> SITION AND IT IS STRONG.

In conclusion he asked that Sutherland succeed him in
case of death:

> OF ALL MY GENERAL OFFICERS HE HAS MOST COMPRE-
> HENSIVE GRASP OF THE SITUATION.

He knew that what happened in the next twenty-four hours
would probably determine the future of Bataan. If the
Japanese broke through the thin protecting cover force, or
bombed the coastal highway, a major disaster would follow,
one that might be the end of USAFFE.

By 7:00 P.M., January 24, trucks, buses and men began
pouring back from the Abucay Line. Just then violent
Japanese small arms and machine-gun fire broke out all along
the front. Though many thought some Japanese spy had
found out about the great retreat, General Nara actually had
no suspicion the American line was being abandoned. He
was simply acting on insistent orders from Homma to finish
the Battle of Bataan at once.

In spite of increasing pressure from Nara, the thin protective shell holding the front lines while their comrades escaped
didn't break. Officers worked up and down this screen, encouraging the men. On the 45th Infantry sector, Major Dudley
Strickler, armed with a pistol and wearing an old khaki

hat instead of a helmet, was going from foxhole to foxhole, urging his men to hold just a little longer.

By midnight the trail to the rear was jammed with buses
full of gaunt-faced Filipinos in blue denims and coconut
helmets; trucks; command cars packed with haggard officers
in filthy uniforms; and marching troops. There was no
moonlight and everyone looked alike. Infiltrating Japanese,
about the same height as the Filipinos, could easily have
joined the march unnoticed.

As traffic neared an important trail intersection near Guitol, it slowed, then crept on again. Men and vehicles were
jammed at the intersection. With no military police to regu-
late the flow to the rear, confusion grew. Units became separated in the nightmare chaos. Officers could do nothing but
keep men and vehicles moving south and pray that no
shells would fall.

Even so there was little shouting, no hysteria. It was dis-
ciplined confusion. The two regiments of the Philippine Division, after continuous but fruitless attempts to plug up the
chopped-off left flank, retreated thankfully. They knew they
had been outflanked and would soon have been surrounded.
The remaining stragglers of Jones' 51st Division also
were slogging back, wondering how they had escaped almost certain destruction. But the men of General Lim's 41st
Division were bewildered and resentful. They had held
the center of the line and thought they were winning the battle of the Abucay Line. Now they were pulling out of positions that had cost the lives of many of their comrades. Why?

At 3:00 A.M. the men of the protective shell up front began
leap-frogging to the rear. They, in turn, were being covered
by the tanks and 75-mm. self-propelled guns of General
Weaver's Provisional Tank Group. Soon the infantrymen
passed through this protective line of tanks. They looked like
walking dead men. Unwashed and unshaven for nine days,
their starved faces were expressionless.

A few minutes later Colonel Imai led a column in pursuit
of the withdrawing Fil-Americans down the trail from the
front. Imai knew he had them on the run at last. He remembered a book of tactics advising commanders to relentlessly pursue a fleeing enemy in spite of fatigue and, consequently, save heavy losses in the next fight.

Weaver's men spotted Imai's column as it burst into the
open. The tanks waited until Imai drew nearer. Then their
37-mm. guns roared. Completely surprised, Imai thought
he'd come upon an enemy artillery position. His men scattered for shelter. While he was preparing an attack, isolated

groups of Fil-Americans drifting back from the Abucay Line ran into the Japanese ranks in the pitch dark. Everyone was confused. Imai and his regimental headquarters dug in as bullets flew from all sides. It was like watching fireworks. Imai sent a message back to Nara: he was surrounded.

The withdrawal continued all through the next day. From dawn to dusk Japanese planes strafed and bombed the trails and coastal road without any opposition. As planes roared down, Filipinos looked up helplessly like sheep in a slaughter pen. They scrambled to the ditches, where there was little cover. American soldiers also scrambled, cursing the Japanese obscenely as they flattened themselves on the ground. Hundreds were killed but the movement to the rear never stopped.

Weaver's tanks and 75's stayed in place, giving the retreating troops security from Imai's frontal attacks, but there was nothing at all to stop Takechi, coming from the east. Fortunately for the Americans he had veered somewhat to the south and was still several miles from the coastal road. If American luck held a few more hours, everyone would escape before the trap shut.

       3 On the other side of Bataan, west of Mt. Natib, Wainwright's entire front line was also in full flight. By noon of January 25 most of the 5000 cut-off men had scrambled down rough trails to the narrow beaches. Their commander, Colonel K. L. Berry, had decided to withdraw down the beaches of the west coast. The road to the rear was still blocked by Colonel Nakanishi's 700 men. It would have been suicide, Berry felt, to try and break through such a strong position with his starving, exhausted men.

It was a gruelling march down the rugged coast in the pitiless tropical sun. Many men threw away their guns and took off their uniforms. The sharp rocks cut the men's sneakers to bits. By dawn almost everyone, including Berry, was barefoot. Then the long line turned, climbing laboriously up a cliff, and headed for the coast road.

Berry halted his men. He wanted to go ahead into Bagac and find out what was happening. Still carrying a Springfield rifle, Berry trudged into the town. He saw a Packard coming down the cross-Bataan road. A tall, thin man got out and approached him. It was "Skinny" Wainwright. Berry wondered what the general would say about retreating without orders.

"Berry, I'm damned glad to see you," said the general.

"I've got all my men on the beaches and in the woods. I came up ahead to find out what's going on."

Wainwright pointed to the south. "Keep going down the road to Trail 9. You'll take up position in there." Then his leathery face broke into a smile. "I'll see that you're mentioned in orders."

By now, January 26, the new American line was almost manned. It lay in the valley between the two great dead volcanoes, just behind the cobblestone road running across Bataan's middle. Along this continuous line from Manila Bay to the South China Sea men were settling into foxholes, resting in dugouts from the arduous retreat and thanking God they'd survived the day's strafings and bombings.

Late that morning Weaver's tanks and 75's were racing through Balanga, heading for the safety of the new line. Though many infantry officers had cursed the tankers for failing to come up to the Abucay Line, they now were grateful for the cover given the foot troops the past two days.

Again the Japanese had missed an opportunity to smash MacArthur with a few accurate artillery barrages and bombings. Though the men of Wainwright and Parker were weak, hungry and riddled with casualties, USAFFE was still intact, still ready to fight.

In his position on the new defense line, Lieutenant Henry G. Lee, Headquarters Company, the Philippine Division, was composing a poem about the Abucay withdrawal. Bataan had been saved, he wrote:

> . . . saved for another day
> Saved for hunger and wounds and heat
> For slow exhaustion and grim retreat
> For a wasted hope and sure defeat . . .

The new American line was also divided in two commands. Once more MacArthur gave Wainwright the west half and Parker the east, but it was stronger and better coordinated. Behind it was an ingenious network of communication and supply trails, cut through the dense jungle just wide enough for a truck. Except for a few connecting trails, most ran from rear to front, south to north.

On the morning of January 26, Brigadier General Clifford Bluemel was walking up one of the most important of these, Trail 2. He wanted to go far front to inspect his sector, the center of Parker's corps. It was more than two and a half miles wide, and to defend it Bluemel had only his own 31st Division and the shattered remnants of Jones' 51st.

Bluemel, as was his custom, carried his Garand rifle like any infantryman. This was no affectation; Japanese snipers hiding behind the lines were gunning for officers. Behind Bluemel trudged his Philippine staff officers, for the general knew more about the trails behind the new line than they did.

Like General Jones, Bluemel had been a terror to junior officers before Pearl Harbor. Convinced a war was coming in the Philippines, he was constantly criticizing with caustic tongue. Many who had disliked him most in days of peace now had a new regard for him. Their baptism in blood on the Abucay Line had made them realize Bluemel's peacetime needling had helped save lives.

The general didn't know he was heading toward a ghost front. Without consulting or even informing him, Parker had pulled out more than half of Bluemel's troops earlier that morning, transferring them to other positions miles to the east. This left a gigantic hole in the center of Bluemel's sector —at the worst possible place. Both sides of Trail 2 were now neatly cleared of defenders.

Bluemel saw two officers coming down the trail from the front lines. Behind them was a column of infantrymen. When they approached, the general saw this was the 1st Battalion of his 31st Infantry Regiment. "Where the hell are you going?" he asked.

"We're looking for Colonel Irwin, sir."

John Irwin commanded the area miles to the right. "Hell," said Bluemel, "he's on Manila Bay."

"We've been ordered to join him."

Bluemel exploded. "Irwin's not commanding this damn division. You're not going to take those goddam troops out of the line."

The battalion commander protested that the order had come from General Parker.

"You're under my command," said Bluemel. "And don't you dare move those men again without my personal orders." The general was incensed. If the Japanese attacked down Trail 2, the entire east half of Bataan could soon be lost. Half an hour later Bluemel discovered recently abandoned foxholes on the right of Trail 2. The 33rd Infantry Regiment was also missing!

Bluemel's anger reached new heights. He couldn't believe Corps Headquarters could be so stupid. More than half of his front was undefended. He scribbled a message to the commander of his remaining regiment, Colonel Johnson: "You will have your reserve battalion occupy sector assigned to 33rd Infantry. That regiment has been taken away. They will move immediately." Then he turned to his intelligence officer, Major Salvador Villa, a man he knew was dependable. "See that there's a man in every foxhole before you return to the CP tonight."

Now he had to plug up the left side of Trail 2. He roamed the lines looking for strays. He ran into sixty-five men of a battalion headquarters battery of the 31st Field Artillery, presently acting as riflemen, and personally led the little group to the front.

"Here you stay and here you die," he told their commander, an eager, young Philippine lieutenant. "I'm going to put in a battalion of the 32nd Infantry on your right with machine guns. Stop the Japs. If you don't, Bataan is finished."

Fortunately for the Americans, General Nara was giving his men a well-deserved rest. His 65th Brigade had been riddled by the fight on the Abucay Line. Of the 7500 overage men more than 2000 were casualties. The others were exhausted, stunned by their first terrible taste of battle.

He was just learning the whereabouts of his missing regiment. A liaison officer, attached to the 9th Infantry, reported that Takechi's men had crossed "impassable" Mt. Natib. Slowed down by the jungle, Takechi had never quite reached the coastal highway. "We haven't eaten for a week," he said.

Nara handed over his personal supply of bread and cigarettes. Then, with amusement, he watched newspapermen interviewing the haggard officer. They would write that, in a brilliant maneuver, Takechi's men had marched over rugged Mt. Natib, completely surprising the Americans and causing the breakthrough of the Abucay Line.

Back in San Fernando, Homma's staff, delighted at MacArthur's sudden retreat, was planning a new assault that would bring a quick end to the irritating Bataan battle. Pressure for immediate results was coming not only from General Terauchi of the Southern Army but also from Tokyo. Everyone wondered what could possibly have delayed such a minor mopping-up operation.

Now at last it looked to Homma as if the embarrassing delays were coming to an end. Unexpected aid had come from the Americans themselves. A secret map of U.S. positions had just been found in an underground room in Manila showing the entire scheme of defense of Bataan. There was a line in red extending across the peninsula just behind the Pilar-

Bagac Highway. This was MacArthur's new main line but it was drawn so sketchily that Homma's intelligence officer figured it was merely the outpost line. About five miles behind this line was another. The intelligence officer deduced that this was the new American main line.

On the basis of this false information Homma devised the attack. General Morioka's 16th Division would continue its successful assault on Wainwright's corps, driving down the west coast. On the east coast, Nara would sweep past the American "outpost line" along Trail 2 and then smash into the "main line." The attack was to start as soon as possible.

It was midnight, January 26. Because of Bluemel's energy and foresight three battalions were thinly stretched across what had been a gaping hole that morning. Every foxhole on Trail 2 was filled and excited young Filipino officers crept from foxhole to foxhole passing on Bluemel's dramatic exhortation: "Here you stay and here you die!" Even so, this area should have been held by a division. Every one of these men would have to do the work of three.

The next morning General Nara got orders from Homma to attack down Trail 2. To Nara it was incredible to expect the 65th Brigade to resume the attack, but he drew up hasty plans and issued them to his regiments at 11:00 A.M. He ordered Takechi to attack at 3:00 P.M. down Trail 2 with Imai's regiment on the left.

The attack started on schedule. Takechi soon reached the cobblestone road that crossed Bataan. On the other side he found the northern terminus of Trail 2 and started down it. For a few hundred yards there was no opposition, then the Japanese were met with such violent fire from Bluemel's men that Takechi had to entrench in a bamboo thicket. When Nara learned this he was perplexed. Assuming Takechi had merely run into the outpost line, he ordered heavier assaults.

At dusk the next day, January 28, Nara's artillery opened up. An hour later it stopped and Japanese infantrymen crept forward, resuming the attack down Trail 2, soon reaching a low embankment. Here the Japanese ran into two strands of barbed wire strung along small trees several feet above the embankment. Bluemel's Filipinos suddenly dashed from their foxholes and bayoneted the invaders. Takechi's men fell back, but a dozen were left hanging on the wires. It was grim, deadly battle and it continued repetitiously till dawn.

In the light of day, the Filipinos holding Trail 2 counted ninety-seven dead Japanese in front of a narrow 150-yard strip. Twenty of these were only five yards from the Filipino foxholes.

When Nara heard of this new setback he suspected the information given him by the 14th Army had been wrong, but he had no other choice. He called for further attacks. Takechi's regiment and Nara's own "Summer" Brigade troops, though discouraged and battle-weary, pushed forward again and again. Each time Bluemel's men threw them back. In three days the bamboo thicket near Trail 2 became a slaughter house.

On the morning of January 31 Nara felt he could not ask Takechi's exhausted men to continue. He ordered his friend to withdraw when dark came. The attack would be taken over by fresh troops. At 5:00 P.M. Japanese planes bombed and strafed Parker's II Corps artillery which had been playing havoc with Nara's entire offensive. An hour later the Japanese artillery preparation began, almost deafening General Nara. Fire was laid systematically along Trail 2 almost back to Bluemel's command post. After an hour and a half the barrage lifted and the infantrymen scheduled to relieve Takechi crept forward under cover of darkness.

Just then Bluemel ordered his division artillery to lay fire on the ford over the river in front of his main line. U.S. shells exploded all along the riverbank. As the stunned Japanese stolidly came forward, machine guns dug in astride Trail 2 riddled the right section of the attack line. The new attackers turned and fled.

Nine Filipinos crept from their foxholes to see what had happened. After 75 yards they stumbled into a Japanese sapper trench extending toward their own lines. It was full of Japanese, long dead. The stink was so sickening the nine hurried back to their own foxholes. It was the end of the attack on Trail 2. Bluemel's thin, stubborn line had momentarily saved Bataan.

13

1 On the day the battle for Trail 2 ended, January 31, Lieutenant Malcolm Champlin, Admiral Rockwell's aide, landed at the tip end of Bataan at Mariveles. He stepped into a battered sedan and was driven by a sailor up the dusty west coast road toward Wainwright's command post.

The general had asked Corregidor for a naval adviser. Four days earlier a second Japanese landing had been made behind his lines, reinforcing the troops that had already landed at Quinauan Point, about halfway between the American front lines and Mariveles. Wainwright feared new Japanese landings and he hoped Champlin's naval training might help him determine when and where they would come.

Only a company of Japanese had landed on the second attempt and they had yet to join up with the original 600 invaders who kept shifting position every night to evade the inexperienced conglomeration of grounded American airmen, Constabulary and Philippine Army troops who were trying to root them out.

The 300 Japanese who had drifted south, near Mariveles, were also still hiding in the dense slopes overlooking that harbor. Even fire from eight 12-inch mortars on Corregidor had failed to dislodge them.

After an hour on the rough coastal highway, a Filipino soldier stepped onto the road and waved Champlin's car to a halt. Vehicles could go no farther; General Wainwright's headquarters were among the trees 300 yards to the right. Champlin walked up a hill into a grove of huge trees on the edge of a ridge. Surrounded by tents were several tables of split bamboo lashed with vines. He recognized the tall, thin man talking to several officers: his new boss, Wainwright.

The general looked up and smiled. "I'm glad to have you here, son. Come over for a chat in the trailer as soon as you're settled." He got up, his loose figure seeming to unravel. He was not the strapping military man Champlin had expected. His face was thin and there was nothing that im-

199

pressed the lieutenant except his eyes. These were quick and piercing.

After settling in a tent Champlin unwrapped the package given him by Rockwell for Wainwright. It was a bottle of Scotch. "Would the general be interested in this?" he asked Wainwright's aide, Captain Tom Dooley.

"Would he!" Dooley's eyes were popping. "Just come with me . . . and handle that bottle with care."

Champlin followed Dooley through jungle vines to a trailer. The lieutenant handed the bottle to Wainwright. "General, Admiral Rockwell sends this to cement Army-Navy relations."

Wainwright took the bottle tenderly, held it up to the fading light and rotated it. "Young man, do you realize that you have here the finest Scotch there is? And that I haven't had a drink for months?"

The next morning Champlin rode up front with Wainwright and Dooley. While a corporal drove up the jungle trail, Sergeant Carroll stood on the running board scanning the sky for planes. Soon they came to the front. After inspecting company command posts and going forward to talk to squad leaders and privates, the general and his party started back home. Japanese artillery fire began to fall, sweeping back and forth across the trail. The car stopped and everyone ran into a clump of woods dotted with foxholes.

While Champlin and the others impatiently waited for Wainwright to pick his foxhole, the general took a cavalry captain by the arm and sat down with him unconcernedly on a row of sandbags and talked.

Champlin had never seen such coolness under fire. When the barrage stopped and the car started off again Champlin said, "General Wainwright, why is it that you, commander of half the troops on Bataan, risk your life the way you did a few minutes ago? It seemed to me you were doing a very foolish thing."

Wainwright smiled slightly, then said in a slow drawl, "Champ, think it over a minute. What have we to offer these troops? Can we give them more to eat? No. We haven't any more food. Can we give them any more ammunition? No, it's running low. Can we give them supplies or equipment or tanks or planes or medicine? No. Everything is running low. But we can give them morale and that is one of my primary duties. That's why I go to the front every day. Now do you understand why it's important for me to sit on sandbags in the line of fire while the rest of you run for shelter?"

The following night, February 1, a bright full moon shone over Bataan lighting up a dozen large barges sailing down the west coast. In them were 700 men of Major Mitsuo Kimura's 1st Battalion, 20th Infantry. Their mission was to reinforce those who had already landed near Quinauan Point in the two previous landings. The combined force of 1500 would then drive south to Mariveles. With this town in Homma's hands, all supplies to Wainwright's corps would be cut off and the Battle of Bataan quickly ended.

The previous landings had completely surprised the defenders. Though the southernmost, only a few miles from Mariveles, had just been wiped out by Philippine Scouts, the other two beachheads near Quinauan Point (now called Quinine by the Americans) were still intact and inflicting heavy losses on other Scouts of the 57th Infantry.

This time a Navy signalman sighted the invasion flotilla long before it neared its goal and telephoned Champlin. The lieutenant hurried to Wainwright's trailer and told the general another landing attempt would probably be made near Quinauan Point. Then Champlin called Navy Headquarters on Corregidor recommending that Bulkeley's PT boats, already on patrol, be sent to the vicinity. In the meantime, Wainwright was rushing the 26th Cavalry to the area and MacArthur's Far East Air Force, four patched-up P-40's, was taking off from the strip near Cabcaben.

As the Japanese barges neared Quinauan Point, Battery D of the 88th Field Artillery and Battery E of the 301st opened up with their 75's and 155's. Machine guns emplaced on cliffs along the coast chattered. Then the four P-40's shot over Mariveles Mountains and found the invaders. After dropping 100-pound fragmentation bombs, they swooped down, strafing the barges with machine guns.

A few minutes later two of Bulkeley's torpedo boats reached the scene. Suddenly MTB 32, carrying the bearded Bulkeley, was blinded by a large searchlight. Two shells screamed overhead, exploding only yards ahead of the boat. They came from a Japanese mine layer covering the landing. The torpedo boat headed directly for the mine layer. Avoiding more salvos, it loosed two of its torpedoes. Bulkeley was sure he had sunk the vessel but it was only slightly damaged.

Americans and Filipinos on the cliffs watched the combined sea, air and land assault on the flotilla in the brilliant moonlight. They were sure the landing had been completely smashed. Several of the barges were sinking, others fleeing south.

But Major Kimura was a man not easily discouraged. The

importance of his mission had been accented by General
Homma himself. Besides there were comrades ashore who
needed help. Though half of his men were lost in the sea
fight, Kimura led the rest to a beach about a mile north of
Quinauan Point. There he was greeted by the 200 men of
the second landing. These two forces consolidated and soon
after midnight disappeared in the dense wooded jungle in
search of the 600 original invaders. The Battle of the Points
was on again.

2 About seven miles to the northeast, another
unorthodox battle was developing in the middle of Wainwright's front lines. This was a densely jungled, hilly area
almost four miles inland from the South China Sea and
about a mile behind the American Main Line of Resistance.
A week previously Homma had ordered the Japanese on
west Bataan to attack Wainwright while Nara was launching
his abortive drive against Parker in the east on Trail 2. Wainwright successfully threw back this attack at all places but
one. Near the center of his line 1000 Japanese, commanded
by Colonel Yorimasa Yoshioka, broke through before the
Filipinos assigned to that area had finished setting up their
defense line. The Japanese continued south for about a mile,
completely undetected by the defenders. This was not too
surprising.

It was easy for 1000 men to go unnoticed in the wild, be-
wildering jungle in the rolling valley between the two great
extinct volcanoes. Tropical vines and creepers draped from
huge mahogany and sprawling banyan trees made the hills a
continuous woody screen; tall cane and thick clumps of
bamboo matted the lower areas. Maps were so crude that
officers couldn't even agree which was the Tuol and which
the Cotar River.

And so Yoshioka's force wasn't detected for three days.
Even when the Japanese were discovered it was thought that
only "seventeen snipers" had infiltrated the lines, but by the
night of the third Japanese landing, February 1, Wainwright
realized a strong enemy force was sitting at the junction of
two important trails a mile behind his front. Already a battalion of Scouts sent to wipe out the "seventeen snipers" had
been hard hit by casualties.

To complicate matters Yoshioka's 1000 men had become
split in two. The Little Pocket, a company, was on top of a
hill 600 yards behind the front line. The Big Pocket, the

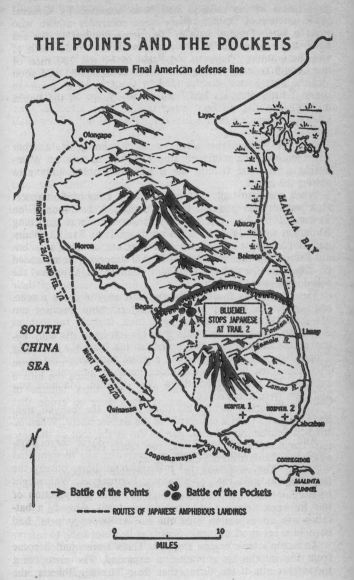

THE POINTS AND THE POCKETS

▬▬▬▬▬ Final American defense line

Layac

MANILA BAY

Olongapo

Moron

Mauban

Bagac

Abucay

Balanga

BLUEMEL STOPS JAPANESE AT TRAIL 2

2

Pantingan R.

Limay

SOUTH CHINA SEA

Mamala R.

Lamao R.

Quinauan Pt.

HOSPITAL 1 ✛

HOSPITAL 2 ✛

Cabcaben

Longoskawayan Pt.

Mariveles

CORREGIDOR

MALINTA TUNNEL

NIGHTS OF JAN. 26/27 AND FEB. 1/2

NIGHT OF JAN. 22/23

N

→ Battle of the Points   ●●● Battle of the Pockets

▬ ▬ ▬ ROUTES OF JAPANESE AMPHIBIOUS LANDINGS

0   10

MILES

main force, was well dug in another 1000 yards farther south at the junction of Trails 5 and 7.

As a further complication Trail 7—a main trail running north-south almost in the exact middle of Wainwright's line—was the boundary between the Right Sector of Wainwright's line, commanded by Brigadier General William Brougher, and the Left Sector, commanded by General Jones. By February 2 little progress had been made by the Scouts trying to wipe out the pockets, even though they attacked time after time shouting their battle cry, "Petay si la!" (They shall die!)

General Wainwright, after narrowly missing death from an ingeniously camouflaged sniper with face painted green during a personal visit to the Big Pocket, ordered tanks to bolster the attack.

When the four-tank platoon arrived a combined infantry-tank assault was planned by the tankers and Colonel Glen Townsend of the 11th Infantry Regiment. Sergeant Leroy Anderson would lead the tanks north up Trail 7 to an enemy gun emplacement at the base of a huge banyan tree. Lieutenant Robert Roberts volunteered to give support with a platoon of riflemen. Lieutenant Willibald Bianchi of Company D asked if he could go along.

The four tanks rumbled up the trail at 4:00 P.M. Anderson's lead tank quickly ran into heavy rifle and machine-gun fire from Yoshioka's camouflaged men. Bianchi ran behind Anderson's tank, firing a rifle with his left hand. As the tank neared the banyan tree, two bullets struck Bianchi's hand. He dropped the rifle but pulled out a pistol with his other hand. Fire had come from a well-hidden machine gun west of the big tree. He ran forward, threw two grenades. Machine gun and crew were knocked out.

Now Anderson swung his tank toward the banyan tree. Soon he was within a few yards of the emplacement. When he tried to depress his 37-mm. gun to fire at the foot of the tree into the nest he found he was too close. Heavy fire rattled against the tank from the banyan tree.

Seeing Anderson was in a vulnerable position, Bianchi leaped to the top of the tank. A Japanese machine gun in the nest chattered. Two bullets thudded into Bianchi's chest but he kept firing at the area around the tree. Suddenly there was an explosion near the turret. Seriously wounded, Bianchi toppled off the tank. Scouts pulled him back to safety.

Anderson's tank engine stopped. There were muffled roars from the interior as ammunition exploded. The crew flung themselves out of the turret, their hair burning. Roberts and his riflemen pinned down Japanese in foxholes behind the banyan tree until the tankers escaped.

The three other tanks roared by, firing their 37-mm. guns. Soon the leader discovered another machine gun on the right of the trail. While the tank fired, pinning down these machine gunners, Lieutenant Edward Stewart crept forward with a Scout. "Throw a grenade," he whispered. The Scout threw one. A few minutes later the same grenade came flying back out of the nest, exploding near Stewart. The Scout threw two more. Both came back.

"Must be a damned octopus in that hole," said Stewart. At a signal he and the Scout threw grenades simultaneously. There was a great muffled explosion. The machine gun was silenced. It was fortunate because the lead tank soon became caught on a stump. The crew had to crawl back to the rear.

A few yards had been punched into the south side of the Big Pocket, but two tanks were lost. It was obvious that a large force somehow had filtered behind the lines. A long, deadly fight lay ahead.

As Bianchi, bloody froth on his lips, was being carried down the trail, he saw his friend, Major Adrianus van Oosten, and stopped the stretcher-bearers. Van Oosten wondered what important message his friend had for him. "Van," said Bianchi, "take care of my camera, will you?"

Late that afternoon Lieutenant Champlin returned to Corregidor. While he was reporting to Admiral Rockwell, Lieutenant Commander F. W. "Mike" Fenno entered the Navy tunnel. He had just brought in 70 tons of 3-inch anti-aircraft ammunition on the submarine *Trout*. Though Fenno had reloaded with fuel and torpedoes, his boat still was too light. Where could he find 25 tons of ballast fast?

It answered a problem that had been worrying Rockwell, Sayre, Quezon and MacArthur for days: the gold and silver they'd brought to Corregidor from the banks of Manila. In a few hours 2 tons of gold bars and 18 of silver pesos were flung into trucks and then down the hatch into the *Trout* like so many sacks of potatoes.

At his house outside the east entrance of Malinta Tunnel, MacArthur was worrying about a much more important problem. The 70 tons of ammunition just brought in by the *Trout* only accented the futility of such meager efforts. He needed large quantities to save Bataan. Washington had to be shaken from its lethargy. It would be a fatal mistake, he radioed Marshall, to continue the present Allied strategy. Instead of building up forces for Australia, the Japanese line of communications stretching over 2000 miles of sea should be attacked. There was only one way to defeat Japan: seek combat, not avoid it.

He wished that those safe and secure in America could realize time was fast running out in the Philippines.

Early on the morning of February 5, Lieutenant Reed of General Brougher's staff called out to the Japanese in the Big Pocket to surrender. The answer was heavy fire.

Wainwright by now realized the job needed special handling. He called a meeting at the command post of the 1st Division. At 10:00 A.M. Generals Wainwright, Jones, Brougher and Segundo conferred. The exasperating command problem had to be straightened out, said Wainwright. He was going to appoint one man, regardless of sectors, to command the operation. He asked Jones how he would tackle the problem.

"They have to be pinched out," said Jones. "First I'd isolate the pockets and throw a cordon around each one." Only then would he launch the main attack. First against the Little Pocket. When that had been wiped out, he'd tackle the Big Pocket.

Though Wainwright and Jones had occasionally clashed, they understood each other. Both believed in personal supervision by generals on the front line.

"All right, Honus," said Wainwright. "You take charge."

The Battle for the Points was also grinding on grimly. Philippine Scout casualties were 50 per cent in some companies. Morale was falling because of hunger and continuous danger from camouflaged Japanese snipers tied to trees. There was no concentrated food; supplies moved slowly through the thick, deadly jungle near Quinauan Point. Commanders were learning that the ability to fight decreased as food decreased.

Tanks were brought up to help but in spite of aggressive efforts, the thick jungle made this a battle of riflemen. The Japanese would have to be rooted out one by one as they were pushed west into the China Sea. By February 7 the Scouts had isolated all the Japanese near Quinauan Point into an area 4000 yards wide. American Air Corps and Philippine Constabulary troops were rushed in to help finish the ugly mopping-up.

At the southern end of this line, on Quinauan Point itself, the end was in sight. The remnants of the 600 Japanese of the first landing had been shoved to the edge of the China

Sea. They were now hiding in caves at the base of a sheer cliff.

Captain William Dyess, who started the war as a fighter pilot, was crouched on top of the cliff with seventy men of his planeless 21st Pursuit Squadron. On all sides were enemy dead—snipers hanging from the trees, riflemen still crouched in their foxholes.

Sergeant Ray Hunt, Jr., formerly a mechanic, stuffed his nose with cotton so he could eat his dinner. He could see a dying Japanese tangled in a trench with two dead bodies, his wound crawling with maggots. The man had three watches on his right arm.

Hunt looked down. A Japanese had darted from a cave and was racing across the beach. Japan is one hell of a long way, he thought, as the man dove into the China Sea. A Scout machine gunner near Hunt slowly put his mess kit down, positioned himself comfortably behind his gun, took deliberate aim and squeezed the trigger. The swimming Japanese became motionless, his body engulfed in a growing circle of red. It was brilliant red, noted Hunt, against an emerald green. Vivid, beautiful and horrible.

A mile to the south, two other Japanese had dived into the China Sea. Still unseen, they were swimming north. Each carried a bamboo pipe containing identical messages from Major Kimura to his commanding general. A bitter battle was going on, reported Kimura, the enemy attacking with infantry and tanks. "The battalion is about to die gloriously," he concluded.

The end came the next day, February 8. Just after dawn twenty of Captain Dyess' grounded airmen left Mariveles in two whaleboats. Covering them were two armored naval motor launches, commanded by Lieutenant Commander H. W. Goodall and armed with 37-mm. and machine guns.

It was almost 8:00 A.M. when Dyess, aboard Goodall's launch, saw sheets hanging down from a cliff. Dyess pointed out caves under the sheets. These, he told Goodall, contained the last stubborn Japanese. The two launches began firing into the caves. Ten minutes later a sailor noticed a flight of Japanese dive bombers coming from the east.

"To hell with the airplanes, sailor," said Goodall. He turned to Dyess. "Where do you want the next shot, Captain?"

The four boats, all guns still firing, sped toward the beach as 100-pound fragmentation bombs burst on all sides. Soon a whaleboat was hit, then a launch. A moment later the second whaleboat was sunk. Just before beaching, Goodall's launch was upset and almost demolished by a near hit.

Dyess and his twenty men swam ashore. While they crept toward the caves from two sides, other American airmen on top of the cliff worked cautiously down through ravines. By noon the caves were cleaned of Japanese. Only one prisoner was taken.

The Battle of the Points was finally over.

3　That same day General Homma called an important conference at his command post in the sugar center of San Fernando. Here it was another muggy day with the heat above 95 degrees. Though he didn't show it, Homma was tormented with worries. The situation on Bataan was desperate, almost catastrophic. He had already lost almost 7000 men in combat and another 10,000 had been stricken with malaria, beriberi and dysentery.

Not a word had yet been heard of the two battalions which had landed behind Wainwright near Quinauan Point. Another battalion had been swallowed up in pockets behind Wainwright's line. On the east coast Nara had been given a bloody nose at Trail 2.

And still Homma was being pressed by Southern Army and Imperial General Headquarters to wind up the Bataan operation in a few days. How was it possible when they'd already robbed him of his only good division, the 48th? He had twice requested that the whole Philippine situation be reviewed. These weren't strong protests, of course, because even a lieutenant general rarely asks for reinforcements. He must do with what he has.

In addition to poor maps, he had been given intelligence reports indicating that the Filipinos were eager to turn on their American conquerors and completely misinterpreting MacArthur's capabilities and intentions. It was almost as though Tojo wanted him to fail. Their enmity was well known. These suspicions were never to be allayed. Three years later in his prison diary Homma would write, "It is reported that Mr. Tojo will be here before long. There is nothing more unpleasant than this. To have to see his face every day will be more than I can bear. . . ." And two weeks later, "At 1:00 P.M. Tojo arrived at the prison. The sight of his face is enough to make me feel disgusted. He came out saying, 'Hello, Your Excellency Homma!' et cetera but I merely nodded." Yet, a week later he wrote revealingly, "Mr. Tojo is being shunned by most of the men and in a way I feel pity for him."

The conference began. General Maeda, the chief of staff, presided as chairman. Homma, as often was the custom of Japanese commanders, played a passive, listening role. Unlike the western military, it was Japanese policy to let staff officers do much of the thinking and planning. It was felt that otherwise they might lose their enterprise.

Homma listened impassively as Maeda outlined the general situation. It was even worse than Homma had suspected. Because of the frightful casualties on the Abucay Line and the triple disasters at Trail 2, the Pockets and the Points, there were now only three infantry battalions on the entire Bataan line! If MacArthur knew, he could smash through and crush the 14th Army.

Others spoke. Major Moriya Wada, then Colonel Tatsuo Haki. The general attack on MacArthur's new line had bogged down, said Haki. To continue with the fast-dwindling forces would be disastrous. Colonel Motoo Nakayama, senior operations officer, disagreed. "The offensive," he said, "should be continued aggressively. However, the main effort should be made along the east coast, not the west."

Maeda cleared his throat. He had first guessed MacArthur's intention to make Bataan a major point of resistance. Homma eagerly waited the views of his most brilliant officer. "I believe the offense should be discontinued. Let us merely blockade Bataan while we occupy the rest of the Archipelago. By that time the men of General Matsukuasa (MacArthur) will be starved and ready to surrender."

As the conference continued in the sultry heat, Homma realized that he couldn't agree with either of the two major views. Maeda's argument for breaking off attack immediately and retreating to safer positions was irrefutable, but it was unthinkable to wait for the Americans to rot on the vine. Tokyo would never stomach such a face-losing tactic. He himself would have to be the one to lose face.

Homma told them a new and much more powerful offense must be launched. To do this he would have to swallow his pride and ask for heavy reinforcements.

The others in the room saw tears running down the big general's face. To Lieutenant Colonel Monjiro Akiyama, Homma was a perfect human being, humanistic and just, who never raised his voice or criticized a man in public. To Wada, he was a humane and literate man who treated younger officers with consideration. As Homma's staff started to file out of the room a telegram was handed the general.

He opened the message. It was from Imperial General Headquarters. Tojo was displeased. Hong Kong had fallen and General Yamashita was about to score one of the greatest military triumphs in Japanese history: he would soon take Singapore. Everywhere there was victory except in the Philippines. Colonel Haki saw a look of supreme agony come over Homma's face. Then the general's head suddenly dropped to the table. Haki and two men carried the unconscious commander of the 14th Army into the next room.

4 Personal conflict between the fighting front and commanders in their homeland wasn't confined to the Japanese that day.

On Corregidor bitter rumors were circulating of abandonment and "sellout" by Washington. Some officers believed Roosevelt and Marshall were going to let MacArthur rot in the Philippines. It was common knowledge throughout the Army that Marshall and MacArthur were not on good personal terms. MacArthur's spectacular skyrocketing after World War I had made him a four-star general and chief of staff, while Marshall, only a year younger, remained a lieutenant colonel. Some said Marshall still blamed MacArthur for not making him a general during the former's regime as chief of staff.

That day MacArthur learned Roosevelt was making a radio speech telling of the thousands of aircraft that would soon be on their way to the battlefront—Europe. Guessing that Quezon would hear it and would be infuriated, the general asked his intelligence officer, Colonel Charles Willoughby, to go at once to the Philippine president and try to placate him.

Quezon was in a tent set up on a slope near the entrance of Malinta Tunnel so he could get fresh air. He was sitting in his wheel chair, angrily listening to the Roosevelt speech, as Willoughby entered. When it was over, Quezon poured out a torrent of violent denunciation in Spanish, a language Willoughby understood. Then the Filipino pointed to smoke rising from the mainland. "For thirty years I have worked and hoped for my people. Now they burn and die for a flag that could not protect them. *Por Dios y todos los Santos,* I cannot stand this constant reference to England, to Europe. Where are the planes this *sinverguenza* is boasting of? *Que demonio!* How American to writhe in anguish at the fate of a distant cousin while a daughter is being raped in the back room."

Willoughby calmed the president, whose breath was coming in gasps, but later in the day Quezon insisted on seeing MacArthur. He was now in a deeply depressed mood. "Perhaps," he said, "my presence on Corregidor is not of value. Why don't I go to Manila and become a prisoner of war?" He was afraid of Tojo's recent promise to give the Philippines independence with honor. "I will defy the Japanese and this will solidify the opposition of all Filipinos."

MacArthur thought this would be a mistake. "I think the Japanese would allow you to go to Malacañan Palace and then let no Filipino near you. They would give out statements coming from you urging Filipinos to surrender." The general also believed Quezon's surrender would be misinterpreted abroad.

"I don't care what outsiders think," flared Quezon, but then calmed down. MacArthur was his good friend, a man to be trusted. "I'll think it over." He wanted to be another Apolinari Mabini, the great national hero, a paralytic prisoner who had refused to take an oath of allegiance during the Filipino-American War.

At this moment a young Filipino second lieutenant was swimming from Bataan to Corregidor to see Quezon. It was Antonio Aquino, elder son of Benigno Aquino, the sugar-cane king and speaker of the Philippine Assembly. Aquino had retreated with the rest of Capinpin's division into Bataan. The 21st Division was now holding a front-line position several miles to the left of strategic Trail 2. Concerned about the increasing tension between Filipinos and Americans, he had conferred with General Capinpin.

"The Americans are forever goddamming this blasted country for the war, the mosquitoes and the poor rations," he told the general. His Filipino enlisted men understandably resented the brusque American attitude. More important, they also felt Americans were getting better food. Aquino then asked permission to go to Bataan and inform President Quezon of the situation.

Capinpin agreed and young Aquino immediately started south in his yellow convertible, already scarred by several shrapnel holes. He finally reached the east coast highway and continued to Cabcaben, a town near the eastern tip of the peninsula.

Just before dusk Aquino started for Corregidor in a small fishing boat. A mile from the rock island, the fisherman refused to go any farther for fear of being fired at by trigger-happy American guards. Aquino stripped, covered himself with heavy oil and tied a bag filled with dozens of ping-pong balls on his back as a life preserver. He knotted his clothes in a ball, then jumped into the water.

In three and a half hours he finally reached the beach not far from the entrance of Malinta Tunnel. After drying his clothes he entered the tunnel and headed for the Quezon family quarters. In the lighted passageway he saw Quezon's two daughters, Nini and Baby. They failed to recognize him at first. He had lost twenty pounds and was tanned dark.

The two girls led Aquino into their father's room.

"Papa," said Nini, "look who swam to Corregidor. Tony Aquino."

Aquino saluted, then, in respect to an elder, kissed Quezon's hand.

"Tony, sit down," said the president. "Let me look at you. How is it in Bataan?"

Aquino's fatigue instantly vanished. He swallowed to keep from choking. "We are doing fine, Excellency. General Capinpin is sending you his regards and prayers for your health." Then he told Quezon of the antagonism between Americans and Filipinos.

The president took it calmly. "You have to know the Americano to understand him. He is gruff and rough but it's just his way."

"There is one other thing, sir. We feel that we should have the same rations as the Americans. We eat only salmon and sardines. One can per thirty men, twice a day."

"What?" Quezon was astounded.

"Yes, sir. One can of salmon for thirty, two gantas of rice and two cans of condensed milk for breakfast."

"Puñeta!" exclaimed Quezon. "I did not know that."

At that moment MacArthur walked in. Aquino stood at attention.

"General," said Quezon, "this is Tony Aquino, the son of Benigno, my secretary of commerce and agriculture."

"How are you, young man?" MacArthur shook Aquino's hand.

Quezon asked Aquino to repeat his story. While the young Filipino was talking, he noticed several American officers standing behind MacArthur shifting in embarrassment.

Quezon turned to MacArthur and said, "I want you to improve the rations."

The general assented. "You did a fine service, young man." He shook Aquino's hand and left.

"If I were forty years younger," Quezon wistfully told Aquino, "I would be with you. I know Bataan, every nook and corner of it. I fought there during the Revolution. God will not forsake us and in the end we shall win. Do not lose hope!"

When he was alone Quezon mulled over what his friend's son had told him. Finally he called for his Cabinet. His mind was made up. "I think I have the answer," he told them a few minutes later. "I'll ask Roosevelt to let me issue a manifesto requesting the U.S. to grant immediately complete and absolute independence to the Philippines." Then he would demobilize the Philippine Army and declare the Philippines neutral. America and Japan would both withdraw their armies.

Manuel Roxas shook his head. He was afraid of the effects of such a proposition on Roosevelt. Vice-President Osmeña agreed with Roxas. "I am sure that Roosevelt would misunderstand our motive."

Quezon's voice rose excitedly in argument. He pointed out that food was running out on Bataan. The starved Filipino troops couldn't possibly hold out much longer.

Hacking coughs silenced Quezon. Osmeña and Roxas realized it was dangerous to try and argue the president out of his quixotic scheme. Further resistance to the plan might bring on a fatal attack. The Cabinet unanimously approved that the message be sent to Roosevelt.

A little later MacArthur received the message. Although he had done his best to calm Quezon's growing fears that America was abandoning the Philippines, secretly he had his own doubts.

He had great personal respect for Roosevelt and knew the President respected him but he still vividly remembered their dispute in 1933 when he was chief of staff and Roosevelt ordered a cut in the Army budget. MacArthur had argued that Army morale would be seriously lowered at a time of national peril. Sharp words were exchanged in a decisive interview at the White House. At last the general stood up and said, "Mr. President, if you pursue this policy which will lead inevitably to the destruction of the American army, I have no other choice but to oppose you publicly. I shall ask for my immediate relief as chief of staff and for retirement from the Army, and I shall take this fight straight to the people." The general saluted, turned on his heel, walked out of the White House and vomited on the lawn. A little later the proposed budget cut was dropped.

MacArthur knew that Quezon could not be dissuaded from sending his alarming message. Perhaps it was for the best. He decided to take a gamble. In addition to Quezon's message, he would send one of his own, painting the real, tragic picture of Corregidor and Bataan. "There is no denying," he wrote, "that we are nearly done."

The Filipinos' attitude, he added, was one of "almost violent resentment against the U.S." He concluded that militarily "the problem presents itself as to whether the plan of President Quezon might offer the best possible solution of what is about to be a disastrous debacle."

Quezon's scheme, obviously, was a wild one, yet perhaps its very wildness would shock Washington into action. MacArthur was risking his whole military career on these two messages, but he was willing to take the gamble.

The next morning, February 9, General Jones was still personally supervising the Battle of the Pockets. By now he was so weak from dysentery he could hardly stand, but he refused to leave the front. The climax of the strange battle was approaching. Colonel K. L. Berry and his 1st Division troops had pinched out the Little Pocket and were now joining in the final assault on the Big Pocket.

There was a new complication. Two days ago General Morioka, in a desperate attempt to relieve his surrounded troops, had ferociously attacked Wainwright's main line at Trail 7, 1400 yards north of the Big Pocket. Just when it looked as though this spirited Japanese drive would break through to the Pocket, Igorots of Colonel Glen Townsend's 11th Infantry counterattacked. Some, clad only in G-strings, rode on top of buttoned-up American tanks tapping with clubs to direct the drivers. The Japanese advance was stopped. By then, however, there was a 600-yard bulge in the line. It had already been nicknamed the Upper Pocket.

While Townsend held off the attack on the main line, Jones was hammering at the Big Pocket from all sides. Now mortars were pounding the trapped men. In the silence after explosions Jones' men could hear the cries of the wounded Japanese. And when night fell they could hear the weird chanting of prayers, soon followed by the steady chopping of trees as the energetic defenders built more defenses and cut more fields of fire.

Inside the Big Pocket five captured Filipino soldiers were lashed to a huge nara tree. The past ten days had been an unbelievable nightmare as they watched the Pocket shrink and their captors get weaker from hunger. At first there had been plenty of water, dipped from the Tuol River at the edge of the Pocket. It was their job to sneak down at night under guard and carry water back to the center, but now the Tuol, actually a large stream, was in American hands. Its banks were already lined with the stinking corpses of Japanese who had been too thirsty for caution.

That night, February 9, the five Filipinos could sense a new attitude in the Japanese. It frightened them. They feared they would soon be executed.

Colonel Yoshioka had just received orders, dropped by plane, to retreat. It was a reprieve from death, for an un-ordered withdrawal was unthinkable. He took a count. Of the original 1000, less than 600 remained and 100 of these were wounded. He consulted with his few remaining officers. They would leave all their horses, bury their three small mountain guns and 47-mm. anti-tank gun and break out to the north the next night. The walking wounded would go with them. The others, naturally, would commit hara-kiri.

5   It was only 3:00 P.M., February 9, in Washington and Franklin Roosevelt, with Secretary of War Stimson and Sumner Welles, was drafting an answer to President Quezon. Roosevelt had been seriously shaken by the Filipino's plan to surrender to the Japanese, particularly since MacArthur and Sayre seemed to have made no effort to dissuade Quezon and had even given the proposal some support in accompanying messages.

The Battle of the Atlantic had just taken a dangerous turn. German U-boats were ravaging shipping along America's east coast. By the end of January, 31 ships totaling almost 200,000 tons had been sunk off the North Atlantic coast. The first week in February the toll had taken a sharp rise. If it continued, and there was no hope it would not, at least 70 ships would be destroyed before the month's end. Saboteurs, apparently, were as busy as the submarines. It was immediately believed, for instance, they were responsible for the mysterious burning of the French liner *Normandie* that same day at her dock at the end of West 49th Street in New York City.

There was also a new disaster in North Africa. Rommel was again loose and threatening to drive the British back to Alexandria.

The President couldn't expect Quezon and MacArthur to agree with the war policy, universally accepted in Washington, that Hitler should be defeated first but they apparently doubted that everything possible was being sent them. The Southwest Pacific had already been sent more than its share of available men and supplies. During January three convoys and the Navy seatrain *Hammondsport* had left San Fran-

cisco and New York for Australia. The *Queen Mary* in Boston
and the *Monterey* and *Matsonia* in San Francisco were being
loaded with reinforcements. By the middle of March 79,000
troops would have left for the Pacific front, almost four times
the number of troops heading for Europe. Most of the few
available planes were also heading toward the Orient.

Roosevelt realized he had to transmit all these facts to
Quezon, but without threat or accusation. The immediate
future of the Philippines rested on the right words.

Quezon received the radiogram on February 10. In it
Roosevelt declared bluntly that the U.S. would never agree
to Quezon's proposal but added that no matter what Quezon
did America would not abandon the Philippines.

> SO LONG AS THE FLAG OF THE U.S. FLIES ON FILIPINO
> SOIL . . . IT WILL BE DEFENDED BY OUR OWN MEN TO
> THE DEATH. WHATEVER HAPPENS TO PRESENT AMERICAN
> GARRISON WE SHALL NOT RELAX OUR EFFORTS UNTIL THE
> FORCES WHICH ARE NOW MARSHALING OUTSIDE THE PHIL-
> IPPINE ISLANDS RETURN TO THE PHILIPPINES AND DRIVE
> THE LAST REMNANT OF THE INVADERS FROM YOUR SOIL.

There was not a single word of recrimination, not even a
veiled threat. The effect on the sick man was overwhelming.
He had long been Roosevelt's friend, ever since the President's days as Under-Secretary of the Navy, but now Quezon
came to the conclusion that he was a great man. Roosevelt
was placing the entire burden of defending the Philippines
on the American people alone.

Quezon swore to himself and God that as long as he lived
he would stand by America regardless of the consequences
to his people or himself. His worries and indecision were
gone. Now he had his course of action.

MacArthur was also reading a message from Roosevelt:

> . . . THE DUTY AND THE NECESSITY OF RESISTING
> JAPANESE AGGRESSION TO THE LAST TRANSCENDS IN IM-
> PORTANCE ANY OTHER OBLIGATION NOW FACING US IN
> THE PHILIPPINES. . . .
> IT IS MANDATORY THAT THERE BE ESTABLISHED ONCE
> AND FOR ALL IN THE MINDS OF ALL PEOPLES COMPLETE
> EVIDENCE THAT THE AMERICAN DETERMINATION AND IN-
> DOMITABLE WILL TO WIN CARRIES ON DOWN TO THE
> LAST UNIT.
> I THEREFORE GIVE YOU THIS MOST DIFFICULT MISSION
> IN FULL UNDERSTANDING OF THE DESPERATE SITUATION

(U.S. Navy Photo)

Battleship Row, Pearl Harbor, as seen from one of the first Japanese torpedo planes.

(Life Phot

The battle that was never fought. Carl Mydans, of Life, *phot graphed this beach on Lingayen Gulf at noon on December 1 when the first major Japanese invasion of the Philippines was su posedly taking place. American newspapers reported 154 Japane vessels were sunk and many of the enemy killed in a fierce thre day battle starting December 10.*

Crew abandoning Prince of Wales *moments before it sinks, D cember 10, 1941.*

(Wide World Phot

Soon to be the first conqueror of a large American force, Lieutenant General Masaharu Homma, the controversial commander of the Japanese 14th Army, steps ashore at Lingayen Gulf, December 24.

Rear Admiral Francis W. Rockwell (left) and his aide, Lieutenant Malcolm Champlin, at Cavite Naval Base.

PEALE IS.

WILKES IS.

DEVEREUX'S COMMAND

PEAC

CAMP ONE

1 Mile

(Wide World Photo)

Wake Island—where the Japanese timetable of conquest was first upset.

Acting on his own initiative, Lieutenant Champlin ordered these Pandacan oil tanks near Manila set afire on December 26 to prevent the Japanese from getting millions of gallons of fuel. For weeks Champlin wondered if he would be decorated or court-martialed.

(Wide World Photo)

Prisoners from Wake in Shanghai. Major James Devereux, Marine commander (left) and Raymond R. Rutledge, civilian worker who threw grenades into Japanese invasion craft. (Wide World Photo)

MacArthur inspects the Abucay line on Bataan, January 10, 1942. To his left, Brigadier General Albert Jones, whose division was reduced to about 100 men two weeks later.

(U.S. Army Photo)

Colonel Susumu Takechi crossed "impenetrable" Mt. Natib and flanked the entire American Abucay Line. His commander, General Nara, recently revealed this was done against his direct orders.

Lieutenant General Akira Nara, former classmate of Coolidge's son at Amherst College. His "Summer Brigade" crushed Jones' division and broke through the Abucay Line.

President Manuel Quezon (left) and Colonel Carlos Romulo. Rumulo later became Philippines Ambassador to the U. S.

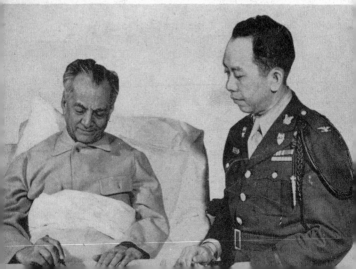

Brigadier General Clifford Bluemel, whose quick thinking prevented General Nara from immediately overrunning the second and final American defense line on Bataan at Trail 2.

Lieutenant John D. Bulkeley, the colorful man of action whose PT boat carried MacArthur through enemy waters to Mindanao on March 11-13.

MacArthur and his chief of staff, Major General Richard K. Sutherland, in Malinta Tunnel, Corregidor, a few days before MacArthur made his bold, dramatic dash to Australia.

TICKET TO ARMISTICE

USE THIS TICKET, SAVE YOUR LIFE
YOU WILL BE KINDLY TREATED

Follow These Instructions:

1. Come towards our lines waving a white flag.

2. Strap your gun over your left shoulder muzzle down and pointed behind you.

3. Show this ticket to the sentry.

4. Any number of you may surrender with this one ticket.

JAPANESE ARMY HEADQUARTERS

投 降 票

此ノ票ヲ持ツモノハ投降者ナリ
投降者ヲ殺害スルヲ厳禁ス

大日本軍司令官

Sing your way to Peace play for Peace

Japanese propaganda leaflets. Japanese "Ticket to Armistice" reads: "The bearer of this ticket wishes to surrender. Killing or harming those surrendering is strictly forbidden. Commander, the Imperial Japanese Army."

Banzai! The 141st Infantry captures Mt. Limay, Bataan, in the final, overwhelming Japanese offensive starting on Good Friday. General Nara honored the regiment's commander, Colonel Takeo Imai (bottom center), by renaming the peak Mt. Imai.

Escapees from Singapore shipwrecked on a small island near Sumatra. A. P. correspondent Yates McDaniel (right rear) and 131 others were forced to abandon their bombed ship the Kung Wo, the previous day, February 13. The girl is Doris Lim, whose flight to freedom would soon end in tragedy.

Vice-Admiral Conrad E. L. Helfrich, the aggressive Dutch commander of the Allied naval forces in the Netherlands East Indies, who was determined to fight the Japanese Navy for Java even though outnumbered.

America's first great humiliation in the Philippines. Major General Edward P. King, Jr. grimly discusses surrender of Bataan with Colonel Motoo Nakayama on April 9. Facing camera (left to right); Colonel Everett C. Williams, General King, Major Wade Cothran and Major Achille C. Tisdelle.

The Death March: 72,000 captured Americans and Filipinos— most of them diseased and near starvation—heading for prison camp. Many were beaten and murdered en route. This picture was stolen by Filipinos from the Japanese during the occupation.

(Wide World Photo)

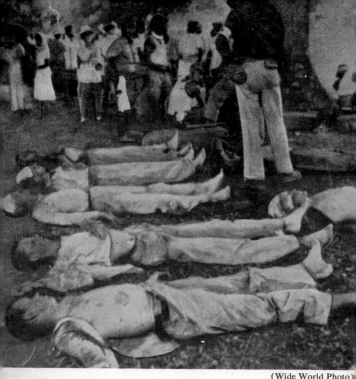

(Wide World Photo)

Five of the approximately 2330 Americans who died on the Death March. Picture stolen by Filipinos.

American and Filipino survivors carry comrades the last mile of the Death March into Camp O'Donnell.

(Wide World Photo)

Americans surrender at the mouth of Malinta Tunnel, Corregidor, on May 6.

Misunderstanding between Lieutenant General Jonathan M. Wainwright and General Homma over surrender terms soon ended this first meeting on May 6 at the Castillo home in Cabcaben, Bataan. Facing Homma (left to right), Wainwright, Brigadier General Lewis C. Beebe and Major Thomas Dooley.

"After leaving General Homma with no agreement between us, I've decided to accept, in the name of humanity, his proposal . . ." In Manila, Wainwright was forced to recite prepared surrender instructions on the night of May 7-8 to those still fighting in the Philippines.

In spite of raging fires the aircraft carrier Lexington, *mortally damaged in the Battle of Coral Sea, was abandoned May 8 with no panic. Some men waiting in line calmly ate ice cream before going over the side.*

Commander Minoru Genda (left), who made the fatal Japanese decision at the Battle of Midway. He is now General Genda, Chief of Staff, Japan Air Self-Defense Force.

"If there is only one plane left to make a final run in, I want that man to go in and get a hit," wrote Lieutenant Commander John C. Waldron, leader of Torpedo Squadron 8, to his men on the eve of the Battle of Midway. Only one member of the squadron, Ensign George Gay, survived the gallant attack the next day.

(U.S. Navy Photo)

TO WHICH YOU MAY SHORTLY BE REDUCED. THE SERVICE
THAT YOU AND THE AMERICAN MEMBERS OF YOUR COM-
MAND CAN RENDER TO YOUR COUNTRY IN THE TITANIC
STRUGGLE NOW DEVELOPING IS BEYOND ALL POSSIBILITY
OF APPRAISEMENT. I PARTICULARLY REQUEST THAT YOU
PROCEED RAPIDLY TO THE ORGANIZATION OF YOUR
FORCES AND YOUR DEFENSES SO AS TO MAKE YOUR RESIST-
ANCE AS EFFECTIVE AS CIRCUMSTANCES WILL PERMIT
AND AS PROLONGED AS HUMANLY POSSIBLE.

Reading between the lines MacArthur knew the Philippines had been definitely, irrevocably written off, their only
value now as a symbol of last-ditch resistance.

The next day, February 11, he replied to Roosevelt. He
would abide by the President's decision. He and his family
would remain in the Philippines and share the fate of the
garrison. He would fight to destruction on Bataan and then
Corregidor, making them names for Americans to remember
forever.

I HAVE NOT THE SLIGHTEST INTENTION IN THE
WORLD OF SURRENDERING OR CAPITULATING THE FIL-
IPINO ELEMENT OF MY COMMAND. . . . THERE HAS
NEVER BEEN THE SLIGHTEST WAVERING AMONG THE
TROOPS.

Morale on Bataan had never been higher. Since the retreat
from Abucay, the Japanese had been consistently stopped.
Filipino soldiers entering Bataan as raw, frightened recruits
had become tough, battle-scarred and dependable. Some
American instructors couldn't believe these were the same
men who had run on the hectic retreat from Lingayen Gulf; a
number of junior officers were even admitting that some
of the early disasters had been caused by their own falter-
ing leadership.

Riddled with dysentery and malaria, their uniforms in
tatters, the half-starved men of Bataan were full of fight
and confidence.

At the Big Pocket General Jones, under protest, was being
carried away on a stretcher. He was so weak from acute
dysentery he could no longer walk. He wanted to stay but he
left knowing the savage battle was all but over. His men
were punching into the Pocket from several sides, unaware
that Colonel Morioka had slipped out the night before with
less than 400 starved men.

The attackers were finding a grisly battlefield. There were

hundreds of graves, some curiously outlined with upright
cigarettes, but many bodies were unburied and the stink of
tropical decay was overpowering. Some dead men were holding hunks of raw horse meat in their hands, their only
sustenance. Huge bluebottle flies rose from the bodies in
clouds. Commanders, seeing this ghastly charnel house, ordered it burned to the ground before disease could spread.
Others like Major Crow tried to prevent some of their own
starving riflemen from digging meat with bare fingers from
sliced-open horses.

Only two live Japanese came out of the Pockets. One with a
broken thigh was taken to Colonel Berry's command post. He
was almost naked, his face skeletal. Berry gave him a pair
of shorts, and a milk shake from the only food available,
sugar and a can of milk. After gulping down the concoction
the Japanese, to Berry's amazement, painfully tried to stand.
He couldn't, bowed his head from a prone position in gratitude, then vomited.

PART 4 DEATH OF TWO EMPIRES

14 *This Naked Island*

1 The keystone of the British Empire in Asia was Singapore, the island at the southern end of the Malay Peninsula. Here East met West. Not far up the peninsula, East— in the form of the 26,000 well-trained men of Lieutenant General Tomoyuki Yamashita—was now surging toward the strategic island determined to drive West into the sea by March 1.

Opposing Yamashita were 86,895 troops under the command of Lieutenant General A. E. Percival, a tall, thin man with two protruding, rabbit-like teeth. Although he was an outstanding staff officer of quiet charm, some observers felt Percival lacked the forcefulness to inspire the assorted British, Indian and Australian units under him.

The clumsy American-built Buffalo fighter in his air force never had a chance against the Zero. Within a week the air above Malaya was Japanese. On the ground Percival was almost as handicapped. There wasn't a single Allied tank in all Malaya because British experts had decreed armor was unsuited for jungle warfare. The Japanese experts felt differently and now their tanks were playing havoc with the defenders. The Indians in particular were terrified by the metal monsters that charged down the roads. Most had never seen a tank before.

By Christmas Yamashita had driven a third of the way to his goal. At 11:20 that morning CBS correspondent Cecil Brown began broadcasting another of his frank reports to

America. "This morning I talked with a number of people and it was not in their hearts to say or even think, 'Peace on Earth—Good Will Toward Men.' The Japanese are too near for that, and most people know that this Christmas Singapore is reaping the terrifying fruits of wishful thinking and unpreparedness. . . . On this Christmas, Singapore has the problem of rectifying almost overnight fifty years of a strange kind of administration of the natives, and one year of military apathy. During that year it was a conviction, almost a certainty, of the military, that Japan would not move, that there would be no war in the Far East. And that conviction carried down to three days before war actually came. That's why this is a grim Christmas in Singapore, because the British out here are getting ready for a war with the war going on, and the Japanese holding northwestern Malaya and dominating the skies over it. The tragedy of this Christmas in Singapore is felt on all sides, I've found, because the British have a capacity for dying with such bravery. . . ."

In spite of the situation many British officials and officers were still confident of victory. The Australians, they reasoned, had yet to see battle and would easily hold the line.

The Australian commander, Major General Gordon Bennett, didn't share such optimism. A brusque, red-haired man, Bennett looked more like a soldier than any other general in Malaya. Though he had won the DSC at Gallipoli, he was an accountant by trade. After several trips to the front he was convinced something drastic had to be done to stop Yamashita. "I have seen a total absence of the offensive spirit," he wrote Australian Army Headquarters in Melbourne. He felt only counterattack and immediate air reinforcements could stop the Japanese.

Bennett's worries were passed on to the Australian prime minister, John Curtin. He, in turn, on that Christmas day cabled Roosevelt and Churchill, then attending the Arcadia Conference in Washington. He begged that reinforcements be sent to Singapore before it was too late. Then, fearing that these two leaders were too engrossed in Hitler to realize how grave the Singapore danger was, Curtin also wired his own minister in Washington:

PLEASE UNDERSTAND THAT STAGE OF SUGGESTION HAS PASSED . . . THIS IS THE GRAVEST TYPE OF EMERGENCY AND EVERYTHING WILL DEPEND UPON CHURCHILL-ROOSEVELT DECISION TO MEET IT IN BROADEST WAY.

Roosevelt and Churchill responded by selecting General

Sir Archibald Wavell as supreme commander of the entire Southwest Pacific area. As many planes, tanks and men as could be spared from the bitter fighting in the Middle East were to be sent to Singapore.

Wavell flew to Singapore Island on January 7 for a brief inspection tour. The previous night 15 Japanese tanks had burst through the front lines of the 11th Indian Division and crossed the key Slim River bridge. They were now less than 250 air miles from Singapore itself. The General rushed north by car. Here he found that the entire III Corps was disorganized, the 11th Indian Division completely shattered. He ordered a general withdrawal of nearly 150 miles to Johore Province where Bennett and his Australians would have to make the final stand on the peninsula.

Still shaken by what he had seen on the mainland, Wavell returned to Singapore to inspect the defenses on the north side of the "Fortress Island." He was shocked to find nothing. There weren't even detailed plans for defense against a land attack. He learned to his consternation that almost all the island's great guns faced the sea and couldn't be turned around to fire at the onrushing Japanese. Far from being impregnable, the island of Singapore was almost naked.

2   Six days later, on January 13, a convoy of large American vessels was approaching the harbor. The word spread: Singapore had not been abandoned; substantial help was finally arriving. Then there was a growing roar as a swarm of Japanese planes appeared in the north. Suddenly dark clouds closed in and before the Japanese could sight the oncoming ships, the storm broke. Many regarded it as a miracle. At any rate, reinforcements were soon unloading: the 53rd British Infantry Brigade, the British 6th Heavy and 35th Light Anti-aircraft Regiments, the 85th British Anti-tank Regiment, and 51 Hurricane fighters.

The wave of optimism increased the next day when control of the front passed to the aggressive General Bennett. Unlike Percival, the Australian thought Yamashita could be stopped by strong shifting lines and frequent ambushes. The purely defensive attitude of the British command, he thought, had to be replaced by strong counterattack methods. There were too many brilliant officers in Malaya, he wrote in his diary, too few aggressive fighters. At last Bennett would have the chance to prove his theories. About 120 miles northwest of Singapore, his Australians were hiding in the dense jungle on both sides of Gemencheh Bridge.

At 4:00 that afternoon a column of Japanese approached the bridge on bicycles, five and six abreast. To the hidden Australians they resembled a huge picnic party. After about 250 cyclists crossed the bridge there was a terrific explosion. Timber, bicycles and bodies were hurled in the air. Deadly fire from concealed Bren guns, Tommy guns and rifles swept the road.

The Japanese, caught completely by surprise, didn't have time to unstrap guns from their bicycles. In twenty minutes the 300-yard stretch of road was littered with dead and dying.

News of this first Australian action in Malaya kindled hopes in Singapore, already revived by the recent reinforcements. And the next morning when the Australians knocked out five Japanese tanks and disabled several others, confidence in ultimate victory returned. Singapore Radio declared the tide of battle was turning, "with the A.I.F. as our sea wall against the vicious flood."

But hope of victory was short-lived. On the morning of January 17 the AP correspondent, Yates McDaniel, hearing ominous stories of a disastrous rout, drove up toward the front. Born in China of American missionary parents, he had been the first foreign correspondent to cover the Sino-Japanese war. Many of his fellow newsmen claimed, with good reason, that he knew more about Asia than any other Westerner. He was a slender man of thirty-five; his high forehead, light brown eyes and delicate, almost transparent skin gave him the aesthetic look of a poet or monk. Yet in spite of his fragile appearance and quiet manner, probably no other white man had traveled through as much of the rugged interior of Asia.

Just before noon McDaniel found General Bennett at the edge of a rubber plantation, about to confer with Percival and Brigadier B. W. Key, the new commander of the re-formed 11th Indian Division. The red-haired Australian was critical of continued withdrawals. He told McDaniel that two days previously the inexperienced 45th Indian Brigade guarding the west coast road at Muar had been attacked and quickly overwhelmed. Australian reinforcements had been rushed to the danger point and were now fighting a stubborn but losing action. With the left flank gone, the entire line was endangered. Though it was the time for counterattack, said Bennett, retreat was still the fashion of the day.

Percival now joined the group. To McDaniel he was a gallant, tragic figure, doomed to failure. Then Brigadier Key arrived. The three generals sat on fallen trees. Percival's high-pitched voice was calm. He was tactful and patient. Key said little, but Bennett spoke angrily, insisting on a more aggressive attitude. After an hour, the meeting broke up and the newsman returned with Bennett to the Australian's field headquarters. It was spartan, a small tent with a simple cot.

"We've got to make counterattacks," reiterated Bennett. "We can't worry about a few of our people being cut off in night operations." His gloom deepened when new reports of further infiltrations on the left flank came in.

On the way back to Singapore, McDaniel stopped his jeep and talked to a group of bedraggled British soldiers. One who had come from Shropshire told of being captured the week before and later escaping. That evening McDaniel wrote a feature story of his trip to the front based on the escaped Tommy. "Wandering along the road today," it began, "I came upon a Shropshire lad."

The British censor refused to pass the story. "You can't mention 'Shropshire,' Yates. It identifies the name of the regiment."

"There is no Shropshire regiment in Malaya."

"The name has to come out," insisted the censor.

"But it will kill the point." McDaniel had to explain it was based on one of Housman's famous poems.

The censor remained adamant.

McDaniel wasn't the only newsman suffering from censor trouble. Nine days previously Cecil Brown of CBS had been arbitrarily banned from broadcasting, not for what he had said over the air but for what he had wanted to say.

The steadily deteriorating Malayan battlefront was intensifying the bitterness between Churchill and Australian Prime Minister Curtin. The next day Curtin, in response to a hurt and testy message from Churchill, sent an equally testy reply:

> WE HAVE CONTRIBUTED WHAT WE COULD IN LAND
> AND AIR FORCES AND MATERIAL TO THIS REGION (SINGA-
> PORE) AND CONSISTENTLY PRESSED FOR THE STRENGTH-
> ENING OF THE DEFENCES, BUT THERE HAVE BEEN SUG-
> GESTIONS OF COMPLACENCY WITH THE POSITION WHICH
> HAVE NOT BEEN JUSTIFIED BY THE SPEEDY PROGRESS
> OF THE JAPANESE. . . .
>
> MY OBSERVATIONS ON CRETE AND GREECE IMPLY NO
> CENSURE ON YOU, NOR AM I PASSING JUDGEMENT ON
> ANYONE, BUT THERE IS NO DENYING THE FACT THAT

AIR SUPPORT WAS NOT ON THE SCALE PROMISED. . . . I
HAVE STATED THIS POSITION FRANKLY TO THE AUSTRAL-
IAN PEOPLE BECAUSE I BELIEVE IT IS BETTER THAT
THEY SHOULD KNOW THE FACTS THAN ASSUME THAT ALL
IS WELL AND LATER BE DISILLUSIONED BY THE TRUTH.

NO ONE HAS GREATER ADMIRATION FOR THE MAGNIFI-
CENT EFFORTS OF THE PEOPLE OF THE UNITED KINGDOM
THAN THEIR KINSFOLK IN AUSTRALIA. NEVERTHELESS, WE
MAKE NO APOLOGIES FOR OUR EFFORT, OR EVEN FOR
WHAT YOU ARGUE WE ARE NOT DOING. THE VARIOUS
PARTS OF THE EMPIRE, AS YOU KNOW, ARE DIFFERENTLY
SITUATED, POSSESS VARIOUS RESOURCES, AND HAVE
THEIR OWN PECULIAR PROBLEMS.

In London Churchill had just arrived from the U.S. in a
flying boat and was examining his accumulated messages.
When he read a report from Wavell revealing that Singapore
was defenseless on its northern shore, he was incredulous.
He was also astonished that no measures worth speaking of
to build such defenses had been taken by any of the Singapore commanders since the war began. In fact they had not
even mentioned to him that they didn't exist.

Like so many others he had put his faith in Fortress
Singapore. He blamed himself. He should have known. His
advisers should have known and told him, but he had never
asked about the matter, busy as he was, because the possibility of Singapore having no landward defenses was as ridiculous as launching a battleship without a bottom. There
was no time for recriminations; the neglect had to be instantly repaired. He hastily dictated a note for the chiefs of
staff:

I must admit to being staggered by Wavell's telegram of the
16th. . . . It never occurred to me for a moment . . . that the
gorge of the fortress of Singapore, with its splendid moat half a
mile to a mile wide, was not entirely fortified against an attack
from the northward. What is the use of having an island for a
fortress if it is not to be made into a citadel? . . . How is it
that not one of you pointed this out to me at any time when
these matters have been under discussion? More especially this
should have been done because . . . I have repeatedly shown that
I relied upon this defence of Singapore Island against a formal
siege, and never relied upon the Kra Isthmus plan. . . .

Not only must the defence of Singapore Island be maintained
by every means, but the whole island must be fought for until
every single unit and every single strong point has been sepa-
rately destroyed.

Finally, the city of Singapore must be converted into a citadel and defended to the death. No surrender can be contemplated.

The urgency long felt in Australia had finally reached 10 Downing Street.

Singapore's 2,000,000 citizens were already getting a severe taste of what war was like. One the morning of January 22 the city, battered by two flights of 50 bombers, was digging out hundreds of dead and wounded from the ruins. Even so, morale was still high. Though thousands of leaflets snowed down from Japanese planes saying that "the Japanese forces desire to refrain from seeing the city reduced to ashes," the general spirit of the conglomerate citizenry was expressed by the sign tacked on Government House: THEY CAN'T STOP OUR CLOCK.

The next day Cecil Brown prepared to leave Singapore. As he stepped in the airdrome bus two strangers recognized him.

"When you get out of here," said the first man, an American, "I wish you would give this place the works."

The other man, an Englishman, agreed. "What they did to you is disgraceful. The people of England should know what has happened here."

At the airdrome a censor examined his stories, broadcasts and diary, then said, "I know all about you, Mr. Brown." The correspondent expected his diary would be confiscated, but the censor said under his breath, "I hope you publish the whole story of Singapore. Publish everything about this country." He winked. "Go ahead, close up your suitcase."

Later that day the spirited exchange between Curtin and Churchill burst out again. The Australian representative in London, Sir Earle Page, had chanced to see a note Churchill had written to his chiefs of staff on January 21. In it Churchill wondered whether the docks and batteries of Singapore shouldn't be blown at once and everything concentrated on the defense of Burma and the Burma Road.

We may, by muddling things and hesitating to take an ugly decision, lose both Singapore and the Burma Road. Obviously the decision depends upon how long the defence of Singapore Island can be maintained. If it is only for a few weeks, it is certainly not worth losing all our reinforcements and aircraft.

Page immediately radioed a copy of this note to Curtin. Now the outraged Curtin was radioing Churchill:

PAGE HAS REPORTED THAT THE DEFENCE COMMITTEE
HAS BEEN CONSIDERING THE EVACUATION OF MALAYA AND
SINGAPORE. AFTER ALL THE ASSURANCES WE HAVE BEEN
GIVEN, THE EVACUATION OF SINGAPORE WOULD BE RE-
GARDED HERE AND ELSEWHERE AS AN INEXCUSABLE BE-
TRAYAL.

When Churchill received this message he was faced with a
difficult decision. Although he was morally certain further
reinforcements to Singapore would be a waste, he ordered
the 18th Division to continue to the beleaguered city as
planned. Later he would write, "The effect that would be pro-
duced all over the world, especially in the United States, of
a British 'scuttle' while the Americans fought on so stubbornly at Corregidor was terrible to imagine. There is no
doubt what a purely military decision should have been."

3   By January 23 all hope of holding any part of
the Malay Peninsula was abandoned. At a conference in
Bennett's headquarters Generals Heath and Key said their
men couldn't stand. Bennett insisted his people could hold but
since the rest of the line was buckling, he too felt withdrawal to Singapore was inevitable.

The retreat was uneventful and by midnight of January 31
almost all of Percival's troops had crossed the 70-foot-wide
causeway that connected the peninsula to the island of Singapore.

Bennett watched the troops trudge across for a while,
then retired to his new headquarters in a cottage on the
island. "Our duty now is to recapture Malaya at the earliest
possible opportunity," he wrote in his diary just before retiring. "We owe it to the nation! We owe it to ourselves!"

By dawn, February 1, the Indians who had fought hard
but to little avail had crossed. Then came the Australians and
the Gordons. Finally a skirl of bagpipes could be heard and
to the tune of "A Hundred Pipers" the battered remnants of
the Argyll battalion, a mere 90 men, marched briskly onto
the bridge. Bringing up the rear was their commander,
Brigadier I. MacA. Stewart, the last man off Malaya. It was a
sight that brought tears to many onlookers.

Demolition squads began laying final depth charges on
the causeway. Just after 8:00 A.M. the charges were touched
off. There was a dull roar. After the smoke and din sub-
sided, those on the island could see water rushing through a
70-foot gap. They thought their fortress was cut off from

the onrushing invaders. Few realized the water in the gap was only four feet deep at low tide.

Two strategic islands had already been scenes of conflict —Wake and Hong Kong. Singapore was much larger, ten times the area of Manhattan. It extended 26 miles from east to west, 14 miles from north to south. At the causeway it was 1100 yards to the mainland. On the west coast the distance across the Strait of Johore narrowed to 600 yards.

Most of Singapore's population was crowded in the south and east. The rest of the island was covered with rubber plantations and jungle growth. There were a few hills but the highest was only 481 feet.

Little happened during the first few days of siege except bombings and intermittent Japanese shellings. Then on February 5 Australians defending the west coast of the island heard sounds of hammering and sawing from the mainland. About 15 miles to the east, in the heart of the city, Singapore's citizens were living without panic in spite of increasing bomb casualties. Although Churchill had called for every man and woman to dig defenses with shovels, almost nothing had been done before the troops arrived. Public concrete shelters had not yet been built, although more civilians had already been killed than in Malta's two years of bombing.

General Percival was taking personal charge of the island's defense. He had two choices: to hold at the beaches or to man the coast line thinly, keeping large reserves for a decisive battle on the island. Though the 200-square-mile island had a coast line of more than 70 miles, Percival decided to defend the beaches. He reasoned that dumps were dispersed and some would certainly be lost if the Japanese got a footing on the island. There was also the morale problem. If the Japanese landed the troops and civilians might panic.

On paper the situation looked better than it was. The Japanese would probably attack with 60,000 men. Now that the entire 17th British Division and 44th Indian Brigade had arrived, Wavell had 85,000, but 15,000 were noncombatants and many of the others were raw, untrained and poorly armed. There was another depressing factor. All but a single squadron of the newly arrived Hurricane fighters had been sent to Sumatra because only one of the four airdromes on the island was out of range of Japanese shells.

Artillery fire from the mainland increased the following two days. On February 8 it rose to such a pitch on the west coast that General Bennett feared it might be a barrage

preparatory to a landing. Early that evening he went to bed
in his bungalow in Bukit Timah, a village on heights a few
miles west of the city. He figured it might be his last good
rest for a long time.

His troops had been dismayed when they walked onto the
fortress island. Except for a half-finished tank trap not a
trench had been dug in their swampy area. They were expected to defend more than 20 miles of the northwest coast,
where the strait was narrowest, with about 2500 men.

The barrage increased. Bennett got out of bed and telephoned his duty officer, Major C. B. Dawkins. "Ask 22nd
Brigade Headquarters if it's had any reports from forward
posts. Tell them to switch on their beach-lights." Bennett
went back to bed, but couldn't sleep. By now the enemy
bombardment was as rapid as drumfire. Again he got up.
Just before 10:30 P.M. he drove to his operations room.

Japanese barges, pontoons, and collapsible boats were at
that moment nearing the northwest coast of Singapore. About
15,000 infantrymen were preparing to hit the beaches defended by Bennett's 2500 men.

Now mortars, set at a fixed elevation on the Japanese
barges, erupted. Their shells fell in front of the oncoming
flotilla. As the barges drew closer, the barrage crept up,
laying a screen of smoke. At 10:30 P.M. the first wave hit
the beach at the end of Lim Chu Kang Road. Australians of
the 24th Machine Gun Battalion sprayed the invaders, setting an ammunition barge afire. In the blazing light several
barges and boats were sunk. Other landing craft beached on a
nearby mangrove swamp area which was lightly defended.

The Australians fought hard all that night but they were
unable to hold back the invaders. In the early morning hours
scores of tanks landed and strong infantry-tank teams
moved inshore. It reminded the Australians of fighting a bush
fire in their own country, with flames encircling those who
tried to put them out. By dawn, February 9, Yamashita
had a firm foothold on the west section of the island, and
was pushing aggressively toward the city of Singapore itself, only 10 air miles to the southeast.

The next day General Wavell flew from his headquarters
in Java and broke through the Japanese air screen around
Singapore. By now the situation was chaotic because of a
series of errors of judgment. Someone had thoughtlessly issued Percival's secret and personal perimeter defense plan
to all the field commanders. Many of these men, exhausted
and distracted by the desperate fighting, were eager to as-

sume the plan was an order to retreat and began falling back to the last-ditch perimeter positions.

Rumors were already spreading of angry scenes at head-quarters: Wavell had severely criticized Percival because the Japanese had been allowed to land; then the ABDA (American, British, Dutch, Australian) chief had become so fed up with Bennett's comments that he told the Australian to "Get the hell out" and take his "bloody Aussies" with him.

It was certainly no rumor that all was not harmonious. When Wavell learned later that morning that many commanders were falling back to the perimeter he ordered a counter-attack which promptly failed. He also issued a Churchill-inspired order of the day:

It is certain that our troops on Singapore Island greatly out-number any Japanese that have crossed the Straits. We must defeat them. Our whole fighting reputation is at stake and the honor of the British Empire. The Americans have held out on the Bataan Peninsula against far greater odds, the Russians are turning back the picked strength of the Germans, the Chinese with almost complete lack of modern equipment have held the Japanese for 4½ years. It will be disgraceful if we yield our boasted fortress of Singapore to inferior enemy forces.

There must be no thought of sparing troops or the civil population and no mercy must be shown to weakness in any shape or form. Commanders and senior officers must lead their troops and if necessary die with them.

There must be no question or thought of surrender. Every unit must fight it out to the end and in close contact with the enemy. . . . I look to you and your men to fight to the end to prove that the fighting spirit that won our Empire still exists to enable us to defend it.

By the following dawn, February 11, Yamashita's men held almost half the island. At 6:00 A.M. Percival was wakened by the chatter of machine guns. The general got up and learned that the Japanese were advancing down Bukit Timah Road and were nearing the Racecourse, about seven minutes by car from the Raffles Hotel.

The general drove up Bukit Timah Road to see what was happening. It was a strange sensation. The sky was covered by the pall of many fires. The great road, usually jammed with traffic, was deserted. Above, Japanese planes hovered, unopposed except for anti-aircraft, looking for targets. He felt naked in the only car driving up the wide road. "Why," he asked himself, "does Britain, our improvident Britain, with all her great resources, allow her sons to fight without air support?"

Later that morning—the anniversary of Japan's greatest patriotic festival, the Foundation of the Empire—planes dropped twenty-nine wooden boxes each about 18 inches long. Each contained a message from Yamashita addressed "To the High Command of the British Army, Singapore," and read:

My sincere respect is due to your army which, true to the traditional spirit of Great Britain, is bravely defending Singapore which now stands isolated and unaided. . . . But the development of the general war situation has already sealed the fate of Singapore, and the continuation of futile resistance would only serve to inflict direct harm and injuries to thousands of non-combatants living in the city, throwing them into further miseries and horrors of war, but also would add nothing to the honor of your army.

Still remembering Wavell's final orders to "fight to the end," Percival did not even send Yamashita a reply.

In spite of planes overhead and shells bursting nearby, civilians walked the streets and queued up outside the cinema in the Cathay skyscraper to see *The Philadelphia Story*. They ignored leaflets fluttering down marked EXTRA saying Roosevelt had just negotiated a separate peace with Japan and had asked the Japanese to declare Singapore a neutral city. Riller's Band still played at the Adelphi Hotel. The Raffles Hotel was jammed with staff officers with nothing to do but sit, drink and carp.

The *Straits Times,* now a one-page newspaper, still pretended there was hope. On the top of each issue was blazoned: "Singapore Must Stand; It SHALL stand—H. E. the Governor." But it was obvious those in command knew the end was near when they ordered 1,500,000 bottles of wine and liquor and 60,000 gallons of samsu, Chinese spirits, destroyed.

Yates McDaniel was amazed at the calmness of the civilians in the face of the deepening rumble of guns. He was now the only foreign correspondent left in the city. His wife had sailed with the others but it had always been his rule to stay as long as communications held out. He passed a wall scrawled in chalk, ENGLAND FOR THE ENGLISH, AUSTRALIA FOR THE AUSTRALIANS, BUT MALAYA FOR ANY SON OF A BITCH WHO WANTS IT. Some Aussie, obviously, was expressing his opinion of the whole campaign.

A little later McDaniel wrote what he thought might be his last story. As he walked toward the Cathay Building to file it, he saw many Europeans, military and civilian, hurrying toward the dock area. They were escaping on a fleet of small coast boats just collected. For a moment he felt impelled to join them, then decided to stay longer. The Singapore story was still alive.

At the Cathay Building he found the British censor packing. "How can I do my job without a censor?" protested McDaniel.

The censor cursed him in a friendly way, but hastily stamped CLEARED BY CENSOR on several blanks. "Write anything you want. Send anything you want. I'm leaving."

McDaniel began to write: "This will probably be my last message from this crumbling fortress. . . ."

4 The next morning the battle increased in ferocity. By 8:00 A.M. Yamashita's tanks were racing down Bukit Timah Road past the Racecourse. In half an hour they reached the Chinese High School on Singapore's outskirts, less than three miles from the city limits. Here they were finally stopped by mixed British and Australians armed only with rifles.

Hearing of the new threat, Percival again drove up to the front to see if this breakthrough was dangerous. One look convinced him to order the Indians and British guarding the northern and eastern shores to fall back and form a tight defensive arc in front of the threatened city.

In his room at the Cathay Building, Yates McDaniel of AP was just finishing a story:

The sky over Singapore is black with smoke from a dozen huge fires this morning as I write my last message from this once beautiful, prosperous and peaceful city. The roar and crash of cannonade and bursting bombs which are shaking my typewriter, and my hands which are wet with the perspiration of fright, tell me without need of an official communiqué that the war which started nine weeks ago 400 miles away is now in the outskirts of this shaken bastion of Empire.

I am sure a bright tropic sun is somewhere overhead, but in my many-windowed room it is too dark to work without electric lights.

Under the low rise where the battle is ranging I see relay after relay of Japanese planes circling, then going into murderous dives on our soldiers, who are fighting back in the hell over which there is no screen of our own fighter planes. But the Japanese are not completely alone in the skies. I just saw two Vildebeestes —obsolete biplanes operating at 100 miles an hour—fly low over the Japanese positions and unload their bombs with a resounding crash. It makes me ashamed, sitting here with my heart beating

faster than their old motors, when I think of the chance those
lads have of getting back. If ever brave men earned undying
glory, those R.A.F. pilots have this tragic morning.

There are many other brave men in Singapore today. Not far
away are A.A. batteries. They are in open spaces because they
must have a clear field of fire. (Please pardon the break in con-
tinuity, but a packet of bombs just landed so close that I ducked
behind the wall, which I hoped would, and did, screen the blast.)
But those gun crews keep on fighting and peppering the smoke-
limited ceiling every time Japanese planes come near, which is
almost constantly.

The all-clear has just sounded—a grand joke, because from my
window I can see three Japanese planes hedge-hopping under a
mile away. I heard a few minutes ago a tragic telephone conversation. Eric Davis, director of the Malayan Broadcasting Cor-
poration, urged Sir Shenton Thomas, Governor, for permission
to destroy the outlying broadcasting station. Sir Shenton de-
murred, saying the situation was not too bad. Davis telephoned
the outlying station and instructed the staff to keep on the air,
but to stand by for an urgent order. We tuned in to that station, and then, in the middle of a broadcast in the Malayan language, urging Singapore people to stand firm, the station went
dead.

McDaniel hurried out of the Cathay Building to file the story
at the cable office. He noted a new spirit in the great city.
British, Chinese and Malayans were working side by side pull-
ing out the wounded and dead from destroyed buildings.
All races were flooding to hospitals to donate blood. Those
British remaining were now doing the unthinkable: their
villas were freely opened as places of refuge to all comers.
Democracy had finally come to Singapore.

It was grimly amusing to hear some of his British friends
at the Singapore Club and the Cricket Club who had gloomily predicted that the Asiatics of the city would panic and
betray them to the Japanese, now praise "their boys" as
loyal and brave. The stubborn fighting of hastily organized
Asiatic defense teams like Dalforce—a motley but formidable crew of Chinese college boys, rickshaw coolies, loyalists
and Communists under the command of J. D. Dalley, a
policeman—was proving what a costly mistake British officials had made in not arming such native groups months
ago.

Black clouds of smoke drifted from the north; the rumble
of big guns was louder; shells were falling closer to the
center of the city. As McDaniel hurried past the white granite
buildings of the city, shored up with sandbags, he saw a de-

jected battalion of Indians sitting in front of their tents in a public park. It shook him.

At the cable office he soon convinced the operator to send his story as an "official dispatch." As he came out, a Chinese girl of nineteen handed him a note. It was from his good friend Wong Hai Sheng, better known as "Newsreel" Wong, the most famous movie cameraman in the Orient, whose picture of a crying baby amidst the wreckage of Shanghai's railroad station had already become a classic. The girl was Wong's niece, Doris Lim. She had been refused passage on the ship that had evacuated "Newsreel" and other newsmen.

McDaniel assured the frightened girl he would get her safely out of Singapore. How was another question. The last convoy of refugees was due to leave any moment. The two hurried to the dock area. It was a hectic scene as 3000 civilians and military crowded aboard the fleet of pitifully ancient boats collected by Sir Robert Scott, head of the British Ministry of Information, Far East Section. Whenever a plane swooped down everyone froze, for almost anything in the air was Japanese.

Deserters from the front were beginning to sneak to the docks, hoping by persuasion, bribe or force to get a passage to safety. The tension was becoming intolerable. These few boats seemed to represent the only escape.

As McDaniel was photographing the scene, Captain Henry Steel, an information officer, told him about an empty craft, the 1700-ton steamer *Kung Wo* from the Yangtse River, which had been serving as a Navy mine layer. McDaniel, Steel and the girl searched the water front and finally located the old coal-burning vessel anchored about one mile off shore. The skipper, a reserve officer, was Scotch and stubborn. Though he promised to take the three when he sailed he refused to leave without definite orders. Another problem was coal. He had only enough for 10 miles.

McDaniel persuaded the Scotsman to steam to a nearby wharf piled high with coal. At the wharf McDaniel, Steel and some officers and men from the *Repulse* and the *Prince of Wales* began stoking coal by hand. The steamer's crew—a strange mixture of soldiers, sailors, Chinese from the Yangtse, and petty officials—was finally urged to help by the increasing roar of battle.

After the coal was loaded McDaniel volunteered to return to the city, learn the military situation and get a technical excuse for the Scotch skipper to leave. Transportation was no problem. The docks were jammed with brand-new cars and tanks. He found a Ford with gas and, accompanied by Doris

Lim, who wanted to pick up her belongings, he drove to the Cathay Building.

Here he learned the defense perimeter was fast shrinking. It was only a matter of hours before the Japanese would break through. Finally he located Vice Admiral E. J. Spooner, in command of all naval forces. The admiral was burning files in preparation for flight that evening in a patrol boat. McDaniel hurried to his own room and grabbed a pack containing two bottles of German Rhine wine, two cameras, a pair of German binoculars, a few biscuits and four tins of Camels. Then he decided to add a paragraph to his last story. Hurriedly he typed:

We have less than fifty per cent chance of getting clear. I am leaving now by car. I swear before I embark to put the car in gear and head it straight for the Straits of Malacca. Do not expect to hear from me for many days, but please inform my wife, Mrs. McDaniel, Hotel Preanger, Bandung, Java, that I have left this land of the living, and the dying.

A few minutes later he and Doris Lim were racing along rubble-strewn streets, littered with unburied dead, to the cable office. Here he filed his final message. As they drove to the docks in the fading light, there was a deep rumble. An ammunition dump, McDaniel guessed, had been blown up. Ominous, black clouds were rising from the fuel dumps on the off-coast islands. McDaniel stopped the car, took several pictures.

As McDaniel and the girl reached the docks, Japanese light bombers began to bomb and strafe everything that moved. Sir Robert Scott's last convoy of refugees was just beginning to move out. It abruptly stopped, hoping for protection from a nearby anti-aircraft battery. At the docks McDaniel explained the situation to Steel and the other officers. They decided first to try and destroy the rows of tanks and cars but a sudden burst of fire from the Kallang airfield less than a mile away discouraged the plan. The breakthrough might come at any moment.

At sunset the Japanese planes left and the Scott convoy slowly headed out of the harbor. The captain of the *Kung Wo* refused to follow since McDaniel had not brought back definite orders to sail.

"But Admiral Spooner is leaving," argued McDaniel. The Scotsman shook his head. He was going to wait for orders. "How can you possibly get orders," said McDaniel, "when there's no one left to give them?"

The captain, unconvinced, insisted on waiting. A few minutes later they could hear the individual cracks of rifles.

At 11:00 P.M. the *Kung Wo* was still anchored, in spite of arguments by McDaniel and Steel and almost hysterical threats by some of the crew. The Scotch captain was stolidly signalling shore with blinkers. A few minutes after 11:00 P.M. an answer finally came: THE COMMODORE OF MALAYA HAS LEFT.

Even with this confirmation of McDaniel's story, the captain was uncertain. He hated to leave without something more definite. After almost an hour of self-debate he reluctantly sounded bells. It was midnight when the old copper-lined steamer slowly headed toward the mine fields.

The ship headed south, threading its way through heavy mine fields and the small islands that hung down from Singapore for more than 100 miles like a string of beads. By dawn, Friday, the thirteenth, the *Kung Wo* was midway through this "1000 Island" chain.

Even the early sun was sweltering, enervating; in another 25 miles they would cross the equator. There were excited shouts. About 30 miles to their right, the west, the green hilly coast of Sumatra had been sighted. This was the first of a group of Dutch-owned long, thin islands, almost nose to nose, that formed a great barrier of about 3000 miles between the Japanese and Australia. The central and most strategic island in this lengthy barrier was McDaniel's goal: Java.

Soon they could hear the roar of approaching Japanese planes, dispatched to sink the final flotilla of ships, launches and boats fleeing from Singapore. The skipper of the *Kung Wo* quickly turned away from Sumatra toward the shelter of one of the "1000 Islands." The little ship zigzagged at top speed, 10 knots, narrowly avoiding falling bombs. Finally one hit the engine room. Another exploded between the bridge and midships. The old ship heeled over and began to list dangerously to starboard as flames leaped up from the engine room. McDaniel saw the one seaworthy lifeboat being lowered over the starboard side. Contrary to British tradition, it was filled with twenty-five crew members. McDaniel alerted a bearded *Prince of Wales* officer.

"By whose orders are you leaving this ship?" shouted the officer.

"The hell with you, sonny boy," shouted a man in the boat. Others gave catcalls.

"I order you to stay aboard."

The lifeboat hit the water clumsily. The crew cut loose,

completely fouling the lines of the pulley system, and rowed off.

The second lifeboat was hastily caulked. Then Doris Lim and all the passengers except McDaniel boarded and, with a junior officer in charge, it headed for a small island seven miles away. It was to return as soon as possible. The third lifeboat, even more rickety, was lowered and promptly sank. Life rafts were tossed over. They disintegrated at once. More planes swept over. One by one they descended, looked over the crippled ship and then, without wasting a bomb or bullet, proceeded to a better target. The afternoon hours passed slowly but still the lifeboat didn't return. Only the copper-lined bottom was holding up the *Kung Wo*.

At 5:00 P.M. McDaniel sighted the approaching lifeboat and suggested to the three officers who had remained that they celebrate. They found four crystal goblets and toasted each other, the British Empire, Singapore and finally the good ship *Kung Wo* with McDaniel's two bottles of *Liebfraumilch*. All agreed that nothing had ever tasted better even though the wine had been heated by the equatorial sun to more than 90 degrees.

They didn't reach the small island until 7:00 P.M. As they waded ashore, the first lifeboat approached. The twenty-five crew members were blistered and almost raving from the heat. They had thought to take along food and liquor, but no water. They were greeted with absolute silence.

It was a night of tension on the malaria-infested island. A minor British official sleeping on the sand next to McDaniel and Doris Lim kept trying to steal the pooled food. He stopped only when threatened with shooting. He then turned his attention to the girl. Again McDaniel and Captain Steel had to threaten shooting.

The next morning, February 14, was hazy and muggy with an ominous heavy mist hanging over the sea. They heard the familiar roar of Japanese bombers. Then through the overcast they saw bombs falling on the smoldering *Kung Wo*. After two direct hits the old ship turned over and sank. The Scotch captain buried head in hands and wept. A moment later someone noticed a patrol launch approaching. The officers held a whispered conference. The Scotch captain said, "If it's Jap and they hail us, I'm surrendering."

McDaniel and Steel asked if they could hide. The Scotsman gave them permission and while the other 130, including Doris Lim, prepared for surrender, McDaniel and Steel crawled into the brush. They peered down at the beach as the launch grew bigger.

Two formations of Japanese bombers flew over McDaniel's little island, completely ignoring the scattered refugee ships below. They kept heading south, soon reaching the coast of Sumatra. The Japanese were not waiting for the fall of Singapore to continue to their next destination on the master schedule of conquest. At a point about 150 miles south of McDaniel these planes debouched 360 picked paratroopers. They drifted down to Palembang, one of the most important oil refinery centers in the Southwest Pacific.

The combined Dutch-British force defending Palembang fought bitterly and by midafternoon it looked as if the paratroopers might be wiped out, but Japanese reinforcements were only 100 miles north of Sumatra in eight transports.

Covering these invasion transports was the 7th Cruiser Squadron of Vice Admiral Ozawa. It was just sighting the remnants of the flotilla fleeing south from Singapore. Five cruisers began to finish the job on the refugees started by the bombers. By dusk more than 20 crowded ships had been sunk with heavy loss of life.

5 In the meantime, Singapore was nearing its end. The day before, on Friday the thirteenth, at a morning conference, Percival's commanders had unanimously agreed that further resistance was hopeless. Even the newly arrived British 18th Division was "Done," according to its commander. Ammunition was rapidly disappearing. The troops were falling back on every front. Morale was low. It was sadly decided to send a message to Wavell in Java urging him to agree to an immediate surrender.

By the next morning, February 14, all of the city was within artillery range of the Japanese. Gangs of armed deserters—mostly from administrative units—wandered the streets, their shirts stuffed with cigarettes and tinned food.

The suffering of civilians was almost intolerable. The green lawns of the Singa General Hospital were now pocked by graves. Inside, the stink of blood and entrails was nauseating. The dead and dying were on beds, under beds, between beds, in the corridors. The operating theatres were butcher shops; doctors and nurses were bathed in blood. Since water was short, instruments were sterilized in dirty water. Nurses had to wash their hands in bottled mineral water.

Percival had just received an answer from Wavell.

YOU MUST CONTINUE TO INFLICT MAXIMUM DAMAGE
ON ENEMY FOR AS LONG AS POSSIBLE BY HOUSE-TO-HOUSE

FIGHTING IF NECESSARY. YOUR ACTION IN TYING DOWN
ENEMY AND INFLICTING CASUALTIES MAY HAVE VITAL IN-
FLUENCE IN OTHER THEATRES. FULLY APPRECIATE YOUR
SITUATION, BUT CONTINUED ACTION ESSENTIAL.

Knowing the situation was hopeless, Percival again radioed Wavell, telling him of the desperate water situation.
The answer was soon received:

YOUR GALLANT STAND IS SERVING A PURPOSE AND MUST
BE CONTINUED TO THE LIMIT OF ENDURANCE.

Surprisingly, some of Yamashita's staff had become so impressed by the accurate British artillery that they were advising their general it was hopeless to keep attacking: there
should be a withdrawal to a safer position. Yamashita
listened, then ordered the assault quickened.

The next morning, February 15, Percival learned that
the entire water system had broken down, with most of
the scanty supply running to waste because of constant pipe
breakage. After attending a Communion service at Fort
Canning, he called a conference of his area commanders at
11:00 A.M.

Percival told them there was almost no petrol, field gun or
Bofors anti-aircraft gun ammunition. Water wouldn't last
much more than twenty-four hours. There were only two
choices: attack and regain the reservoirs or surrender.
Each of his commanders said a counterattack was out of
the question.

It was time for Percival to make the hardest, most momentous decision of his life. He made it quickly. He said
he would ask the Japanese to cease fire at 4:00 P.M. and send
a deputation into the city to discuss terms of surrender.

Now he was handed a message from Wavell.

SO LONG AS YOU ARE IN POSITION TO INFLICT LOSSES TO
ENEMY AND YOUR TROOPS ARE PHYSICALLY CAPABLE OF
DOING SO YOU MUST FIGHT ON. TIME GAINED AND DAM-
AGE TO THE ENEMY OF VITAL IMPORTANCE AT THIS CRISIS.

WHEN YOU ARE FULLY SATISFIED THAT THIS IS NO
LONGER POSSIBLE I GIVE YOU DISCRETION TO CEASE RESIST-
ANCE. BEFORE DOING SO ALL ARMS, EQUIPMENT AND TRANS-
PORT OF VALUE TO ENEMY MUST OF COURSE BE RENDERED
USELESS. ALSO JUST BEFORE FINAL CESSATION OF FIGHT-
ING OPPORTUNITY SHOULD BE GIVEN TO ANY DETERMINED
BODIES OF MEN OR INDIVIDUALS TO TRY AND EFFECT ES-

CAPE BY ANY MEANS POSSIBLE. THEY MUST BE ARMED. IN-
FORM ME OF INTENTIONS. WHATEVER HAPPENS I THANK
YOU AND ALL TROOPS FOR YOUR GALLANT EFFORTS OF
LAST FEW DAYS.

Relieved to get official approval, Percival sent a surrender
party up the Bukit Timah Road toward the lines of the Japanese 5th Division. Then he dispatched his last message, a
telegram to Wavell:

OWING TO LOSSES FROM ENEMY ACTION, WATER,
PETROL, FOOD, AMMUNITION PRACTICALLY FINISHED. UN-
ABLE THEREFORE TO CONTINUE THE FIGHT ANY LONGER.
ALL RANKS HAVE DONE THEIR BEST AND ARE GRATEFUL FOR
YOUR HELP.

Yamashita and his chief of staff, Lieutenant General
Suzuki, were watching the battle from the heights near
Bukit Timah. Suzuki pointed out a Union Jack fluttering in
the breeze atop Fort Canning. It would take a week of hard
fighting to capture that hill, he said. Behind Singapore was a
small fortified island. To the left was Fort Changi. To seize
them would be no simple matter. All in all it would
take many days to break through the last defense line.

Just then a front-line commander telephoned that the
British were sending a flag of truce.

Lieutenant Colonel Ichiji Sugita, who had written the
surrender message of February 11, drove forward and met
the British surrender team. "We will have truce," he said
in Japanese, "if the British Army agrees to surrender. Do
you wish to surrender?"

Captain Cyril H. D. Wild, the British interpreter, was tall,
blue-eyed, the son of the Bishop of Newcastle. He said, "We
do."

Sugita told Wild to bring Percival and his staff to the
same place for a meeting with General Yamashita. The British
agreed, returning to their lines.

At about 4:45 P.M. Sugita again drove to the front lines.
Here he met Percival, Wild and several other British officers.
In two cars the party proceeded toward the Ford factory
just north of Bukit Timah village. Sugita sat next to Percival
and introduced himself in broken English. "We fought for
two months. Now we're coming to the end. I compliment
you on the British stand."

Percival said little. These were probably the most bitter

moments in his life. In faraway England his daughter, Margery, was celebrating her twelfth birthday.

At the factory the surrender party dismounted from the two cars. With Percival carrying a white flag, the group entered the new Japanese headquarters. A few minutes later Yamashita arrived.

"We have just received your reply," said Yamashita in Japanese. "The Japanese Army will consider nothing but surrender."

A Japanese, formerly a university professor, interpreted falteringly in his poor English. Colonel Sugita and Captain Wild, both of whom had picked up some of the other's language, also tried to help.

"I fear we shall not be able to submit our final reply before 10:30 P.M.," said Percival. His thin face was red, his eyes bloodshot.

Yamashita, annoyed, raised his voice. "Reply to us only whether our terms are acceptable to you or not. Things have to be done swiftly. We're ready to resume firing."

The vague, disjointed discussion continued with Sugita now acting as interpreter. Partially because of Sugita's imperfect English and Wild's poor command of Japanese, and partially because of Percival's natural reluctance, no agreement could be reached. To Sugita, the whole scene, though tense and critical, was somewhat comical.

Finally Yamashita said impatiently, "Unless you do surrender, we will have to carry out our night attack as scheduled."

When Wild translated this a look of amazement came over Percival. "Cannot the Japanese Army remain in its present position? We can resume negotiations again tomorrow at 5:30 A.M."

"What!" Yamashita again raised his voice. "I want the hostilities to cease tonight and I want to remind you that the question is strictly a matter of this."

"We shall discontinue firing by 8:30 P.M.," said Percival almost in a mumble. "Had we better remain in our present positions tonight?"

Yamashita told him to keep his troops in their positions. All firing would cease at 8:30 P.M. Then the British would disarm all but 1000 men to keep order in the city. "You have agreed to the terms," continued Yamashita, still annoyed by Percival's vagueness, "but you have not yet made yourself clear as to whether you have agreed to surrender or not."

Percival cleared his throat and nodded.

"If you've accepted our terms," said the exasperated Yamashita, "we want to hear 'yes' or 'no' from you! Surrender or fight!"

"Yes," said Percival faintly. "I agree." Then he added, "I have a request to make. Will the Imperial Army protect the women and children and British civilians?"

"We shall see to it. Please sign this truce agreement."

At exactly 7:50 P.M., after fifty nerve-racking minutes, Percival signed.

Both generals left the factory. The two exhausted interpreters remained to iron out the details. Before they started work Sugita gave Captain Wild, with whom he now felt a friendly bond, two packages of food.

As agreed, that night at 8:30 the roar of battle abruptly ceased. The sudden silence was strange, uncanny. Singapore —the City of the Lion—was dead. At St. Andrews Cathedral wounded were lying in the nave and the aisles. Doctors and orderlies moved about their work murmuring softly. When the Right Reverend John Leonard Wilson, Bishop of Singapore, heard of the surrender he led a short service. In conclusion a medical corps major played the organ while everyone sang "Praise My Soul, the King of Heaven."

The Battle of Singapore was over, the most publicized fortress in the world captured. It was the worst disaster and largest capitulation in British history. In seventy days Yamashita, at the cost of 9824 battle casualties, had punched down the Malay Peninsula 650 miles. The British had lost 138,708, including more than 130,000 prisoners. They had also lost an empire.

That night the waters below Singapore were dotted with launches, patrol boats and assorted small craft carrying off several thousand last-minute escapees, including General Gordon Bennett, Brigadier Paris of the 12th Indian Brigade and V. G. Bowden, the Australian Government representative. Farther south the remnants of Scott's convoy were desperately making for the north coast of Sumatra or hiding in the "1000 Islands." Already the majority were captured or dead.

The 132 from the *Kung Wo* were still alive, still uncaptured. The patrol launch had not been Japanese, but a cabin cruiser piloted by a Scotch planter. He had promised to send a rescue boat to the little island the following night if possible.

Now on the night of February 15 McDaniel and the others were anxiously waiting. Finally just before 10:00 P.M. the newsman saw a flashlight signal—two long, two short. It seemed to be about a mile away.

"Can you swim?" he asked Doris Lim. She couldn't, but with the help of McDaniel and Steel, she thought she could make it. These three and less than 60 others began wading toward the signal over the sharp coral. After three hours of wading and swimming McDaniel and his two companions and about half of those who'd risked the trip finally reached a dingy ferry launch and were hoisted aboard, completely exhausted. The Malayan skipper waited another half-hour for laggards, then headed southwest.

About three hours later they crossed the equator. At sunrise the little launch approached the lush green hills of the northern coast of Sumatra. When the skipper found the mouth of a river, the Indragiri, he headed inland to the southwest. He told McDaniel that the Japanese had landed on both ends of the long island. There was only one way to escape: cross to the southern side. They would have to go up river as far as possible by launch, then travel by foot, oxcart or car the rest of the way across Sumatra to Padang on the southern coast. Here they might be lucky enough to get passage on a ship going to Ceylon or Java.

McDaniel hoped it would be Java. His wife was there, waiting for him.

That morning the Japanese were triumphant. The leading paper, *Asahi Shimbun*, headlined its story of Singapore: GENERAL SITUATION OF PACIFIC WAR DECIDED.

In an interview Colonel Hideo Ohira, chief of the Press Division, Imperial Headquarters, said, "To seize Singapore Island in as little time as three days was only possible with our Imperial Army. Japan is the sun that shines for the world peace. Those who bathe in the sun will grow and those who resist it shall have no alternative but go to ruin. Both the United States and Britain should contemplate the 3000 years of scorching Japanese history.

"I solemnly declare that with the fall of Singapore the general situation of war has been determined. The ultimate victory will be in our hands."

Singapore was given a new name, Shonan, "Bright South."

1   Yates McDaniel watched the dark shore line slip by rapidly on his left. It was almost dawn of February 19 and this was the southern coast of Sumatra. By a series of chances verging on the miraculous, Doris Lim and McDaniel were aboard a British destroyer speeding east toward Java. They had crossed Sumatra by cart, bus and car to Padang. Following a tip in a local bar, they had ridden a trolley car to the nearby port of Emmahaven and boarded the destroyer the previous afternoon. Now they would hug the coast until late dusk; then turn left, north, and try to break through the dangerously narrow strait between Sumatra and Java under cover of darkness. Their goal was Batavia, the Javan capital which lay on the north side of that slender 800-mile-long island.

More than half of the other escapees from Singapore were already dead or captured. V. G. Bowen, the elderly Australian Government representative, was captured, made to dig his own grave and shot; Admiral Spooner, formerly commodore of Malaya, and Air Vice-Marshal Pulford were shipwrecked and dying on a malaria-infested little island with sixteen others. Many had reached Padang, like McDaniel, only to be sunk en route to Ceylon or Java.

McDaniel was cheered by stories of the entirely different attitude in Java. Everyone in Sumatra had talked of the stubborn Dutch defense of their Indies empire. It was refreshing to hear of people who still believed the Japanese could be beaten, but there were also rumors of difficulties between the Dutch and the U.S. Asiatic Fleet. The Dutch admiral, Helfrich, wanted to fight but the American admiral, Hart, thought resistance was suicidal.

McDaniel was coming to another crumbling empire.

General Sir Archibald Wavell was in a gloomy mood at his headquarters in Bandung, 80 air miles from Batavia, high in the mountains of central Java. The ABDA commander had been told by Churchill and Roosevelt to defend the Malay Barrier. This was fast becoming a barrier in name only. The left flank, Singapore, had collapsed. The center, Java, was being deftly set up by the Japanese for a knockout blow.

Java was already isolated. To its west, Sumatra was being swallowed up by paratroopers and a recently landed convoy. A few miles to its east, another advance invasion convoy had just anchored off the exotic island of Bali. And Wavell had no doubt that large invasion convoys were already heading for Java itself. He was still in pain and somewhat crippled from a recent accident. Returning to Java on February 10 from his last Singapore trip he had fallen from a quay in the dark and broken two small bones in his back.

The steadily worsening relations between the Dutch and the U.S. Navy hadn't improved his mood. He could see both sides. He admired Hart, a thin, wiry, elderly man who was calm and cool, reserved and frugal in words. Wavell also had great admiration for the outspoken and stubborn Helfrich, a short, rotund, balding man of intense energy. But since the Dutch admiral was determined to fight the Japanese before they landed on Java, Wavell supported Helfrich. Then, too, the Briton could never forget the ready and willing help the Dutch had given him in the defense of Singapore. Without hesitation they had weakened their own small forces to send submarines, planes and men to Malay.

Fortunately the understandable conflict between Hart and Helfrich was soon over. After much behind-the-scenes maneuvering in Washington President Roosevelt had been apparently convinced that the sixty-four-year-old Hart was too tired and unaggressive to command the ABDA Navy. Five days previously it had been officially announced that Hart had requested relief because of ill health. Helfrich was given the job and Hart was already on his way home.

At his quarters nearby, Vice-Admiral Conrad E. L. Helfrich still believed the Japanese could be beaten, but not by running away. Like Wavell, he admired Hart. What really had alarmed the Dutchman was Hart's assumption that the defense of the Dutch East Indies was already a lost cause. Helfrich's own little fleet had proved the Japanese could be hurt. His handful of submarines alone had already sunk more tonnage than the combined U.S. air, surface and underwater forces.

Helfrich had been told the unimpressive American record was due in large part to explicit instructions to fight warily. In his opinion U.S. cruisers and destroyers had been sent too far south to fight the enemy properly. It wasn't until January 24, after much needling by Helfrich, that the American surface ships made their first attack. The heartening results of that raid in Makassar Strait—three transports sunk in a brilliant and daring raid by four U.S. destroyers—only proved his point. The Jap could be beaten. And the place to do it was not on the beaches of Java but in the waters to the north.

    2 Japanese naval officers were just as amazed as Helfrich at their almost totally unopposed parade south past the Philippines. Except for stubborn but minor Dutch and Australian resistance they presently held all Borneo, the Celebes, and had strong footholds in Sumatra and New Britain.

The main goal in the Southwest Pacific was Java. Its fall would mean the end of the Indies campaign. Conquest had to come like lightning before the vast oil, tin and tungsten resources could be destroyed by the Dutch. Without the oil of the Indies the entire war machine could run dry.

Two great invasion convoys were converging on Java from both sides. The previous day the Western Force had left Indo-China in 56 transports, their destination the west end of Java. The Eastern Force—40 transports carrying the outfit taken from General Homma, the 48th Division—was just leaving the southern Philippines for east Java. The two forces, each protected by powerful cruiser and destroyer units, were due to land February 27.

Helfrich was willing to do anything to stop, or even delay, the invasion of Java. Half of his four-nation fleet, under his countryman, Rear Admiral Karel W. F. M. Doorman, was now steaming east along the southern coast of Java toward Bali. Helfrich had just learned of the Japanese landing on this famous island and was determined to try and wipe out the beachhead. If the Japanese could hold Bali, it would be a great step toward the conquest of Java. About the same size as Singapore Island, it was separated from the eastern end of Java by the narrow Bali Strait. There was an even more important channel on the other side of Bali. This was Lombok Strait, wide and deep, the main gate through the barrier of islands that lay between the Japanese and Australia.

For many centuries pirates had plundered these strategic waters. This "Strait of the Red Peppers" divided the two continents. Bali on the west was pure Asian. Lombok, only 25 miles to the east, had different trees and plant growth, different birds and animals. The skull-shaped island was a strange, transitional spot where Australian forms of life were already replacing the Asiatic.

By late afternoon Helfrich knew that if the vital Bali beachhead was to be wiped out, Doorman's force would have to do it that night. Java-based American bombers had made eighteen sorties on Bali that day, but only negligible damage had been done to the 2 Japanese transports and their 4 escorting destroyers.

Helfrich and Doorman drew up a hasty, simple plan. Since every minute was vital, they figured there wasn't time to concentrate forces. The attack would have to be made in three waves. First 2 light cruisers and 3 destroyers would turn north, darting through Lombok Strait in a hit-and-run assault; then would come a light cruiser and 4 destroyers; and finally, to mop up anything still afloat, 5 torpedo boats.

It was deep dusk when the British destroyer carrying Yates McDaniel and other refugees from Singapore rounded the east end of Sumatra and began its dangerous dash north through the narrow channel between the two islands, Sunda Strait.

As it grew dark, tension rose. Just before 10:00 P.M. McDaniel saw a dramatic cone rising from the water ahead and to the left. This was the island volcano of Krakatao, whose spectacular eruption in 1883 had sent tidal waves all the way to Hawaii. In an hour they would be passing through the narrowest part of the strait, the 14-mile gap between Sumatra and Java. Aeons ago the two islands had been one. Then came a terrific volcanic explosion cutting it in half and giving birth to Sunda Strait.

On the other end of Java, the first wave of Doorman's Bali attack force was just turning up into the rips lacing the southern entrance of Lombok Strait. The light cruiser *De Ruyter*, with Doorman aboard, led the pack, its main guns trained to starboard. Next came another Dutch cruiser, the *Java*, her guns aimed to port. Three miles astern was a Dutch destroyer closely followed by 2 U.S. destroyers.

At 10:20 P.M. the *Java* sighted enemy ships on the left. They were difficult to make out due to the background of the 10,000-foot cone of sacred Mount Bali but looked like 3 cruisers. Five minutes later the *Java* opened fire.

The 3 "cruisers" laying off Bali were a Japanese Army transport, emptied of troops and just getting under way for Makassar, and 2 destroyers. These quickly swept the sea with their searchlights. Finally pinning down the 2 Dutch cruisers, they fired.

The *De Ruyter*, its main guns facing the wrong direction,

didn't fire a shot in return but the *Java* scored a hit on the transport. As the 3 Allied destroyers raced north to join battle, the Dutch cruisers completely unharmed continued through Lombok Strait and turned left, heading home for Surabaja.

The 3 Allied destroyers were not as lucky. In less than an hour the Dutch ship was sunk and the 2 American destroyers turned around returning to the south.

Two hours later, at 1:15 A.M., February 20, the second Allied wave headed north into the strait. They sped in column—4 American destroyers and the Dutch cruiser *Tromp*—at 25 knots.

The original Japanese destroyers were now joined by 2 more. They raked the Allied column as it passed through the strait, heavily damaging the *Tromp* and the U.S. destroyer *Stewart*. One Japanese destroyer was slightly damaged with seven men dead. Another suffered a serious hit in the engine room, killing 60, but steamed off safely under her own power. Based on damage alone it was a lopsided Japanese victory. More important, the Japanese beachhead on Bali was not even molested.

Even so, Helfrich was already receiving optimistic reports. Doorman reported that the 5 torpedo boats of the third wave had seen nothing: Lombok Strait was clear. This news heartened Helfrich, but he was not overly jubilant. The Japanese still controlled Bali and its main airport. Soon it would be a base for air attacks on Java.

It was dark when the British destroyer carrying McDaniel cleared the strait between Java and Sumatra. It rounded the western tip of Java and proceeded up its north coast for 100 miles. It was sunrise by the time the ship docked at Batavia. The sun was already hot as he and Doris Lim walked to Des Indes Hotel, the AP headquarters. Here he learned his wife had gone on to Australia. He was also handed a note from "Newsreel" Wong, who had left the day before in a mass exodus of civilians and officials: "Help Doris. On way to Ceylon, then Calcutta."

McDaniel, exhausted after the strenuous escape from Singapore, found a bed and fell asleep. Almost immediately he was awakened. It was a direct phone call from New York City. AP wanted a story of his adventures.

Ninety air miles inland, in mountainous Bandung, General Wavell was reading a radiogram from the Combined Chiefs of Staff in Washington ordering him to defend Java with the utmost resolution:

EVERY DAY IS OF IMPORTANCE. THERE SHOULD BE NO
WITHDRAWAL OF TROOPS OR AIR FORCES OF ANY NATION-
ALITY, AND NO SURRENDER.

3 By the morning of February 22 the two Java
invasion convoys were within six sailing days of their destination. As the moment for landing drew nearer, other
powerful Japanese naval units were converging on the
Southwest Pacific area: 4 battleships, 5 carriers, 9 heavy
cruisers, 7 light cruisers and 52 destroyers.

Wavell didn't know the exact composition of the Japanese
Java Invasion Forces, but he was certain his tiny ABDA fleet
would be far outnumbered. That day he sent a realistic
message to Churchill.

I AM AFRAID THAT THE DEFENCE OF A.B.D.A. AREA HAS
BEEN BROKEN DOWN AND THAT DEFENCE OF JAVA CAN-
NOT NOW LAST LONG. IT ALWAYS HINGED ON THE AIR
BATTLE. . . . ANYTHING PUT INTO JAVA NOW CAN DO LIT-
TLE TO PROLONG STRUGGLE: IT IS MORE QUESTION OF
WHAT YOU WILL CHOOSE TO SAVE. . . . I SEE LITTLE FUR-
THER USEFULNESS FOR THIS H.Q. . . . LAST ABOUT MY-
SELF. I AM, AS EVER, ENTIRELY WILLING TO DO MY BEST
WHERE YOU THINK BEST TO SEND ME. I HAVE FAILED YOU
AND PRESIDENT HERE, WHERE A BETTER MAN MIGHT PER-
HAPS HAVE SUCCEEDED. . . . I HATE THE IDEA OF LEAVING
THESE STOUT-HEARTED DUTCHMEN, AND WILL REMAIN
HERE AND FIGHT IT OUT WITH THEM AS LONG AS POSSIBLE
IF YOU CONSIDER THIS WOULD HELP AT ALL.

GOOD WISHES. I AM AFRAID YOU ARE HAVING VERY DIF-
FICULT PERIOD. BUT I KNOW YOUR COURAGE WILL SHINE
THROUGH IT.

The next day the situation in Java looked even worse. The
damaged *Stewart,* improperly braced on keel blocks by
Dutch workmen, had rolled over in drydock and was ordered
scuttled. The oil situation was also getting desperate, even in
the heart of one of the world's great oil-producing centers.
Most storage facilities were inland. Those on the coast were
inadequate and by now the native crews had fled to the
hills because of incessant air raids.

The Allied air defense, never strong, was now so depleted
it could offer little resistance. The Dutch Air Force, originally
composed of 200 outmoded or obsolete bombers and
fighters, was down to a few battered planes; there were a

few British planes, leftovers from the disaster in Malaya. Of the 111 planes which America had rushed to Java, only 23 heavy bombers and a few fighters remained. First 11 Flying Fortresses, survivors of the Philippines campaign, were thrown into the defense of the Netherlands East Indies. For weeks they were the only heavy bombers operating against the invaders. Then 38 B-17E's and 12 two-engine bombers began arriving in driblets after being ferried halfway round the world from MacDill Field. Though these planes went on missions almost every day and did everything from bombing at 30,000 feet to strafing from 1500, to date they had sunk at most 5 transports and 2 tankers. This poor record was understandable: many of the crews and some of the pilots had had almost no previous experience with the Flying Fortresses or LB-30's; 26 bombers were lost on the ground because of poor anti-aircraft protection, air warning and fighter cover; because of the violent tropical storms and lack of intelligence only about half the bombers ever reached their assigned targets.

The story was almost the same for the American pursuit fliers. Of the 83 P-40's which flew up from Australia only 39 had arrived. (Several pilots had never before stepped into a P-40.) Though the survivors knocked down their share of Zeroes, they were too few to do anything but slow down the hordes of enemy planes.

On the evening of February 23, Yates McDaniel took Doris Lim to the docks at Batavia and put her aboard a ship bound for Ceylon. He had persuaded the British consul general that she was a British citizen. It was a fast modern passenger ship and Doris was delighted, even though it would mean running the Japanese gantlet without a convoy.

Now McDaniel had only himself to worry about, but before leaving for Australia he had to make sure he wasn't missing a big story in Java.

In Bandung, Wavell was just getting word of another setback. Strategic Timor, at the eastern end of the long barrier of islands between the Japanese and Australia, had been captured. Both ends of the barrier were now in Japanese hands. Java, in the middle, was isolated. One of the richest prizes in the world, she lay completely exposed to conquest —except for Helfrich's four-nation fleet.

In spite of the sounds of disaster on all sides of him, the admiral still refused to give up hope. He wired London that the British and Americans were much too pessimistic:

SUNDA AND BALI STRAITS ARE STILL OPEN. IT IS STILL
POSSIBLE TO SUPPLY US BY SHIP. IT IS NOT TOO LATE. BUT
WE MUST ACT WITH EXTREME SPEED, GRIM RESOLUTION
AND TAKE ALL RISKS.

Gloom at Bandung deepened in the next few days, culminat-
ing on February 25 when Wavell dissolved ABDA and turned
over the final defense of the Netherlands East Indies to the
Dutch governor general. After bidding a solemn good-bye
to his Dutch friends, Wavell went to his quarters to pack. His
next stop was India, where he was to be commander-in-
chief. Was he going off to command another sinking ship?

Helfrich now was solely responsible for stopping the sea
invasion. The decisive moment was approaching. At mid-
morning word came that a great Japanese convoy with strong
escort was moving south down Makassar Strait and would
apparently reach eastern Java in two or three days. Doorman,
defending this end of the island, would need reinforcements.
At 11:25 A.M. Helfrich ordered all available fleet cruisers
and destroyers in Batavia to steam east to Surabaja to bolster
Doorman's heavy cruiser, 2 light cruisers and 7 destroyers.

Helfrich knew he could not stop the Japanese, but the
Combined Chiefs in Washington had ordered him to defend
Java until the end and if he couldn't stop the Japanese, at
least he could hurt them. It was his duty to kill as many
Japanese soldiers as possible before they got ashore. He
would fight on the Java Sea regardless of consequences.

That afternoon Yates McDaniel watched the 5 ships of war
file out of Batavia's naval base, Tanjok Priok, to reinforce
Doorman in what would undoubtedly be the last gallant defense of Java. They were a brave sight, their ensigns flapping:
the big British cruiser *Exeter*, famous for her battle with the
Graf Spee, the Australian light cruiser *Perth*, and three trim
British destroyers. They looked potent and confident as
they steamed east, but McDaniel recalled how powerful the
Prince of Wales, the *Repulse* and their destroyer escorts had
looked sailing out of Singapore for their rendezvous with
disaster.

Now McDaniel headed for the commercial docks. The
Java story was about over and he was leaving at sunset on a
Dutch cattle boat. The chances of getting through safely
were ridiculously small but McDaniel knew this was his last
chance. He got only blank looks when he asked the ship's destination; he hoped it was going to Australia. If it did, he
wondered if this would be an evil omen for the Allies.

First he had seen Singapore die; now Java was falling. Would Australia be next?

    4 By late morning of February 26 the two Japanese convoys were within striking distance of their destinations. The Western Assault Convoy of 56 transports, escorted by 2 light cruisers, 2 flotillas of destroyers, and covered by 4 heavy cruisers, was about 250 miles from the west end of Java.

The Eastern Assault Convoy of 40 transports, escorted by a light cruiser and 6 destroyers, was less than 200 miles from its goal, east Java. Additional protection was also nearby: two heavy cruisers, a light cruiser and 7 destroyers. Over-all commander was the able but cautious Rear Admiral Sokichi Takagi.

Helfrich knew the Western Assault Convoy was also approaching but he had decided to concentrate almost his entire force at Surabaja under Doorman to try and stop the greater danger from the east. Just before noon these eastern invaders were sighted by two Allied planes about 175 miles northeast of Surabaja. When Helfrich got this report he radioed Doorman to sail out of port after dark with his entire force and attack. A decisive duel between Doorman and Takagi was inevitable and imminent.

A few hours later Helfrich received a sharp jolt. An R.A.F. plane reported another large invasion convoy off the west end of Java. Though the convoy was apparently heading north, away from Java, Helfrich knew this was the Western Assault Convoy, ahead of schedule and marking time.

Helfrich had almost nothing to throw against this second threat—only the light cruiser *Hobart*, 2 antique cruisers and 2 equally old destroyers—but he ordered them to set sail from Batavia at dark and engage the enemy.

A little later Helfrich was told by Lieutenant General L. J. van Oyen, the Dutch air chief and now head of the combined ABDA air fleet, that the bulk of his force, the Americans, were leaving in spite of his definite orders to fight to the very end. Already U.S. ground crews were on trains heading for Tjilatjap, a town on the southern coast of Java, where a freighter would take them to Australia. It almost amounted, said van Oyen bitterly, to desertion. Colonel Eugene Eubank, who had ordered this evacuation, was only following specific instructions from his chief, General Brereton, who had flown on to India.

Soldiers of all colors and many nationalities—English,

Australian, Chinese, Dutch, Indian, as well as Americans—were swarming into the escape port of Tjilatjap. It was obvious to almost everyone that Java was fast falling.

Many miles from the frantic scene, Churchill was writing a last message to the commander of those British and Australian troops chosen to stay behind and fight the land battle of Java.

> I SEND YOU AND ALL RANKS OF THE BRITISH FORCES WHO HAVE STAYED IN JAVA MY BEST WISHES FOR SUCCESS AND HONOUR IN THE GREAT FIGHT THAT CONFRONTS YOU. EVERY DAY GAINED IS PRECIOUS, AND I KNOW THAT YOU WILL DO EVERYTHING HUMANLY POSSIBLE TO PROLONG THE BATTLE.

At 6:30 that evening Doorman sailed out of Surabaja with his 14 ships. He was a tall, dark-haired man with slightly drooping shoulders. Helfrich esteemed him highly as a tactician with great presence of mind in a crisis. Like Helfrich he was ready to die for his queen. Like all the other Dutch in Java he was also fighting for home, family and future.

The shadowy column nosed north into the Java Sea through the violet light of early dusk. Then it turned due east, beginning its night sweep in search of Takagi's transports and warships.

The column was an inspiring sight, and most of those aboard the assorted ships felt reassured to be in such proud company, but it was a patchwork fleet. Each national group was actually a distinct and separate task force, with no common doctrine, philosophy or technique. And Doorman's last hurried instructions before sailing had been, necessarily, vague and incomplete. It was, thought Lieutenant (junior grade) H. S. Hamlin, Jr., of the *Houston*, like eleven all-stars playing the Notre Dame football team without a single practice session together.

At 8:55 P.M. Helfrich cabled: YOU MUST CONTINUE YOUR ATTACKS UNTIL ENEMY IS DESTROYED. He wanted Doorman to know that he must attack at any price—at once. Delay might be disastrous. Only in the early moments would the Allied fleet enjoy numerical advantage.

Doorman saw nothing in his sweep along the coast. At dawn he radioed Surabaja for air protection. None was available. A few hours later enemy bombers harassed but did not damage the fleet. Exhausted and discouraged by the fruitless night search, Doorman headed back for home.

That morning the seas off the southern coast of Java were dotted with ships fleeing toward Australia. Only two were heading north and these, bound for Tjilatjap, were loaded with American fighter planes. The freighter *Seawitch* carried 27 P-40's in her hold. The U.S. aircraft tender *Langley* was bringing 32 ready-to-fly P-40's and 33 Army Air Force pilots. The two ships were traveling without a convoy in a desperate race to reach Java before it was too late.

The *Langley*, in the lead, was due to dock that afternoon. Its crew knew that approaching Java in daylight was dangerous, but Helfrich, with Admiral Glassford's approval, had insisted the risk be taken. The hours saved might be critical. The ABDA fleet still had no air cover for the coming battle in the Java Sea.

At 8:00 A.M. a lone Japanese reconnaissance plane spotted the *Langley* and alerted the newly captured airfield on Bali. At 9:55 A.M. 16 Betty bombers and 16 Zero fighters took off.

Seven of the bombers attacked the *Langley* at 12:10 P.M. but Commander R. P. McConnell, the aircraft tender's skipper, ordered hard right rudder and the bombs fell to port. When the remaining Betties struck, McConnell again avoided the bombs. At 12:15 the group of nine bombers sharply wheeled and once more attacked. This time the *Langley*, built in 1922 as America's first aircraft carrier and later the mooring ship for the famed dirigible *Shenandoah*, was hit five times. Planes on deck burst into flame.

Half an hour later the Zeros strafed the deck planes briefly, then left when they saw a great explosion. At 1:32 P.M. McConnell ordered the ship abandoned.

On the north side of Java, Admiral Doorman's 14-ship striking force was still en route back to its base. But at 2:27 P.M. just as his flagship, the light cruiser *De Ruyter*, entered Surabaja Harbor, he got a message from Helfrich to attack an enemy force east of Bawean Island. This was a point some 90 miles north of Surabaja.

There was no time to make an operation plan. Since the fleet didn't have a common code of tactical signals, Doorman handed an order to an American liaison officer on the *De Ruyter*. The order was translated and transmitted to the *Houston*, which relayed it over voice radio to the American destroyers. The British and Australians got the news by flashing light in plain English and signal flags. It was:

FOLLOW ME, THE ENEMY IS 90 MILES AWAY.

1 Doorman's fleet quickly turned around and headed out to sea again. There was rising excitement in every ship. The 3 British destroyers, screening abreast, led the way to the northwest. Then came Doorman in his flagship, *De Ruyter*. Behind in column were the famous British heavy cruiser *Exeter;* the American heavy cruiser *Houston*, the host of Roosevelt on four cruises; the Australian light cruiser *Perth;* and finally the Dutch light cruiser *Java*. To the left of the cruisers was a second column: 2 Dutch destroyers followed by a quartet of ancient American four-stack destroyers.

Seamen and officers of all four nations were thankful at least to have something on the water to fire at. The past month they had all been pounded by bombs. Soon would come the chance to fight back. Men rushed to their battle stations. There was no time to eat. The enemy might be just over the horizon.

Doorman had no planes to catapult from his cruisers to search out the enemy. They had been left ashore the day before since he'd expected only a night action. He would have to grope his way forward in a deadly game of blindman's buff. Once more Doorman radioed to Surabaja for air cover. Helfrich, who had previously asked in vain for command of all air forces, added his weight to Doorman's request, but it was denied. There were only eight Dutch fighters available, asserted the air commander, and these were already assigned to accompany bombers on a late-afternoon attack on Takagi's approaching transports. Doorman could either turn back or steam ahead into battle without air protection. The 14 ships continued northwest.

Admiral Takagi had two advantages. He wasn't blindfolded. Three float planes had already reported that Doorman was heading for him. He also had a slight numerical edge—17 ships to 14. Both admirals had 2 heavy cruisers but Takagi's

13 destroyers gave him a decided edge against Doorman's. The Dutchman's only advantage was in light cruisers, 3 to 2.

As Doorman headed toward him, Takagi guessed correctly that the Dutchman's primary purpose was to sink the transports. He ordered the 40-ship convoy, which was heading south for the Java coast, to turn away. He placed Rear Admiral Shoji Nishimura's Destroyer Squadron 4—the light cruiser *Naka* and 6 destroyers—south of the convoy as a screen. Just east of Nishimura were Takagi's own 2 big cruisers, the *Nachi* and *Haguro*, his knockout punch. And farther east was Rear Admiral Paizo Tanaka's Destroyer Squadron 2, the light cruiser *Jintsu* and 7 destroyers. By 3:15 P.M. Takagi was ready, waiting for the groping Doorman.

Even so, the report that a strong enemy fleet was racing north to the attack had taken Takagi aback. According to Air Intelligence, the ABDA fleet had been battered to bits by incessant air raids and was too badly damaged to fight.

It was a clear, bright day. On Takagi's big cruiser, *Haguro*, some of the men thought they could smell the fragrance of nearby Java. They had read much of this exotic land and were eager to see it firsthand. Midshipman Hachiro Kimura, a graduate of the Naval Academy only twenty-three days before Pearl Harbor, stood on the bridge. Like everyone else on the *Haguro* he was excited and tense. The men, dressed in white fatigues and steel helmets, visited the ship's shrine and tied *hachimaki* tightly around their foreheads. The officers, wearing white dress uniforms and baseball caps, were straining to be the first to see the enemy.

But Tanaka's force, a few miles to the east, was nearer. At 4:00 P.M. a lookout on his flagship, *Jintsu*, sighted mastheads about 17 miles to the southeast. Word spread through the ship. Everyone was in high spirits. Victory again would be on the side of Japan and the Emperor.

A minute later those on *Haguro* also got their first glimpse of the enemy. Midshipman Kimura could see only the lofty masts of the *De Ruyter*. It looked terrifying with its strange, odd-shaped superstructure, like something from Mars. Kimura had never before experienced such a weird feeling of fright. He knew the *Haguro* was faster and had 10 great 8-inch guns, but the *De Ruyter* began taking the shape of some prehistoric monster as it grew bigger.

The *Electra*, the middle of the 3 British destroyers birddogging in front of the Allied cruisers, sighted Tanaka's destroyer flotilla at 4:12 P.M. She reported to Doorman:

ONE CRUISER, UNKNOWN NUMBER LARGE DESTROYERS
BEARING 330°, SPEED 18, COURSE 220°.

Those on *Electra* couldn't see that a few miles behind and
a little to the west of Tanaka were Takagi's 2 big cruisers.
And several miles farther west was the destroyer flotilla of
Admiral Nishimura. All these Japanese forces now turned
and began speeding almost at right angles toward Doorman's
two parallel columns like three great arrows.

In a few minutes Doorman guessed that the oncoming
enemy was trying to cross the bows of his formation and
ordered the cruisers to flank speed of 26 knots. The 2 Dutch
destroyers, unable to make this speed, fell back. Behind, the
4 American destroyers also slowed when Doorman ordered
them to stay in line.

Takagi's 2 big cruisers, *Nachi* and *Haguro,* closed to within
28,000 yards of the Allied column. At 4:15 P.M. their 8-inch
guns blasted. Geysers exploded harmlessly in front of their
targets, *Exeter* and *Houston.*

At 4:16 P.M. the 2 Allied heavy cruisers opened fire with
almost a single crash. It was an unequal duel. The 2 Japanese
ships each had 10 8-inch guns. *Houston's* No. 3 Turret had
been wiped out and 46 men killed in the bombing of
February 4, reducing her big guns to 6. Thus with *Exeter's*
6, Doorman had only 12 big guns against 20.

As the big guns of the *Houston* roared, shaking the ship
violently, Lieutenant Hamlin, turret officer of No. 1, looked
through his periscope. He saw splashes falling around their
target, a heavy cruiser. A second salvo came down on the
enemy. Hamlin saw the dull red glow of bursting shells, so
different from the orange flash of gunfire. From the waist
of the Japanese ship a cloud of smoke burst up, and then,
back aft, a bright orange flash that looked like a burning turret.

He turned to the voice tube leading to the gun chamber.
Inside they were working like a team of perfectly drilled
acrobats and had no time to watch the show. "We've just
kicked the hell out of a ten-gun Jap cruiser!" he shouted.

The men in the gun chamber cheered.

Now Tanaka in the light cruiser *Jintsu* led his 7 destroyers
in an attack at the head of the Allied line. *Electra* was
straddled, geysers rising on both sides. Commander C. W.
May coolly twisted the ship, avoiding another near miss. It
was almost as if he'd been a mind reader. Again he turned

and shells burst in fantastic greens, yellows and reds where the destroyer had been a moment before.

Gunner T. J. Cain felt exhilarated and didn't know why. Others on *Electra* shared his feeling. In a bombing they sometimes got the jitters, But this shelling had put everyone in a kind of holiday mood. It was quite extraordinary.

Behind the British destroyers, Doorman's 5 cruisers kept on course with the *Houston* and *Exeter*, the only ones with guns big enough to reach the Japanese, providing all the fire power. Next to last in this line, on the *Perth*, Paymaster Lieutenant-Commander P. O. L. Owen was watching the battle from the after end of the quarter-deck. He was in the battle by accident. Assigned to the *Hobart*, he had missed boarding that ship in Batavia because of an air raid. Captain Waller of *Perth*, an old friend and former commander, had invited him aboard as a temporary guest.

Japanese salvos began to straddle *Perth*. Though he had undergone much bombing in the Mediterranean, this was Owen's first taste of shell fire and his reaction was quite different from that of Gunner Cain. He remembered Waller, a veteran of two fierce surface engagements, once telling him, "I'd rather 1000 bombing attacks than to stand one enemy shelling." Now Owen knew what he meant. It was awesome. He and his three-man machine-gun crew stood watching in tense fascination as tight salvos lobbed around their ship, first 25 yards short, then 25 yards over. He could see the black streaking track of each shell as it winged toward them: for a split second the shell would become a black image just before it struck the water. It was a phenomenon not seen, he guessed, by many men.

It was extremely taxing to be a mere spectator. The guns of *Perth* were silent, out of range. Owen became incensed that Doorman didn't order the light cruisers to turn into the enemy and get in close enough to fight.

Ahead, on the *De Ruyter*, Doorman wanted to do just that since his only superiority—3 to 2—was in light cruisers; but he had a more immediate problem. Takagi's 3 forces were closing in. The 2 heavy cruisers, particularly, were gaining fast. Doorman could see that if he continued his course, Takagi would soon pass across the head of his column, "crossing his T." By this classic maneuver the Japanese would bring their broadsides to bear on the column of Allied cruisers who could retaliate only with their forward guns. Consequently, at 4:21 P.M. Doorman swung his cruiser column 20 degrees away from the Japanese to the left. His destroyers followed suit.

The Japanese also turned. Soon the two great enemy fleets were traveling almost parallel, heading west with Doorman in between Takagi and the Java coast line. Observing this spectacular scene from grandstand seats were Americans in 3 A-24 dive bombers and 10 escorting P-40's. They were on their way to bomb the 40 transports Takagi was presently trying to shield from Doorman. Their leader, Captain Harry Galusha, instead of skirting the action, became so fascinated by what he saw below that he led the formation right across the battlefield. Several of his men began to complain vocally that he had more nerve than brains, but Galusha, though he was supposed to be after transports, was looking for a carrier. If he found one, he was going after it. He counted 12 Japanese warships. Then to the north 6 cruisers. And beyond them, farther north, was clustered a great flotilla of transports, the Eastern Invasion convoy.

Finding no carriers, Galusha turned north and attacked the transports. Though his bombers claimed 3 victims, not a single Japanese ship was sunk or even badly damaged. It was unfortunate for the Allies that the P-40's accompanying Galusha had not been assigned to Doorman, as he and Helfrich had requested. They could well have won the battle of Java Sea for the Dutchman, if only by knocking down the 3 persistent Japanese float planes that were giving Takagi's gunners such tremendous advantage by correcting fire in the increasingly smoky battle area.

A few minutes later Takagi ordered Admiral Nishimura's destroyer flotilla to launch a torpedo attack. Nishimura, in the light cruiser *Naka*, dashed toward Doorman's column followed by 6 destroyers. At 4:33 P.M. *Naka* loosed torpedoes from a distance of 16,000 yards, then swung sharply away from the enemy. The 6 Japanese destroyers behind did the same and a swarm of long-range torpedoes headed toward the Allies. These, newly designed, had the astounding range of 30,000 yards and since they were propelled by oxygen, left no tell-tale trail of bubbles.

Two minutes after this school of torpedoes was launched, Doorman abruptly turned toward the enemy, trying to reduce distance for the benefit of his light cruisers. But by the time the move was executed all Doorman's attention was diverted to self-preservation. The torpedoes recently launched by Nishimura began appearing on all sides. The Allies, who had no torpedoes of such range, were sure a wolf pack of submarines had suddenly attacked. Many of these torpedoes exploded prematurely, giving rise to excited reports of sinkings by both Japanese and Allied observers, but none actually found a target.

At 5:00 P.M. Admiral Takagi sighted smoke from his transports. Realizing the battle had drifted dangerously near the invasion convoy, he ordered everyone to attack simultaneously, at once, even though his big cruisers were more than 20,000 yards from the enemy. In the next few minutes almost 50 torpedoes were launched by *Haguro* and the two destroyer divisions. The distance was too great. All missed.

The area was now black with smoke from Japanese destroyers laying a screen between the two opposing cruiser columns. Doorman was blinded; only *Exeter* had radar. But Takagi could still look over the smoke screen with his float planes.

Tanaka ordered his flag torpedo officer, Commander Yasumi Toyama, to launch another torpedo attack. Toyama signaled the order. One destroyer answered cockily by flag, "It's simple, exactly like a maneuver." They all felt the same. There was nothing to it. At 5:07 P.M. Tanaka's squadron launched their torpedoes. At the same moment the *Haguro* began shooting with its 8-inch guns at the biggest target in the line, the *Exeter*.

Every sea battle has its moment of decision. In the Battle of Java Sea it came at exactly 5:08 P.M., a sudden stroke of bad luck for the Allies, good luck for the Japanese. One of *Haguro*'s shells crashed through an anti-aircraft mount on the *Exeter*, pierced the ship's decks without detonating and landed in the boiler room. There was a tremendous explosion and in one stroke 6 of *Exeter*'s 8 boilers were cut out. The big cruiser, her speed halved, lurched and turned hard left so the *Houston* just behind wouldn't pile into its stern.

Captain Rooks of *Houston*, assuming Doorman had ordered a simultaneous turn of all cruisers to avoid torpedoes, also quickly swung to port. The lurch almost sent Lieutenant Hamlin to the deck. His No. 1 Turret rumbled as it trained around trying to keep on target. Six hundred yards ahead he saw *Exeter* moving at only five knots. Something drastic must have happened. It gave him a sick feeling.

Houston strained as she heeled sharp over to avoid ramming the British ship, the screws shaking her as she went astern. A few hundred yards behind the American ship, Captain Waller of *Perth* also assumed Doorman wanted a left turn to let torpedoes comb the line and was sharply moving to port. So was the *Java*.

Hamlin grabbed the phone, heard the gunnery officer, Commander A. L. Maher, say calmly, "Check fire. *Exeter* has

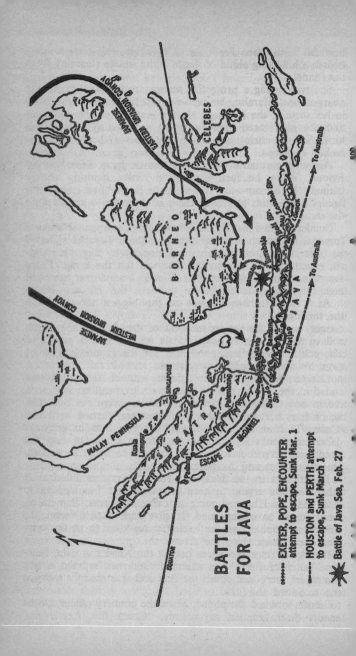

BATTLES FOR JAVA

••••••• EXETER, POPE, ENCOUNTER attempt to escape. Sunk Mar. 1

———— HOUSTON and PERTH attempt to escape, Sunk March 1

✴ Battle of Java Sea, Feb. 27

JAPANESE WESTERN INVASION CONVOY

JAPANESE EASTERN INVASION CONVOY

CELEBES

BORNEO

JAVA

SUMATRA

MALAY PENINSULA

SINGAPORE

Kuala Lumpur

Palembang

ESCAPE OF EXETER

Sunda Str.

Bantam

Batavia

Bandung

Tjilatjap

Banjermasin

Soerabaja

Bali Lombok Str.

LOMBOK

To Australia

To Australia

EQUATOR

Macassar Str.

been hit." Just then *Perth* swept by again, this time to starboard, a billowing cloud of dense white smoke steaming from her funnel.

She was laying a protective screen around *Exeter*. As she charged past Hamlin, he saw a beautiful snow-white "bone in her teeth"—the foam at her bow—and from the yardarms and the gaff, three huge battle flags streamed straight behind. She was firing rapidly. It was one of the finest sights he had ever seen.

Ahead, Doorman in *De Ruyter* was steaming alone and oblivious. When he finally saw the melee behind, he too turned left. By now the entire Allied fleet—except the damaged *Exeter*—was steaming south in disorder to get clear of the smoke-engulfed area.

Suddenly the water was crisscrossed by the wakes of many torpedoes. The cruisers began zigzagging and dodging as destroyers rushed about like bird dogs. Many believed they'd run into another nest of submarines. These were the long-range torpedoes launched by Tanaka's destroyer squadron eight minutes previously.

At 5:15 P.M. there was a great explosion in the middle of the milling Allied ships. The Dutch destroyer *Kortenaer* had caught one of the torpedoes in the waist. Hamlin saw her roll over on the port beam, break in two like a jackknife. The stern section stuck up, the propellers slowly turning over. Men were clinging to the rudder.

Commander T. H. Binford, in charge of all four American destroyers, saw the disaster from his flagship, *Edwards*. *Kortenaer*'s skipper, Lieutenant Commander A. Kroese, was a friend. He exclaimed, "Oh, my God, there's my friend 'Cruiser'!" In less than a minute there was nothing except debris and an oil slick. As the *Houston* was passing the wreckage, several saw a Dutch sailor, clinging to a stanchion, wave his arm in cheerful salute.

Doorman knew he had to re-form his cruiser line before other disasters struck. "ALL SHIPS FOLLOW ME," he signaled at 5:20 P.M. and headed southeast. Five minutes later he altered course to northeast so the line could pass between the smoke-encircled *Exeter* and the Japanese and gave the crippled ship a chance to escape.

Though *Exeter* was momentarily protected from the Japanese heavy cruisers by smoke, Doorman realized the enemy destroyers were maneuvering for another torpedo attack on the wounded ship. He ordered the three British destroyers to dash forward through the smoke and try to stop the enemy destroyers before they got started.

At 5:25 P.M. the men of *Electra* heard the calm voice of their skipper, Commander May, come over the phone. "The Japanese are mounting a strong torpedo attack against the *Exeter*. So we are going through the smoke to counterattack."

The other two British destroyers were far behind and May felt he could not wait. *Electra* instantly darted northwest through the smoke. Soon she was in the open, alone and naked to the approaching *Jintsu* and her seven destroyers.

Electra fired rapidly at *Jintsu*. Her aim was good and *Jintsu* was hit, with one dead and four wounded, but the odds were too great. In seconds the water around *Electra* was spouting with near misses and straddles. The little destroyer rocked. The stink of Japanese explosives fell on the crew with the spray. Still she fired at *Jintsu*. The crew saw two hits spark on the Japanese flagship's hull. They yelled but their triumph was cut off by a deafening explosion. Their own ship staggered from a hit below the bridge. All communications from bridge to ship were cut. Then a second and third shell hammered home. Escaped steam screeched from the after-boiler room. *Electra* shivered, stopped at 5:30 P.M. She was a floating target for an entire destroyer division.

Electra began to sink but her gun crews stayed at their stations and continued to fire. Finally a message was passed from the bridge: "Prepare to abandon ship."

With *Electra* knocked out of the way, *Jintsu* and two destroyers dashed through the smoke screen to attack the *Exeter*. In a wild melee the Dutch destroyer *Witte De With* and the remaining two British destroyers rushed forward to protect the damaged British cruiser.

It was 5:40 P.M. The late afternoon was dark from smoke of battle in spite of the brilliantly forming sunset. Doorman ordered *Exeter* to retire to Surabaja with *Witte De With* as escort. In the confusion the two ships turned south and escaped. Now Doorman had only 10 ships to match Takagi's 17. Worse, he had only *Houston*'s 6 big guns to duel with Takagi's 20 8-inchers.

Under cover of the smoky battlefield, Doorman formed a new line with his remnants. Behind *De Ruyter* were *Perth*, *Houston*, *Java* and the 6 destroyers. A few minutes later the line broke out of the smoke into the clear. He could see Takagi's big cruisers, *Nachi* and *Haguro*, steaming parallel but in the opposite direction about 19,500 yards away.

Fortunately for the Allies, Takagi had no idea the *Exeter*

was out of action and that he enjoyed overwhelming superiority. Even so he was pleased with the action. Not one Japanese ship had yet been sunk or even seriously damaged. He radioed the invasion convoy, standing off not far to the north, that it was now safe to head for Java.

Many of his junior officers, like Midshipman Kimura, were not at all happy. They felt Takagi should have moved in much closer and wiped out the Allies. They also felt much of the fault should fall on Takagi's senior staff officer, Captain Kou Nagasawa, the one in charge of the whole operation. Stories were already circulating about Nagasawa's behavior under fire: he was so terrified he hung onto the compass every time a near miss from one of *Houston*'s crimson-dyed shells shot up a terrifying blood-red geyser.

Even so Nagasawa was now advising Takagi to move in closer. The 2 Japanese cruisers closed in slightly on Doorman and fired. Two shells hit the *Houston*. Both were duds. The American cruiser was forced to answer with slow fire. All ammunition in Turrets 1 and 2 was gone. Men were now having to transfer heavy 8-inch shells from disabled Turret 3 as the ship zigzagged and careened.

At about 5:50 P.M. Takagi saw Doorman's line turning in a counterclockwise circle and ordered his 2 big cruisers to launch a gun and torpedo attack. Five minutes later Tanaka's destroyer flotilla emerged from the smoke and also sighted Doorman turning. Within three minutes torpedoes were launched.

The Dutch admiral saw these torpedoes coming and at 6:00 P.M. ordered everyone to swing south. The torpedoes churned past harmlessly. By now the primitive Allied radio communication system had completely broken down and Doorman was reduced to visual signals which were almost useless in the smoke and haze. To make matters worse, the direct voice contact of both *De Ruyter* and *Houston* with the American destroyers was gone.

At 6:06 P.M. Commander Binford finally saw a flashing signal from Doorman: COUNTERATTACK. While Binford on *Edwards* was leading his 4 American destroyers to the north, he got another signal from Doorman: CANCEL COUNTERATTACK. Then a third: MAKE SMOKE.

It was just 6:09 P.M. and the sun was setting. In the churned-up battlefield behind Binford, *Electra* was beginning to sink. Gunner Cain, wounded in the leg, calmly limped to his cabin. His wife had recently sent him photos and he'd need them for company if he were captured. Once he had the pictures, he noticed the tilting walls of his cabin and became seized with sudden panic. Terrified of being trapped, he dashed up to the deck. There he met Steward Gretton, who held out a half-bottle of whisky. "Sorry about the shortage of glasses, sir, but I thought you'd care to join me in a drink."

Cain refused. They'd soon be in the sea and Scotch would only add to their thirst. The steward looked at Cain's wounded leg. "Doesn't seem much else left to do, sir," he said. "Don't you think it's time we left?"

The water around the foundering ship was soon dotted with swimmers and men on floats. A shout suddenly went up near Cain. It turned into a cheer. The skipper, Commander May, was leaning over the bridge waving.

The men in the water shouted. "Come on, sir, jump!" *Electra* shuddered.

"She's going," shouted several. "For God's sake jump!"

May waved again then calmly turned away.

"He's going to leave from the port side," said Cain.

"But he's leaving it too bloody late," cried Gretton. The ship plunged, her stern momentarily rising steeply. She disappeared, her white ensign flying from the gaff. Cain wept.

The battle was still on not far away. At 6:15 P.M. Doorman signaled Binford: COVER MY RETIREMENT. The American destroyer commander wasn't sure what Doorman wanted but he decided the best thing was to attack. Leading with *Edwards*, Binford put his 4 old destroyers in column, and steamed between the Allied battle line and the *Nachi* and *Haguro*. By flag he ordered those following to prepare for torpedo attack. Two almost collided in the smoke, but the 4 ships finally got into the clear as Binford led them head-on toward the big Japanese cruisers. Then he swung the column parallel to the cruisers for a broadside attack.

At 6:22 P.M. Binford ordered all starboard torpedoes fired even though it was 10,000 yards to the Japanese cruisers. The column reversed and a few minutes later the rest of Binford's torpedoes, those on the portside, sped to the north.

Takagi saw the wakes of the approaching torpedoes and dodged. Now in sight of the Surabaja lighthouse, he began worrying about mines and submarines. To be on the safe side he again radioed the convoy, 30 miles northwest of him and presently heading for Java, to reverse course. Half an hour earlier he had thought Doorman was shattered, yet the Dutchman was still leading his ships in good order. What were the Allies going to do next? Return to Surabaja for fuel? Or swing around and try to hit the convoy? Takagi broke the engagement and began retiring to the north. He would wait until darkness—the time preferred by Japanese naval commanders to attack.

Doorman saw this retirement dimly through the smoke and at 6:30 P.M. radioed Helfrich in Bandung, ENEMY RETREATING WEST. WHERE IS CONVOY? Helfrich radioed back that he had no current information; Doorman would have to make a guess.

At 6:31 P.M. Doorman signaled, FOLLOW ME, and headed to the northeast, but nine minutes later changed his mind and turned to the northwest. Hours earlier American fliers had sighted the Japanese convoy and radioed back its position. The information was never passed on to Helfrich or Doorman. Helfrich later was to term this state of affairs a "scandalous lack of coordination."

2   The present lull was a welcome relief to those on *Houston*. The crew was served tomato juice and cold Vienna sausages. The men were deafened; their faces pocked with powder burns. Excitement of battle was passing and many realized they were on the point of exhaustion, but there was also a sense of exhilaration. *Houston* had done well, scoring several hits. She herself had only been hit by two duds. The captain had pulled them through again, handling the cruiser like a destroyer in the heat of battle. The men below were near collapse. More than 70 had passed out from heat exhaustion in the torrid fire rooms during the fight.

Two destroyers, *Electra* and *Kortenaer*, had been sunk and *Exeter* and her escort, *Witte De With*, were out of action but the men felt the enemy had been hurt worse. They agreed, generally, that Doorman was right in tenaciously hunting the convoy.

On the *Jintsu* a civilian servant was serving tea to Admiral Tanaka. The destroyer commander was pleased with the battle. At least 4 or 5 Allied ships must have been sunk. The Japanese losses were remarkably low. Not a ship had been sunk, and only the destroyer, *Asagumo*, badly damaged.

The men were eating canned bamboo sprouts; fresh meat and vegetables had long disappeared. They were anxious to get the battle over so they could pick up fresh fruit and vegetables in Java.

On the heavy cruisers some junior officers were still criticizing Tagaki for being influenced by Nagasawa's extreme caution. Takagi, they argued, should have remembered the old saying of the Japanese Navy, "Let the enemy cut the skin, if you can cut the meat."

At 7:26 P.M. Doorman was still blindly groping for the convoys to the west-northwest. His aim was almost perfect. The 40 Japanese transports were only 20 miles away but a minute later he sighted *Jintsu* and 3 destroyers on the port beam. At the same time, a plane from *Jintsu* dropped a flare behind the Allied column. The Dutchman, guessing these ships were a protective screen between him and the convoy, decided to make a wide circle around the *Jintsu* group. He turned south toward Java.

Tempers began to fray as the tension built again. At 9:00 P.M. *De Ruyter* reached shoal water and swung right to parallel the coast of Java. The other cruisers followed. So did the 2 British destroyers, *Encounter* and *Jupiter*.

The 4 American destroyers hesitated. They were low on fuel and out of torpedoes and Binford had to make a sudden and hard decision. "I'm not going in there after Doorman," he told *Edwards'* conning officer, Lieutenant William Giles. "That Dutchman has more guts than brains." He told Giles to turn left and lead the four destroyers to Surabaja, only 50 miles to the west, where they could refuel. Since he couldn't contact Doorman directly, Binford radioed shore and asked them to relay the message.

Doorman didn't know he was now leading his line dangerously close to a mine field laid only that afternoon by the Dutch themselves. On every ship men were straining their eyes looking through periscopes, range finders and binoculars for the forest of masts that would mean a convoy. Nothing could be seen. Then suddenly at 9:25 P.M. there was a great explosion at the end of the line. The British destroyer, *Jupiter*, was enveloped in flames. Some guessed she had been torpedoed by a submarine. She had most likely hit a drifting Dutch mine.

Doorman turned north in hopes he was heading for the Japanese convoy. A feeling of anxiety spread as the ships plunged into the dark unknown. What had hit the *Jupiter* might hit them any moment. This feeling turned to terror at 9:50 P.M. when a single parachute flare floated down and brightly lit the entire column. It was a strange game. Doorman, stalking the convoy, was himself being stalked by an enemy specifically trained and psychologically suited for night battle and whose planes could easily follow his phosphorescent wake. Two minutes later six more flares, looking like hobgoblins, straddled Doorman's line at right angles.

Many felt they were steaming straight into a trap as *De Ruyter* kept doggedly heading north. At 10:17 P.M. *Perth* heard men in the water shouting in a strange tongue, perhaps Japanese. Just behind, *Houston* also heard the foreign cries but to be on the safe side dropped a raft and flare.

The shouting men were survivors from the jackknifing *Kortenaer*, sunk in the afternoon battle. A few minutes later *Encounter*, drawn by the flare, stopped and picked up 113 survivors, including Binford's friend, Commander Kroese.

Fortunately for Doorman, Takagi was now also in the dark, for his float planes had left. The Japanese commander quickly altered course to south, hoping to throw himself between Doorman and the convoy.

It was almost 11:00 P.M. The wounded *Exeter* and its escort, *Witte De With*, had safely anchored in Surabaja. Other survivors of the great battle, the 4 American destroyers of Commander Binford, were just entering the harbor, when a radio order came from the Dutch shore station, relayed from Doorman, to return to Batavia for fuel and torpedoes. Binford turned his column west. Then he stopped. It made no sense. He held a conference by voice radio with the skippers of the other ships.

Commander Edward Parker, considered one of the Asiatic Fleet's ablest and most aggressive destroyer commanders, said, "It'll be suicide going to Batavia. We'd meet Jap destroyers and cruisers in the daylight."

"I know there's no oil there," said Binford. "Or torpedoes." He suggested they fuel to capacity in Surabaja and clear the docks by daylight. "Do any of you have any more comments or suggestions?"

All agreed. Binford radioed Doorman he would proceed south as ordered after he had refueled in Surabaja. The column again reversed course and steamed back into port.

At this same time the rest of Doorman's fleet was about 100 miles to the northwest in the middle of the black Java Sea. It was in column formation with *De Ruyter* in the lead, heading north still in search of the Japanese convoy. A few moments after 11:00 P.M. lookouts on *De Ruyter* saw the 2 big Japanese cruisers on their port beam heading in the opposite direction. The Dutch cruiser fired. A moment later *Perth, Houston* and *Java* fired. Takagi's cruisers answered. The sky was bright with bursting star shells.

Firing stopped abruptly and there was an awesome silence.

The 4 Allied cruisers continued to steam north in column at high speed. In *Perth*, immediately behind Doorman's flagship, Commander Owen was peering into the darkness from the quarter-deck. He could see nothing and wondered if they'd been firing at phantoms. It was eerily quiet. All he could hear was the swish of water, the throb of the screws. The deck pulsated with life and it gave him a feeling of hope. He wondered if the first light of day would bring them in sight of the Jap convoy. Like everyone else on *Perth* he was eager to tear into the transports. Java was the last stand. If it fell, their homeland, Australia, would probably be conquered.

The Allied sailors did not realize that the *Nachi* and *Haguro* had just reversed their course and were now running a little behind and parallel to Doorman's column. They put on speed, quickly drawing abreast of the Allies. At 11:22 P.M. from 10,000 yards *Nachi* loosed 8 torpedoes and *Haguro* 4.

Doorman's cruisers steamed on, oblivious of the torpedoes speeding toward them. Lieutenant Hamlin standing at his battle station on *Houston* saw a sudden blaze ahead at 11:36 P.M. It came with the terrifying abruptness of a huge cigarette lighter. The *De Ruyter* was on fire! A moment later rockets shot up from the stricken ship. Fire had reached her pyrotechnic locker.

From his station in the after director, it looked like a Fourth of July celebration gone crazy to Lieutenant Joseph Dalton. It was impressive, horrifying. It didn't seem possible any human could survive such a holocaust.

In *Perth*, yards behind the *De Ruyter*, Owen was still dazed by the mighty column of incandescent flame that had suddenly shot up ahead. It was fantastically brilliant, a solid, gigantic mass of white flame—the most frightening thing in his life. He was thrown to his feet as *Perth* violently sheered off. From the deck Owen could see they had just barely missed hitting the blazing ship.

Just behind *Perth*, Captain Rooks had been waiting to see what Waller of *Perth* would do. Making a lightning decision, he too ordered a sharp turn. The *Houston* reared and shook as men were thrown against the forward bulkheads. The ship heeled dizzily from the turn and "crash stop" but it skimmed safely past the *Perth*.

Then at 11:40 P.M. there was another tremendous explosion, this time just behind the *Houston*. The other Dutch cruiser, *Java*, was burning furiously. In minutes she stood vertically with bow up. Hundreds of her crew were falling or jumping into the dark sea. With frightening abruptness the ship plunged out of sight. There was momentary quiet and the almost 500 seamen struggling in the water were heard shouting three cheers for Her Majesty the Queen.

The survivors of the blast on *De Ruyter* were assembled on the bow. There was another great explosion and the huge superstructure that had so terrified Midshipman Kimura vanished as if by magic. With *De Ruyter* went the tenacious fleet commander, Karel Doorman, and 366 officers and men.

Captain Waller of *Perth* was now senior officer of the Allied fleet. One of Doorman's last orders had been to leave any survivors "to the mercy of the enemy." He made his decision quickly. Ordering *Houston* to follow, Waller raced to the southeast. Takagi gave chase but when the 2 Allied cruisers abruptly turned toward Batavia, the Japanese were fooled and didn't follow.

The Battle of Java Sea, the greatest surface engagement since the Battle of Jutland, was over. It was a complete Japanese victory. Takagi lost no ships, suffered comparatively little damage and successfully protected his convoy. Doorman lost 3 destroyers, 2 light cruisers and his life.

He had also lost Java.

1 Doorman's tragic seven-hour-long battle did accomplish two things: it delayed both invasion convoys twenty-four hours. By dawn of February 28, however, the Western Convoy of 56 transports was closing in on the western tip of Java, preparing to land late that night. The Eastern Convoy, although badly worried the day before by the nearby rumble of the great sea battle and harassed by Allied bombers, still had all 40 transports afloat. They were heading south toward the central coast of Java, expecting to land about midnight.

The 10 battle-worn Allied ships surviving the classic sea fight were concentrated that morning at Batavia and Surabaja. Their crews were haggard and exhausted.

All the Allied destroyers and the crippled *Exeter* were at Surabaja. Here Commander Binford, in charge of the American destroyers, was talking on Green Line, the secret telephone to Admiral Glassford's headquarters in Bandung. "I've got four ships and 700 men. The bottom's dropped out. I want to get out of here and go to Australia. If we stay twenty-four hours, it will probably be too late to escape."

"I'll tell the boss and let you know," replied Glassford's operations officer.

Binford returned to the *Edwards*. By this time he had acquired another destroyer, the *Pope*. She had missed the battle because of minor repairs but was now ready to sail. The afternoon wore on with no word. Anger and resentment against the mountain-based Asiatic Fleet headquarters of Admiral Glassford rose. To men like Lieutenant William J. Giles, Jr., of the *Edwards*, it appeared that the Allied ships in Surabaja were being hemmed in like rats in a trap, while the headquarters people, safe in their mountain hideout, twiddled their thumbs.

Finally Binford went ashore and again called Bandung.

"We sent you a signal," was the answer. "We told you to go to Australia. But the *Pope* has to wait and help escort the *Exeter*."

"If she does, she's a goner." With half her boilers out, *Exeter* had little chance of escape.

"That's too bad. *Pope* wasn't in the battle and still has her torpedoes. She has to escort *Exeter*."

At 5:00 P.M. *Edwards*, with Binford aboard, led the other 3 U.S. destroyers out of Surabaja. As they passed the moored *Exeter*, the crews lined the decks, lustily cheering their allies on the crippled cruiser for their gallant fight the day before. Then, with Lieutenant Giles navigating, the 4 slender ships turned right, to the east. Under cover of darkness, they would soon make a dash for freedom through the narrow Strait of Bali.

Two hours later *Exeter* escorted by *Pope* and the British destroyer *Encounter* began their attempted escape. First they headed north toward Borneo. *Exeter* was too big to follow the Americans through Bali Strait and the trio was trying to circle around the Japanese Eastern Convoy, now about to land 100 miles west of Surabaja. The next night the 3 ships would turn left and try to get through Sunda Strait at the west end of Java.

Near this end, at Batavia, the other 2 survivors of the battle, *Perth* and *Houston*, were just leaving the naval base. Like *Exeter* they were going to try and run the gantlet of Sunda Strait. They left behind a city of the dead. The docks of Batavia were still smoking from bombings. Sheds, godowns, ships in the harbor were gutted. There was no sign of movement.

The *Houston* was far from the spick and span ship so loved by President Roosevelt. The admiral's cabin, occupied by the President on his four cruises, looked like the scene of a drunken brawl: furniture was scattered, mirrors cracked; large hunks of soundproofing torn from bulkheads and overhead were lying on the deck. In every cabin and wardroom, concussions from the 8-inch guns had emptied drawers, spewed clothing from lockers, torn pictures and clocks from walls.

There was more serious damage. Water seeped into the hull from plates badly sprung and leaking from near misses. Yet most of the men had that strange feeling enjoyed by most sailors. They felt their ship was immortal. Already reported sunk twice by the Japanese, the *Houston* had been nicknamed "The Galloping Ghost of the Java Coast." The rumor was they were bound for California. Soon they would see their families.

Ahead of *Houston* was the *Perth*. Her skipper, Captain

Hector Waller, was stocky, with heavy shoulders and thick legs; a dour, unemotional man with a high forehead. His crew felt he would get them through safely if anyone could.

At 8:00 P.M. the mine fields covering the port were cleared and a voice came over the intercommunication system. "This is the captain speaking. We are sailing for Sunda Strait and will shortly close up to the first degree of readiness relaxed. Dutch air reconnaissance reports that Sunda Strait is free of enemy shipping. But I have a report that a large convoy is about 50 miles northeast of Batavia moving east. I do not expect, however, to meet enemy forces."

Unlike the men of *Houston*, many on this ship had a feeling of foreboding in spite of Waller's reassuring words. The ship's mascot, a cat named Red Lead, had tried to jump ship at Batavia, sneaking down the gangway to the godowns three times. The men remembered other bad omens. Three days previously, during an air raid at Batavia, the portrait of the Duchess of Kent, who had renamed the ship *Perth* in 1939, had been knocked to the deck. Then someone recalled they had two chaplains aboard. One was bad enough.

As the 7000-ton *Perth* zigzagged toward the strait at 22 knots, Paymaster "Polo" Owen, wearing white shirt and shorts and a blue Mae West, walked to his action station, a .5 machine gun, in the stern. He was uneasy. He felt like a pawn moved by an unknown force. By chance he had gone through the Battle of Java Sea on the wrong ship. Now what was coming? Certainly the Japanese, sweeping down on Java from two sides, wouldn't let them escape.

The narrowest point of Sunda Strait, where only 14 miles divide Java from Sumatra, was already alive with Japanese warships: 2 light cruisers and 8 destroyers. And a few miles to the north were the aircraft carrier *Ryujo*, 4 heavy cruisers and several destroyers. This powerful aggregation was protecting the 56 transports of the Western Convoy, just now dropping anchor at the western tip of Java in Bantam Bay.

Soon the 2 escaping Allied cruisers would round the tip of Java, turn left into Sunda Strait and continue on a course which would take them between the moored Japanese transports and this formidable battle escort.

The sea was calm, the air still and a full moon shone from a clear sky. It was another hot, sensuous tropical night. At 10:39 P.M. a patrolling Japanese destroyer sighted the 2 Allied ships as they neared the western tip of Java. In a few minutes 6 Japanese destroyers and a light cruiser were streaking toward Bantam Bay to protect their anchored transports.

Perth and *Houston*, unaware they were steaming into

ostile waters, were now turning left, heading south into the
arrow strait. Suddenly at 11:06 P.M. Captain Waller sighted
a vessel five miles ahead. "Challenge," he ordered, but he still
wasn't worried. "It's probably one of our corvettes patrolling
the strait." The chief yeoman signaled with his Aldis lamp.

The mystery ship was one of the Japanese destroyers
guarding the transports in nearby Bantam Bay. She answered
with her pale green lamp. No one on the *Perth* could understand the message.

"Repeat the challenge," said Waller.

In response the Japanese destroyer turned away and began
to lay a smoke screen in front of the transports massed in
Bantam Bay.

"Jap destroyer," said Waller, recognizing her silhouette.
"Sound the rattles. Forward turrets open fire."

A minute later Polo Owen, asleep at his station in the
stern of *Perth,* was wakened by a far-off popping noise. He
looked up and saw two rockets, one chartreuse, one scarlet,
falling lazily. Seconds later the 6-inch guns far forward
blasted. Owen jumped to his feet, donned his anti-flash gear.

Suddenly the two big guns only 10 yards forward swivelled
and aimed dead astern just over his head. There was a mighty
roar, and as fire from the two bores licked out Owen was
blown to the deck. He flattened, face down, to avoid the
simmering heat as salvo after salvo lashed out overhead.

The 2 Allied cruisers were now dashing south past Bantam Bay and its transports, their guns blazing at 4 enemy
destroyers.

At 11:26 P.M. *Perth* was hit in the forward funnel. Six
minutes later a shell exploded near the flag deck, but as the
cruiser swung to the right toward Sumatra, damage control
reported her wounds were only superficial.

In Bantam Bay there was alarm in the crowded transports.
On board the transport *Ryujo Maru,* headquarters for General Hitoshi Imamura of the 16th Army, the general's aide
was startled from his reading by the crash of guns. Only a
few minutes before he had felt disappointed that the landing
had been made without the firing of a single gun or rifle.

More Japanese warships were already racing to help the
embroiled destroyers. From the south 2 destroyers met the
Allied cruisers head on, launching torpedoes at 11:40 P.M.
From the northwest the light cruiser *Natori* and her 2 destroyers rapidly approached. Soon *Houston* and *Perth* had
so many targets that unengaged destroyers began to dart in
to very close range and light up the Allied ships with blue
searchlights.

At 11:48 P.M. ominously large geysers shot up all around *Perth*. Two heavy cruisers, *Mogami* and *Mikuma*, were also converging from the northwest, their salvos dropping dangerously close. Two minutes later *Perth's* luck ended. A shell smashed into the ordinary seamen's mess from the starboard side near the waterline. Within ten minutes the gunnery officer told Waller there was almost no 6-inch ammunition left. The captain made an instant decision. He would make a run for it through Sunda Strait. As the *Perth* headed full speed south, a Japanese destroyer raced in, threw a searchlight on the cruiser.

"For God's sake, shoot that bloody light out," called Waller. *Perth's* 4-inch guns spoke. The light vanished. Suddenly at five minutes after midnight the deck heaved. A torpedo had ripped into the starboard side near the forward boiler room. The ship rapidly began to lose life. A moment before she had been almost human, bounding and swaying. Now she was sluggish, as if dead tired.

Near the stern at his machine-gun position, Polo Owen heard the great crash forward. Then terrifying silence. He ran to the port torpedo space. Empty. There was nothing he could do. It was bloody awful. He went back to his gun. It was torn and twisted. Suddenly a second torpedo hit. The ship seemed to go to pieces. It was, thought Owen, like standing on a match box.

On the bridge they were picking themselves up from the deck. The second torpedo, they guessed, must have hit on the starboard side almost under them. Water and oil gushed onto the bridge, bowling over several men.

"Christ," said Waller. "That's torn it. Abandon ship."

"Prepare to abandon ship, sir?" asked the gunnery officer.

"No. Abandon ship."

Polo Owen and three sailors were trying to untie stacked rafts. The knots, tightened by the blast of the big guns, were like iron. "Anyone got a knife?" he asked.

The sailors ran forward. Owen followed them. *Perth* was moving slowly, her screws thumping, one almost out of water. From below he could hear the grinding tear of objects sliding across the heeling ship. He saw escaping steam ahead. He looked over the side, then climbed the rail and dove. In mid-air he suddenly realized he'd forgotten to inflate his Mae West. Treading water, he bent his head and tried to blow into the valve. He kept sinking and finally ripped off the life preserver in disgust. The water was warm, peaceful, pleasant. He took off his shirt and shorts and emptied his bowels. It was a great relief.

A few miles to the east, there was panic among the transports huddled together at Bantam Bay. Four were already sinking. Eight torpedoes aimed by the cruiser *Mikuma* at the *Houston* had sped by their target and exploded against friendly hulls. One of these unlucky transports was *Ryujo Maru*, headquarters ship of the 16th Army. General Imamura, his aide and hundreds of soldiers leaped into the warm water. The general and his aide grabbed pieces of wood, for neither wore life jackets. Suddenly the aide heard a grinding noise. He looked up and saw *Ryujo Maru* listing badly. The grinding increased as automobiles, freight and tanks rolled off the deck into the water with a dreadful sound.

To the northwest, the cause of all this, the heavy cruiser *Mikuma* was firing her big guns at *Houston*, which was already damaged by a torpedo. At 12:15 A.M. a salvo ripped into the U.S. cruiser's after engine room, scalding to death the entire force. The ship slowed down as steam geysered through gaping holes in the deck.

In Turret 1 Lieutenant Hamlin was looking through his periscope for targets. There was a tremendous jar. His head hit the periscope.

"Turret 2 is hit," said a voice over the phone, then added, "Fire in Turret 2!"

With one eye Hamlin tried to estimate the range to a blinding searchlight. His guns roared, the salvo fell short.

"Fire in Turret 2 magazines," said the telephone voice. If her ammunition were touched off, Turret 2 would be ripped out of the ship.

"Flood Turret 2," said the gunnery officer, Commander Al Maher, calmly.

Hamlin fired another salvo from Turret 1, this one 1000 yards longer.

"Fire in the small arms magazine," a voice on the phone told him

Hamlin was too busy to be worried. He had his target in a 1000-yard bracket. He split the difference and fired again.

"Fire in Turret 1 magazine," announced someone from Plotting Room in a strained voice.

At the same time Hamlin heard his own talker say tightly, "Fire in the magazines!" Then he heard Maher's calm voice: "Flood Turret 1."

"One, Aye, Aye," answered Hamlin. In a split second he decided to flood the magazine five stories below him but keep the upper powder room and shell room dry so he could shoot six more salvos.

"Flood the magazines," he told his talker.

In the confusion, he was misunderstood and sprinklers also began to spray the upper powder and shell rooms. Now there was only one salvo left. Hamlin carefully aimed at the searchlight and fired. It blinked out.

"Turret 1 out of action," Hamlin told Maher.

"Very well, stand by."

It was just 12:25 A.M., March 1. Fires from Turret 2 were licking high, illuminating the entire area.

Several miles away *Perth* was writhing as if in pain. She righted herself for a second, then rolled over and sank.

The *Houston* was also nearing the end of her life. The ship had slowed to 6 knots. All engines were quiet. On the bridge someone asked, "Are we abandoning ship?"

Captain Rooks nodded. His executive called out, "Abandon ship!" At 12:33 A.M. the bugle signal sounded. Officers began filing down from the conning bridge, Rooks in the rear.

In the forward engine room, Lieutenant Robert Fulton had felt the shock of the two torpedo hits. They were much lighter than the near bomb miss of February 4 which had broken the gauges, yet the engine order telegraph which signaled the speed to be made was now swinging crazily, moving without apparent sense. Though he was making full speed, the order from the bridge was constantly changing. The signaled speed from the control engine room aft also changed erratically. He wondered what was wrong, but no communication to the after engine room was possible, for all four telephone circuits were dead.

Then an order came to abandon ship. It didn't make sense to Fulton. The forward engine room was unharmed; they were making full speed. "Call back to the bridge and verify," he told the talker. "Tell them we cannot contact the after engine room, but we are in good shape." Soon confirmation of the order to abandon ship came. Fulton ordered the fires under the boilers to be killed. The throttles of the two engines were left open so that the 400 pounds of steam pressure would be bled from the system. Finally the engineers filed calmly up through two hatches to the mess hall above the engine room, and through the starboard catapult tower to the quarterdeck.

Hamlin and his crew were abandoning Turret 1. As he walked aft down the slanting deck, he was amazed to see the men either standing around quietly drawing life jackets or lining up without confusion at their stations, in spite of the rain of shells dropping all over the foundering ship.

Rooks stood at the head of a ladder leading to the main

deck. He was bidding good-bye to his men, wishing them good luck. Suddenly there was a blazing glare a few feet aft of the captain, as a 5-inch shell exploded. Rooks was dead.

Word of the captain's death passed quickly. Ensign C. D. Smith saw Rooks' Chinese cook, Tai Chi-sah, nicknamed Buddha, sitting in front of his cabin and told him to jump overboard. The Chinese shook his head. "Captain die, ship die. Now Buddha die."

There were only three men on the *Houston*'s forecastle. The list was getting worse and the ship was rolling peculiarly, so Hamlin left the ship. Once in the water he swam as fast as he could, for he was sure she would plunge any moment. One hundred yards away a torpedo whirred past. Then there was a blinding flash as it hit the side of the *Houston*. Hamlin doubled up from a blow in the stomach. He couldn't breathe. A shell burst nearby. Another painful shock.

Lieutenant Joseph Dalton was near the incinerator trying to get men to take their shoes off and leave before it was too late. The men were calm and there was no shouting; many seemed reluctant to leave the sinking ship.

By now it was only 10 feet to the sea. He jumped. It felt like a warm bath but the oily crust was nauseating. Since he had no life jacket, he struck out for a floating mattress. Clusters of men, most without jackets, were struggling around him. Spotting a raft, he began herding men toward it. Shells began falling nearby. He lifted his chest high out of the water to relieve the concussion. Even so it felt like a mule kicking him. He drifted on the mattress through fuel oil, then through a pool of gasoline which was dissolving the oil. He finally reached the raft and began ripping the mattress to pieces to make a sail. In the glare of searchlights he saw *Houston* listing, blazing.

Hamlin, still gasping for breath, turned around for a last look at the *Houston*. She lay dead in the water, her sides riddled with shell holes. Her guns stuck out crazily at odd angles. A bright orange flame sizzled and crackled halfway to the top of the foremast. He remembered the ship when he had first joined her, just after a cruise with President Roosevelt. She shone then with new paint, her brass and steel glistened.

The ship rolled gently to her side. The crackling flames went out with screaming hisses. Hamlin turned and swam as hard as he could to get out of the suction. Others, farther away, watched the *Houston*'s yardarms dip near the water. The cruiser paused and the Stars and Stripes seemed to wave defiantly from the mainmast. Then the big ship shuddered and slid out of sight. It was 12:45 A.M.

There was sudden, terrifying quiet. The battle was over. Survivors of the two Allied cruisers were swimming for shore. Of *Houston*'s 1000 men, less than half were still alive and many of these were drowning. About half of *Perth*'s crew of 680 were also alive but some of these were choking to death in the oily sea.

Japanese survivors of the torpedoed transports were crawling onto the sandy beaches of Bantam Bay. General Imamura's aide, exhausted and dispirited, was looking for his chief. At last he saw the general, his face black from oil, sitting on a pile of bamboo. The aide hurriedly limped to the general. "Congratulations," he said, "on the successful landing."

2   On the other, the eastern, end of Java, Lieutenant Giles was plotting *Edwards'* course as she led the 3 other American destroyers through the narrows of Bali Strait at 28 knots. He hugged the shores of Bali so the ship wouldn't stand out so clearly in the bright moonlight. When heavy clouds suddenly shrouded the full moon Giles knew his mother was praying for him. At 2:05 A.M., just as *Edwards* was clearing the strait and entering the Indian Ocean, he sighted a destroyer on the port bow, then another.

Commander Binford also saw them. "There are two ships on our port bow about 700 yards," he announced over voice radio to the three ships behind. "They may be destroyers. I don't know if they've seen us but I'm not opening fire. I'm trying to get out undetected. But if they shoot, return fire immediately."

There was silence for fifteen minutes, then the Japanese began firing, their shells passing over the American destroyers and hitting the beaches of Java.

The Americans returned fire.

"Breakers ahead," cried a lookout on *Edwards*.

Giles called out, "Full left rudder!"

Binford, hearing this, called to the helmsman, "Full left rudder!"

The *Edwards* came hard left, heading for the enemy ships, with the 3 American destroyers following. Several minutes later her skipper, Commander H. E. Eccles, brought *Edwards* 30 degrees to the right. Again Giles called for hard left rudder, again the ship missed the reef by yards.

Binford ordered smoke. As Japanese gunfire ceased, the

4 ships headed south for half an hour, then turned sharply to the west as if bound for Tjilatjap. Binford now stopped the smoke and headed south for Australia. Soon the last of the smoke blew away. No enemy was in sight. The old destroyers were safe.

For several years the families of those on *Houston* and *Perth* had no idea what had happened to their loved ones on the night of February 28, 1942. They knew only that the two ships had mysteriously disappeared somewhere off Java with all personnel listed as "missing in action."

Most United States naval authorities secretly concluded Captains Rooks and Waller and all their men had died, but by dawn of March 1, almost half were still alive. Some were swimming in the warm, oily water east toward nearby Java; some were heading south toward the tiny islands in the middle of Sunda Strait; some were just hanging on grimly to floats.

The oldest man on *Houston* was clinging to the spare airplane pontoon with a dozen others. This was Commander G. S. Rentz, the portly, gray-haired chaplain. When the pontoon began to sag dangerously, Rentz, near exhaustion, quietly swam away. A seaman brought him back. After two more attempts to leave were frustrated, he gasped, "You men are young with your lives ahead of you. I'm old and have had my fun."

He said a prayer for the men and then, before anyone could stop him, dropped out of sight. He had left his life jacket on the pontoon. Seaman First Class W. L. Beeman put it on.

Lieutenant Fulton, the engineer, was swimming toward a beach with three others. None of them knew it was Bantam Bay. Lieutenant Dalton's raft was still half a mile from the same bay. In the daylight he could see dozens of anchored transports, surrounded by many landing craft. One of these approached and started towing the raft to a larger ship. While the *Houston* men sat in the bobbing raft wondering what their fate would be, officers in the Japanese craft began to argue. Then the raft was suddenly cut loose and it began drifting southwest in a heavy current. Dalton saw a man in the Japanese ship's fantail lift his automatic rifle as if to shoot them. It was disconcerting but the Americans were now too tired to try to hide. The Japanese didn't shoot.

Though Dalton and the others paddled furiously to reach Java, the current was too strong. Several tried to swim toward shore and had to be hauled back.

The *Perth* survivors were even farther south. Polo Owen, in almost exactly the middle of the strait, was approaching Toppers Island. He and Petty Officer Tyrell were hanging onto a wood and metal recreation seat, once on the deck of the *Perth*. The morning sun made Owen's eyes sting. His eyelashes were stiff with oil. The seat began breaking up as it headed for the little mound-like island. The two men saw a plank and swam for it.

They drifted past Toppers, heading for the larger island of Sangiang, and Owen could see a white beach and palm trees. Then a fresh current began swinging them away from this island past men floating face up in their life jackets, knees drawn up as if in sleep. All dead.

Now Owen could see the blue haze of conical Krakatoa 20 miles away. Tyrell was muttering something and Owen thought, I can't last much longer. He wondered what drowning would feel like. After the horrors of the past few days it would be pleasant. He let go the plank and sank. Something rammed against his chin. Owen came up and saw Tyrell jerking the plank frantically and shouting, "For God's sake, don't leave me!"

All Owen could think to say was, "Sorry." He saw Tyrell's head slowly disappearing. He jerked the plank. Tyrell popped to the surface and said slowly, "I couldn't help it."

Owen wondered who the man was. What was his name? Then he thought, this is madness. He prayed for shelter from the blistering sun, asked God to restore him to his family in Australia.

On the north coast of Java, the Western Invasion Force was disembarking 100 miles west of Surabaja. Ever since midnight the broken-down remnants of the ABDA air force had been making sporadic raids on these transports. The efforts of the American, Dutch, New Zealand and Australian fliers were gallant but useless.

At dawn of March 1, the U.S. 17th Pursuit Squadron, composed of veterans of the hopeless Philippines campaign, was making its last Java mission. Nine battered P-40's—with blistered tires, worn brakes, shaky engines—approached the coast flying low. They saw 30 transports along the beach, with many small boats ferrying back and forth. Ashore lines of men, like rows of ants, were heading into the hills. This was the same division that had landed at Lingayen Gulf in the Philippines.

Heavy anti-aircraft fire from ships and beach caught the nine planes in a deadly cross fire. Three were hit instantly.

One, piloted by Lieutenant Cornelius Reagan, burst into flame and headed for the beach. Lieutenant Robert McWherter, on his wing, signaled Reagan to follow him to the beach and bail out. Reagan waved. He rolled back the canopy of his P-40, reached forward, lit a cigarette on the flaming motor and put it to his mouth. Then he crashed.

A few barges were sunk but only six planes returned—a typical Java mission.

On the southern coast of the long island, the *Seawitch* was unloading its 27 crated P-40's at Tjilatjap. When a group of stranded American airmen, veterans of the disillusionment of the Philippines, saw this, they laughed derisively. According to the rumor of the moment, the *Queen Mary* was Java-bound, loaded to the gunwales with P-40's. It was the same old story—too little, too late. Even the 27 P-40's were useless. There was no time to assemble them, and the pilots to fly them would soon be leaving for Australia. They were dumped, still crated, into the bay.

While Japanese were landing at Bantam Bay and on the north coast of the island, Java was already disintegrating. In Bandung the British admiral, A. F. E. Palliser, Helfrich's chief of staff, telephoned Commodore Collins at Batavia, telling him to send all British warships to Tjilatjap at once and then leave Batavia himself. At 8:30 A.M. the British naval base staff left the city in a truck and car convoy and headed for the south. Half an hour later Palliser and the American commander, Glassford, came to Helfrich's headquarters. They asked him to cancel his order to fight to the end.

Helfrich doggedly insisted he was only following the explicit orders of the Combined Chiefs of Staff. "I am going to fight as long as there are ships. A large concentration of submarines in the Java Sea could still be successful. The enemy will make another attempt to land tonight near Rembang. Even if he succeeds I'll attack the next wave of transports."

"I have instructions from the Admiralty," said Palliser, "to withdraw His Majesty's ships from Java when resistance will serve no further useful purpose. This time, in my judgment, has come." He was sending his ships to Ceylon at once.

"Do you realize you're still under my orders?" said Helfrich angrily.

"I do, of course. But in this vital matter I cannot do other than my duty as I see it."

"Have you forgotten the enormous support I gave the British cause in Malaya? All of my fighting fleet—my cruisers, my destroyers, my submarines, my air—all of it was placed at your disposal. And to our great loss. I did much more to defend Singapore than the British Fleet has done to defend the Netherlands East Indies. Now when I ask you for the same sacrifice I made, when my newest submarines went into that hell on the east coast of Malaya and the west coast of Borneo and when my surface vessels protected your convoys . . . now you can refuse!"

"I am grateful for your support but I cannot alter my decision."

Helfrich turned to Glassford. "What do you intend to do?"

Although the American agreed with Palliser that it was useless to fight, he said, "My instructions are to report to you for duty. Any order you give me will be obeyed at once."

Helfrich sighed heavily. "You may give your ships any orders you wish, Admiral Palliser," he said. Then he turned to Glassford. "You will order your ships to Australia." The Dutchman thanked the American effusively for his help.

3 At this same moment the last 3 ships to survive the Battle of Java Sea were about 60 miles south of Borneo. The damaged *Exeter* and her 2 destroyer escorts were slowly heading northwest hoping to escape south through Sunda Strait that night. But Captain O. L. Gordon of *Exeter* already realized this was a forlorn hope. A few minutes previously, at 9:35 A.M., the masts of 2 enemy heavy cruisers had been sighted to the south.

The Japanese cruisers belonged to the victor of the Battle of Java Sea, Admiral Takagi. They were *Nachi* and *Haguro* and, with 2 destroyers, were moving in for the kill. Another powerful force was coming from the other side. Alerted by Takagi, Vice Admiral Ibou Takahashi, commander-in-chief of the Third Fleet, was approaching from the north with 2 heavy cruisers and 2 destroyers.

In between these two forces, *Exeter* and her 2 escorts writhed trying to escape. At 10:10 A.M. Captain Gordon turned the *Exeter* to the southeast while the destroyers *Pope* and *Encounter* laid down a smoke screen. Speed was increased to maximum, 25 knots, but the 4 big Japanese cruisers closed the trap and at 10:20 A.M. opened fire. *Exeter* replied while *Pope* and *Encounter* began firing at 4 converging Japanese destroyers.

By 11:00 A.M., though no real damage had been done, the *Exeter* was hopelessly trapped. Five minutes later she loosed torpedoes in a desperate strike at Takahashi's 2 cruisers. The range was too great.

Salvos from the Japanese cruisers were falling closer. Soon *Exeter* was bracketed. *Pope* and *Encounter* darted around the slow ship, trying to distract attention. Lieutenant Commander Welford Blinn of *Pope* launched 4 torpedoes at Takahashi's cruisers, then swung around and aimed 5 more at Takagi's force.

Even so, the Japanese moved closer, and at 11:20 A.M. an 8-inch shell parted the one remaining steampipe of *Exeter*. Almost immediately the big ship slowed to 4 knots. *Pope* and *Encounter*, realizing nothing could now be done, raced to the east to save themselves.

Exeter's main engines had stopped, so had the dynamos. Her turrets were frozen, with silent guns pointing in different directions. The steering gear was useless. All power had failed. The inside of the ship filled with smoke as the forward boiler room burst into flame from escaping fuel oil.

The order was given to sink the ship. Magazine flood valves were opened; the engine rooms were allowed to flood through the condensers; and all watertight doors opened. Down below the fire raged and the ship began to list as black smoke poured out from her funnels.

To Lieutenant Commander George Cooper, the first lieutenant, standing at the rear of the bridge, she still seemed defiant, like a stag at bay. Men were cutting down Carley floats; timber was being cast adrift. Shells were falling all over the ship from close-range fire. Cooper saw the after superstructure catch fire as projectiles whined overhead sounding like the song of the Valkyries.

The ship was beginning to heel over and she was only making slight headway. Men began going over the side in groups, drifting astern. The executive officer, calmly walking around the ship, came up to Cooper on the quarterdeck. "This is it," he said in an impassive voice. "Best of luck, Number One."

Cooper threw his binoculars on the deck and jumped from the quarterdeck into the sea. He saw a destroyer closing on the starboard beam of *Exeter*. It fired a torpedo. It was a good shot, hitting her right amidships. The big cruiser shuddered a bit and almost instantly flopped to starboard until her funnels and masts were horizontal. The white ensign was still flying from the masthead.

As *Exeter* put up her forefoot as a final sign of defiance and began to plunge, everyone in the sea spontaneously cheered. Then there was only a great swirl of water, smoke and steam.

Ten miles to the east the other British ship, *Encounter*, was also trapped and sinking. As men dropped over her sides, the *Pope* raced toward a heavy rain squall just ahead. At 11:50 the old American four-stacker plunged into protective darkness, but she too was doomed. Ten minutes later she was sighted by a float plane from one of the cruisers and at 12:30 P.M. 6 dive bombers from the nearby aircraft carrier *Ryujo* appeared overhead.

Commander Blinn zigzagged his ship, avoiding 10 dive-bombing attacks. On the eleventh drop, a bomb just missed the side of the ship abreast No. 4 torpedo tube. It exploded underwater, ripping a large hole below the waterline and knocking the port shaft seriously out of line.

Six high-level bombers from *Ryujo* began attacking from 3000 feet. While Blinn was maneuvering to avoid the second level bombing attack, his damage control officer reported flooding was beyond control. Blinn ordered watertight doors and ports opened. After the wounded were put in a boat, Blinn ordered demolition charges set off in the engine rooms to insure sinking the destroyer. Finally the ship was abandoned.

At about 1:00 P.M., shells from Takagi's rapidly approaching cruisers fell all around the ship. A salvo hit *Pope*. It disappeared, stern first, in fifteen seconds. Now there wasn't a single Allied ship afloat on the Java Sea.

George Cooper of *Exeter* was just being hauled aboard a Japanese destroyer. The decks were crowded with 300 survivors. When the destroyer steamed away Cooper and others pointed to the hundreds of men still struggling in the water, but the officers on the bridge took no notice. It was terrible to see messmates being left to drown but Cooper knew there was nothing he could do. He looked up at the Japanese skipper. He was smoking, occasionally giving an order otherwise he was completely impassive and never looked at his 300 prisoners. He showed no signs of jubilation, relief or even fatigue. He might have been on a pleasure cruise having just stopped to give his crew a bathe.

The sea carnage had also spread to the waters south of Java. By the end of the day the Southern Striking Force of Admiral N. Kondo owned the waters below Tjilatjap and was relentlessly cutting down transports and warships fleeing Java. The U.S. Navy oiler *Pecos*, carrying all the survivors of *Langley*, was sunk 400 miles south of Java. Although the U.S. destroyer *Whipple* raced in to pick up 232 men from the sea, the rest had to be left to their death. *Whipple* escaped but two other four-stackers, *Pillsbury* and *Edsall*,

vere caught by Kondo's battleships and carriers that afternoon and sent to the bottom.

By midnight the last flyable American plane was getting
ready to leave the dying island of Java. It was an OB-30—
the British export version of the B-24—and it was dangerously loaded with 35 passengers. At 12:30 A.M., March 2, the
plane with its load of airmen left the Jogjakarta (now known
as Jockstrap) field. The frustrating, hopeless American air
effort in Java was over.

That same dawn, a flying boat left a lake near Bandung
for Ceylon. In it was Admiral Helfrich. He took with him
only a small valise. Behind lay his family, friends and
possessions. Ahead was an unknown future. He felt like a
raw ensign.

By midmorning Japanese of the Western Invasion Force
were rapidly converging on Batavia and Bandung from two
sides. The Eastern Force was already halfway to Surabaja
and well on the way to Tjilatjap. Enemy resistance was being wiped out with little trouble. It puzzled General Imamura.
He had expected a long, arduous campaign. Was he walking
into a trap?

Commander Shukichi Toshikawa of the 5th Destroyer
Flotilla was talking to Imamura's chief of staff. He had
been chosen, he explained, to apologize to the general for
torpedoing his four transports and dumping him in Bantam
Bay.

"Don't tell General Imamura," said the chief of staff in
alarm. "He thinks the American cruiser *Houston* did it. Let
her have the credit." To this day official records have done
just that.

The survivors of *Perth* and *Houston* were still scattered
around Sunda Strait. Polo Owen and Tyrell, each hanging
desperately to the end of a plank, were near the end of
their endurance. Then Owen saw something black to the
left. Tyrell blew his shrill whistle. He blew until he was
winded.

Finally he cried, "I can see it there. It looks like a boat.
Christ, it's a boat. Now it's gone . . . gone . . ." His head
started going under water.

"Don't go. We'll be picked up. Hang on, for God's sake,"
cried Owen. As Tyrell's head rose from the water, Owen
grabbed the whistle. He blew it over and over again.

Finally an Australian voice shouted, "For Christ's sake,
stop blowing that bloody flute. We 'eard you the first time."
In a moment Owen was in the bottom of a boat with Tyrell
beside him. Owen sighed with contentment when he felt

something solid between him and the sea, then passed out.

The largest group of *Houston* survivors had been captured on the beach of Bantam Bay. Since landing, Lieutenants Hamlin and Fulton had been toting boxes and cases from the beachhead to assembly points. Fulton noticed many of the cases had soda bottles from Saigon tied to them. Now in the darkness the *Houston* men were pulling rickshaws filled with ammunition and dogcarts loaded with luggage up a road. Most of the men had lost their shoes and their feet were cut and bleeding. They were heading toward Serang, on the road to Batavia, but they didn't know where they were going or what their fate would be when they got there.

4   That day General Gordon Bennett, the red-haired Australian commander, arrived in Melbourne after a thrilling escape from Singapore by native boat, launch and plane. When he called on Lieutenant General V. A. H. Sturdee, the Australian chief of general staff, his reception was cold.

"Your escape was ill-advised," said Sturdee. He returned to his work, leaving Bennett standing in the middle of the room.

Bennett had returned to a far different Australia. Eleven days previously the war had landed squarely on her front door. In a devastating daylight raid, 81 planes from the 4 carriers of Admiral Nagumo, of Pearl Harbor fame, had almost wiped out Darwin, the main seaport in north Australia. The U.S. destroyer *Peary* and 8 other ships had been sunk, 9 damaged and 22 Allied planes destroyed. Only 5 Japanese had been shot down.

At one frightening stroke the Australian people were suddenly forced to realize they were wide open to invasion. New Britain was gone. Half of New Guinea was gone, the rest apparently going. Java and Timor were being gobbled up.

Fearsome posters pictured a brutal Japanese soldier coming across the sea out of a rising sun with one hand grabbing the map of Australia. Across it was written: THE WORD NOW IS MUST.

People were confused and divided. "People are unhappy about Darwin," wrote Sir Keith Murdock in the Sydney *Sun.* "They know that workers were holding stop-work meetings a day or two before the raid. They know that ships that should have been cleared with proper appliances and labor are still lying in the harbor exposed to bombs. Australia has pegged out a tremendous claim upon the world. She asks now that she be allowed to hold a vast land for her seven million white people. Let us then seize the chance, for if we cannot rise to this occasion, then assuredly we can never rise to any occasion."

Not long after this Yates McDaniel landed in Australia where he was reunited with his wife in Melbourne and made chief of bureau of the AP for the Australian area. One morning, while still recovering from his narrow escapes, he was awakened by an insistent knock. It was "Newsreel" Wong. Hearing that McDaniel had arrived in Australia, he had immediately flown from Ceylon.

"Where is Doris?" he asked.

McDaniel became concerned. Her ship should have long since reached Ceylon or India. He told Wong the name of the ship. The two men went downtown and checked with shipping experts. There was no news at all. They wouldn't learn until after the war that Doris Lim's ship had been sunk soon after leaving Java. Not a passenger survived.

By the morning of March 3, the waters below Java were a graveyard of Allied ships as Admiral Kondo made this a Japanese sea. In addition to merchant ships, the British destroyer *Stronghold* was sunk and the convoy being escorted by the Australian gunboat *Yarra* was being hemmed in. Yet in spite of the shocking toll, many ships were stealing past the mighty Japanese force to Ceylon and Australia.

The land battle for Java was coming to a sudden humiliating end, too. The Allies were scattered and disorganized. Some groups battled desperately; other groups did almost nothing. Nobody knew what was going on as the two great invasion forces converged on the key cities of Java. On March 5, at a conference of senior Allied officers at Bandung, Lieutenant General H. ter Poorten, commander of the ABDA army, said guerrilla warfare was impossible. The Indonesians were too hostile to the Dutch. Three days later ter Poorten broadcast a message telling everyone to lay down arms.

The last message to the outside world came from a dispatcher at Bandung's commercial radio station. Just before it was destroyed he said, "We are shutting down. Good-bye till better times. Long live the Queen!"

Java was gone. Like all other fortresses cut off by sea— Guam, Wake, Hong Kong and Singapore—she had fallen. The final sea and land battles had cost the Japanese 1 mine sweeper, 4 transports, a number of barges, a few damaged warships and less than 1000 lives. The easy victory, however, had its pitfalls. The Japanese had learned little, many top commanders concluding that their present equipment and tactics were good enough for future operations.

The Allies had suffered a humiliating and devastating defeat. Defense had been hopeless from the start, but it had not been a completely useless, senseless gesture of bravado. The Americans, British, Dutch and Australians had kept faith with each other. Abject surrender, as in France, might have demoralized the entire Southwest Pacific. In spite of bitter arguments and recriminations, there was still an underlying spirit of unity among the members of defeated ABDA and now all their eyes hopefully turned toward the only remaining bastions inside the new Japanese Empire—Bataan and Corregidor.

18

". . . And I Shall Return"

1 The stalemate in Bataan continued through February. In Tokyo, Prime Minister Tojo was becoming more impatient with each passing day. Militarily Bataan was of little importance, but its propaganda value for the enemy was constantly rising. It had to be liquidated quickly. About a month earlier Homma had informed higher headquarters that the Bataan campaign could not be concluded successfully without heavy infantry and artillery reinforcements. Although these were already arriving, and training for the final attack was under way, Tojo doubted Homma's ability to draw up a plan that would bring the quick success so sorely needed.

The prime minister called in his secretary, Colonel Susumu Nishiura, one of his young advisers. Tojo explained the problem, pointing out that he didn't want to violate procedure by speaking directly to the army chief. "Perhaps," suggested Tojo, "you could convey my worries to Colonel Hattori?" This was Takushiro Hattori, army operations officer for Imperial General Headquarters. As prime minister and minister of war Tojo had no direct voice in actual combat operations. Even suggestions had to be made subtly. He knew he could trust Hattori, who had once been his private secretary. Hattori was not only one of the most brilliant young officers in the Army but one of the ablest military diplomats.

That day Nishiura visited Hattori. They had studied together at military school when both were youths and had always remained close friends. Hattori, already worried about

Bataan, put his entire staff to work. Within a week his desk was piled with detailed staff reports and plans. After assimilating all this material, he decided that the most unexpected place of attack was Mt. Samat, a rugged hill 1920 feet high sitting just behind the center of the American line. Hattori's plan was simple: a concentrated air and artillery bombardment on a two-and-a-half mile sector in front of Mt. Samat, followed by a full-scale infantry drive through the hole. According to his calculations, resistance would be soon crushed and the Americans would surrender.

The plan was approved by his chief, General Sugiyama. Now the Hattori plan had to be presented to General Homma's staff so subtly they would think it was their idea and thus save face. Hattori called in Lieutenant Kumao Imoto, briefed him on the plan, and ordered him to fly to the Philippines. Then Hattori checked his personal schedule. He was due to make an inspection of the Southwest Pacific in early April with Sugiyama. He would juggle the schedule so he could be in the Philippines during the attack. For once he'd like to see one of his plans in operation.

2 After the elimination of the Pockets, the American and Filipino defenders had had little to do except patrol, train for future operations, and strengthen the long line across the peninsula. For a time morale continued to be high. The men had been heartened by reports of Japanese collapse. A communiqué from Corregidor stated that Homma had commited hara-kiri because of his failures in Bataan; Yamashita, the "Tiger of Malaya," had taken his place. This false story became embellished with details: Homma had chosen for the suicide MacArthur's apartment in the Manila Hotel, where funeral rites had also been held.

Food, however, had become the main interest in Bataan. Many front-line troops were getting only a third of a ration a day. They were walking skeletons, coming closer each day to actual starvation. The efforts to bring supplies to Corregidor and Bataan through the Japanese sea blockade had failed. Ships and submarines had brought in little more than 1000 tons of ration, only enough to feed Bataan's 80,000 soldiers and 26,000 civilians for four days.

By now most of the carabao (water buffalo) had been eaten. Early in March, while Navy Lieutenant Champlin was talking to Wainwright, a cavalry captain informed the general that the supply of fodder for the remaining 250 cavalry horses and 48 pack mules was almost gone.

"I knew this was coming, Captain," said Wainwright. One of the horses was his own prize jumper, Joseph Conrad. "We have a lot of men who also are short of food and horse meat is not so bad." He paused, then said, "You will begin killing the horses at once. And I want you to kill Joseph Conrad first." As he turned away and started back to his trailer, his eyes were filled with tears.

The hungry men were vulnerable to the most debilitating ailments. Quinine was almost gone, and they were now located in one of the most malaria-infested areas in the world. Over 500 were hospitalized in the first week of March alone. An epidemic of catastrophic proportions threatened to break out momentarily. Already base hospitals, collecting stations, field stations and aid stations were overflowing. It was a common sight, General Clifford Bluemel wrote his wife, to see men stricken with malaria lying helpless and untended beside their foxholes.

Weakened by their constant fight against hunger, malaria, dysentery, beriberi, dengue and scurvy, most of the men became concerned only with the struggle for existence. Their minds were dangerously idle, making them prey to doubts, fear and enemy propaganda. Until recently most had believed the optimistic reports from MacArthur's headquarters that an enormous supply of food, planes, ammunition and reinforcements would soon arrive. These official reports to the front-line troops had given rise to a series of fantastic rumors. Some men actually believed the convoy was bringing an entire cavalry division of Negro soldiers who would gallop into Bataan on snow-white horses. Others believed it was bringing a special group of sharpshooters commanded by the World War I hero, Sergeant York.

But by now only the most naïve believed the "mile-long" convoy was coming. And Sergeant York and his squirrel-shooters had become a standard joke. Such rumors had been displaced by disillusionment. Americans wrote disparaging poems about Roosevelt and "Dugout Doug"; many Filipinos were asking themselves what they were doing on Bataan, away from their loved ones. All the front-line troops griped about the rear echelons. Those in the service areas, they complained with justification, had more steel helmets and food than the fighters. Only one in four at the front had a blanket, shelter half or raincoat and about 20,000 were shoeless.

Everyone on Bataan griped about those on Corregidor who were "living off the fat of the land." This came to a climax when a waybill for three anti-aircraft batteries which were receiving Corregidor-type rations was made public. Among the items for this relatively small group were: a case of ham and bacon, 24 cans of lard substitute, peas, tomatoes, corn, peaches, 24 bottles of catsup, 50 cartons of cigarettes and 600 pounds of ice. The luxury items grew with every telling as the story spread all over Bataan. To men existing on rice and perhaps a little monkey or iguana, it made those responsible for such inequities worse than the Japanese. The 50 cartons of cigarettes alone were more than an entire infantry division was getting. A man was lucky to get one cigarette a day at the front.

By now the Japanese propagandists had changed their early tactics and were no longer trying to turn the Filipinos against their American "masters." It was obvious that the great majority of Filipinos were fond of Americans and the American way of life. The appeal was now aimed at hunger, home and sex. Colored pictures of food were dropped. Then came menus from the Manila Hotel, the Panciteria Antigua and the Maritima Steamship Company. Stamped across the menus in red were the words: DON'T YOU WISH YOU COULD ENJOY THIS?

Other leaflets pictured a tearful mother calling to her son or a surrendered soldier enjoying a sumptuous meal surrounded by his smiling wife and children.

The crudest leaflets featured sex. The most effective of these was a "striptease" series. First, the picture of the face of a beautiful woman was dropped from planes. Next came a view of the same woman from the waist up, with a shawl just covering her large breasts. The third showed the woman, full length, draped seductively with a shawl. In the fourth picture, the shawl was gone. The final picture showed the sex act.

Although most of the propaganda leaflets were thrown away or used in the latrines, they had an undeniable psychological effect. By the first week in March morale on Bataan had dropped dangerously. The verse of correspondent Frank Hewlett, who had spent much time up front with Wainwright, expressed what most men on Bataan—Filipinos and Americans alike—were thinking:

> We're the battling bastards of Bataan:
> No momma, no poppa, no Uncle Sam,
> No aunts, no uncles, no nephews, no nieces,
> No rifles, no guns or artillery pieces,
> And nobody gives a damn.

3 On the morning of March 10, Wainwright drove up front in a bantam car to see how the front-line troops were getting along. It was clear and hot. A perfect day for strafing, thought Lieutenant Champlin, who sat next to the general. But when no planes appeared. Champlin relaxed and put on sunglasses. As Wainwright began quizzing his two aides, Pugh and Dooley, on cavalry tactics, Champlin was thinking of the off-the-record talk he and the general had had the night before. After Champlin had promised not to repeat their conversation, Wainwright said, "The Army high command has made three major military mistakes here in the Philippines. Ranking officers failed to visit troops in the front lines when all we have to offer our people is morale. Second: we shouldn't have had to rely on half-trained Filipinos. More troops should have been sent from the U.S. before the war." The last mistake he blamed on MacArthur. "We should never have discarded the Grunert plan of retreating into Bataan for that grandiose scheme of getting the Japs at the beaches with a paper army."

Champlin happened to look into the glare of the sun. For a moment he couldn't move or speak. A black speck was hurtling directly toward the jeep. The speck grew larger. It developed wings which began to dip from side to side.

Champlin finally found his voice. "Get the hell out of the car! Quickly!"

The other three officers looked at Champlin as if he were crazy. It reminded the Navy man of a slow-motion movie. He yelled again, then released the safety strap across the general's seat, seized him by the scruff of the neck and leaped out of the car. The two tumbled down a ditch into a thorny bush.

Champlin looked up at the road and saw bullets spattering into the empty car. Aiming a Garand rifle he had borrowed that morning from Wainwright, he fired at the strafing plane.

After several passes the plane left. Heads popped up from vines and bushes. "Jesus," said Dooley, looking at Champlin with wide eyes, "that was a close one."

Champlin looked at Wainwright, sitting calmly on the ground with an amused expression on his face, his eyes twinkling. "You kind of like that gun, don't you, son?"

"Yes, General, I guess I do."

"It's yours. Take it and thanks. He'd have gotten us if you hadn't spotted him coming out of the sun."

"But, General," said Champlin, "this gun is Government Issue."

"Who's fighting this war? The pencil-pushers in Washington or you and me?"

That noon, Wainwright and his aide, Major Johnny Pugh, were on a motor launch heading for Corregidor. MacArthur had asked to see the commander of I Corps immediately. Soon the two men were in MacArthur's office inside Malinta Tunnel. "General MacArthur is going to leave here and go to Australia," said his chief of staff, General Sutherland. "He's at the house now and wants to see you. But I'll give you a fill-in first."

Wainwright listened intently as Sutherland explained how Roosevelt had been trying to persuade MacArthur to evacuate the Philippines since February 22. "Until yesterday the general kept refusing. He plans to leave tomorrow evening by torpedo boat for Mindanao." A Flying Fortress would then take him to Australia. "You will be placed in command of all troops on Luzon," continued Sutherland. "If it's agreeable to you, General Jones will get another star and take over your I Corps." After explaining that Colonel Beebe would be promoted to general and made MacArthur's deputy, carrying out his orders from Australia, Sutherland said, "You look hungry, Skinny. Have some lunch and then we'll go up to the house."

"Nope, I think not." Wainwright jerked his thumb toward Bataan. "We only eat twice a day over there."

The two generals walked out the east end of the tunnel, then through the scrub jungle for half a mile down the island's polliwog tail to a small gray house. MacArthur came out on the porch, grinned and held out his hand. "Jonathan," he said as they shook hands, "I want you to understand my position very plainly." He was leaving, he said, only because of insistent, repeated orders from Roosevelt. At first he had told his staff he would refuse, but they convinced him that defying the President's direct order would bring disciplinary action. "I want you to make it known throughout all elements of your command that I'm leaving over my repeated protests."

"Of course I will, Douglas," said Wainwright.

"If I get through to Australia, you know I'll come back as soon as I can with as much as I can." Then he warned of the necessity of greater defense in depth. "And be sure to give them everything you've got with your artillery. That's the best arm you have."

The two were quiet for a moment. In the distance the dull

rumble of battle from Bataan could be heard. Wainwright was thinking of the dwindling ammunition and food supply, his air force of two battered P-40's, of the spreading malaria and dysentery and lack of medicine. He said, "You'll get through."

"And back," MacArthur added with determination. He gave Wainwright a box of cigars and two large jars of shaving cream. "Good-bye, Jonathan." They shook hands warmly. "If you're still on Bataan when I get back, I'll make you a lieutenant general."

"I'll be on Bataan if I'm alive." Wainwright turned and slowly started back to his launch.

As darkness fell the following day, March 11, MacArthur stepped onto the porch of his house and approached his wife. Even those on Corregidor who disliked MacArthur thought she was modest, charming and courageous. "It's time to mount up, Jeannie," he said quietly. MacArthur, Mrs. MacArthur, their four-year-old son, Arthur, a Chinese nurse and Major Charles Morhouse stepped into a car and were driven to the north Mine dock. To Morhouse it was like a dream. The day before he had been surgeon of the Provisional Air Corps Regiment on Bataan. Though he had never met MacArthur before, the general had chosen him to be the attending physician on the rigorous trip to Australia.

The MacArthur party walked along the wide, concrete pier, then up a gangway to PT Boat 41. Its commander was the colorful, bearded Lieutenant John Bulkeley. Following Mrs. MacArthur, the Chinese nurse, Ah Cheu, carried Arthur aboard. MacArthur shook hands with Major General George Moore, chief of harbor defenses. "George, keep the flag flying. I'm coming back." MacArthur stepped aboard. Then came Major Morhouse, General Sutherland, Navy Captain Harold Ray. The last man aboard was MacArthur's aide, Lieutenant Colonel Sidney Huff. He waved to Colonel Frederick Ward and called out, "We're coming back up here, Freddy."

The PT boat slowly pulled away from the pier. MacArthur was standing, looking back at Corregidor. At that moment, the loudspeaker near Ward crackled. It was Carlos Romulo, the "Voice of Freedom," broadcasting to troops all over the Philippines. MacArthur took off his familiar field marshal's cap and raised it in farewell to the few on the pier.

It was about 8:00 P.M. by the time PT 41 reached the mine field protecting Corregidor. An hour later three other PT boats, carrying Admiral Rockwell and twelve more of MacArthur's staff, met Bulkeley's boat at the edge of the field.

Suddenly, with Rockwell's craft leading, the four boats sped south with a great roar. A searchlight from Corregidor blinked on, lit up the boats and suddenly was doused.

Rockwell's boat, PT 34, piloted by Lieutenant Robert B. Kelly, exchanged places with Bulkeley when clear of the mine fields, then soon fell behind the leader. "Don't you think we're getting a little far apart?" said the admiral. Kelly tried to close up the gap, but the engine was full of carbon.

"Damn it," said Rockwell as the gap grew, "let's close up." Kelly sent a whispered order to the engineers to disconnect the throttle and push the carburetors up by hand. In a moment, PT 34 roared wildly past Bulkeley's boat. Rockwell, worried by this erratic performance, looked at Kelly dubiously. It was only then that the young lieutenant revealed the poor condition of his boat.

"My God," said the admiral softly. He then noticed Kelly sighting along his fingers as they passed an island. "Don't you have a pelorus?" Kelly did not. "I suppose Bulkeley's boat has better means?" It didn't apparently. "How in hell do you navigate?" asked Rockwell sharply.

"By guess and by God, sir," said Kelly with a smile.

By midnight all four boats had become widely separated. Just before dawn the lieutenant junior grade in command of PT 32 scanned the horizon with his glasses. "Jap destroyer," he cried excitedly, pointing behind them at something approaching fast in the murky light. "She has 5-inch guns. If we resist it means the lives of all the men in the boat."

"We're damned well going to resist," said Brigadier General Hugh Casey, MacArthur's engineer, and one of the boat's five passengers. The excited young skipper shouted commands to man machine guns and prepare torpedoes for launching, then himself cut the lashings and pushed overboard all the reserve gas drums.

By now the other vessel was closing in from behind. Brigadier General Spencer Akin, the signal officer, was about to drop overboard a laundry bag filled with code devices. The sailors at the machine guns and torpedo tubes were preparing to attack.

"That's one of our boats," cried out Casey.

A moment later the "destroyer" they had narrowly missed attacking pulled alongside. It was Bulkeley's boat. MacArthur, wearing gold cap and a fieldjacket, was standing, soaking wet. Beside him were his wife, also wet but smiling, and Ah Cheu holding Arthur. The boy, though wet and seasick, was not crying. With jaw set, he was a small imitation of his father.

MacArthur asked Casey to come aboard to discuss their immediate future. They were still far from the first rendezvous, a small island of the Cuyo group, and it would soon be broad daylight. After a short conference, it was agreed that though it was risky to continue, it was even more dangerous to wait until dark.

The two boats didn't reach the island rendezvous until 4:00 that afternoon. Waiting in a cove in the sweltering sun was Rockwell's boat. Here a second conference was held. MacArthur wondered if he and his family should make the rest of the trip by submarine. One was scheduled to appear at this same spot the following day just in case its services were needed.

"We'd better get the hell out of here fast," advised Rockwell. There was even the chance, he said, that the submarine wouldn't appear. Sutherland agreed.

Bulkeley warned them that the next lap would be even rougher than the first, since the weather might worsen. Rockwell, anxious to get moving, assured MacArthur the weather was going to be good.

The general turned to his chief of staff. "Dick, I can't do anything to Rockwell. But if it's rough tonight, I'll boil you in oil."

The men in the boat which had dumped its spare fuel were distributed between the other two boats and an hour before sunset, with Rockwell leading, they started toward Mindanao. Within an hour a Japanese cruiser loomed up in the northeast. The two boats turned, hiding in the glaring rays of the setting sun. Half an hour later, with tropical suddenness, it was pitch-dark. Rockwell led them back to the east and they slipped along the coast line of Negros Island.

A wind sprang up, lightning zigzagged across the sky. Rockwell was steering through the narrow passage in the Mindanao Sea without charts, guided only by instinct and the smell from nearby islands. Bulkeley stayed behind letting the other boat run interference. He navigated by bubble sextant and bearing, using the only charts of the little flotilla. Fortunately both boats broke into the Mindanao Sea without running aground. Here huge 15-foot waves crashed against the frail craft.

In the first boat, Rockwell stayed on the bridge with Kelly even though foaming waves smashed over the cockpit, soaking everyone. As the waves grew in size he remembered his advice to MacArthur. "The general's going to give me hell for this in the morning."

At dawn, March 13, the island of Mindanao was sighted. "Good navigation, Kelly," said Rockwell. "I wouldn't have believed it possible."

The two craft roared along the coast at top speed. At 7:00 A.M. Bulkeley's boat, now in the lead, headed for the Bugo dock, near the Del Monte pineapple factory.

Colonel William Morse, waiting on the dock with a guard of U.S. soldiers, saw a tall figure in the bow of the first boat. It reminded him of the picture of Washington crossing the Delaware. The sun glistened on the gold-braided visor of the man's cap. There was no other cap like this in the world.

"Hello, Morse," called MacArthur in an unconcerned voice. His face was pale, his eyes dark-circled. Obviously dead-tired, he squared his shoulders and stepped off the boat. Excited Filipinos began to appear magically. The general turned to Bulkeley. "Commander, I'm recommending a Silver Star for all members of your crew. You've taken me out of the jaws of death and I won't forget it." Then he turned to Morse and asked where he could relieve himself.

Tall, bespectacled Major General William Sharp, commander of the Mindanao forces, drove MacArthur up the mountain road to the south. In an hour they reached the vast, sprawling Del Monte pineapple plantation. Four Flying Fortresses were scheduled to be waiting here for the general's party.

Sharp explained with some embarrassment that the planes had not as yet arrived. The following day a lone, patched-up Flying Fortress landed at Del Monte. Four had left Australia. Two had turned back with engine trouble, one had crashed in the sea off Bugo. These had been the best planes the U.S. Army commander in Australia, Lieutenant General George Brett, could scrape up. He had tried to borrow four of the dozen brand-new Flying Fortresses assigned to Vice Admiral Herbert Leary, commander of the Australia-New Zealand Force.

"I'd like to help you, Brett," Leary had said, "but it is quite impossible. We need those planes here and can't spare them for a ferry job, no matter how important it is."

When MacArthur saw the only B-17 that had safely reached Del Monte he was incensed. A veteran of the Philippine campaign, it was obviously worn-out. Its turbo superchargers wouldn't operate; the expander tube on the right brake had ruptured from age. The general was also not at all impressed with its pilot, Lieutenant Harl Pease, Jr. He told Sharp he flatly refused to ride in a brokendown crate piloted by an "inexperienced boy." (Pease, in spite of his youthful looks, was already well-seasoned by combat and regarded by fellow fliers as one of the best pilots in the Southwest Pacific.)

MacArthur sent a blistering radiogram to General Brett asking for other planes. He also radioed General Marshall:

THE BEST THREE PLANES IN THE UNITED STATES OR HAWAII SHOULD BE MADE AVAILABLE WITH COMPLETELY ADEQUATE EXPERIENCED CREWS. TO ATTEMPT SUCH A DESPERATE AND IMPORTANT TRIP WITH INADEQUATE EQUIPMENT WOULD AMOUNT TO CONSIGNING THE WHOLE PARTY TO DEATH AND I COULD NOT ACCEPT SUCH A RESPONSIBILITY.

When Brett got this message, he once more called on Admiral Leary, this time determined to be more forceful. To his amazement, Leary didn't raise a single objection. A radiogram from Washington had seen to that, evidently. Brandnew bombers were instantly made available, but it took another day to prepare them for the long flight.

The resultant delay was causing increasing nervousness at Del Monte. By now everyone in north Mindanao knew MacArthur was there. Since Japanese were already entrenched in the southern part of the island, General Sharp was expecting enemy raids momentarily.

Heavy guards surrounded the homes and clubhouse of the Del Monte compound. By the evening of March 15, the new plans from Australia still had not arrived and the tension was becoming intolerable. Captain Allison Ind, formerly Brereton's intelligence officer, went out for a walk that night. He was a small man with an alert, inquisitive mind. After some argument he persuaded a sentry from Texas to let him go outside the ring of American guards. It was quiet and peaceful in the strange Cagayan countryside. Suddenly he heard the crunch of a boot on gravel. Against the stars he saw the black figure of a man wearing a cap. He knew there were no Americans outside the ring of guards; Filipinos would wear straw hats. The cap could only belong to a Japanese. He silently dropped to the ground, pulled out his long-barreled pistol. He put the gun under his left armpit to muffle the sound and softly cocked it. The figure was now standing stockstill as if listening. Slowly Ind raised the gun until the sights were in position. His target was the crown of the cap. He began to squeeze the trigger, already filed down to a hair release. He knew he couldn't miss at this short distance.

Then a second figure appeared and he heard a woman say, "I don't hear it now." Ind recognized the voice of Jean MacArthur. He felt the strength drain from him. "It's Ind, General," he said weakly.

"Where are you, Ind?" asked MacArthur.

"In the plantation, sir. I mistook you for a Japanese infiltration party. I almost shot your ears off."

Mrs. MacArthur gasped when she saw the gun, but the general only laughed softly. "Well, you better get up here and we'll decide who's going to escort whom back to the compound."

The next night, March 16, three new B-17's arrived from Australia. At 9:30 P.M. Captain William Monay, maintenance officer in charge of the flight, telephoned the commander of the Del Monte fields, Lieutenant Colonel Elsmore. "Okay, Ray, we're all set up," he said. A few minutes later blacked-out cars left the compound with the MacArthur party, heading for Airfield No. 1.

Monay escorted MacArthur and his family to a plane. He checked their luggage. Everyone, regardless of rank, was allowed 35 pounds. MacArthur did not ask for an extra allowance. One of the engines coughed, refused to start. MacArthur and the others filed out of the plane. The general strolled toward an officer standing nearby smoking.

"Have you another cigar? I left mine in my quarters at the plantation."

He lit up a cigar and sat on a bench next to Colonel Morse. The general talked to the little group of his hopes. He said there was a great army of Americans waiting for him in Australia. "I'm going to get help for you."

Captain Monay approached, told MacArthur he would have to transfer to Captain Frank Bostron's plane. The general nodded and soon his party was aboard. Several enlisted men brought out a mattress and put it aboard the plane for Mrs. MacArthur and Arthur. Then Bostron taxied the plane to the end of the field. The engines roared and the Flying Fortress rumbled down the short runway. Suddenly at the end of the plateau it dipped out of sight. Monay stopped breathing. But seconds later the big plane rose and began climbing. Monay sighed, "Thank God!"

Before the second plane was in the air, rumors were spreading. Someone, hearing an enlisted man remark that the mattress he'd helped put aboard MacArthur's plane was heavy, started a story that it was filled with thousands of gold pesos. In a few hours there were a few men willing to swear they saw chests of drawers and even a huge refrigerator loaded on the general's plane. These groundless stories were soon to be whispered all over America by MacArthur's detractors.

At 9:00 the next morning the two big planes approached Batchelor Field, 45 miles south of Darwin, Australia. They set down with ponderous grace. MacArthur had broken through the Japanese blockade. Now all that remained was the long, uncomfortable trip across the northern wasteland of Australia. "It was close," he said to those anxiously waiting on the runway. "But that's the way it is in war. You win or lose, live or die—and the difference is just an eyelash."

Major Morhouse got something to eat, then went to the office of the base commander. As he entered, MacArthur, wearing only long underwear, shirt and shoes, was walking up and down haranguing the base commander.

"What's the matter?" asked Morhouse.

"They're just too damned lazy to do what I want," said MacArthur angrily. "I want to take a train to Daly Waters and drive overland to Alice Springs. Mrs. MacArthur is tired of flying."

"General," said Morhouse, "I'll do everything I can to keep Arthur alive but I'm not sure he'll survive that 800 miles of desert."

MacArthur stopped pacing. "Do you mean that, Doc?"

"Yes."

"Get the plane ready," he said quietly.

It was none too soon. As the MacArthur party was loading on Major R. H. Carmichael's B-17 the red-alert sirens went off. Zero fighters were approaching the field. Carmichael took off quickly, keeping the plane at tree-top level until he was out of range of the Japanese planes.

Soon the MacArthur plane was over the desert. It looked to Major Morhouse like an artist's drawing of Mars. He noticed MacArthur looking thoughtfully over the side at the desolate wilderness. Three hours later the plane touched down at Alice Springs. MacArthur put a hand on Morhouse's shoulder. "Thank you, Doc," he said gratefully.

Here the general was met by enthusiastic reporters. When they asked him for a statement, he quickly scribbled a few lines on the back of a used envelope.

The President of the United States ordered me to break through the Japanese lines and proceed from Corregidor to Australia for the purpose, as I understand it, of organizing the American offensive against Japan, a primary object of which is the relief of the Philippines.

I came through and I shall return.

Since his family was too sick and exhausted to go farther by plane, MacArthur now transferred to a train. Even this was by no means modern, running on narrow-gauge tracks, but the next leg of the journey was through far less arduous country. MacArthur ordered his deputy chief of staff, Brigadier General Richard Marshall, to fly ahead to Melbourne and learn the true state of affairs in Australia.

Near sunset of the third day of the long trip, the MacArthur train finally reached the wide-gauge tracks where a luxurious private car was waiting. MacArthur's deputy chief of staff was also waiting with a detailed report. Marshall told the general there were only 25,364 Americans in Australia. And not one of these was an infantryman. Further, there were no tanks and many of the 250 planes were practically wrecks. But this wasn't the end of bad news. There were only about 7000 trained Australians on hand to defend their country from an invasion that could come momentarily.

The general's knees buckled as if he had been struck. His face drained of blood, his lips twitched as if in pain. "God, have mercy on us!" he whispered. He had left three times as many troops on Bataan alone and had assumed he was coming to command a great army.

He paced the corridor of his car all night.

4 President Quezon was still in the Philippines even though he had escaped from Corregidor by submarine almost three weeks earlier than MacArthur. The president was reluctant to leave his people. It wasn't until the night of March 18, after weeks of pleading by his own staff and the worried local American commanders, that he consented to let Commander Bulkeley take him by PT boat to the island of Mindanao, but here again Quezon dallied. Instead of driving directly to Del Monte and taking a plane for Australia, he insisted on making a visit to the picturesque Moro town of Dansalan on the shore of Lake Lanao. Finally, after another week's persuasion from his most steadying influence, Vice President Osmeña, he agreed to motor to the pineapple plantation.

At Del Monte, General Sharp was a badly worried man.

MacArthur had impressed on him the importance of getting Quezon safely out of the country. The Japanese already controlled the southern part of the island and might seize Del Monte in a surprise attack at any hour. When the general learned that Quezon was finally coming, he ordered Colonel Morse to move out with two truckloads of Air Corps troops and escort the president on the last lap of his trip.

On the night of March 23, Morse was waiting in the blacked-out town of El Salvador. To his amazement he saw approaching from the west a long line of brilliantly lit-up cars. It was the Quezon party, but the president was missing. He had stayed behind to rest. Half an hour later a lone car appeared carrying the exhausted president. He swore angrily at the roads, demanding that the district engineer be dragged out of his bed so he could personally fire him. He refused to go another foot on such a miserable highway. While the even-tempered Osmeña and his staff tried to persuade him to continue, the argument grew so loud that lights went on all over El Salvador. Townspeople sleepily crowded out to the streets to look at their president.

At last Quezon consented to proceed slowly. Each bump was agonizing to the suffering man. After 20 miles the caravan reached Cagayan. Quezon again refused to go farther. He would sleep at the Bishop's palace. But Father Edralin, pastor of the cathedral, told Quezon that Bishop Hayes was away and he had no authority to allow anyone to stay at the palace.

"In that case," said Quezon, "we will occupy your quarters."

Edralin regretfully informed him church law permitted no women in his quarters. Again a loud argument broke out. Again lights popped on and citizens gathered. Finally Colonel Morse persuaded the president to continue to Del Monte. The roads, said Morse, were much better from this point on and General Sharp had prepared very comfortable quarters for the president and his family at the plantation.

On March 25, the Flying Fortresses for the Quezon party had still not arrived from Australia. That noon Morse got an excited call from General Sharp. He rushed to Sharp's headquarters near the plantation clubhouse. "Quezon has disappeared," said the agitated general. "He's taken his wife and son and daughters."

Morse finally found the Quezon family far in the hills at the home of Mr. Crawford, manager of the plantation. Since the president refused to return to the compound, Morse sent for several truckloads of Air Corps men so a cordon could be placed around the house. The colonel spent the rest of the afternoon talking to the president. "Everyone gets help from Roosevelt except the Philippines," said Quezon with asperity. "If I can get to Australia perhaps I too can get some help."

On the night of March 26, three B-17's landed at Del Monte. Colonel Morse accompanied Quezon and his family to Airfield No. 1. The dying man, still reluctant to leave his people, was helped aboard a plane. To many American enlisted men it appeared as if he were being forcibly pushed into the Flying Fortress. They would have given anything for a place. This was to be Quezon's first ride in a plane and the idea of flying terrified him. In addition, he had heard alarming stories about the difficulty of breathing at high altitudes.

As with the MacArthur flight, Captain William Monay was in charge. Ironically, history repeated itself. One of the engines of Quezon's plane wouldn't start. The presidential party was transferred to another plane. To Monay's relief all four motors of this one started, but a moment later there was a sputter and then silence.

Colonel Elsmore and Monay ran to the plane as passengers started to disembark and learned that Quezon had ordered the pilot to cut the motors. The president couldn't find his chaplain and refused to fly until he was aboard.

Elsmore explained that Father Ortiz was aboard in another compartment. Quezon confirmed this and the plane finally started down the runway. As it took off and its wheels slowly retracted, Elsmore and Monay looked at each other with relief.

The volatile president lived to reach Australia but he was destined to die in America.

5 Wainwright was now on Corregidor. The War Department had made him commander-in-chief of all forces in the Philippines, promoting him to lieutenant general.

When MacArthur learned this on March 21 he radioed Washington that he had already planned to divide the Philippines in four separate commands, giving Wainwright jurisdiction only over Bataan. MacArthur himself would control the islands from his headquarters in Australia through a deputy chief of staff on Corregidor. The general explained this plan was based on "special problems" because of "the intangibles of the situation in the Philippines."

Some of MacArthur's staff, including Sutherland, were

rivately more outspoken. In their opinion, Wainwright was
ot qualified to take over-all command of the islands.

The following day, Marshall sent his reply. Conciliatory in
one, there was no specific criticism of MacArthur's plan.
Yet Marshall made it quite evident that Wainwright would
etain over-all command unless MacArthur objected strenu-
usly. MacArthur did not. Accepting the inevitable with
ood grace he radioed:

> HEARTILY IN ACCORD WITH WAINWRIGHT'S PROMOTION
> TO LIEUTENANT GENERAL. HIS ASSIGNMENT TO PHILIP-
> PINE COMMAND APPROPRIATE.

In spite of this surface harmony, command trouble was
lready brewing. A few days later Wainwright radioed Mar-
hall directly that there was only enough food on Bataan
o last until April 15. If supplies didn't reach him by then,
e said, "the troops there will be starved into submission."

When MacArthur read a copy of this message he sent a
critical comment to Marshall on April 1.

> IT IS OF COURSE POSSIBLE THAT WITH MY DEPARTURE
> THE VIGOR OF APPLICATION OF CONSERVATION MAY HAVE
> BEEN RELAXED.

Most of the men on Bataan would have agreed with Wainwright. They were starving and they knew it. By now they
had been told that MacArthur was in Australia. Among
Americans, opinion was divided. Some thought he had done
the only practical thing, yet many enlisted men and junior
officers felt he had abandoned them. Sarcastic poems were
passed from foxhole to foxhole. One of the favorites was
sung to the tune of "The Battle Hymn of the Republic."

> Dugout Doug's not timid, he's just cautious, not afraid,
> He's protecting carefully the stars that Franklin made.
> Four-star generals are rare as good food on Bataan.
> And his troops go starving on.
>
> Dugout Doug is ready in his Chris-Craft for the flee
> Over bounding billows and the wildly raging sea.
> For the Japs are pounding on the gates of old Bataan.
> And his troops go starving on.

While many Americans on Bataan deeply resented Mac-
Arthur's already widely publicized remark, "I shall return,"
regarding it as extremely egotistic, others joked about it

good-naturedly. In the Provisional Air Corps Regiment, a standard joke was, "I'm going to the latrine. But I shall return!"

Filipinos, almost unanimously, still regarded MacArthur as the greatest man alive. "I shall return" to them was a personal guarantee from the American they most trusted that the Philippines would eventually be freed.

By April 1 it was obvious to everyone on Bataan that the long lull was coming to an end. General Homma had recently dropped beer cans, festooned with red and white ribbons, containing a demand for surrender.

Addressed to His Excellency, Major General Jonathan Wainwright, they read:

We have the honor to address you in accordance with the humanitarian principles of "Bushido," the code of the Japanese warrior. . . . Your Excellency, you have already fought to the best of your ability. What dishonor is there in following the defenders of Hong Kong, Singapore and the Netherlands East Indies in the acceptance of honorable defeat? . . . The joe [sic] and happiness of those whose lives will be saved and the delight and relief of their dear ones and families would be beyond the expression of words. . . .

Wainwright didn't answer. He knew heavy enemy reinforcements had landed; patrols were becoming more aggressive; skirmishes were flaring up along the outpost line; and Japanese planes, absent for a month, were appearing in increasing numbers.

Wainwright realized this was to be a powerful, all-out attack and his front-line strength was at a new low. He could do nothing about that. Disease and starvation were taking a fantastic toll. A thousand men a day were entering hospitals. Almost 75 per cent of the front-line troops had malaria. Perhaps even more serious, men were surly, physically exhausted and almost numb from privation. And there was no hope that any more food would reach Bataan.

The night of April 2, Good Friday Eve, was calm and peaceful along the Fil-American front. To the north 50,000 Japanese, including 15,000 fresh troops from the 4th Division and the Nagano Detachment, were massed for attack. Behind them 150 heavy guns, howitzers and mortars were ready to lay down the most devastating barrage of the campaign. Colonel Hattori's plan would be tested the next day.

"Our four groups have been brought into line and on a front of 25 kilometers ten flags are lined up," wrote General Homma in his operational diary that night. "Artillery is

plentiful. . . . There is no reason why this attack should
not succeed."

Opposing Homma were about 80,000 Americans and Filipinos. But only 27,000 of these were even listed as "combat effective." And of the 27,000 "effectives" about three-
fourths were weak from malaria; all were on the edge of
starvation.

In the Fil-American front lines some men were reading
a poem just written by Lieutenant Henry G. Lee of the
Philippine Division. Of all those writing down their thoughts
the past few months, Lee's poems dug deepest.

> I see no gleam of victory alluring
> No chance of splendid booty or of gain.
> If I endure—I must go on enduring.
> And my reward for bearing pain—is pain.
> Yet, though the thrill, the zest, the hope are gone,
> Something within me keeps me fighting on.

1   The next morning dawned clear and warm. It was April 3, the opening day of the great Japanese attack. It was also a Japanese national holiday, the anniversary of the death of the first Emperor, Jimmu.

General Nara of the 65th Brigade looked south at a rugged jungle-covered hump called Mt. Samat. American and Filipino soldiers were stretched out between this hill and Nara. Soon the greatest artillery barrage of the campaign would rip up the two and a half miles in front of Samat. Then his soldiers, led by tanks, would attack. If lucky he would be standing on top of Samat in a week or ten days.

Nara's face was gaunt. Since landing on the Philippines his weight had tumbled from 150 pounds to 110. He prayed that this great offensive would be the last. General Homma had told him if all went well, they would completely crush the Filipinos and Americans in three or four weeks. If the offensive lasted longer, his already battered brigade would probably collapse.

He again carefully scanned the northern slope of Mt. Samat. This rugged part of the jungle line was held by the troops of General Vincente Lim. It was ironical. He knew Lim well and liked him. They had been classmates in 1928 at the Fort Benning Infantry School.

Lim's 41st Division woke up that morning little suspecting that their entire division line and a portion of the outfit to their right, Capinpin's 21st Division, was the two-and-a-half-mile front so carefully selected by Colonel Hattori in Tokyo.

The center of this stretch, where the weight of Nara's attack would come that afternoon, was held by the 42nd Infantry Regiment. Major Rigoberto Atienza, until a few days ago Lim's inspector general, had recently arrived to take over as regimental commander.

"We can expect an overcast sky this afternoon," he told the regimental supply officer. "This is Good Friday. In my childhood, my grandmother used to tell me that it becomes cloudy in the afternoon in token of the world's sympathy for the sufferings of Christ. I've observed it since and found it to be so."

"That's superstition," said the supply officer.

Suddenly at 9:00 A.M. a shell burst on the forward slope of the ridge only 50 yards ahead. Fragments rained down. Other shells fell thick and fast as Atienza and several of his staff huddled in a dugout. After half an hour, Atienza telephoned his three front-line battalions. "Prepare for an attack," he told them, assuming this was a preparation barrage.

The Japanese artillery was only registering. At 10:00 A.M. they began firing for effect. Shells seemed to explode on top of each other. The Filipinos had never seen anything like this devastating barrage. To those Americans who had served in World War I, it seemed as intense as the heaviest German barrages.

Bombers of the 22nd Air Brigade roared overhead, dumping load after load on the tiny selected area. Defenses painstakingly built in the long lull were churned to rubble. The men huddled in their foxholes. It was terrifying but they were safe. Then, near noon, other planes passed, dropping clusters of sticklike objects. When they hit, dry leaves and bamboo burst into flame. Incendiaries. At first some of the men joked about the burning brush and lit cigarettes on the flaming bamboo. It was fun, a welcome change from the weeks of boredom. More incendiaries dropped. Since the rainy season was yet to start, the fires spread rapidly. Suddenly the men found they were surrounded by licking flames. The heat was intolerable, the flames leaped higher.

The men jumped from their foxholes and ran back to the second line of defense. Here their terror increased. Cover had been blasted away until most of the ground was as barren as No Man's Land of World War I. Shells again shrieked, exploding on all sides. They leaped into the bald craters. But soon, whipped by a sudden breeze, the fire leaped over the barren stretches to the lush jungle growth beyond. Hundreds were cremated. The others ran farther to the rear like frenzied animals, spurred by the smell of burning leaves, wood, clothes, leather and flesh.

Masked by this confusion of smoke and flame, the Japanese infantry and tank attack started at 3:00 P.M. Nara's 65th Brigade smashed directly at Atienza's line. Already his regiment and the regiment to its right were running pellmell to the rear.

Late that afternoon, Atienza prepared to move back to a safer command post. As he was throwing papers and one change of clothing into a musette bag, dazed men began streaming into the area. They were led by a captain.

"No more, sir," cried the captain. "We're licked!" His eyes were wild. His arms waved like a windmill.

"What's happened?" asked Atienza.

"There's no more use. Our lines are gone! Our men have been roasted alive or hit directly by shells!" His eyes were crazy with fright. His clothes were torn, burned; his hair askew.

"Shut up!"

"No more, sir. No use, I tell you." Now the captain was surrounded by officers and men.

Atienza knew he had to prevent a panic. He drew his .45 and pointed it at the captain. "Shut up, goddam!"

The other only cried, "You can kill me if you want but we're beaten!"

Atienza slapped him. The captain reeled. Atienza drew back his hand again as the other shook his head vigorously.

"I'm sorry, sir," he finally said in a wavering voice.

"So am I," said Atienza. He took the captain by the arm, led him into a tent and gave him a cigarette.

Just before dusk, General Parker, still commander of the corps on the east half of Bataan, learned that a great hole, almost three miles wide, had been torn in his lines just in front of Mt. Samat. He had only about 600 men in reserve and he ordered them to plug up the gap.

Homma didn't get details of the Filipino rout until that evening. Delighted and surprised, he ordered Nara to take advantage of the sudden breakthrough and sweep west of Mt. Samat the next morning. Fresh troops from Shanghai were told to circle east of the mountain.

April 4 opened with another fierce Japanese artillery and air bombardment. By dusk Nara had cut past Mt. Samat on the west and the Shanghai men on the east. The Japanese were already more than a day ahead of schedule.

When Wainwright went to Corregidor, he had turned over command of all forces on Bataan to Major General Edward King, Jr., a modest man, an intellectual. He was an artilleryman of wide experience; an extremely able soldier, reasonable and realistic. King was well-liked by junior officers and enlisted men for he was as courteous to a second lieutenant or private as to a fellow general. He looked and acted more like a professor than a military leader, giving orders in a quiet, undramatic way.

It was this modest man's unhappy job to try to patch the tremendous hole in the east half of the Bataan line. His first step was to turn over the most carefully hoarded unit in Bataan, the all-American 31st U.S. Infantry, to General Parker.

On the night of April 4, the eve of Easter Sunday, this well-trained American outfit moved forward through the jungles to help plug up the hole. Lieutenant Robert Taylor, the regimental chaplain, walked with the men. As the line wound up the east side of Samat in the darkness, a sergeant stopped ahead of Taylor and pointed to the sky. There was the Southern Cross, shining brilliantly. It was startling and beautiful.

"If more people in the world would march under the Cross," said the sergeant, "we'd have less wars." Then he turned and headed north toward the quiet battleground.

Easter dawned hot. While many Americans and Filipinos worshipped at dawn services, shells and bombs began to fall. Then at 10:00 A.M. an assault on Mt. Samat itself began. In less than three hours the Japanese planted the Rising Sun on top of the little mountain. At last they had a commanding view of the shattered American lines. More important, the 41st Field Artillery, which had been slowing the attack with its accurate fire, was now forced to evacuate the southern slopes of the mountain. The artillerymen rolled their guns over the cliffs, destroyed equipment and then ran to the rear. The Japanese were not far behind and by mid-afternoon had taken almost all of the strategic mountain.

Less than seven air miles to the southeast, a jeep was wildly careering up the coastal road toward the town of Limay. The driver was Captain Tom Dooley. Next to him sat General Wainwright. The jeep stopped in a cloud of dust on a wooded hill. Then Wainwright climbed a trail to General Parker's II Corps headquarters.

Parker and his officers, hollow-eyed from lack of sleep, were poring over maps. Wainwright saw that a great wedge had been driven in the lines. Two divisions were practically destroyed. Parker's staff decided that only a strong counterattack would restore the ground. A plan was worked out. Tomorrow morning a general counterattack would be launched.

Wainwright approved the plan but he had misgivings. It was a plan born of desperation. The men were dead on their feet, starved and depressed. It was, however, the only

chance. A few minutes later Dooley and Wainwright heade
back for Cabcaben and the boat to Corregidor. Dooley drov
so hard he broke an axle.

The American High Command still didn't know the Jap
anese had already stormed over Mt. Samat and were comin
down the other side.

2   April 6 was to be the day of decision fo
everyone on Bataan.

The desperate Fil-American counterattack was a gallan
conception. It seemed incredible that any of the men woul
allow themselves to be led back into what was obviously
hopeless battle; yet in the first minutes of April 6, unit
were actually moving out to attack, if not with enthusiasm
at least with a grim determination to do what had to b
done.

The counterattack west of Mt. Samat soon collapsed. Th
result was utter confusion. By midday this entire left hal
of Parker's corps had disintegrated. Nothing remained to sto
Nara from sweeping south to the end of the peninsula ex
cept the rugged terrain itself.

The counterattack east of the little mountain started unde
even worse auspices. Unknown to Parker the left flank o
the troops scheduled to make this attack, Capinpin's divi
sion, had been crushed the night before and the genera
himself captured. An hour before dawn three exhausted of
ficers from Capinpin's division staggered into the lines o
the unit to their right, the 31st U.S. Infantry Regimen
The three Filipinos told Lieutenant Colonel Jasper Brady
the commander of the American unit, that the 21st Divisio
had completely disintegrated.

Brady had only 800 men. Realizing that even if his attac
was successful he didn't have enough troops to hold th
entire rear line of a division, he tried to call Sector heac
quarters by phone. The line was dead. He called the unit o
his right, the 31st Division of General Clifford Blueme
Telling Bluemel his troops were still at the line of departur
he asked the general to confirm his action.

"Like hell," was Bluemel's tart answer. "Why didn't yo
attack as ordered?"

Brady explained.

"The preparatory and supporting fire by my artillery
coming as scheduled," said Bluemel. "And my 51st Comb
Team is ready to accompany your advance."

Brady again asked Bluemel to confirm his action.

"Not by a damned sight. Don't pass the buck to me," retorted Bluemel. "I advise you to launch your counterattack immediately. If you refuse to attack, I'm going to report your action to your Sector commander."

"Sir, I've tried but I can't raise General Lough's headquarters."

"Then I advise you to report your failure to counterattack to General Parker." Bluemel hung up. He had his own problems. He had asked Parker twice the day before to let his outflanked troops fall back to the banks of the San Vicente River. Twice Parker had refused.

Late that morning Bluemel finally got a line through to II Corps. He told Parker of Brady's failure to attack. (Neither general knew that by this time Brady had finally contacted his own Sector and been ordered to cancel the counterattack and hold his present position.)

Again Bluemel asked if he could fall back to the southern bank of the San Vicente and dig in. The answer was no. Instead he would form a line on the second ridge in front of the river. Bluemel hung up and swore. This had been Brady's line of departure for the abortive counterattack. It was a poor position with no field of fire; there had been no reconnaissance or preparatory work. It was typical of Corps, he thought, to give orders without having personal knowledge of the terrain.

Bluemel set up his line, personally going from position to position. At 4:00 P.M. the peppery general got a call from Corps ordering him to form a new line on the south side of the San Vicente River. Bluemel was justifiably irate. It was too late to lay out any preparatory work. It would soon be dark. Several officers were rushed back to the river to make a hurried reconnaissance. Finally Bluemel started his troops to the rear, patrolling the columns to see that order was maintained.

At 5:00 P.M., while making a reconnaissance south of Trail 2, he found a small group of disorganized, demoralized soldiers from the 31st U.S. Infantry. He talked to them, explaining the new mission, and placed them in the position their regiment was supposed to occupy. Then he started back toward his command post. Half a mile south of the San Vicente River he met bedraggled men from his own division, moving farther to the rear. Gesturing belligerently with his rifle, Bluemel shooed them to the front. As he drove them up the trail like cattle, other retreating men were met. They just stared dumbly when Bluemel asked what outfit they were from. When he called for officers, no one moved forward. Pointing with his rifle toward the enemy, he ordered them all to turn around and join the movement back to the north.

By midnight, after frantic efforts by Bluemel, his signal officer, Captain Matt Dobrinic, and several others, a ragged but recognizable line was formed on the southern bank of the San Vicente. At last the general lay down to rest.

Colonel Takushiro Hattori, the planner of the offensive, had been watching the day's action from the heights of Mt. Samat. West of the mountain he saw Nara's troops streaming through, bypassing scattered American units, pushing relentlessly to the south. On the other side of the mountain he saw the main attack of the day, the assault of the Shanghai troops on General Bluemel's assortment of defenders. The Fil-Americans here were falling back across the San Vicente River. It was a sensational victory already with everything working exactly as he had imagined. It was a parade.

The day of decision had turned into a day of disaster for the Americans. By nightfall Homma's men had punched in the entire left half of Parker's Corps and were threatening to drive the east half into Manila Bay. Only the hurried line set up by Bluemel on the San Vicente stood between Homma and victory.

3   April 7 was another hot, clear day.

Japanese bombers ranged the American rear that morning. Lieutenant Hattie Brantley, a nurse at General Hospital No. 1, watched planes circling over the great white cross of sheets that marked the hodgepodge hospital area. It was located in a field at the top of the steep, zigzag road near the southern end of Bataan in a settlement vaguely reminiscent of the former summer capital and thus called Little Baguio. The white cross didn't reassure her. A week ago a bomb had actually hit the sheets.

About 10:00 A.M. there was a weird whistling noise. A bomb landed on an ammunition truck on the road in front of the hospital. There was a frightening roar, then the spatter of shrapnel, pebbles and earth on the tin roofs.

In the Orthopedic Ward nurses and corpsmen quickly cut traction ropes so the wounded men could roll out of bed. Father Cummins went to the middle of the room and raised his arms. He asked everyone to repeat the Lord's Prayer.

A moment later other bombs hit the mess area, and the doctors' and nurses' quarters. There was a banshee shriek

of tearing tin and wood. Iron beds doubled, breaking jagged-
ly like matchsticks. The patients began screaming.

Near by, Nurse Brantley heard another bomb fall. This
one was even closer, shaking the earth and raising a cloud
of dust and smoke. Hearing the scream of patients, she realized a ward set up in a large open space and roofed by
burlap had been hit directly; dozens must be dead, more
dying. She ran for help into the Orthopedic Ward. Here
open panic was threatening to break out. Then she saw
Father Cummins climb onto a nurse's desk. Even in the
roar of planes his voice could be heard in prayer. The
patients quieted. A feeling of comfort came over Lieutenant
Brantley. It was now out of her hands, she realized. She
began to cry. Others were crying too.

A moment later, the priest climbed down from the desk.
"Somebody take over," he said quietly. "I'm wounded."

Up front the entire left half of Parker's front was gone.
But the right, the east half, though weak and shaky, still
held. General Bluemel only slept an hour after setting up
the San Vicente line. Then with two Filipino staff officers, he
headed back to the front for another inspection. Less than a
mile from the river he met large groups of men from his
own division shuffling to the rear. They told him they were
going to Lamao.

"There's no food in Lamao," said Bluemel. The general
and the two Filipino officers herded the men back to their
positions. After looking over the positions of the all-
American unit, Bluemel walked back to his command post
and slept an hour. When he awoke, he once more headed
back north to the line. And once again he met retreating
men of the 51st Division.

"Why did you desert?" he asked. No one answered. He
waved them back to the river. They turned and disconsolately
trudged to battle.

A truck came from the front at high speed. Bluemel
stood in the middle of the trail, signaled it to halt. Without
slowing it roared toward the general. He jumped back just
in time. A minute later a truck column approached. Again
Bluemel signaled the leading truck to stop. It slowed and
an American of the 31st U.S. Infantry leaned out and shouted,
"The San Vicente Line has broken!"

Bluemel never thought he'd see American soldiers running
like that. Soon great crowds of Filipinos surged toward him.
He gestured with his rifle. "Form a line on both sides of
the trail." Shells began to explode along the road. The men,

shouting in terror, ran past Bluemel. He grabbed at them, but no one paid any attention to the irate general.

Bluemel walked back to his command post, ordered it moved to the rear and dispatched an officer to Parker's Corps with the bad news. He hopped in a jeep and returned north toward the disintegrating San Vicente Line. If he hurried perhaps he could rally some of the units and put up some kind of resistance. Trail 2 was filled with demoralized, sick, retreating men. Most had thrown away their arms and equipment. Shells again hit the trail and Bluemel parked the jeep, heading forward on foot. Soon he found a fairly intact battalion and told its commander to place it along a low ridge. He hurried toward the ridge to select the actual positions. As soon as Bluemel finished putting the battalion in place, shells began to fall once more. When the smoke cleared Bluemel discovered his newly placed battalion had vanished. It was the last known unit of his own 31st Division. The general remembered how courageously they had stopped Nara at the other end of Trail 2 two months before. Now through lack of medicine, food and clothing they had become an uncontrollable mob. More than half were sick with malaria and dysentery. He realized he could expect no more from the shattered Philippine Army units.

Bluemel helped load wounded on shelter halves. They were carried to the last division bus and driven off. His jeep and driver had disappeared. He was alone. Except for a few men of his staff he was all that remained of the 31st Division.

Rifle fire broke out to the right rear. Japanese were obviously converging from two directions. There was nothing else to be done at the San Vicente River. He turned and walked down Trail 2, following the rest of the retreating mob.

He met more of his staff officers. Something had to be done to prevent a complete rout. He told them to quickly reorganize the nearby Americans of the 31st U.S. Infantry Regiment and have them move through the underbrush in a column of files a few yards from each side of the trail. They were to guide on him as he moved slowly down the trail. This would prevent the column from attracting planes.

It was done and the movement to the rear continued in good order until an open space in the trail was reached. Here one battalion of Americans hurried across the open spot and proceeded down the trail. The next battalion followed, and before Bluemel could catch up to them, both battalions cut to the left through underbrush, and disappeared into an overgrown stream bed.

Bluemel angrily sent his Filipino staff officers to the stream. They called over and over again, "31st Infantry!" No American answered.

Now only Bluemel and four Filipino officers were left to stop the oncoming Japanese on Trail 2. The angry general hurried south with Japanese patrols only a few hundred yards behind. Soon he saw ten American enlisted men of the 31st U.S. Infantry coming out of the brush. Bluemel collared them, ordering them to beat the brush on both sides of the trail. After 500 yards they flushed an American ma'or.

"I'm going to the junction of Trails 2 and 10," Bluemel told the embarrassed major.

"Don't," the other warned. "It's open country and can be bombed. Go across country through the underbrush and avoid the junction." Bluemel pulled out his map and began to examine it. When he looked up the major was gone. So were the ten enlisted men.

Bluemel and his four Filipinos continued toward the junction in spite of the major's advice. Soon they saw a scout car approaching from the south. It stopped. "Do you know where I can find General Bluemel?" called a cavalry officer.

"Right here," said the general.

The newcomer said he was Major William Chandler of the 26th Cavalry. "Colonel Vance is waiting at the junction of Trails 2 and 10 with the 26th Cavalry. We have orders to report to you, sir."

This was the first good news Bluemel had heard in two days. "Tell Vance to stay where he is." He motioned Chandler to get moving. "We'll follow on foot."

Bluemel quickened his pace down the trail. He crossed a stream. There, to his amazement, he found the two missing battalions of the 31st U.S. Infantry and the ten enlisted men. He told them in terse, direct language to report immediately to the trail junction.

Before Bluemel reached the junction, rifle shots broke out behind him. The Japanese had caught up and now occupied the ridge just behind Bluemel's retreating troops. Late that afternoon Japanese attacked the junction in force. Bluemel knew his few hundred men couldn't hold long. He looked at the map. About a mile to the rear was the Mamala River. This would have to be the next delaying point.

The trail to the Mamala was jammed with masses of Filipinos and Americans and trucks of the 26th Cavalry. Suddenly shells exploded and Japanese dive bombers swooped down. One bomb hit an ammunition truck. The exploding ammunition momentarily blocked the retreat. As Bluemel hugged the dirt, he thought his ears would burst from the explosions. Then came an even louder roar. Fragments flew past Bluemel killing several men. Something walloped his leg.

"Are you hurt, General?" asked Vance.

Bluemel pulled up his trouser leg. "No blood. I'm all right."

The withdrawal became a panic. He thought, What do you do with a mob?

That afternoon Wainwright, on Corregidor, telephoned King at his Bataan headquarters near Hospital No. 1. The two desperately tried to figure some way to stop the Japanese breakthrough in the east half of Bataan.

Wainwright pointed out that the Fil-American front lines on the west half of the peninsula were completely intact. In fact there was still almost no activity at all on this side of Bataan. Why, he suggested, shouldn't these relatively fresh troops turn right and attack to the east? Perhaps they could even form a new line all the way across Bataan.

King was reluctant but Wainwright could see no other solution. He ordered the desperate plan carried out. King, in turn, telephoned Albert Jones, the new commander of Wainwright's former corps, now recovered from dysentery and promoted to major general.

The outspoken Jones promptly and bluntly told King that the attack ordered by Wainwright was senseless. It could not possibly be launched. His men were so weak from hunger and sickness, they couldn't even climb the steep cliffs of the Pantingan River, let alone fight their way up. Besides, said Jones, how could he possibly mount such an attack in time? A three-way telephone connection was then set up and the discussion continued among Jones, King and Wainwright. Finally Wainwright said with some exasperation that he was leaving the decision up to King and hung up.

It didn't take the Bataan commander long to agree with Jones. King ordered Jones to pull back his corps in four phases so he wouldn't be outflanked by the breakthrough on the other side of the peninsula.

Late that afternoon King asked his chief of staff, Brigadier General Arnold Funk, to take a boat to Corregidor and tell Wainwright that surrender might come any moment. A few hours later Funk, a big man, wearily entered Wainwright's office in Malinta Tunnel. He told of the physical deterioration of the men, of the collapse of Parker's entire left wing, then said, "General King sent me here to tell you he might have to surrender."

Funk's face, thought Wainwright, was a map of the hopelessness of the Bataan situation. He knew as well as King and Funk of the suffering of the men of Bataan; he knew they were on the verge of starvation. But on his desk was a radiogram MacArthur had sent three days before.

> I AM UTTERLY OPPOSED UNDER ANY CIRCUMSTANCES OR CONDITIONS TO THE ULTIMATE CAPITULATION OF THIS COMMAND. IF FOOD FAILS, YOU WILL PREPARE AND EXECUTE AN ATTACK UPON THE ENEMY.

He also had orders from Roosevelt forbidding surrender "so long as there remains any possibility of resistance." Wainwright studied the exhausted Funk, then said in his slow drawl, "General, you go back and tell General King he will *not* surrender. Tell him he will attack. Those are my orders."

Funk hesitated. Among fellow officers he was well known as capable, outspoken. There were tears in his eyes when he said, "General, you know, of course, what the situation is over there. You know what the outcome will be."

"I do."

Funk slowly, wearily turned and walked out.

       4   The only general anywhere near the front lines in Parker's crumbling corps that April seventh was Clifford Bluemel. Assuming command of all troops in the area, he ordered a general retreat starting at 9:00 P.M. to the Alangan River, which was only seven air miles from the end of Bataan. He wrote an order to Colonel Vance, still holding along the Mamala River: the 26th was to cover the entire movement, pulling back as soon as the last of Bluemel's varied units departed.

At 9:00 P.M. the mass retirement began. It was so dark Bluemel ordered that each man hang onto the shirt of the soldier ahead. "Move slowly," he said. "Fifty yards at a time, then stop."

It was a slow, punishing march. Most of the men hadn't eaten for two days. The sick and wounded, unable to keep up, dropped by the side of the trail, groaning in agony, yet knowing they had to be left behind. Occasionally rifle shots burst out from the north and men pushed frenziedly against those ahead, trying to make them go faster.

By dawn, Bluemel had set up a defense line along the Alangan River for several miles. On paper it was a formidable force but actually he had only about 1400 men. On his right there was a big gap of 1500 yards and the defense line didn't resume until it reached the east coast highway. Here were 1200 assorted troops commanded by Colonel John Irwin, supported by the 21st Field Artillery, a few fixed naval guns, and the last three 155-mm. guns of the 301st Field Artillery.

Bluemel was dead tired, as was everyone else on the line. In addition he felt the weight of the entire defense on his shoulders. If he relaxed even momentarily it might collapse. He finally made telephone contact with Parker's headquarters and told II Corps' operations officer that there was a gaping hole to the right. He urged the immediate dispatch of Beach Defense units to fill in the hole.

"Troops will be sent up after dark."

"That'll be too late. You can be damned sure the enemy will find that big gap before dark and rush through." He was told of Irwin's 1200 men guarding the East Road to his right. The entire line was now under Bluemel's command, said Parker's staff officer. Bluemel was all that was left of II Corps. What would he need to assist him? "I need four staff officers, communication personnel and equipment from II Corps."

"Use your own staff."

"I have only two Filipino staff officers. Like me they've been without food since breakfast of 6 April and have had about one and a half hours' sleep a night. I have no communication personnel or equipment. The 31st Signal Company disappeared."

"Well, you'll have to take staff officers from the troops with you. Use their communication equipment and personnel."

Bluemel was disgusted. There were at least thirty American officers on the II Corps staff who'd been eating and sleeping regularly, yet not a damned one could be spared for the fighting line. He said, "Since you're not sending me any troops until after dark to fill the gap, I can't possibly hold the line. What line do you want me to hold next?" His tone became sharper. "This time I'd like to send out officers from every unit to make a daylight reconnaissance."

The answer was brusque. "Hold your present line."

"Damn it, I told you it was impossible. Not unless the gap is filled immediately."

"Hold *that* line."

Bluemel angrily banged down the phone and went out to

inspect his Alangan River line in daylight. The south bank was a steep slope covered with cogon grass almost three feet high, with patches of underbrush and a scattering of trees. When Bluemel saw Japanese observation planes buzzing overhead, he guessed his men had been seen digging new positions. He again telephoned Parker's headquarters stressing the importance of filling the 1500-yard gap to the right. He repeated his request for staff officers and communication equipment. Nothing was available.

At 11:00 A.M. planes suddenly swooped down on the Alangan dropping incendiary bombs. The dry cogon grass and bamboo thickets burst into flames. Bluemel's men jumped from their foxholes, beat out the flames, and resumed their positions.

A few miles to the right, other bombers hit Colonel Irwin's men on the East Road just as they were digging foxholes. The men fled and had to be rounded up by Irwin's officers. Another wave of bombers appeared. Again the starved, exhausted men ran to the rear. Again they were brought back to the front, some at pistol point. More attacks followed. Each time fewer men returned to the front lines. By about 3:00 P.M., though the Nagano Detachment had not yet even appeared, Irwin's line was completely deserted.

At the same time, the troops from Shanghai were already probing defenses on the Alangan River. As the general had predicted, they soon found the great gap and began filtering behind Bluemel's lines.

While Bluemel was standing on Trail 20, a bus approached from the rear, filled with men of the 2nd Platoon, Company G, 4th Philippine Constabulary.

"We are to report to General Bluemel," said a sergeant. "I'm General Bluemel."

The men in the bus were silent. "Well, who the hell is in command?" asked Bluemel. Finally the sergeant said he was and the men started reluctantly filing out with their barracks bags.

"You won't need those," said Bluemel.

At that moment, Lieutenant Colonel Smyth of the Provisional Tank Group arrived. "Can you use any tanks?" he asked Bluemel.

Bluemel cheered up. After telling the new platoon to form up and wait for him, he took Smyth forward to locate places for the tanks.

As the two officers were returning to the bus, small arms broke out from the front and the right. The Japanese began to close in. The 2nd Platoon, which had just debussed and formed a line, broke as one man for the rear. Bluemel chased them but they were too fast. He returned to Smyth.

"I'll send three tanks immediately," said the tanker and left.

The fight continued until dusk. No reinforcements arrived as the Japanese began to encircle the 26th Cavalry. An American officer reported from the front that the 31st U.S. Infantry had now fallen back and the Philippine Scouts of the 57th, enveloped on both flanks, were also having to withdraw.

At that moment five Japanese tanks rumbled down Trail 20 toward the embattled 26th Cavalry. The cavalrymen and the Philippine engineers of the 14th Battalion didn't panic, keeping up such heavy fire that those in the Japanese tanks didn't dare come out to remove the overturned trucks forming a roadblock.

Though the tanks were momentarily stopped, Bluemel knew he had to pull back the rest of his people quickly or be completely surrounded. He ordered the stubborn engineers to withdraw. The 26th was to cover them and then follow.

It was pitch-dark as Bluemel and his staff, now mostly cavalrymen, started toward the rear. The general headed down Trail 20, hoping to find other units he could use in a new defense. Just after 9:00 P.M. the exhausted little group reached a stream. Here the general found the 57th Infantry and the all-American unit. He was told General Parker wanted to talk to him on the phone.

It was Parker's operations officer. "Form a line on the Lamao River."

"Where the hell is the Lamao River?"

"It's the stream near your phone."

Bluemel was not too tired to be angry. "Why in the devil didn't you designate this position this morning as I asked? I could have had a daylight reconnaissance. Now it's too damned dark. None of my people know a thing about this terrain. Why in hell didn't your staff of thirty make a reconnaissance for us? Why aren't they here to guide my troops into position or at least give us some advice?"

There was a pause. "It was not known how you desired to put the troops in."

"I'm willing to put them in any damn way as long as they get in. The least you can do is send me four of your staff officers and help me get my people into position."

"I'm sorry, we can't spare anyone."

Bluemel blew up. "We can't hold a line here! It's an impossible situation you've given me. I'm nearly all in and so are my officers and men. And I've told you before we haven't eaten for almost three days. If you want any fighting up here you'd better send me 1600 'C' rations and some small arms ammo." He hung up, disgusted. His muscles ached as he slowly, wearily walked to the little river. He took off his shoes and stuck his feet in the cool water. It was a wonderful feeling. He leaned over, scooped up water with his hands and bathed his dirt-encrusted face.

1 That night the Japanese were steadily pressing down the eastern half of Bataan. A few hours earlier Colonel Takeo Imai, one of Nara's regimental commanders, had planted a large flag on top of Mount Limay. Now from the same heights he was looking south to the end of Bataan at occasional flashes of light. The enemy was probably blowing up equipment and munitions in desperation. Beyond he could even make out the dark outline of Corregidor Island. Occasionally angry spits of fire came from its heights where giant cannon were trying to stop the advance by interdicting the east road.

Fleeing in front of the relentless Japanese columns, Americans and Filipinos poured out of the jungles in hundreds of places and were being jammed into the toe of the peninsula. They came by trail, across the rugged valleys, by the main road. No one knew what was going on in the mass confusion and desperation. A strange dull terror drove many of the men. They were numb, exhausted, terrified and yet listless. Many didn't realize they were on the edge of starvation and delirium. Many didn't know they had malaria or dengue. Those with dysentery, of course, knew it. The humiliation of their affliction had long passed, in the general agony.

Sergeant Frank Bernacki and twenty-eight men of the Provisional Air Regiment were guarding the four bridges between Lamao and Cabcaben on the east road. Men suddenly streamed across the first bridge, kept going south. They were Americans, Philippine Scouts, Philippine Army men. All were frantic.

"All hell's broken loose!" an American sergeant shouted to Bernacki. "The lines have broken just down the road! Get out!"

Bernacki hesitated. This meant the Japanese advance guard was rolling down the east coast highway toward him. He finally got an officer on the phone. "What should I do?" he asked.

"Grab your sack and take off."

"Shouldn't we fight?"

"Hell, no. Save your tail. I'm going to try and get to Corregidor." Bernacki gathered his twenty-eight men. They drove several buses onto the road, tipped them over. Then with the help of a dozen civilians, they built roadblocks with logs. Men fleeing from the front continued to come through but though occasionally he could hear the chatter of a machine gun, no Japanese appeared.

Bernacki put his men in a truck and drove south to Cabcaben. Here the road turned due west. He followed it past Hospital No. 2 and up hills to Hospital No. 1, sitting on the right of the road at Little Baguio. The road became more and more jammed as it suddenly dipped down a harrowing zigzag. Finally Bernacki reached the last town on Bataan, Mariveles. It was a madhouse. A few boats were preparing to take the privileged to Corregidor. Other vessels were being towed out in the bay and sunk. Great mobs of disorganized troops from a dozen units clustered at the sides of the road.

Bernacki saw a brigadier general halting the path to the docks. "No one can go to Corregidor," he shouted. "We've had it," he told Bernacki wearily. "We're waiting here for the Japs to kill us or capture us. If you've got guns, tear them apart."

Out of the bay, the diesel tug *Manapala* was towing the submarine tender *Canopus* to its final rest. The battered old ship's valves were opened and *Manapala* headed back toward shore. Many felt a personal loss as they watched *Canopus* slowly sink. The "Old Lady" had been one of the bright spots in the Bataan campaign. Here a man could enjoy a real shower bath and a drink of cold water and eat a good meal on white linen.

The remnants of Lim's division were heading south on foot, by truck and bus. Major Atienza was lucky. He was in a bus. Near Mariveles it reached the division's final assembly point. Near a clump of three mango trees he and his companion, Captain Manuel Tinio, spread blankets. The two lay down to sleep, but Atienza soon awakened. He felt a chill. Thinking it was the night wind, he buttoned his shirt collar and put on his khaki cap. He grew more chilled.

Tinio awoke and felt the major's brow. "You're burning with fever, sir," he said and wrapped his towel around Atienza.

The major began to shake. He knew he had malaria. Fires were burning down below in Mariveles, reddening the sky. He could hear the dull thuds of explosions. Suddenly the earth began to shake violently.

It was a severe earthquake, felt all over the southern half of Bataan. Some in their dazed condition thought this was the end of the world.

At the Cabcaben airstrip, the earthquake was rocking the last American plane on Bataan just as its motor was being warmed up.

"Quit shaking this plane," the pilot, Lieutenant Roland Barnick, shouted to the five passengers huddled on the bare floor behind him.

The plane, a navy amphibian, had been hauled from the bottom of Mariveles Harbor several months previously. Since then Captain Joe Moore, a former P-40 pilot, had used it to fly in supplies, medicine and mail. Since he always included several boxes of candy on each trip, it became known as "The Candy Clipper."

The rickety Grumman Duck creaked as it waddled down the bomb-pocked strip. Finally it lifted heavily and a moment later was skimming a few feet above Manila Bay.

Barnick turned and shouted at Carlos Romulo, who had been broadcasting the "Voice of Freedom" from Corregidor until Wainwright ordered him to leave. "Last man out of Bataan, eh, Colonel?"

Japanese searchlights now picked up the lumbering plane and bullets began ripping through the wings.

"Our own guns are shelling us," shouted one of the crew, looking out a small window at the disappearing outline of Bataan.

Barnick raised the ship to 70 feet. When it refused to go any higher, he hurriedly penciled a note and handed it back to the passengers. They instantly began throwing overboard all baggage, steel helmets, sidearms and lastly parachutes. "The Candy Clipper" rose another 50 feet and headed for the south.

2   On Corregidor, the distraught Wainwright was getting only disjointed scraps of information, but he knew from the chaotic reports that his eastern corps was collapsing. He remembered MacArthur's definite instructions to launch a last desperate attack. At 11:30 P.M. he telephoned General King.

Though he must have known his orders could not be followed, Wainwright said, "Launch an offensive with Jones' I Corps northward toward Olangapo." This, he explained, would take the pressure off Parker's disintegrating corps on the east.

Wainwright now radioed MacArthur in Australia. The troops on Bataan, he said, were fast folding up and the weakened men no longer had the power of resistance.

Near the tip end of Bataan at his headquarters near Hospital No. 1, General King was mulling over Wainwright's recent order. It placed King in an impossible situation. If he obeyed, the resultant attack would end in a suicidal slaughter. The red-haired general called Jones. "I have just received orders to launch an immediate attack with your Corps."

Jones said he was in the midst of a withdrawal to the Binuangan River as ordered. "Any attack is ridiculous, out of the question. My men are too weak."

King didn't argue. He told Jones to forget the attack and hung up. It was now time to make the final ugly decision. The situation was chaotic and helpless. Any more fighting would lead to needless killing. He called for his chief of staff, General Funk, and his operations officer, Colonel James Collier.

The three men conferred at midnight in the narrow, flimsy headquarters building. They reviewed the tactical situation, considering all possible lines of action. At last King asked the key question: "Will I be able to stop the Japanese from reaching the high ground above Mariveles?"

The other two shook their heads. No matter what resistance was put up, they said, the Japanese would reach Mariveles by the next evening.

King hesitated. Wainwright was hamstrung by MacArthur's explicit order to attack until the end and Roosevelt's "no surrender" message. It was up to King to make the decision on his own, with the full knowledge that he was disobeying orders.

"I have decided to surrender Bataan," he said. If he ever got back to the States, he was sure he'd be court-martialed, but the lives of his 78,000 soldiers were far more important.

It was not a surprising decision yet it hit Collier "with a terrible wallop." Tears came to his eyes. He saw the other two men were also crying.

"I have not communicated with General Wainwright," said King, "because I do not want him to be compelled to assume any part of the responsibility."

Now began the bitter mechanics of surrender. Two bachelors, Colonel E. C. Williams and Major Marshall Hurt, volunteered to drive to the Japanese lines as emissaries. Unit commanders were warned that surrender would take place at 6:00 the next morning. Parker heard the news almost at once for his headquarters was practically next door to King's. He telephoned Bluemel.

"If the Lamao River line can be occupied," Parker said, "it'll only be necessary to hold it until morning."

"What's going to happen then?" asked Bluemel.

"A car carrying a white flag will go through the lines on the east road at daylight."

"Do you mean we're surrendering?"

"Yes. There must be no firing after the car passes through the lines. Did you get the ammunition and rations?"

"I got the ammo. No rations."

"I'll check personally."

The nurses at both hospitals were being warned to pack. They would leave in half an hour for Corregidor. At Hospital No. 1, in Little Baguio, the nurses didn't want to leave their patients.

"The patients will follow you," said their commandant, chubby Colonel Duckworth. "And so will the doctors. I'll see you all in San Francisco soon."

The two dozen nurses piled into a bus and soon were heading down the dangerous zigzag to Mariveles. Traffic was growing thicker and they seemed to creep. Dust filled the bus, irritating their throats. On all sides were glares of fire and rumbles of explosions. It reminded Lieutenant Brantley of Dante's Inferno. Strangely she didn't feel a part of the hell around her. She was numbed.

The nurses at Hospital No. 2, located several miles east of Little Baguio, also protested. What would happen to the patients? In surgery alone there was a long line of dying men waiting for operations. The doctors had to force the nurses to leave. Lieutenant Lucy Wilson had another reason for wanting to stay. The next day she was supposed to marry Lieutenant Dan Jopling of the 200th Coast Artillery. She and three other nurses got into a garbage truck and it slowly started west toward Hospital No. 1 on the way to Mariveles. It stalled. A half-track pushed until it started again. As they approached Little Baguio and the other hospital, there was a tremendous roar. The earth shook. Rubble rained on all sides. The sky lit up fantastically. Other explosions followed. The line of traffic stopped. Lieutenant Wilson was dazed. There were flames all over. The whole world seemed to be on fire.

The TNT warehouses were being destroyed. The sky was fantastic with bursting shells, colored lights and pillars of rainbows as several million dollars' worth of explosives and ammunition erupted.

General King, in his headquarters not far away, had just received a telephone call from General Jones.

"For crying out loud, Ned," said Jones, "what's going on?"

"The ammunition dump is blowing up," said King calmly. He didn't bother to say that the roof had just literally been blown off overhead.

"Hell, I can feel the ground shaking all the way up here. It must be an earthquake."

"I hate to tell you this, Honus, but I'm surrendering at 6:00 A.M. They're shelling the hospital. Parker's Corps is gone. There's nothing else I can do. Put white flags all along your line. You'll have to destroy your artillery and machine guns and stand by for further orders."

"I don't see what else you can do," agreed Jones. "I'll spike the artillery, but I'm saving the machine guns. At the last minute we can throw the bolts in the jungle."

"Use your judgment, Honus," said King in a hopeless voice.

Jones wasn't the only one who thought the great explosion at 2:00 on the morning of April 9 was another earthquake. Many on southern Bataan could feel the earth rocking sickly.

Clifford Bluemel felt the tremor. He was so tired he hoped the earth would open and swallow everyone and end the chaotic mess. His phone rang. It was Brigadier General Lewis Beebe from Corregidor who said, "I'm trying to get in touch with King and Parker." The explosion had temporarily severed all wire communications in the Little Baguio area. Bluemel could hear Wainwright shouting in the background. Skinny, he knew, rarely used the phone because of partial deafness.

The providential call gave Bluemel a chance to pour out his troubles. He said he'd asked for staff officers and got none. He also explained how impossible it would be to hold the Lamao River line. After a slight pause he heard Wainwright shout, "Tell Bluemel to use his own judgment and take whatever action he deems best. Whatever he does will be approved by General Wainwright."

Wainwright was visibly concerned about the counterattack he had ordered King to make; King hadn't yet reported what was going on. When the conversation with Bluemel ended, Beebe again tried in vain to make contact with King. Wainwright told him to try Jones directly. Jones answered the phone and told Beebe that the order to attack had never been given by King.

"Well, stand by," said Beebe. "You'll probably receive instructions to attack at any minute."

Not long after this, King learned about the call to Jones and realized he would have to face the situation squarely. At just 3:00 A.M. he called Corregidor. Beebe again answered for Wainwright.

"I want a definite answer as to whether or not General Jones will be left in my command *regardless* of what action I may take," said King. Beebe passed on this question to Wainwright.

"Tell him he's still in command of all forces on Bataan," answered the distraught Wainwright. For some reason he never asked King about the attack Jones was supposed to make.

And King still did not tell his superior he was going to surrender the next morning, that two emissaries were now almost ready to leave for the front.

Three hours later King called Corregidor and at last revealed what he had done. Lieutenant Colonel Jesse T. Traywick, Jr., night duty officer at Corregidor, hurried to Wainwright's tunnel quarters.

"Sir," he said, "General King is going to surrender!"

Wainwright was speechless.

"He's sent an officer to the Japanese to arrange terms."

"Go back and tell him not to do it!" While Traywick hurried back to the office, Wainwright waited anxiously.

Traywick returned, his face sober. "It's too late," he said.

"They can't do it! They can't do it!" Then Wainwright got hold of himself and went to his office, where he sent a message to MacArthur.

AT 6 O'CLOCK THIS MORNING GENERAL KING . . . WITHOUT MY KNOWLEDGE OR APPROVAL SENT A FLAG OF TRUCE TO THE JAPANESE COMMANDER. THE MINUTE I HEARD OF IT I DISAPPROVED OF HIS ACTION AND DIRECTED THAT THERE WOULD BE NO SURRENDER. I WAS INFORMED IT WAS TOO LATE TO MAKE ANY CHANGE, THAT THE ACTION HAD ALREADY BEEN TAKEN.

By dawn many assorted small boats were approaching Corregidor from the smoldering, defeated peninsula. In all about 2000 were escaping. The nurses from Hospital No. 1 had already landed and were anxiously waiting for their friends from Hospital No. 2. What had happened to them?

Delayed by the spectacular explosions at the ammunition dump, most of these nurses were just loading into a motor boat at Mariveles, but Lieutenant Lucy Wilson and three others were still stranded. Their garbage truck wouldn't move and they had been forced to walk several miles to a beach. Here, a passing interisland boat had just seen them and pulled in to the shore. Soon they, too, were on their way to Corregidor. Lieutenant Wilson watched Bataan disappear. This was the day she was to have married Dan Jopling and she didn't even know if he was still alive.

King's chief emissary, Colonel Williams, was then passing through the American front lines. His jeep proceeded north on the coastal road displaying part of a white sheet attached to a bamboo pole. In Williams' pocket was a typewritten, signed letter of instructions from King ordering him to try and arrange a meeting between Homma and King. If this was not possible, Williams himself was empowered to surrender all the Bataan forces.

A patrol of about thirty Japanese suddenly rushed on the road, bayonets flashing. The jeep stopped. The Japanese hesitated, then started to rush the car with fixed bayonets. Their commander, a noncom, abruptly changed his mind and ordered the others to withdraw. He approached the jeep with a hand grenade. As he was about to pull the pin, a Japanese lieutenant burst out of the jungle and ordered him to stop. After a hurried conference, the lieutenant and half a dozen men climbed onto the jeep and Williams' driver was told by sign language to head north toward Lamao.

Soon the two Americans were brought to Major General Kameichiro Nagano, commander of the detachment attacking down the east coast highway.

"I've been sent forward by General King to contact General Homma to discuss surrender terms," Williams told a Japanese interpreter.

Nagano agreed to arrange a meeting between King and Homma at Lamao at 11 A.M.

"I'll report back to General King and tell him of the arrangements," said Williams.

Nagano shook his head. Williams was to be held prisoner. The driver would take back the message. After his driver left with oral instructions, Williams became more worried about the letter from King authorizing him to surrender Bataan. He kept his hand in his pocket and surreptitiously began tearing it into fragments. The first time he was alone he was determined to eat the pieces.

A little after 9:00 A.M. the stocky King, wearing his last clean uniform, headed up front in a jeep. With him were his two aides, Majors Achille Tisdelle and Wade Cothran. One hundred and fifty yards ahead another jeep carried Major Hurt and Colonel Collier. Though both cars displayed sheets tied to bamboo poles, several planes swooped down, bombing and strafing. The jeeps stopped and the Americans flung themselves in a ditch. The surrender team started again. Just before reaching Lamao another plane dove, but at the last moment its pilot saw the white flags. Instead of firing, he wagged his wings. The Americans continued 100 yards to Lamao bridge. Here they saw Japanese infantry drawn up in columns of twos on the other side of the bridge.

As Japanese guides escorted the Americans to the Experimental Farm Station, King recalled Lee had surrendered to Grant at Appomatox on that same day. He even remembered what Lee had said, just before the ceremony: "Then there is nothing to do but to go and see General Grant, and I would rather die a thousand deaths."

At last he knew exactly how Lee had felt.

He saw a Japanese general sitting at a long table with Colonel Williams, in front of a small building. It was Nagano. The Japanese commander motioned King to sit down, explaining through an enlisted interpreter who knew little English that he wasn't authorized to conclude surrender arrangements. A representative from General Homma would soon arrive.

In a few minutes a shiny Cadillac drew up. Tisdelle recognized it as belonging to his friend, Juan Elizalde. Colonel Motoo Nakayama, Homma's senior operations officer, stepped out with his own interpreter. King rose to greet the newcomer but Nakayama ignored him and sat at the head of the table. King again sat down, hands in front, back erect. Tisdelle had never seen his general look more like a soldier.

The new interpreter spoke to Nakayama, then turned to King and said in a German accent, "You are General Wainwright?"

"No. I am General King, commander of all forces on Bataan."

Puzzled, the interpreter conferred with Nakayama, who was also puzzled, and finally said, "You must go and get General Wainwright."

"I don't represent General Wainwright, only myself. I have no means of getting in touch with him."

There was another conference. "For what purpose have you come?"

"To secure terms for the force in Bataan."

Nakayama was confused and displeased. "You'll have to get General Wainwright," said the interpreter. "The Japanese cannot accept surrender without him."

Patiently King repeated he represented only those on Bataan and could not communicate with Wainwright. He knew the lives of many depended on his words and manner. "My forces are no longer fighting units. I want to stop further bloodshed." He asked that he be permitted to return to head-quarters so he could send couriers to all his units. He also requested an armistice of twelve hours and permission to evacuate his men as prisoners of war in his own trucks and cars to their prison camp.

Nakayama spoke sharply to his interpreter. "Surrender must be unconditional," said the interpreter.

King kept his temper. "Would you consider these provi-sions? Give me permission to notify forward elements. It would save lives on both sides if the Japanese stayed in posi-tion. The movement of prisoners of war would be facilitated by using our trucks and cars."

"Surrender must be unconditional."

"Will our troops be well treated?"

"We are not barbarians. Will you surrender uncondi-tionally?"

King knew further delay would mean more unnecessary deaths. He nodded.

"Please hand over your sabre," said the interpreter.

"I left it behind in Manila."

After a brief, concerned conference the interpreter said a pistol would be acceptable. King placed his pistol on the table. So did the other Americans.

Nakayama rose, got into the Cadillac and was driven off. The American officers were taken in their jeeps another 17 miles farther north to Balanga, the capital of Bataan. Behind the sprawling Balanga Elementary School, King was led to some chairs and tables under a large tree. Japanese newsmen snapped many pictures of the captured general. Then Colonel Nakayama began to ask questions.

How many Japanese prisoners of war did King have? When King replied only about sixty, the Japanese were surprised there were that many. Talk switched to Corregidor. King insisted he didn't know how many troops were there. Or how many guns.

"Where are the guns placed?"

"I don't know."

"Why does a general officer have so little information?"

"I may give you any information you ask concerning my former command, but I am unable to give you any information concerning the defenses of Corregidor."

Nakayama pressed the point. "Does this mean you don't know anything about Corregidor or refuse to answer?"

"It means that I will not give any information about the defenses of Corregidor." King calmly crossed his leg, drew out a cigarette and lit it.

The Japanese interpreter leaned over the table, knocked the cigarette out of King's hand and yanked his leg down. "Sit at attention," he ordered. King did.

A black and white map of the lower tip of Bataan and Corregidor was laid on the table.

"Show where the tunnel leads from Mariveles to Corregidor," asked a Japanese staff officer.

King was amused. "There's no such tunnel."

"There must be." King shook his head. "Well, I am positive you have caverns near Mariveles where are stored all the large reserves of artillery." King truthfully denied their existence. "There are such caverns," insisted the Japanese officer, pointing to the cliffs on the eastern side of Mariveles. "Do not lie. Your artillery has been destroyed many times yet you kept bringing out additional artillery." King again shook his head.

The Americans were brought to a little house across the road. Two privates standing at the door as guards grinned. One came forward and offered King a pack of cigarettes. Half an hour later an amiable officer took off his cap, bowed and introduced himself as Colonel J. Takasaki. "Ah so, now for you the war is over and we are all friends."

King nodded politely. "Yes, for us the war is over but we are not friends. We are your prisoners."

"Oh, no. We are friends. Have you eaten?" When the colonel learned they hadn't, he spoke to an orderly. In a minute the man returned with heated evaporated milk. Warm San Miguel beer and more cigarettes were also brought in.

Takasaki rose. "Shortly I will come back and you and you," he said indicating King and Williams, "will come with me. I am going to take you for a ride." He smiled pleasantly and went out.

3 Though almost everyone else in II Corps was waiting to be captured, Bluemel was still fighting. He had pulled back his dwindling forces from the Lamao River line. Now, at noon, he was somewhere near Trail 20. Though lost, he did know the Japanese were on two sides. He ordered his people to deploy and hold off the attackers.

Several worried and annoyed American officers approached Bluemel. "General," said one, "the High Command surrendered at daylight. Here it is noon and you're starting a fight. Everyone else has surrendered but you."

Bluemel told them they could do what they wished. He was going to keep fighting. A moment later one of the officers pointed at several white flags flying over Bluemel's own lines. The general looked at them, benumbed from exhaustion. His uniform was ripped. He wore only one star. The other had been torn off his shoulder. He had done everything he could. He threw his rifle on the ground and waited for the Japanese to come.

Men were waiting all over the southern end of Bataan in huddled groups. Many were weeping unashamedly, Filipinos and Americans alike. Tears came mostly from the humiliation of surrender but partly from the relief of thinking that the torture was finally over.

Sergeant James Madden and 300 other American airmen were sitting at the side of the road halfway up the steep zigzag going up to Little Baguio. Their commander told them all sick men should get into a parked six-by-six truck. Madden helped a friend, whose ankles were painfully swollen from beriberi, into the truck just as Japanese soldiers appeared. Shouting and swinging their rifle butts, they chased everyone from the six-by-six.

Madden's commander, somewhat shaken, told his men to line up in columns of twos. When the group started up toward Little Baguio, the Japanese shouted angrily and made them head back toward Mariveles. The airmen were puzzled. Rumors flew. They were going to be shipped to Japan. They walked down the steep zigzag road, finally reaching the airfield near Mariveles. By now there were about 3000 captives packed in the dusty field.

They sat in the hot sun, puzzled, fearful and confused. After a long wait Japanese soldiers approached and began stripping the captives of blankets, watches, jewelry, razor blades, mess equipment, food and even toothbrushes. When the looting was over, the prisoners were herded onto the road. Four and five abreast they started once more up toward Little Baguio.

Men of the 200th Coast Artillery were also being looted in another part of Mariveles. A Japanese enlisted man took an amethyst ring from the man Lucy Wilson was supposed to marry that day, Lieutenant Dan Jopling. Another looter took a ring from the man standing next to Jopling just as a Japanese officer passed. The officer grabbed the ring from the soldier, saw it bore the University of Notre Dame insignia.

"Whose is it?" he asked.

The Notre Dame man, a former football player named Tonelli, said it was his. The officer smashed the enlisted man in the face with his fist and politely handed the ring back to Tonelli. "What year did you graduate?" he asked.

"1935."

"I graduated from Southern California in '35," said the Japanese amiably. He noticed the white mark on Jopling's finger. "Which one took it?" Jopling pointed out the looter. The officer walked over, struck the man several times and returned with the amethyst ring. "If you have anything of personal value," he advised, "hide it."

Groups were being rounded up all over the tip end of the peninsula. Lieutenant Colonel Allen Stowell was still at the communication center of Parker's headquarters watching a puzzled Japanese officer examine the switchboards. The Japanese rang every line, got no answers, and finally said to Stowell, "Code, code."

When Stowell said nothing an enlisted man approached, held a pistol to the American's head. Stowell scratched his head. "Code? Oh, yes." He wrote out the International Code.

This partially satisfied the Japanese officer. "More, more," he insisted.

Stowell pulled out an obsolete code book, Division Field Code No. 4. The Japanese officer was so delighted he ordered the enlisted man to lower the pistol.

About five miles farther east, Lieutenant Tony Aquino of Capinpin's division was sitting on a tree trunk near the Cabcaben airstrip. He still had his yellow convertible Buick, his birthday gift. Now it had no fenders or mudguards, was splotched with green paint; its top was ripped off, headlights smashed. It reminded Aquino of a skull with the eyes gouged out, only the sockets remaining.

To the south he heard dull metallic clanking, then a burst of machine-gun fire. Tanks! He and the others braced themselves. They were unarmed, their weapons stacked or thrown away. Without warning Zeros dove, roaring down at treetop level. Amazingly, no one moved for cover. The men waved their white flags.

This was a mistake. The last plane made a steep climb, turned back and dove, its guns blazing. Aquino jumped behind a tree trunk. He pulled out his rosary and began to pray automatically, "Oh, my God, I am heartily sorry. . . ."

The plane left. Several bodies littered the ground. Now Aquino again heard the roar of the approaching tanks. Dots of dust sprang upon the road. He saw they were machine-gun bullets.

"Let's get the hell out of here," someone shouted. Aquino flung himself down the decline at the side of the road. He jumped wildly across a 12-foot-wide stream. His heart pounding, he felt like a hunted deer. He wanted to do something but his mind was blank with fear.

A loudspeaker blared out, "Hiripino sordiars! Come hya and surrenda. We are youar frengs. Japang wirr nota kirr you. Come hya!"

Aquino saw a friend come out of a thicket waving a white flag and expected to hear gunfire, but there were no shots. The Filipinos were like children, at first fearful of a stranger with candy. Seeing there was no danger, they trustingly approached. Aquino still held back, suspecting the Japanese were waiting for a large number to appear before opening fire with the tanks.

"Hiripino sordiars," shouted a Japanese officer standing in the turret of a tank, "Japan come to riverate you from the Americang oppressors. Go home now. Manira go."

At the word "home," everyone crowded around the tank. A Filipino field grade officer stepped forward, saluted the Japanese officer as a token of surrender. The Japanese saluted and everyone knew all was over. The Filipinos cheered wildly. The Japanese officer smiled and waved his arms. The Filipinos waved back. That was it. The game of war was over. They jumped with joy and embraced each other.

Aquino and his friends piled into the battered Buick and started east toward Cabcaben. Jubilantly they made plans for the future. Aquino said everyone was welcome to spend the rest of their lives at his hacienda. They passed another group of Japanese and waved happily, expecting another friendly welcome, but a sentry shouted at them to stop and advanced with a rifle. The Japanese motioned them to get out of the car, pointing to the nearby Cabcaben airstrip, already jammed with prisoners. Aquino took a last sad look at the Buick, and marched with the others toward the field. His fear was returning.

    4   On the west half of Bataan, in Wainwright's former corps, the front lines were still intact, but General

Jones had spiked his big guns and placed white flags all along his front. Even so he had ordered his men to return any Japanese fire. They were to keep fighting in spite of the white flags, until definite arrangements were made with a Japanese surrender team.

It was now dark and Jones hadn't been able to reach the Rock by phone or radio all day. Communications with King at the tip end of Bataan were also out. He had no idea what he was supposed to do. An American general from one of his units ran wild-eyed into the command post crying, "All is lost!" Jones put the general to bed and sent General Fidel Segundo to take over the leaderless men.

On Corregidor, Wainwright still had no idea what was going on in Bataan. He was somewhat cheered by a message from Roosevelt giving him belated permission to surrender.

> AM KEENLY AWARE OF THE TREMENDOUS DIFFICUL-
> TIES UNDER WHICH YOU ARE WAGING YOUR GREAT BAT-
> TLE. THE PHYSICAL EXHAUSTION OF YOUR TROOPS
> OBVIOUSLY PRECLUDES THE POSSIBILITY OF A MAJOR
> COUNTERATTACK UNLESS OUR EFFORTS TO RUSH FOOD
> TO YOU SHOULD QUICKLY PROVE SUCCESSFUL. BECAUSE
> OF THE STATE [OVER] WHICH YOUR FORCES HAVE NO
> CONTROL I AM MODIFYING MY ORDERS TO YOU. . . .
> MY PURPOSE IS TO LEAVE TO YOUR BEST JUDGMENT
> ANY DECISIONS AFFECTING THE FUTURE OF THE BATAAN
> GARRISON. . . . I FEEL IT PROPER AND NECESSARY THAT
> YOU SHOULD BE ASSURED OF COMPLETE FREEDOM OF
> ACTION AND OF MY FULL CONFIDENCE IN THE WISDOM
> OF WHATEVER DECISION YOU MAY BE FORCED TO MAKE.

Wainwright radioed Roosevelt that since all communications with Bataan had been cut he had no knowledge of the terms arranged by General King. But he concluded:

> OUR FLAG STILL FLIES ON THIS BELEAGUERED ISLAND
> FORTRESS.

In Melbourne, MacArthur was reading a prepared statement to reporters: "The Bataan Force went out as it would have wished, fighting to the end its flickering, forlorn hope. No army has done so much with so little, and nothing became it more than its last hour of trial and agony. To the weeping mothers of its dead, I can only say that the sacrifice and halo of Jesus of Nazareth has descended upon their sons, and that God will take them unto himself."

The fighting, except for flurries of defense on the western half, in Jones' area, was all over on Bataan, but it was not to be the end of suffering for the 76,000 sick and starving Fil-Americans.

1   King's surrender of over 76,000 men including
12,000 Americans, was the greatest capitulation in U.S. military history. Except for the patients in Hospitals No. 1 and
2, all these men were now starting or about to start on the
long trip to their prison camp at Camp O'Donnell, a few
miles north of Clark Field. The first part of this odyssey, the
55-mile stretch between Mariveles at the tip end of Bataan
and the sugar center of San Fernando, would soon be recorded in the minds of Americans and Filipinos as one of
the major atrocities of the war. It would be called the Death
March.

Many of the 70,000 participants began the march at the
airstrip near Mariveles on the morning of April 10. Even
though groups of prisoners were leaving at intervals, the
airfield kept getting more congested, for thousands of other
Americans and Filipinos were streaming into Mariveles from
another direction, the road coming down the west coast.

Adding to the confusion were 26,000 civilians, crowded
like sheep into the tip end of the peninsula since early
January. Japanese guards soon gave up all hope of organization. Their officers had told them it would be a simple
operation. They were to round up about 25,000 prisoners
and bring them back by foot to Balanga. There, trucks would
be waiting to take them to their prison camp. The guards'
orders had been hurried and brief, for King's surrender
had come as a surprise to the high command. Homma had
figured the final attack would take about a month.

Homma had assigned the job of handling prisoners to
Major General Yoshikata Kawane, his transportation officer.
Kawane had presented his plans to Homma ten days before
the attack began. It was divided in two phases. Colonel
Toshimitsu Takatsu was responsible for the first, assembling
the prisoners at Balanga. No transportation was planned
since the farthest point, Mariveles, was only 19 miles away,
a day's march to Japanese soldiers. It wouldn't even be necessary to issue food to the prisoners since they could use

heir own rations. Kawane told Homma he would personally
upervise the second phase: the trip from Balanga to the
rison camp. He could spare only 200 trucks but these would
•e enough to shuttle the prisoners the 36 miles to San
Fernando. Freight trains would then take the men to Capas,
a little town about 13 miles north of Clark Field. From
here they would be marched 8 miles to their new home,
Camp O'Donnell.

The feeding arrangements were no problem, said Kawane.
The prisoners would eat the same rations as Japanese troops.
They would be fed not only at Balanga and San Fernando
•ut at two points between, Orani and Lubao.

"What about the sick and wounded?" Homma had asked.

Kawane said Major Hisashi Sekiguchi was setting up two
field hospitals, one at Balanga and the other at San Fernando. If the staff and equipment they were momentarily expect-
ng from Japan arrived, a third hospital would be set up in
•etween. At any rate medical units, aid stations and "resting
•laces" would be established every few miles.

Homma approved.

Unfortunately the plan was based on several fallacies.
Homma knew Wainwright's men were low on food but he
had no idea they were on the point of starvation. He also
vas ignorant of the defenders' alarming disease toll since
he malaria rate in south Bataan was many times greater
han in the Japanese lines, only a few miles north. He also
niscalculated how his own men would react as guards of
his defeated horde. But his greatest miscalculation was numerical. Homma's staff had assured him there were only
25,000 or 35,000 Fil-Americans in Bataan.

In Mariveles civilians and soldiers were separated into two
columns.

A Japanese officer was shouting reassurances. "The papers
ie about prisoners being shot. The Imperial Japanese Army
vill take good care of you. You will get good food and
reatment. At Balanga you will be picked up by trucks. We
vill abide by the Geneva Pact."

Groups of 300 were started off. Some had no guards.
Other groups had as many as four. Some merely had one
guard leading the way on bicycle.

Sergeant Frank Bernacki's group was halted near the air-
trip in front of a small building flying an American flag.
"Face the flag," shouted a Japanese officer. The group, most-
y U.S. airmen, turned and watched the Stars and Stripes

lowered and the Rising Sun raised. Then the march con
tinued.

Not far behind, Colonel Ray O'Day, instructor of Gen
eral Capinpin's division, had already thrown away his bed
roll, and was carrying only a musette bag. Soon Japanese
from the north began passing. These were rougher than their
captors, looting as they passed. Two saw O'Day's gold Scottish Rite ring and motioned for him to hand it over.

"Wife, wife," he said, but they insisted. He had to suck
his finger till the ring slid off. A few minutes later he was
robbed of his personal papers and half a dozen ration cans.
When O'Day protested, the looter threw him back five cans
but kept the letters and pictures.

Another Japanese, seeing this, looked at O'Day sympathetically and said, "So sorry, so sorry," and passed by.

The line of prisoners wound up the zigzag road toward
Little Baguio. The ditches were littered with burned trucks,
battered self-propelled mounts, rifles and abandoned equipment. O'Day stopped to rest. An American soldier plodded
by and said, "How you making it, Pop?" For the first time
he felt old.

Now they passed Hospital No. 1, sitting at the top of the
hill. Over it flew the Rising Sun. Guards were patrolling the
area, keeping other Japanese from molesting or looting the
patients. A tank commander, finding that Colonel Duckworth
had given medical treatment to forty-two Japanese prisoners,
had kept his promise to treat the hospital staff with consideration.

The columns continued, passing King's former headquarters, then the side road to Hospital No. 2. Here there was
no protective and grateful commander. It was already commandeered by a Major Sekiguchi. When the hospital commander requested more food for his staff and patients, Sekiguchi had said, "Your own forces didn't feed you adequate-
ly and I don't choose to feed you any more than you've
been receiving." Several truckloads of food and medicine
were at that moment being driven away.

American doctors rushed to Sekiguchi, protesting this
mass looting. "Do you have receipts for the food and medicine?" he asked. When they answered in the negative he
said, "Ah, so, since you don't have a receipt, it is quite obvious the Japanese Army didn't take it."

A small group of Filipino doctors and a detachment of
unwounded Philippine Scouts began to file out of the hospital area, up the road. They had been ordered to join the
march to the north. Immediately a rumor spread around the

rawling wards under the trees: the Japanese were freeing ll Filipinos.

Lieutenant Colonel Jack Schwartz, chief of surgery, hured from ward to ward begging the wounded Filipinos to tay, telling them it was a hoax. Japanese guards, evidently ager to rid themselves of responsibility, began encouraging he patients to start up the trail. Some guards actually ordered patients to leave, removing casts from the wounded, ushing them out of the area. Five hundred Filipinos, too veary to get out of bed, stayed, but about 5000 others, inected by mass hysteria, hurried down the dusty trail. Amutees chopped off limbs from trees for crutches and hobled away, their dressings unravelling. Men with critical belly vounds staggered toward freedom. Soon the main highway vas clogged with the maimed and wounded. Within a mile heir hysteria dissipated and they realized they had been nisled, but it was too late to return. Before long the ditches vere lined with dead and dying.

The march continued east toward Cabcaben. Sergeant ames Madden was in one of the first groups, having left Mariveles the night before. His throat ached from dust. Near he town his group saw a stream and rushed for it. The guards let the prisoners drink and wash themselves and their clothes. An hour went by and still they weren't herded back o the road. A feeling of gaiety passed from man to man. They talked of the war and agreed it would all be over in a year at the most. Abruptly they were shocked to silence by a series of roars. Shells from big Japanese guns emplaced ust behind them were flying over their heads toward Coregidor. Puffs of smoke appeared on that rock island as the hells exploded. The gaiety was over.

A few minutes later Madden heard a sound like milk trucks —hundreds of bottles rattling in wire cases. These were mortar shells from Corregidor. Madden and the others dropped, seeking cover as explosions tore up the ground.

American shells were also landing around Hospital No. 2. While Colonel Schwartz tried to calm his remaining patients, there was a tremendous explosion. Dust, foliage, trees flew into the air. Several shells had landed directly on or near Ward 14. Schwartz headed through the cloud of dust toward a chorus of terrified screams and moans.

At Cabcaben guards hastily reorganized the marching groups. Here the road turned north and headed straight up the east coast of Bataan. Ordinarily this was a scene of beauty. On the left was towering Mt. Bataan, the peaks of its time-eroded crater usually wreathed in cool-looking

clouds. On the right were the blue-green waters of Manil
Bay. Everywhere was lush green tropical growth: banan
trees, each topped by its purple phallus; occasional cocoanu
trees bent in modest grace; nipa palms whose long leave
swayed slightly like beckoning fingers.

Now there was no beauty. The colorful foliage was cov
ered with a heavy coat of chalk. The road itself was a con
tinuous, swirling dust cloud as an almost steady line of Japa
nese artillery, tanks and trucks came down the peninsula
from the opposite direction. Many of the infantrymen in
trucks jeered at the prisoners. Some began a cruel game
swinging at the marching men with long bamboo poles
knocking off their helmets and hats. Only occasionally a
Japanese, usually an officer, would stop the sport and apologize to the conquered. Sergeant Leon Wolf, of the 14th Ordnance, saw a Japanese officer run up to an American tank
commander and hug him. They had been classmates at
UCLA. They chatted a moment, then went off in different
directions.

Another motorized column of Japanese appeared. Somewhere its occupants had found golf clubs and with shouts
of laughter began swinging them at the hapless marchers
With each mile treatment grew more brutal as Japanese combat troops thinned out and rear-echelon units took their
place. Sun and dust made the marchers' thirst almost unbearable. Lieutenant Tony Aquino of Capinpin's division
made a sign to one of his guards, cupping the palm of his
hand.

The guard grunted and made a motion like slapping a fly
from his nose. Aquino knew it meant "No." In the middle
of the afternoon, the group rested near an irrigation ditch
At last the guard motioned permission to drink. The Filipinos scrambled along the ditch ducking heads into the running water.

When Aquino had drunk his fill he looked up to see the
guards laughing, and pointing at the ditch a few yards up-
stream. A moment later the Filipino saw what had amused
them. In the stream lay a naked corpse, intestines spilling
out, face swollen, covered with maggots. Aquino vomited
three times.

On this same dust stretch some Americans and Filipinos
were hit by gun butts, wrenches and clubs when they tried
to drink from ditches, streams or even the footprints of carabao. Yet some few lucky ones were actually stopped by
Japanese foot soldiers going in the opposite direction and
given water from their canteens. There appeared to be no

rhyme, reason or consistency to the actions of the Japanese. Only one thing was clear to the marchers. Things were steadily growing worse.

2   As the men of Parker's corps headed slowly up the east coast of Bataan, the great majority of Jones' men on the other side of the peninsula were still waiting in their jungle bivouacs or foxholes. It wasn't until dark that a Japanese car displaying a white flag approached Jones' headquarters.

Jones issued orders for his men to stack arms. He felt relieved, as if a tremendous load had been lifted from his shoulders. At 9:00 the next morning Jones and his chief of staff, Colonel William Maher, were driven south, back toward Mariveles. He was brought to Lieutenant General Susumu Morioka, his old antagonist of the 16th Division. They conversed pleasantly for several minutes.

"Who's going to win the war?" asked Morioka.

"We are, of course."

Morioka smiled. "*You* won't."

"Not me," said Jones. "But I have four boys at home who will."

Morioka laughed.

Jones' front-line troops were now heading over jungle trails and on the cobblestone road bisecting Bataan toward the east coast town of Balanga. Those in the rear were following their commander south toward Mariveles down the west coast road. Among these were Brigadier General Luther Stevens, commander of the Left Subsector, I Philippine Corps, and his chief of staff, Colonel Edwin Aldridge. Great numbers of Japanese troops were streaming toward them from Mariveles.

Their staff car was stopped by a shouting Japanese officer. When Aldridge opened the door, the Japanese kicked his right leg. Then he kicked the American in the face and yanked him out of the car. As the dazed Aldridge turned to get his possessions he was booted in the rear.

At that moment a truck carrying Colonel Don Bonnett and his officers of the 71st Philippine Regiment drove up and stopped. The Japanese officer seized a long bamboo pole and began to swing viciously at the Americans, splitting open Colonel Bonnett's head. Everyone was shoved into the truck. About 10 miles from Mariveles, the vehicle was stopped and the twenty-two American officers led up a side road. They were told to sit on the ground. They were tied together, two by two. Soon a Japanese captain who spoke some English noticed the group. He released Stevens and his aide; but as Stevens was untying his officers, another officer ordered Stevens and his partner retied.

In the meantime the main march up the other side of Bataan on the east road was growing. Most groups made the march from Mariveles to Balanga in two or three days. Attempts at bringing order out of chaos failed and with each mile the guards became more confused and irritated—and, consequently, more brutal. As the starving, disease-ridden prisoners staggered slowly up the dirt road in the blistering sun toward the capital of Bataan, guards urged them to hurry so the schedule could be maintained.

A young American soldier next to Sergeant Floyd Grow was panting desperately, unable to keep up the pace. Finally he fell out of ranks, shouting wildly, "I want him to shoot me!" The guard pushed him back into line. Again the youngster fell back. Again the guard pushed him in place. The American stumbled, fell and couldn't get up. The guard shot the young soldier.

Grow passed an American sitting in a culvert, his hands extending toward him in supplication. He started for him, then saw his countryman was stiff with rigor mortis.

There was little shade for the marchers on the long stretches between towns. Chalk from the road, stirred by the marchers, clung to the men's sweating bodies, stung their eyes, turned their damp beards to a dirty white. When Japanese motor columns rumbled down the center of the road, clouds of dust swirled blindingly.

The countryside was a bleak, terrifying desert. Thousands of bombs and shells had stripped the rolling hills of trees and foliage, leaving scarred, blackened stumps. Dirty clouds of smoke still rose to the left where woods were smoldering from the cataclysmic Good Friday bombardment. The afternoon heat was deadly and men threw themselves, when guards permitted, into each filthy stream.

The first group stumbled into Balanga at 2:00 P.M., April 11. Then at irregular intervals, other groups of soldiers and civilians approached the cool-looking Talisay River on the outskirts of the city. Some guards let their prisoners rush to the water, drink, bathe and rest on the banks. Others stolidly drove their men past, even though they piteously cried for water.

Once in the suburbs, there was shade at last from the sun. Palm and banana trees formed a green comforting arch.

Fantastically beautiful tropical flowers—reds, purples, blues —brightened the dust-covered roadway.

Many of Jones' men were also pouring into Balanga from the cross-peninsula cobblestone road and the capital of Bataan had already become a confused mass of shouting Japanese guards and milling prisoners. No one knew what was going on or who was in charge. Orders were given, then countermanded or forgotten.

Here ended Phase One: a dismal failure, completely disorganized, uncoordinated, inadequately supervised, with an alarming lack of discipline. Now Colonel Takatsu's responsibility ended. General Kawane's began.

A semblance of organization began to appear. For the first time in three days an attempt was made to feed the prisoners. Even so confusion continued and in some ways became more intolerable for the marchers. Some groups were fed a handful of rice and salt as they left Balanga as well as given water and marched in good order with proper rests. Others missed this first meal, were shooed away from every artesian well and marched either too fast or too slowly. A few guards were kind; more were indifferent or cruelly careless; others were outrightly sadistic.

Rank made little difference in the treatment at Balanga. While Colonel Harrison Browne, chief of staff of the Philippine Division, was being looted, he heard a groan. Turning, he saw his commander, Brigadier General Maxon Lough, on his knees. A Japanese lieutenant was viciously swinging a four-foot hardwood club at the general's head.

Browne and Captain Joseph Sallee, Lough's aide, helped the general to his feet and dragged him under a mango tree. An American doctor patched Lough's wound and Browne gave his commander a drink of whisky from a shampoo bottle.

General Jones was driven to the Balanga schoolhouse about this time. He wasn't beaten up but late on that afternoon of May 11 he was placed at the head of a column marching to the next point, Orani, about 11 miles due north. Jones protested. He wanted his men to ride. The guards paid no attention to him. The transportation situation was already going to pieces. Prisoners were swamping Balanga and it was obvious there would be more than twice the 25,000 expected plus thousands of civilians. There were less than 200 trucks for the job and many of these were being repaired. In fact in all the 14th Army that day there were only 230 trucks in running order.

Scores of U.S. trucks and cars were being picked up every

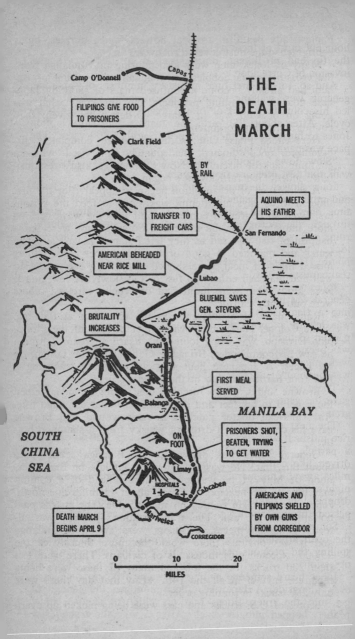

THE
DEATH
MARCH

Camp O'Donnell — Capas

FILIPINOS GIVE FOOD
TO PRISONERS

Clark Field

BY
RAIL

AQUINO MEETS
HIS FATHER

TRANSFER TO
FREIGHT CARS

San Fernando

AMERICAN BEHEADED
NEAR RICE MILL

Lubao

BLUEMEL SAVES
GEN. STEVENS

BRUTALITY
INCREASES

Orani

FIRST MEAL
SERVED

Balanga

MANILA BAY

SOUTH
CHINA
SEA

ON
FOOT

PRISONERS SHOT,
BEATEN, TRYING
TO GET WATER

Limay

HOSPITALS
1 + 2 +

Cabcaben

DEATH MARCH
BEGINS APRIL 9

Mariveles

AMERICANS AND
FILIPINOS SHELLED
BY OWN GUNS
FROM CORREGIDOR

CORREGIDOR

0   10   20
MILES

hour but most of these were transporting Japanese soldiers to the tip end of Bataan in preparation for the amphibious invasion of Corregidor.

And so, for the first time in history, numbers of American generals were walking toward a prison camp. General Jones led his column. Ahead of him a guard was pedalling a bicycle. After about 200 yards the guard would stop, motion Jones to hurry up his men and pedal another 200 yards. The pace was painfully fast.

"Slow down," shouted someone from the rear. "We can't walk that fast. Men are dropping out."

Jones slowed the march. The guard pedalled angrily back and motioned the general to hurry. It was pitch-dark by the time they reached Abucay. In a few miles they passed through the burned-out village of Mabatang, its charred ruins still giving off a faint acrid smell. Many instinctively looked to the left at the rising hills toward rugged Mount Natib. Here on the Abucay Line they had received their first real baptism of battle.

Jones' party didn't reach Orani until after midnight. The general was held aside while the other prisoners were pushed into a rice paddy enclosed by barbed wire. Finally Jones was led to a corner in the crowded enclosure. Men were packed so tightly they had to draw up their knees. The stink was overpowering. Near Jones was an open latrine, crawling with maggots. The whole area was covered with feces. It was, he thought, another Andersonville.

There was water but no food. An American enlisted man gave the general a handful of uncooked rice. "Keep several grains on your tongue," he advised.

The next morning Jones and the others were fed lugao, rice mush. It was sticky and tasted like paste but no one left a particle. They were lined up in the scorching sun and driven like cattle toward the next main station, Lubao, 16 miles away. This march was much harder than the previous night's for it was under the blazing tropical sun. Men dropped out, falling into the ditches. Every time the group passed through a village, the marchers called, "Water!"

Sometimes civilians would bring out cans of water from the open artesian wells, but the guards shoved them aside, spilling the precious water to the road. Water became an obsession.

Jones heard someone calling his name from a truck as it drew alongside. A Japanese officer motioned the general to get into the truck. Jones and his chief of staff, Colonel Maher, hopped into the back. After a mile the truck drew up to a nipa hut, brilliant with purple bougainvillaea. Inside were Generals King and Brougher and several high-ranking Filipinos. Guards led King and Jones to the rear where photographers were waiting.

"Take off your sunglasses and helmet," ordered an officer.

Jones looked at the Japanese levelly. He was tired of following their orders and said bluntly, "No." He expected a beating, but the Japanese merely shrugged his shoulders and told the photographers to snap their pictures.

Other groups following Jones into Orani were not so lucky, the enclosure growing more and more filthy. Half of the men had dysentery. So far there had been only isolated cases of brutality but as the foot traffic piled up, it became more general.

Sergeant Floyd Grow's chief guard was lining up his men at the side of the road, not far from Orani. "You Americans are soft," he said. "I was born and raised in San Francisco, I know. Take off your clothes. I'm going to give you the sun treatment." The men obeyed. "Now stand at attention." The men stood in the blistering sun, sweat rolling down their naked bodies.

The roadside began to be dotted with the dead. They soon became swollen to monstrous size by the heat. Crows tore open these cadavers with their beaks, often fighting each other for the nauseating meat while buzzing hordes of fat, green flies covered the remnants. Most of these men had died of disease, hunger or exhaustion. Some had been murdered.

Lieutenant Tony Aquino's group had been marching for hours without rest or water. Their legs were swollen, their eyes burned. An American ahead of Aquino fell, the sharp stones of the road cutting his face. A guard ran up, kicked him in the ribs to make him get up. The American slowly rose on all fours, then dropped exhausted. The guard kicked harder. The prisoner—blood dripping from his mouth, face covered with bruises—again tried to get up. He extended his right hand to the Japanese in a pleading gesture. The guard slowly, deliberately placed the tip of his bayonet on the side of the American's neck, and quickly jabbed.

For a moment, the American squatted in the road suspended like a fly on a pin but when the bayonet was suddenly yanked free, he fell inertly. It was a picture Aquino would never be able to erase from his memory. The Japanese sank his bayonet into the limp figure once more and angrily motioned the horrified onlookers to continue their march.

Sergeant Jack Cape of the 31st U.S. Infantry had a sadistic

guard who only let his charges drink from ditches or carabao wallows. Near Orani one man collapsed from dysentery. Two American comrades dragged the man along, but soon were too weak to continue. The man was dropped. Cape saw the Japanese guards hand the two Americans shovels, motioning them to give their fallen friend the coup de grâce. When they refused, the guard raised his pistol. The men hit their comrade with shovels.

A mile later two other Americans were staggering dazedly. They fell. Cape saw guards kick them to make them walk, and when this was useless, run them through with bayonets.

Colonel Edwin O'Connor saw a guard push a staggering Filipino off the road, and shoot him. A little later another Filipino began to scream crazily. A guard led him to a bush. O'Connor heard a shot, then saw the guard emerge from the underbrush alone. The man walking next to O'Connor was a big American. One of the guards took a violent dislike to him, jabbing him constantly with his bayonet and once cutting him across the face.

Sergeant Calvin Graef of New Mexico saw two American airmen fall out from exhaustion. Guards beat the two fallen men with bamboo clubs until their heads were pulp.

By now occasional beheaded bodies could be seen in the ditches. With every few miles, their number increased. Lieutenant Colonel Allen Stowell could tell only by size if they were American or Filipino since the bodies were turning from brown to black. After counting twenty-seven headless corpses, Stowell told himself, "You've got to cut this out." He began marching with eyes straight ahead.

Although many were too dazed and crazed to do anything but scramble toward the nearest water, whether in ditch, well or wallow, others figured ways to keep their bodies from dehydrating. Colonel Edwin Aldridge found a five-gallon oil can in a roadside house and half-filled it with water. He and nine comrades were taking turns, two at a time, carrying the can.

Those in Sergeant Charlie James' group were making water bottles of bamboo sections. James himself drank only from wells so he wouldn't get dysentery. To combat thirst he kept a can-opener key under his tongue. At one stream he saw a Filipino soldier sitting, looking vacantly. Blood was running from bayonet wounds in his sides.

Ironically the ranks of the marchers were being swollen by escaping soldiers sneaking down to the coastal road from the mountains. Many joined the long march not realizing they were heading for prison camp.

Though most civilians were being trucked out, others were walking. Mothers had covered the faces of older daughters with dirt to make them unattractive. Even though it was known that General Homma punished rapists severely, Japanese soldiers crept up to the civilian resting places after dark and tried to drag girls back to their camps.

The atrocities that began on the Balanga-Orani stretch increased during the 16-mile lap to Lubao. The road, pocked by bombing, made walking difficult.

General Clifford Bluemel was now marching next to General Stevens. They were at the head of the column, eating dust, a common humiliation for officers. A truck approached from the north. As it passed, a Japanese soldier leaned out and swatted Stevens in the face with a bamboo stick. Bluemel saw his comrade's glasses falling, caught them. He grabbed the staggering Stevens and led him to the side of the road. They sat talking, while Stevens tried to clear his head. A guard came up, pointed a revolver at Bluemel's chest, motioning him to get up. When Bluemel started to argue, he saw the hammer go back and the gun turned to Stevens. Bluemel helped Stevens to his feet. When Bluemel realized his friend couldn't continue he led him toward a rice paddy. Stevens protested, knowing Bluemel was risking death. Just then another guard ran at the two men with fixed bayonet, thinking they were trying to escape. When the guard saw the blood on Stevens' head he merely prodded Bluemel back into line with the bayonet.

Stevens crawled into the irrigation ditch at the side of the road and hid beneath some undergrowth. He lay motionless as the column disappeared. But for Bluemel's courage, he knew he might be lying on the road with a bullet in his head.

Not far behind, Sergeant Robert Franklin was watching a Filipino soldier dart from the road to a guava tree. As the man climbed to pick the fruit, there was a shot. The Filipino fell, dead.

Resting not far away at the side of the road without shade was a mixed group of Filipinos and Americans. Their guards told them to get up but the Filipino next to Captain Joseph Revak was too weak to rise. A guard prodded him. Though he tried, the man couldn't get up. The Japanese pulled out his pistol and, to Revak's horror, shot him. They marched and then, since the line straggled out, again stopped for a rest. This time it was Revak who couldn't get up. A guard motioned with a rifle but the American didn't care. "Go ahead and shoot," he panted.

The guard stood over him. Revak was unable to move a muscle, but when he saw the rifle swing toward him, he felt a surge of strength and staggered to his feet. Half-conscious, he wobbled up the road.

At another resting place, a few miles farther north near the base of Bataan, Corporal Roy Castleberry watched two civilians dig a hole in the hard, dry ground. Beside the hole lay a delirious American captain. The captain passed out as he was laid in the hole. Suddenly he came to, realized he was being buried alive and began to crawl desperately out of his grave. A guard ordered the Filipinos to hit the American with their shovels. They refused. Then the guard raised his rifle as if to shoot them. The Filipinos, faces twisted in agony, hit the American, rolled him into the hole, and covered him with dirt. A moment later a hand rose from the grave. The fingers moved feebly, entreatingly.

The marchers crossed the strategic bridge at Layac and turned east toward San Fernando. At last they were leaving Bataan peninsula. This stretch of road was straight, unshaded. Hundreds dropped in their tracks. Some, maddened by thirst, risked their lives to run to the adjoining sugar cane fields. They chewed the cane, then threw the pulp away. Others behind, not willing to take the chance of getting shot, picked up the chewed cane and tried to get its last moisture. The men were so dehydrated that most were unable to urinate. To those who could, the few drops burned as if a hot iron had been shoved up their penis, yet at the same time brought unspeakable relief.

It was on this long stretch that Captain Ed Dyess, formerly a fighter pilot, saw six Filipinos in his group make a dash for an artesian well. As they neared the water, the guards loosed a rifle volley. Four fell dead. Two, badly wounded, crawled, eyes glassy, toward the bubbling well, hands outstretched. The guards fired again. Now all six were dead.

A few miles later the Dyess group reached the outskirts of Lubao, a spraddling city of 30,000. Dyess saw a weird object draped over a barbed-wire fence. When he drew closer, he realized it was a Filipino soldier, abdomen slit open by a bayonet. His bowels were draped like grayish purple ropes along the wire.

Soon they were passing in tragic parade through crowds of waiting Filipinos. Civilians risked their lives to throw out boiled eggs, fried chicken wrapped in banana leaves or pieces of panocha, brown hard sugar. Others placed pots of rice

and cans of water in the road. Some guards did nothing.
Others kicked over the rice and water vats and swung rifles
at those throwing food.

A few civilians were selling food but the great majority
wouldn't even take the money offered them. The streets were
lined with weeping people. Though Japanese guards hurried
up and down the lines, old women swathed from crown to
ankle would pull staggering marchers from the line, stand
over them with their long skirts. When the guards had
passed, the exhausted American or Filipino would be hidden
in a nipa hut. Some Filipino soldiers, their tattered uniforms
looking civilian, would dart into the crowd, grab a girl, pos-
ing as a husband, or seize a baby, holding it as a father.

The men passed the large church near the edge of town
and then were herded into a large corrugated tin building,
a rice mill. Inside were several rotting bodies and piles of
feces. There was one water spigot for the several thousand
men jammed into the 150-by-70-foot building but only those
nearby could worm their way through for a drink. There
was room only to sit, huddled. Doors and windows were
shut and ventilation had to come from cracks in the walls.
Men often found themselves next to dying or even dead
comrades.

When the mill was packed, the overflow was formed in
groups outside. Here also there was a single water spigot.
The water dribbled in a continual thin stream as men, desperate for water, crowded into line for a few drops. The
guards here treated everyone badly. Colonel K. L. Berry
saw an American and a Filipino arguing at the spigot.
Guards rushed at the American with bayonets. He dodged
but was soon caught. So was the Filipino. Both were tied
to a tree and shot. Later Berry saw a guard beat a Filipino
over the head with a pickhandle until his brains oozed out.
He wondered what his "crime" had been. Colonel Aldridge
knew. He had seen the Filipino glare at the guard a moment
before.

Sergeant James Madden was at the spigot when a young
American, not even twenty, was dragged into the area by
two guards.

"Why did you try to get away?" asked the interpreter.

"I was trying to get into the hills and join the guerrillas.
I know what's going to happen to Americans."

He was led across the road, tied to a tree with hands
behind his back. Two guards knelt down, aimed their rifles
and fired. The bullets hit the tree. They aimed again. This
time their guns jammed. An officer ran up, shouting and

waving a sabre. The two guards stood at attention as the officer slapped them with the palm of his hand. The guards loosened the American's hands and made him kneel. Murmurs of shock came from the prisoners across the street but there was not a single sound of protest. The officer forced the American to get off his knees and walk into the bushes. A moment later the Japanese returned, his sabre dripping blood. He walked across the street, pushed aside Madden and the others at the spigot and washed his red sabre.

3 Most of the marchers stayed overnight at Lubao, but some remained two days and a few three or four. There were usually two meals daily, a handful of rice and a dash of salt. Those outside the corrugated rice mill crowded together, victims of the suddenly cool nights and ferocious mosquitoes. At least they had air.

The final lap to San Fernando was the shortest, about nine miles, and the cruelest. There was almost no cover. Here the asphalt, churned up by tanks and trucks, was melting in the sun. Those thousands without shoes, or with shoes in tatters, felt as if they were walking over hot coals. By now a mile was endless to these diseased, dehydrated, starving men. They passed field after field of sugar cane; many glanced longingly to the northwest at the rugged Zambales Mountains, symbols of freedom.

Several thousand Filipinos escaped on this stretch. For Americans it was a much more difficult choice. Few knew the country or could speak Tagalog. The Filipino could quite easily become assimilated in the next village. The American, even with tanned face, was conspicuous by his size, manner and voice.

Sergeant Frank Bernacki, formerly of the Air Corps, was one American lured by the Zambales. Tanks with *Singapore* scrawled on their sides approached. While the guards were waving at the tankers, Bernacki whispered to other Americans around him, "I'm leaving. Anyone want to go with me? I hear Thorp has $50,000 with him." There were rumors that a Captain Claude Thorp had escaped from Bataan two months earlier with a large sum of money given him by MacArthur to set up guerrilla groups.

No one wanted to go. Bernacki crawled alone into the snake-infested cane. The leaves were sharp. It was hot, dusty, almost suffocating as he crawled on all fours through tangled vines. He passed out.

Nearby, another airman, Sergeant Ray Hunt, was driven to escape by desperation and hatred. Normally 160 pounds, malaria and starvation had lowered his weight to 100 pounds. As the marchers crossed a bridge, he suddenly dashed into a deep ditch and hid in thick foliage. He heard someone say, "Don't look! Do you want him to get shot?" Finally the footsteps of his group faded out. He crawled along the ditch and to his amazement saw two more Americans, face down, frozen in terror. Hunt touched one of the men on the leg, then softly spoke. It was a corporal named Chatum. The other man was an artilleryman, a Captain Jones.

Hunt wanted to leave the ditch. The others argued. Even so, Hunt rose slowly and called to several Filipino farmers across the river. After a few minutes one approached. "Are there any Japs around?" whispered Hunt.

"Stay down," the other warned and left. He returned soon and led the three Americans to a bamboo house on stilts, a buhay. Here was another American, a Lieutenant Kerry. The four could watch the march through the weave of the bamboo walls. They saw an American bayoneted.

Filipinos visited the men several times a day bringing water, rice and a crude sugar. One boy offered to hide Hunt in a nearby fishpond. "I will make you well again," he promised. "I'll keep you safe until the Americans return."

Another boy told them of an American civilian still in a nearby hacienda and offered to guide them there. The four Americans were loaded into a cart with solid wooden wheels and covered with hay. All that day a carabao pulled them toward the northwest, toward the jagged Zambales Mountains.

Marchers were staggering the last mile of the 55-mile trek into the sugar center of San Fernando. At the outskirts of town, trucks lined the road, forcing the men to pass by one at a time. It was a gantlet. Japanese soldiers in the trucks swung their rifle butts as the Filipinos and Americans staggered past.

Farther on, the streets were lined with civilians. Although guards tried to hold them back, many defiantly ran to the passing men with jars of water and baskets of food. A Filipino girl threw Sergeant David Duran a ball of rice. He saw a guard rush toward her, batter her in the face with his rifle butt. This ball of rice was his first food since joining the march.

People from all over Luzon were looking for loved ones, hoping to find a relative alive in the ragged, pitiful parade. The great crowd moaned and wept in public sympathy as

e skeleton army dragged by. Occasionally a wife, a child
r father would spot a Filipino soldier and rush to his side.
ven though guards would push these civilians away, there
as little open brutality.

Most of the men were fed rice balls. Here also were water
nd crude medical care. The men were penned in various
laces: in a pottery shed, at the "Blue Moon" dance hall,
a empty lots, in old factories, in school buildings and yards,
nd in the large cockpit arena near the railroad station.
Colonel Aldridge, sitting at the edge of the jammed cockpit
rena with General Stevens, watched a group of young air-
en stumble toward the entrance as if it were the gates of
eaven. One reached the threshold, then fell in, dead. The
thers in the same group were at the point of death. All
ad dysentery.

Lieutenant Aquino's group was taken to an old vinegar
actory, a great concrete-block structure of Spanish archi-
ecture with a galvanized roof. Aquino, 150 pounds when
e left for war in his new yellow convertible, now weighed
9. He flopped on a matting of straw and slept fourteen
ours. When he awoke he was pulled out of the stifling
actory by a guard, marched into a Japanese barracks, and
ed upstairs to a room. Inside were his father and a Japanese
olonel. Father and son embraced.

"Thank God you are alive," said the elder Aquino after
long pause.

"How are Mother and the kids, Papa?"

"Everyone is alive. We were so worried." The father, one
f the leaders of the new "Quisling" Laurel government,
ntroduced the officer as Colonel Ota of the *kempeitai*, the
ecret police.

"Mr. Aquino is a good friend of Japan," said Ota in a
British accent. "He will help form your government with
apanese guidance. To thank him, we the benevolent Japanese people tell him that his son can go home with him."

At first Lieutenant Aquino wondered if his release was
ome sort of pay-off. "Colonel Ota," said the young man,
"I thank you for your kindness and your esteem for our
amily but I have to refuse to go home. I cannot desert my
nen. If you really mean to help me, give all of us food
nd medicine."

"Your father was right," said the colonel. "He said you
would refuse. Please accept my apologies for the way you
ll have been treated." He left.

Now Benigno Aquino quietly told his son that President
Quezon had ordered Laurel and other leading Filipinos to

appear to collaborate with the Japanese. The young ma
looked at his father and was convinced he could never be
traitor. The elder Aquino said that he and other top nativ
officials were working with General Homma for early re
lease of all Filipinos from prison camp.

"Hurry, Papa, we are dying like flies."

The two drank tea and ate cookies. When Colonel Ot
returned the elder Aquino said, "Good-bye, son. I will tel
your mother to come and see you." They embraced. A
young Aquino was leaving, his father handed him a packag
of food wrapped in banana leaves. Lieutenant Aquino re
turned to the vinegar factory, gathered his men and passe
around the food; each got only a mouthful. A few minute
later the doors of the factory were opened and Japanese
guards entered with wheelbarrows full of rice.

Most stayed one or two days in teeming San Fernando
but a few were marched directly to the railroad station and
without being given food or water, loaded into small boxcars
7 feet high, 33 feet long and 8 feet wide, similar to the
French 40 and 8. One hundred to 115 were shoved into
each car, then both doors closed. Men were forced to stand
in the steamy interior. The stink of the disease-ridden was
unbearable as the trains slowly headed north on the three-
to-four-hour trip to Capas.

While Sergeant James Madden's car was still in the San
Fernando yards, suffocating men in the rear kept shouting
"Open the door!" The shouts turned into weeping, screaming. Suddenly there was a crash as the engine backed into
the line of boxcars. One of the doors sprung open. A guard
with a gun ran over when he heard the moaning. He
climbed into the packed car but kept the door open. Even
with one door open those in the rear could barely breathe
as the train headed north.

Without discussion or plan, the strong ones voluntarily
moved to the rear of the car, allowing the sicker ones to
breathe the sweet, fresh air. It was a miracle, though
Madden, that men who had suffered so much could retain
their humanity. As the hours passed, men rotated in the
jammed car without argument.

Most of the cars were kept locked and many died. Sergeant Charlie James was in the back of his car. He was
lucky. Near his nose was a small crack in the hot steel wall.

"I'm smothering," moaned someone.

"Shut up, we can't do anything about it," said someone
else.

"Save your breath," said a third. "You're using up oxygen."

Men with dysentery were unable to control themselves; others vomited on their comrades. Some fainted from the smell. Some died but were still kept erect by the pressing mob. At every stop, the more friendly guards opened the locked doors. Filipinos crowded around, passing out bottles of water, tomatoes, bananas, rice, eggs, coffee, sugar cane. Those Americans who had previously regarded Filipinos as inferiors began to appreciate their courage and humanity. Occasionally a prisoner would make a break from one of the cars, mingling with the crowd. There were so few guards and the crowds were so belligerent, that not many of these escapees were caught or even chased.

At the town of Capas, the men were unloaded. The fresh air was like elixir. Here again hundreds of civilians were waiting with food and water. Some guards allowed food to be passed out; others kicked over baskets of food. It was about eight miles over a shadeless, dusty road to the prison camp, O'Donnell. Yet the men were happy to be again in the open. They were buoyed too by the tremendous surge of friendliness they had received all the way from San Fernando. The men staggered toward the barren plains. For a change there were no brutalities. Many of the guards were sympathetic on this stretch and even helped the weaker marchers.

At last the prisoners saw a maze of tumbledown buildings, some only half-built, sitting out on a great plain in loneliness. This was Camp O'Donnell, where perhaps the misery would be over.

They passed through a gate flanked by towers armed with machine guns. A long barbed-wire wall extended in both directions. They were marched up a hill and seated on the ground in the blazing sun in front of a building flying the Japanese flag. After a long wait, the commandant of the hastily established camp would speak to each group through an interpreter.

"The captain, he say Nippon has captured Javver, Sumatter and New Guinyah," a fat interpreter told Captain Ed Dyess' group. "Captain, he say we soon have Austrayler and New Zealer. The captain, he say America and Nippon enemies. Always will be war until America is Nippon's. Captain, he say you are not prisoners of war. You will be treated like captives. He say you do not act like soldiers. You got no discipline. You do not stand at attention while he talk. Captain, he say you will have trouble from him."

Each group learned in the first minutes at Camp O'Donnell

that their sufferings would continue indefinitely, or until death

As the great sprawling march was nearing its end, the Manila Sunday *Tribune* of April 19 printed many picture of the masses of prisoners and civilians coming out of Bataan. There was also a Japanese-inspired story:

The task of making observations upon the tragic aspect o marching war prisoners from the Bataan front, where they sur rendered on April 9, to San Fernando, Pampanga, previous to their entrainment to their permanent concentration camp is a sa one; hence, our effort to avoid details about the whole episode
So the public would not get the wrong impression from such an enigmatic remark, however, we make it plain that the Im perial Japanese Forces, whose business is clearly to prosecute the present war to its successful termination, are going well out o their way to feed and help 50,000 men who once were their enemies beyond most reasonable men's expectations.
If, in spite of the humane treatment the Japanese are giving these prisoners, the latter are too weak to reach their destina tions, we have only the high command of the American force to blame for surrendering when many of their men had already been terribly weakened by lack of food and by diseases.

Although General Homma now knew there were more than double the expected number of prisoners, he was no told by General Kawane that the general health of the cap tives was so dangerously low that they were near starvation
Assuming General Kawane could handle the march of pris oners, Homma was presently devoting his time and attention to the assault on Corregidor. In fact he was so involved with invasion plans, he was not even aware of the thousands of lives lost on the road to San Fernando. During these days he was isolated in his headquarters at Balanga and his only trips were south to the tip end of the peninsula
He didn't learn until two months later that more Fil-Americans had died on the long march than on the battle-fields of Bataan. Of the approximately 70,000 men who started, only 54,000 reached Camp O'Donnell. No one will ever know the exact death toll since many of those un-accounted for escaped. Even so, according to a consensu of responsible survivors, 7000 to 10,000 men died on the march from malaria, exhaustion, starvation, beatings or exe-cution. Of those dead, about 2330 were American.
Most survivors were convinced the march was cruelly, pur-posefully planned and executed.
There had been little plan at all. About half of the pris oners rode in trucks from Balanga to San Fernando and

suffered little. Some who walked saw almost no brutalities and were fed, if not well, at least occasionally. Yet others a mile behind were starved, beaten and killed by brutal guards.

Brutality to the Japanese enlisted man was a way of life. He was used to being slapped and beaten by his officers. He, in turn, slapped and beat from habit. He had been indoctrinated to obey swiftly and without question. When Americans and Filipinos failed to understand his orders or were too weak to follow them, he often resorted to violence and even murder. There was almost a complete failure of guidance and leadership from above.

The Japanese soldier despised those Fil-Americans who had surrendered. "Do not fall captive even if the alternative is death," read his soldier's manual. "Bear in mind the fact that to be captured not only means disgracing the army, but your parents and family will never be able to hold up their heads again. Always save the last round for yourself."

Another motivation for brutality was revenge. This act had always transcended other human ties in Japan, justifying any action.

Whatever the causes, no man who marched would ever forget the horrors and torture. Few would ever forgive. The Death March was to become a focal point of hate and revenge to Americans and Filipinos.

PART 6

FROM HUMILIATION TO VICTORY

22

"But Not in Shame"

1 About dawn on the morning of April 18, some 650 miles northeast of Japan, a reconnaissance plane flew low over the U.S. carrier *Enterprise* and dropped a beanbag containing a message to Admiral Bill Halsey, commander of Task Force 16. An enemy patrol ship was 42 miles ahead and the pilot was sure he had been sighted. Halsey swore and signalled the bad news to a nearby carrier, the *Hornet*.

A harsh alarm immediately sounded on the *Hornet* and sailors ran to their battle stations. Awakened by the noise, Army pilots and crewmen soon learned that Task Force 16 had been sighted by a Japanese picket ship and they would probably have to take off in their sixteen B-25 Army bombers at once instead of that evening, as planned, when they would be within 500 miles of Japan.

It was a jolt for the fliers. Everything had been precisely planned, to the last gallon of gas. They were to bomb Tokyo and three other cities that night, then continue west to China where they would land at dawn.

Finally Colonel Jimmy Doolittle, leader of the fliers, came down from the bridge after a conversation by blinker signals with Admiral Halsey on the *Enterprise*. "Come on, fellows, let's go," he said. Surprise was gone; they would have to bomb in daylight and 150 miles had been tacked on to their route. Just then a voice from the *Hornet's* bullhorn boomed, "Army pilots, man your planes!"

As Commander John Ford, the famous movie director,

and his crew took pictures, mechanical donkeys pushed and pulled the twin-ruddered B-25's into position. The deck was wet, green water breaking over the carrier's ramps.

Ten extra five-gallon cans of gasoline were loaded into each plane. Then the main tanks were topped. Though gauges read "Full," Navy men rocked the bombers in case any bubbles had formed in the wing tanks. Even an extra quart might mean the difference between life and death.

Doolittle was to be the first to go. At 7:24 A.M. he gave his engines full throttle. They roared until some of his anxiously watching pilots were afraid he'd burn them up. Blocks were pulled from the plane's wheels and it rolled forward until the left wheel was resting on a white line that ran down the port side of the deck. The left wing of the bomber was far over the side of the carrier as it clumsily wobbled forward into the heavy wind, engines roaring, flaps down.

The other pilots watched tensely. Doolittle would have to time his take-off perfectly. If he didn't leave the deck at the apex of the *Hornet*'s heavy pitch he would probably plummet instantly into the sea. The B-25 gained speed and took off just as the bow of the carrier was lifted high by the heavy sea.

There was a cheer from the Navy as the Doolittle plane circled and passed low over the *Hornet*. It headed straight for Tokyo; there wasn't enough gas to wait and fly formation.

The other bombers started taking off, each "sweated" into the air by every man in Task Force 16. All went well until the last plane slowly headed toward the starting line. Suddenly Aviation Chief Machinist Mate Thomas Respess and others holding down its nose, were horrified to see one of their group blown like a tumbleweed by the preceding plane's blast into the spinning left propeller of their plane. The man's left arm was chopped off by one blade. Another hit him in the rump knocking him clear.

The pilot felt the jar and glancing back saw the injured man lying on the deck. Rattled, he put his flap control lever back in retract instead of neutral. As the plane roared down the short runway, the flaps slowly came up. Consequently when the plane left the deck it dropped down out of sight.

Respess was sure it was going to crash. Then he saw it skimming only feet above the waves. Ponderously it rose, turned and followed the other planes.

Thirteen planes were to drop their four bombs apiece on strategic targets in Tokyo. Single planes were to hit Nagoya, Osaka and Kobe. Doolittle reached Tokyo first. At noon he buzzed so low over a ball park, the game was broken up. There was no effective opposition from fighters or anti-aircraft as plane after plane swept over the city.

Only moments before Doolittle arrived, a mock raid had been staged and the citizens of Tokyo thought the American attack was just the realistic climax. Children in schoolyards and people in the crowded streets waved at the passing planes, mistaking their circular red, white and blue markings, similar to those used by the Allies in World War I, for the Rising Sun.

For more than fifteen minutes no air alarm was sounded. The picket ship *Nitto Maru*, just before it was sunk by Halsey that morning, had warned of the approaching carriers but Imperial Headquarters had not expected an air raid until the next day. Not one American plane was shot down and soon fifteen were roaring toward China. A single plane was heading across the Sea of Japan toward Vladivostok.

Since little damage was done, the raid caused no panic. To the people it was only as if a meteor had hit Japan, but their leaders were worried. It proved, argued men like Foreign Minister Togo, the falsity of the military assurances of the inviolability of the imperial capital. Four fighter groups were assigned to protect Japan from future raids. The High Command ordered the China Expeditionary Army to cease other operations and root out enemy bases in the Chekiang area. More important, they began to be obsessed by the island of Midway, the probable base of the attack. It had to be taken.

The effect in the Allied world was just as important. With the fall of Bataan had come the lowest point in morale and world standing. Doolittle's epic flight, although causing little physical damage to Japanese objectives, was a pledge that America would soon attack. Allies on every battlefield, in every prison camp were roused with new hope. American newspapers blazed the story in their biggest headlines, with the Los Angeles *Times* composing the most original: DOO-LITTLE DID IT. Naturally the Navy's key role in this raid was not revealed, Roosevelt merely stating that Army planes had taken off from Shangri-La.

One plane, piloted by Lieutenant Edward York, landed safely in Vladivostok where it was impounded by the Russians. The other 15 either crashed in China or were abandoned in mid-air. Of the 80 Doolittle fliers, two were drowned and one was killed when his parachute only partially opened. Eight were captured.

The men who had sent bombers over Chungking, Singapore, the Philippines and hundreds of unprotected cities ordered these eight brought to trial for their "inhuman" acts. The trial—conducted solely in Japanese and lasting less than half an hour, during which the eight men were not advised of the charges, given interpreters or even informed it was a court-martial—found all eight guilty. Five were given life imprisonment, one eventually dying of malnutrition. Lieutenants Hallmark and Farrow and Sergeant Harold Spatz were executed. But first, according to popular rumor in Japan, these three were used in medical experiments.

2 While Doolittle was bombing Tokyo, a radiogram was received by Lieutenant Colonel Orin Grover at Del Monte on the island of Mindanao. Corregidor was badly in need of medicine. A plane had to be sent immediately. For the past few months a small band of fliers—including Captains Harold Slingsby, Dick Fellows, Joe Moore, Hervey Whitfield and Bill Bradford—had been operating a taxi service, "The Bamboo Fleet," between Bataan, Corregidor and Del Monte in worn-out military and private planes.

Now there was only one plane left, the ancient Bellanca once belonging to the Philippine Air Taxi Company. Captain Bradford, nicknamed "Jitter Bill," knew it well for he had been general manager and senior pilot of the organization. Seven years older than the legendary Paul "Pappy" Gunn and a veteran of World War I, he was the most experienced pilot in the Philippines. Five weeks previously he had logged his five thousandth hour over the islands when he took Colonel Arthur Fischer out of Corregidor in the desperate attempt to fly live cinchona seed to the United States and save quinine for the Western world. And only two days before, he had snatched Colonel Carlos Romulo and two others out of Iloilo the morning the Japanese landed on the island of Panay.

Because of his experience Colonel Grover asked Bradford what he thought were the chances of flying up to Corregidor. "Exactly zero," was the reply. In addition to Panay, the Japanese now occupied most of Cebu. For practical purposes, the entire Visayan Group was Japanese. Grover wired this information to Corregidor. The answer came the next day: send a plane regardless.

Someone would have to fly the slow, unarmed, ten-year-old Bellanca up through enemy territory to the Rock. After the few qualified pilots were rounded up, Captain Benny Putnam handed Bradford a deck of cards. "Shuffle and cut," he said. The low man would have to make the trip. Bradford shuffled, cut. He drew a card and put it in his pocket. The others drew and showed their cards. Then Bradford slowly pulled out his card, the deuce of diamonds. He was low man.

Captain William Monay, an interested onlooker, drew Bradford aside. "I saw you stack the deck," he whispered.

Bradford denied this, pointing out that only a fool would willingly take on such a mission. "But," he added, "the others there wouldn't have a chance of getting into Corregidor. I know where to make that last dogleg turn and find it in the dark."

Several hours later Bradford took off with old Number Nine heavily loaded with medicine. The first lap to the island of Negros, sandwiched between Japanese-occupied Panay and Cebu, was suspenseful but uneventful. His big worry as he touched down at Bacolod was who owned the island. Fortunately Americans ran out to refuel his ship but the Japanese were expected any day. Early the next morning he took off for the last, dangerous lap. It was only a three-hour trip to Corregidor and he wanted to land just at dawn.

As he approached Luzon clusters of twinkling lights marked villagers arising in the pre-dawn, but as he passed by, the lights blacked out in alarm. The coastline was shrouded in white stratus, distorting familiar landmarks. He fanned the Bellanca away from shore for he was ahead of schedule and was without lights or radio. He now had to mark time until dawn could bring enough visibility for recognition and a landing.

When light came with tropical abruptness, he found himself half an hour from Corregidor. He headed northeast, at full throttle, flying just above the rollers with a thin layer of mist a few feet overhead half covering him. When he was still several miles from the Rock the plane abruptly burst into sunlight. He sped along the torn-up southern coast of the polliwog-shaped island of rock expecting to be shot down by friendly guns. No shots came. He nervously glanced behind, half expecting to see a Nip fighter on his tail. It didn't seem possible that he had lumbered through enemy territory at 80 miles an hour and was still in one piece. He flared old Nine up in a climbing turn over the island's tadpole tail, took another hurried look around for bandits and then settled down on the rough, scarred surface of Corregidor's tiny airstrip, Kindley Field. As his wheels touched, a man ran out, frantically waving him to a revetment. Bradford guided the patched-up old plane to her resting place, cut the switch and sat shakily in silence.

By the time he was in Malinta Tunnel and the precious medicine unloaded, air raid signals were shrieking. He reported to Wainwright.

"Brad," said the general, shaking his hand, "I thought you'd get through. Glad you made it. Congratulations."

Bradford was startled by the change in the general and the others he knew since his last trip. Their faces were gaunter, more drawn. Everyone had the look of doom.

The shelling had done it. Until the fall of Bataan, the bombing had been tremendous yet caused relatively few casualties. The shelling was churning the entire island into a no man's land.

Though morale was still fairly high, few of the 13,000 on the island had hopes of being saved. The men's favorite theme song was "I'm Waiting for Ships That Never Come In." Others sarcastically asked if the chalked V's on many of the men's helmets stood, not for Victory, but for Victim.

On the day Bradford arrived, a new threat began to menace those living outside the tunnels. Japanese 240-mm. howitzers had been dragged from Cavite to Bataan. Now their high-angle fire was blasting Corregidor's hitherto unreachable 12-inch mortar pits. The number of dead and wounded rose alarmingly.

Japanese fire increased, coming to a tremendous climax on April 29, Emperor Hirohito's birthday. In addition the 260th air alarm was sounded that day and bombers began to hit Malinta Hill. The combined attacks continued through the afternoon. Grass fires sprang up, two ammunition dumps were blown to shreds. By dark, most of the island was covered with thick clouds of smoke and dust.

A few hours later two Navy PBY's broke through the blockade, landing on the bay several miles south of Corregidor. After medicine and 740 mechanical fuses were unloaded, 50 people were selected to fly south to safety: 30 nurses, 3 civilian women and 17 men. "Jitter Bill" Bradford was one of the men. His Bellanca had crashed in an attempted night take-off with three passengers. He shook hands with Wainwright, who had come to the dock to say goodbye, and said, "Wish you were coming with us."

Wainwright smiled wryly, "I couldn't." A pretty nurse, Lieutenant Juanita Redmond, embraced the gaunt, weary general and kissed him. "Oh, thank you, General," she said.

Wainwright stood on the dock and watched the two heavy

flying boats skim across the water, slowly rise and disappear in the south. Then he walked back to Malinta Tunnel.

Those who thought the bombardment on the Emperor's birthday was the greatest the Japanese could muster were mistaken. Each day the pounding increased. General Homma knew he had to knock out the big mortars of Batteries Geary and Way before his invasion fleet could sail from Bataan.

By the morning of May 2, Battery Way had only two guns but Geary was intact. Near noon, Private Ralph Houston, an aid man, was sitting in Geary's projectile room. Its thick, squat guns were silent for the moment and he decided to stretch his legs. He walked through the open steel doors. The underbrush was torn up, the terrain unrecognizable. Suddenly there was a terrific roar. He was momentarily in total darkness. Dazed, he turned around. What had been the powder room was now a great hole, steaming smoke. He ran to the wreckage. Behind the crater he heard voices. Men were entombed. He shouted that he was getting help, then, in spite of the bombardment, ran from the heights of Topside down the hill toward Malinta Tunnel.

Everyone on Corregidor knew something terrible had happened. The explosion had rocked the island like an earthquake. It was the end of Battery Geary. The barrels of its eight 10-ton mortars had been tossed about like matchsticks, one landing 150 yards away on the pock-marked golf course. Corregidor now had little except its beach defenses to hold off the landings everyone knew were imminent.

Life outside Malinta Tunnel was hazardous and rugged, but at least there was fresh air and light. Those in the tunnel suffered from an intolerable tension. The 1000-bed hospital was packed and fresh casualties were being placed in aisles. Its odor, the smell of death, pervaded the laterals. Dust and dirt, loosened by every hit on Malinta Hill, showered the thousands of inhabitants. When the blowers were off during air attacks, the air soon became fetid, the heat almost unbearable. Huge black flies, roaches and other insects infested the place.

Many, suffering from "tunnelitis," refused to step foot outside the tunnel. These were nicknamed "tunnel rats," and according to sarcastic comrades had become shelter-shocked. There was still food for six to eight weeks but the two meals a day were meager, giving little real nourishment. By now private hordes of food and liquor had been consumed. The hundreds of bottles of wine and whisky recovered from Quezon's sunken yacht were almost gone. Some of the men at

he batteries were making their own "raisinjack" and "jungle
uice" from raisins and prunes.

In the tunnel, tempers were short; arguments sprang up
over trifles. Most felt life had to be lived day by day. Gambling was widespread, with fantastic stakes. Money was only
paper. Jam sessions attracted big crowds. While some turned
to religion in what they knew were their last free moments,
a few, lucky enough to find willing women, took them outside during the night. In spite of bombing and shelling, there
was still occasional love-making on Corregidor.

The next day, May 3, Wainwright was told the water supply was dangerously low. He wired MacArthur:

SITUATION HERE IS FAST BECOMING DESPERATE.

That afternoon, in the hospital latrine, Lieutenant Lucy
Wilson was talking with an amputee patient, Lieutenant
Louis Lutich. He was a friend of the man she was supposed
to have married on Bataan, Dan Jopling. She asked Lutich if
he knew whether Jopling was alive or dead. Lutich didn't
know. While they were talking she was told to report to the
chief nurse, Captain Maud Davison, and guessed it was because she had recently told off an amorous colonel. She was
wrong. She had been selected to leave in the last transportation to freedom.

After dark Lucy Wilson, ten other Army nurses, one Navy
nurse, a civilian wife, six Army colonels and six naval officers were taken in a boat toward the edge of the mine
field. Suddenly there loomed up directly ahead an indistinct
shape which, after some hesitation, was identified as a submarine, the *Spearfish*.

Its commander was Lieutenant James C. Dempsey, who
on February 8, 1942, had commanded the old S-37 in a
night surface attack against a division of four Japanese destroyers; that night S-37 became the first U.S. submarine
ever to sink an enemy destroyer. This was Dempsey's first
patrol in command of the *Spearfish*, and so far at least two
Japanese freighters had been sunk. Enroute to the base in
Australia from the South China Sea, Dempsey only knew
that he was to rendezvous that night at a point just off the
mine fields about three miles from Corregidor.

Shortly after twilight *Spearfish* had surfaced and commenced charging batteries while lying-to at the rendezvous.
Now Dempsey, who was not even certain that the Rock was
still American, saw a boat approaching. This was not the
appointed rendezvous time and the boat was flashing an in-

correct identification signal. Was it manned by Japs or friends? Was this a trap? Should he open fire on the boat and attempt a getaway on the surface? The storage batteries had been under charge only ten to fifteen minutes and Japanese patrol craft had last been sighted a few miles distant from the rendezvous point. Then he heard an unmistakably American voice, southern-accented: "Submarine Ahoy," and saw American women among the boat's passengers. They wore khaki slacks and shirts or old dresses and no make-up, but after thirty-five days on patrol, they looked to Dempsey and his crew like beautiful girls from the Ziegfeld Follies.

While Dempsey anxiously scanned the horizon, the twenty-five manifested passengers and two later-discovered civilian stowaways, who were in the boat to assist in transferring the cargo to the submarine, filed down the narrow hatch. Dempsey, sensing danger, warned everyone to hurry. Finally passengers and cargo were aboard. *Spearfish* headed out on the surface. It was none too soon. As the full moon burst through the clouds, shells began to fall on Corregidor. Explosions and fires lighted up the entire area so brightly that Japanese patrol craft could be seen heading toward *Spearfish*. Dempsey sounded the diving alarm. The *Spearfish* submerged, rigged for "silent" running and commenced maneuvering to evade the enemy.

There were no manuals to guide Dempsey in the complex problems so many women presented. The incident would later become the basis for the movie *Operation Petticoat*. When bunks were assigned in the cramped submarine, one sailor, thinking Lucy Wilson was a child because of her pigtails, patted her paternally and said, "You can sleep with your daddy." But being the last on the manifest, she got no bunk. She slept on the floor.

3 Homma's artillery attack reached new heights the next day, May 4. In an almost continuous drumfire, 16,000 shells exploded on Corregidor in twenty-four hours. At times it sounded like fire from gigantic machine guns.

In the little whitewashed office he had inherited from MacArthur, Wainwright was writing a message to Marshall answering Washington's request for a frank estimate of the situation.

IN MY OPINION THE ENEMY IS CAPABLE OF MAKING ASSAULT ON CORREGIDOR AT ANY TIME.

SUCCESS OR FAILURE OF SUCH ASSAULT WILL DEPEND

ENTIRELY ON THE STEADFASTNESS OF BEACH DEFENSE
TROOPS. CONSIDERING THE PRESENT LEVEL OF MORALE,
I ESTIMATE THAT WE HAVE SOMETHING LESS THAN AN
EVEN CHANCE TO BEAT OFF AN ASSAULT. I HAVE GIVEN
YOU, IN ACCORDANCE WITH YOUR REQUEST, A VERY FRANK
AND HONEST OPINION ON THE SITUATION AS I SEE IT.

The situation the following morning was critical. Morale
was low. Those in the tunnels were psychologically battered,
physically debilitated. Almost everyone was overwhelmed by
the psychosis of doom. Those on the outside had different
problems. Many had a bitter unreasoning hatred of the "tunnel rats," and could not see why they had been forced to
stay outside for weeks in shallow foxholes, serving no apparent purpose. As usual in a fighting situation, the combat
troops got less than those they protected.

The wonder is that there was any morale at all among
the beach defense troops. Of the 4000 in number at the fall
of Bataan, there were today little more than 3000 effectives
because of the heavy shell casualties. Of these about 1300
were well-trained fighters from the 4th Marine Regiment.
The rest was a conglomerate force of Filipino fliers and artillerymen and American refugees from Bataan.

In spite of the tremendous shelling of the past few weeks,
the justified gripes, and the obvious weakness of their own
forces, many of these men thought they could hold Corregidor. Even so, there were some who had to be regularly dug
out of the bushes or chased out of the tunnels and put back
in their foxholes. That most men stayed in place was a trib-
ute to the competent leadership of Marine Colonel Samuel
Howard and his officers and the fighting spirit of his men.

Across North Channel in Bataan, General Homma was
giving final instructions for the storming of Corregidor. He
was already several weeks behind schedule. A malaria epidemic had suddenly struck his troops in the infested river
valleys of southern Bataan, soon exhausting the quinine supply.

The Corregidor invasion troops were hardest hit by malaria, their strength dropping as much as two-thirds. When it
looked as if the entire operation might have to be indefinitely postponed, 300,000 quinine tablets arrived from Japan
by air and the epidemic was halted.

That evening Homma watched anxiously as his landing
craft slowly left Lamao carrying 2000 men of the 61st Infantry and several tanks of the 7th Tank Regiment. They

were to land in two waves on the north beach of Corregidor's polliwog tail and push west toward Malinta Tunnel. The next night reinforcements of about 3000 men and tanks would land on the north shore of the polliwog's body, Topside. The two forces were supposed to converge, crushing everything between them.

All went well until the fleet neared Cabcaben. Here the commander, Colonel Gempachi Sato, who was with the first wave, the 1st Battalion, discovered to his dismay that the 2nd Battalion, the second wave, had somehow drifted to his right instead of staying on the left. He ordered the 2nd Battalion to hang back, and then move over to the right to its proper place.

The men of the 1st Sea Operations Unit, who were handling the boats, began to get confused. These high-spirited veterans of Singapore had imagined this would be a simple operation and knew little of the tides and currents that were presently raising havoc with their boats. Since the tide had flowed west when they left Bataan, they assumed the current off Corregidor would also be west. Now they were discovering it went east. Colonel Sato and the 1st Battalion were approaching Corregidor half a mile east of their destination. Lagging far to the rear, the 2nd Battalion was innocently heading for a point almost a mile east of its beach.

A heavy Japanese covering barrage began to fall just west of the intended landing points. The defenders dug in and waited, suspecting something would soon happen. At 11:00 P.M. they saw the dim, bulky shapes of boats slowly nearing North Point. Every gun on the tail end of Corregidor loosed a deadly barrage on the already confused invaders. Two 75-mm. guns, commanded by 1st Lieutenant Ray Lawrence and saved for such an emergency, finally revealed their position east of North Point, sinking boat after boat. Joining in the carnage were 37-mm. guns. Though the few remaining Corregidor searchlights were quickly shot out by Bataan guns, tracers lit up the entire north shore like a Fourth of July display.

The slaughter was sickening even to tensely watching beach defense officers. Half of Sato's 1st Battalion never reached the shore. Finally just before midnight, his tardy 2nd Battalion began to land near North Point. The moon had risen and the clouds cleared. Artillery from Topside began to dig up the beach area, then the last 12-inch mortar of Battery Way spoke. It was also light enough for men at Fort Hughes, on nearby Caballo Island, to open up with their mortars, 3-inchers and 75's.

The Japanese of the 2nd Battalion crouched helplessly as
their craft headed for the beach. To them it seemed as if a
hundred big guns were raining steel on their heads. Most of
the boats were sunk or leaking badly. Off shore 90 yards, a
lieutenant gave his men the signal to jump into the water
and wade to the beach. They leaped overboard, but the
water was still deep and many, weighed down by almost
100 pounds of equipment, were dragged underwater and
drowned. When he reached the shore the lieutenant counted
his men. Seven of every ten were missing.

In spite of the terrible losses, Colonel Sato began to lead
the remnants of his two battalions yard by yard toward the
east mouth of Malinta Tunnel.

At midnight, a U.S. Marine runner burst into the tunnel
office of Major George Moore, commander of Harbor Defenses, reporting breathlessly that probably 600 Japs had
landed.

Moore telephoned Wainwright. "The Nips are landing out
near North Point!" Then Moore ordered the men manning
the island's big guns to report to the tunnel as infantry reinforcements. Not long after 3:00 A.M., Wainwright was
informed the Japanese had seized Battery Denver, a Marine
anti-aircraft gun pit scarcely a mile east of the tunnel. A
few minutes later the general was handed a radiogram decoded on a ruled sheet of paper.

DURING RECENT WEEKS WE HAVE BEEN FOLLOWING
WITH GROWING ADMIRATION THE DAY-BY-DAY ACCOUNTS
OF YOUR HEROIC STAND AGAINST THE MOUNTING INTEN-
SITY OF BOMBARDMENT BY ENEMY PLANES AND HEAVY
SIEGE GUNS.

IN SPITE OF ALL THE HANDICAPS OF COMPLETE ISOLA-
TION, LACK OF FOOD AND AMMUNITION YOU HAVE GIVEN
THE WORLD A SHINING EXAMPLE OF PATRIOTIC FORTI-
TUDE AND SELF-SACRIFICE.

THE AMERICAN PEOPLE ASK NO FINER EXAMPLE OF
TENACITY, RESOURCEFULNESS, AND STEADFAST COURAGE.
THE CALM DETERMINATION OF YOUR PERSONAL LEADER-
SHIP IN A DESPERATE SITUATION SETS A STANDARD OF DUTY
FOR OUR SOLDIERS THROUGHOUT THE WORLD.

IN EVERY CAMP AND ON EVERY NAVAL VESSEL SOLDIERS,
SAILORS, AND MARINES ARE INSPIRED BY THE GALLANT
STRUGGLE OF THEIR COMRADES IN THE PHILIPPINES.
THE WORKMEN IN OUR SHIPYARDS AND MUNITIONS

PLANTS REDOUBLE THEIR EFFORTS BECAUSE OF YOUR
EXAMPLE.

YOU AND YOUR DEVOTED FOLLOWERS HAVE BECOME
THE LIVING SYMBOLS OF OUR WAR AIMS AND THE GUAR-
ANTEE OF VICTORY.

FRANKLIN D. ROOSEVELT

Wainwright carefully folded the message. He would always
treasure it. Then he wrote a reply:

YOUR GRACIOUS AND GENEROUS MESSAGE OF MAY 4 HAS
JUST REACHED ME. I AM WITHOUT WORDS TO EXPRESS TO
YOU, MR. PRESIDENT, MY GRATITUDE FOR THE DEEP AP-
PRECIATION OF YOUR GREAT KINDNESS. . . . AS I WRITE
THIS AT 3:30 A.M. OUR PATROLS ARE ATTEMPTING TO LO-
CATE THE ENEMY POSITIONS AND I WILL COUNTERATTACK
AT DAWN TO DRIVE HIM INTO THE SEA OR DESTROY HIM.
THANK YOU AGAIN, MR. PRESIDENT, FOR YOUR WONDER-
FUL MESSAGE WHICH I WILL PUBLISH TO MY ENTIRE
COMMAND.

At 4:30 A.M. Colonel Howard sent his last infantry reserves, the 500 untrained sailors of the 4th Provisional Battalion, into the battle just east of the tunnel. These men had
been waiting at the tunnel's mouth for several hours, watching a steady parade of wounded men brought back from the
front. It was a sight to shake experienced troops.

Led by their commander, Major Francis Williams, the
500 sailors, armed only with rifles, filed toward the dark
battleground. One of their officers, Army Captain Harold
Dalness, had been among the 2000 to escape Bataan the
night before its surrender. He felt relieved to get out of the
gloomy, depressing tunnel where every trouble was enlarged.
The noise was suddenly terrific. At first Dalness thought it
was the change from tunnel to open air. Then he realized
their avenue of approach was being heavily bombarded.

Shells dropped among the men causing scores of casualties. There was momentary confusion as sailors scrambled
for shelter, but in ten minutes Williams and his officers re-
assembled the sailors. Shaken by their sudden baptism in
blood, the men allowed themselves to be led forward. Dalness was astonished. Experienced infantry troops might have
rebelled. These untested Navy men were showing unbelievable courage.

When they were 200 yards from the thin American line,
Williams ordered the two leading companies to form a line

of skirmishers. They moved forward briskly to the left until they reached the front line. The next two companies moved to their right through the confusing darkness.

In spite of chaotic and deadly fighting, the newly reinforced line held. A few minutes before dawn, Williams went from company to company, encouraging the men. The whole line, he said, would attack at dawn. At exactly 6:15 A.M. Williams' sailors, together with the Marines of Headquarters and Service Company, moved forward. The attack completely surprised the dug-in Japanese, who were waiting for plane and tank support. They fell back on both flanks, but men on a small hill in the center held, their machine gun taking a heavy toll of Americans.

One of Williams' company commanders, Navy Lieutenant Bethel Otter, crept forward with five volunteers. When the six men were within 25 yards of the gun position, they threw their grenades. Several hit the target directly, knocking out the machine gun, but before the position could be occupied, other Japanese ran forward and killed Otter and four of his men.

After the first quick advances, the Americans could make little more headway for there were no supporting weapons to assist their attack. By 9:00 A.M., after gaining 300 yards, the entire line was pinned down. Williams sent a runner to the tunnel to get reinforcements and artillery support. Neither was available. For an hour the Americans could do nothing but hold. Every time a squad moved, heavy artillery fire from the big Japanese guns on Bataan would fall.

Then at 10:00 A.M. Dalness heard the ominous rumble of tanks. Three pushed forward. The awesome sight panicked some of the defenders. A few started toward the rear. Noncoms and officers stopped them and a rout was prevented.

When Wainwright heard Japanese tanks were moving against men with no anti-tank defenses, he knew he had to make up his mind fast. He went over the position in his mind: most of his seacoast guns were destroyed; 46 of the 58 beach defense 75-mm. guns were knocked out; communications were gone.

In his imagination he could see a tank nose into the tunnel and attack the wounded and nurses. Leaning on the stick he carried because of a game leg, he walked into his headquarters and called for Generals Moore and Beebe.

"We can't hold out very much longer," he told them. "Maybe we could last through this day but the end certainly must come tonight. It would be better to clear up the situation now, in daylight."

It was 10:15 A.M. when he ordered Beebe to broadcast a previously prepared surrender message. "Tell the Nips," he said in a voice choked with emotion, "that we'll cease firing at noon."

The men of Corregidor were ordered to destroy all arms greater than .45 caliber. Now Wainwright radioed Major General Sharp, commander of the Visayan-Mindanao Force, releasing to his command all the Philippines except Corregidor and its three neighboring islands. Sharp was told to report immediately to MacArthur for any further orders. "I believe you will understand the motive behind this order," he added. By doing this, Wainwright hoped he could confine the surrender to the four fortified islands in Manila Bay.

At 10:30 A.M., Beebe, in a tired but clear voice, broadcast the surrender message in English, over the "Voice of Freedom" radio station. Then it was broadcast in Japanese.

While guns were being spiked, codes burned, and radio equipment smashed and more than 2,000,000 pesos in paper money cut up with scissors, Wainwright was composing his last message to Roosevelt.

WITH BROKEN HEART AND HEAD BOWED IN SADNESS BUT NOT IN SHAME I REPORT TO YOUR EXCELLENCY THAT TODAY I MUST ARRANGE TERMS FOR THE SURRENDER OF THE FORTIFIED ISLANDS OF MANILA BAY. . . .

THERE IS A LIMIT OF HUMAN ENDURANCE AND THAT LIMIT HAS LONG SINCE BEEN PAST. WITHOUT PROSPECT OF RELIEF I FEEL IT IS MY DUTY TO MY COUNTRY AND TO MY GALLANT TROOPS TO END THIS USELESS EFFUSION OF BLOOD AND HUMAN SACRIFICE.

IF YOU AGREE, MR. PRESIDENT, PLEASE SAY TO THE NATION THAT MY TROOPS AND I HAVE ACCOMPLISHED ALL THAT IS HUMANLY POSSIBLE AND THAT WE HAVE UPHELD THE BEST TRADITIONS OF THE UNITED STATES AND ITS ARMY.

MAY GOD BLESS AND PRESERVE YOU AND GUIDE YOU AND THE NATION IN THE EFFORT TO ULTIMATE VICTORY.

WITH PROFOUND REGRET AND WITH CONTINUED PRIDE IN MY GALLANT TROOPS I GO TO MEET THE JAPANESE COMMANDER. GOOD-BYE, MR. PRESIDENT.

1 At 11:00 A.M., in the Navy tunnel, Commander Melvyn McCoy wrote out his final dispatch and handed it to a radioman. "Beam it for Radio Honolulu, and don't bother with code."

> GOING OFF AIR NOW. GOOD-BYE AND GOOD LUCK. CAL-
> LAHAN AND MCCOY.

The Army radio operator, Corporal Irving Strobing, was still maintaining constant contact with WTJ in Honolulu. He was afraid to let them go for even a second. Since concussion from the shelling had knocked out most of the lines, Strobing was now keying directly at the transmitters near the west mouth of the tunnel.

> NOTIFY ANY AND ALL VESSELS HEADED TOWARD THIS
> AREA TO RETURN TO THEIR HOME PORTS.

After this radiogram was sent out in the clear Strobing was told there would be no more official messages. Wanting to keep in touch with the outside world as long as possible, he began sending out his personal account of the last moments of Corregidor.

> WE ARE WAITING FOR GOD ONLY KNOWS WHAT. . . .
> LOTS OF HEAVY FIGHTING GOING ON. GENERAL WAIN-
> WRIGHT IS A RIGHT GUY AND WE ARE WILLING TO GO
> FOR HIM BUT SHELLS WERE DROPPING ALL NIGHT
> FASTER THAN HELL. TOO MUCH FOR GUYS TO TAKE. . . .
> CORREGIDOR USED TO BE A NICE PLACE BUT IT'S HAUNTED
> NOW. . . .
> THE JIG IS UP. EVERYONE IS BAWLING LIKE A BABY.
> THEY ARE PILING DEAD AND WOUNDED IN OUR TUNNEL.
> . . . I KNOW NOW HOW A MOUSE FEELS, CAUGHT IN A
> TRAP AND WAITING FOR GUYS TO COME ALONG AND FIN-
> ISH IT UP.

At noon all American guns were ordered to stop firing. Colonel Paul D. Bunker went outside and lowered the post flag, twice shot down and replaced under fire in the past few weeks. As a white flag went up, Bunker burned the Stars and Stripes. Half an hour later, when Japanese fire continued, Beebe repeated his radio broadcast.

Fire persisted and Wainwright was forced to send Marine Captain Golland Clark, Jr., forward with an interpreter, a flag bearer and a musician. When the four men approached the front lines at about 1:00 P.M., the musician blew his bugle while the flag bearer waved a white sheet. Firing finally ceased, and the surrender team walked into the Japanese lines. Soon they met Colonel Motoo Nakayama, Homma's senior operations officer, who insisted that Wainwright meet him.

Within an hour Wainwright, General Moore, Colonel Pugh, Major Tom Dooley and Moore's aide, accompanied by Captain Clark, were riding east in a Chevrolet. At Denver Hill they got out of the car and advanced on foot past the dead and dying. Colonel Nakayama, preceded by a private and an English-speaking lieutenant, came from the other side.

The two parties met near the top of the hill. There was a brief silence, then the Japanese private snatched the field glasses that were around Colonel Pugh's neck.

"We will not accept your surrender unless it includes all American and Filipino troops in the whole archipelago," said the Japanese lieutenant.

"I do not choose to discuss surrender terms with you," said Wainwright. "Take me to your senior officer."

Colonel Nakayama came forward.

Wainwright said he was only surrendering the four islands in Manila Bay. When this was translated, Nakayama replied with an angry torrent of Japanese. He had explicit orders from Homma to bring Wainwright to Bataan only if the American agreed to surrender all his troops.

Back in Malinta Tunnel, Corporal Strobing was tapping out another message to Honolulu.

MY NAME IS IRVING STROBING. GET THIS TO MY MOTHER, MRS. MINNIE STROBING, 605 BARBEY STREET, BROOKLYN, NEW YORK. . . . MY LOVE TO PA, JOE, SUE, MAC, CARRY, JOYCE AND PAUL. ALSO TO ALL FAMILY AND FRIENDS. GOD BLESS 'EM ALL. HOPE THEY WILL BE THERE WHEN I COME HOME. TELL JOE WHEREVER HE IS TO GIVE 'EM HELL FOR US. GOD BLESS YOU.

Strobing added ZZA, STANDBY, but it was the last word from Corregidor. WTA/WVDM was finally off the air.

At WTJ Honolulu, the man who had been listening, Arnold Lappert, wept over his key.

In his headquarters on Bataan, Homma was in agony, believing the entire invasion had failed miserably. Then a staff officer reported that a white flag was waving over Corregidor. Homma at first refused to believe the good news. Only an hour previously he had learned that 31 boats had been sunk during the first invasion and the second landing, consequently, would have to be cancelled since there were only 21 landing craft left. When the general was convinced the white flag was not an American trick, he was so relieved he radioed Nakayama to disregard former orders and bring Wainwright to Bataan at once.

At 4:00 that afternoon, a Japanese assault boat scraped against a small dock in Cabcaben. Wainwright, leaning on his cane, stepped onto Bataan. It was a strange, bitter feeling to be once again on this peninsula of tragic memories.

Two cars drove the Wainwright party up the road, so recently the scene of the agonizing march of American and Filipino prisoners. Soon the cars stopped and Wainwright was led to the home of Silvestre Castillo. It was a small house, painted blue, surrounded by a luxuriant growth of mangroves. Pocked with fragment holes, it was the only standing structure in sight.

Wainwright, Beebe and the four other Americans—Colonel Pugh, Major Dooley, Major William Lawrence and Sergeant Hubert Carroll—waited on the open porch. To the south, out in Manila Bay, they could see Corregidor still erupting with shell bursts. A strong wind from the bay whipped up dense clouds of sand and dust. They waited tensely. A Japanese orderly brought cold water which they gratefully drank. After half an hour a group of Japanese newspapermen and photographers arrived.

The Americans were lined up on the lawn in front of the house and their pictures taken. At 5:00 P.M. a Cadillac came around the sharp curve from the north and stopped with a jerk near the house.

General Homma, looking crisp and military in olive-drab uniform, stepped out of the car. His shirt, brilliantly white, was open at the collar. On his chest were rows of decorations. At his side hung a sword.

Wainwright was a striking contrast to the barrel-chested, heavy-set Homma. Over six feet tall, he weighed only 160 pounds and looked as thin as a crane to the newsmen. His uniform, his best, was simply a khaki shirt and trousers. He wore no decorations or sword.

"Welcome to Cabcallo (Cabcaben)," said Homma through his interpreter, a lieutenant. Though he could speak English, Homma wanted his staff to understand the conversation. "You must be very tired and weary."

"Thank you, General Homma," said Wainwright.

They went to the porch and sat around a long table, Homma in the middle, facing Manila Bay. On his right was Major General Takaji Wachi, who had relieved Maeda as chief of staff, and Colonel Nakayama on his left. Behind the latter stood the interpreter and behind Homma was newsman Kazumaro Uno.

Across the table sat Wainwright with Beebe and Dooley to his left, Pugh and Lawrence to his right. The American commander handed a signed surrender note to Homma. The Japanese commander, without glancing at it, passed the note to his interpreter, who read it aloud. The note surrendered only the four islands in Manila Bay.

"I can not accept your surrender unless it includes all American and Philippine troops on the archipelago," said Homma.

"I can only surrender my men on Corregidor and the three other fortified islands. The troops in the Visayan Islands and Mindanao are no longer under my command. They are commanded by General Sharp, who in turn is under General MacArthur's high command."

Homma was annoyed. Did Wainwright take him for a fool? He turned to his interpreter. "Tell him we've heard broadcasts from Washington confirming his position as commander-in-chief of American forces in the Philippines."

Wainwright played out the game, insisting he only commanded the harbor defenses.

Homma was shrewd. "Ask him when he released Sharp from his command."

"Several days ago," replied Wainwright. "Besides, even if I did command General Sharp's troops I have no means left for communicating with them. I have destroyed my radio equipment."

"Send a staff officer to Sharp," answered Homma. "I will furnish the plane."

But Wainwright refused, insisting he had no authority over Sharp.

Homma lost all patience. He banged the table with his fists, then said slowly in a cool, controlled voice, "At the time of General King's surrender in Bataan, I did not see you. Neither have I any reason to see you if you are only the commander of a unit of the American forces. I wish only to negotiate with my equal, the commander-in-chief of American forces in the Philippines. Since you are not in supreme command, I see no further necessity for my presence here." He started to rise.

"Wait!" said Pugh in alarm. He quickly conferred with Wainwright and Beebe.

Wainwright, defeat etched deeply on his face, slowly nodded in assent. "In face of the fact that further bloodshed in the Philippines is unnecessary and futile, I will assume command of the entire American forces in the Philippines at the risk of serious reprimand by my government following the war."

Homma was not convinced of Wainwright's sincerity. He said sternly in Japanese, "You have denied your authority and your momentary decision may be regretted by your men. I advise you to return to Corregidor and think this matter over. If you see fit to surrender, then surrender to the commanding officer of the regiment on Corregidor. He in turn will bring you to me in Manila. I call this meeting over. Good day." He nodded slightly and walked back to his Cadillac.

The Americans' confusion was compounded by a vague translation of Homma's final statement. Wainwright nervously chewed the cigarette in his mouth to a pulp; Beebe was speechless.

"General," said Dooley earnestly to Wainwright, "you'll have to arrange something. At your command all troops on Corregidor and the other harbor islands disarmed this afternoon. The Japs will slaughter our unarmed people."

Wainwright, leaning heavily on his cane, walked over to Colonel Nakayama, who had been detailed to take the Americans back to Corregidor, and asked, "What do you want us to do now?"

The Japanese interpreter translated this to Nakayama then replied, "We will take you and your party back to Corregidor, and you can do what you damn please."

In the meantime, Colonel Pugh had buttonholed a friendly young Japanese lieutenant who formerly taught school in Osaka, and asked him what Homma had really said. "Wainwright should return to Corregidor," explained the Japanese, "and either resume fighting or surrender to the Japanese commander there."

Pugh hurried toward Wainwright, who was angrily walking up and down the yard, still burning from the rude treatment. After Pugh explained the situation, both men approached Colonel Nakayama.

"General Wainwright will surrender the entire American forces to General Homma unconditionally," said Pugh. "Take us to General Homma and General Wainwright will dispatch me to Mindanao to instruct General Sharp to comply with his demands."

Fortunately newsman Uno, who had been raised in Utah and was sympathetic, was standing next to Nakayama. He translated. It took a moment for Nakayama to make up his mind, then he said, "I shall go with you to Corregidor and safely turn you over to the commanding officer there. You will stay for the night. First thing tomorrow morning you will go to General Homma with a new surrender and an understanding to contact the other American forces in the Philippines."

The Wainwright party, Nakayama and Uno were driven to the Cabcaben pier in a car and a beer truck. It was getting dark as they headed for smoldering Corregidor in the Japanese assault boat. Uno, noticing an American lying on the heap of luggage, asked, "What's the matter?"

"I'm not feeling well." It was General Beebe; he was seasick.

Colonel Nakayama turned to Uno. "This is what the Japanese soldier eats in place of candy. Give some to the Americans."

Uno passed the candy. Beebe didn't want any. Wainwright took several. So did Pugh, who ate one and said, "Not bad." Uno didn't agree. They tasted like dog biscuits to him.

Finally they approached the looming outline of Corregidor. The boat ground to a halt near North Point. Sergeant Carroll and another American soldier jumped into the chest-high water and started carrying Wainwright to shore. When they tripped, Wainwright waded the rest of the way. Beebe, deathly sick, was also carried to shore. Seeing he was too weak to stand, Nakayama ordered a halt while the general rested. Finally the group started up a steep bank toward the road, Beebe helped by two soldiers.

They walked up the road with Nakayama in the lead. Next came Uno with a flashlight. The stunted woods were only charred wood. The earth was churned by shells. Bodies lay in grotesque positions. It was a frightening scene.

Wainwright was shocked to see many campfires all over Corregidor and guessed the Japs had landed reinforcements. He was even more shocked to find the main Japanese line within 100 yards of the eastern entrance of Malinta Tunnel. He was led around Malinta Hill to the destroyed market place of San Jose in the middle of the island. Here he was introduced to Colonel Sato. The commander of the invasion force told the general that the Japanese controlled the area between the west entrance of Malinta and Morrison Hill on Topside. The tunnel had already been occupied and cleared of all Americans except those in the hospital. Now Colonel Sato was about to attack Topside.

Wainwright, convinced most of the men on Corregidor would be slaughtered if he didn't surrender unconditionally at once, agreed to sit down with Sato and draw up a document based on Homma's demands. At midnight Wainwright signed in the feeble light. He felt drained of energy as he was taken to the west entrance of Malinta Tunnel, past solemn groups of Americans and Filipinos. The weight of surrender was heavy. Many of his men reached out to seize his hand. Some patted his shoulder and said, "It's all right, General, you did your best."

His eyes were full of tears by the time he entered the tunnel. It was an added blow to find the laterals filled with Japanese. He went to General Moore's office and said he had surrendered totally. Moore agreed nothing else could have been done.

"But I feel I have taken a dreadful step," said Wainwright gloomily. He and Pugh went to his quarters, escorted by a sentry. The two flopped on their cots and slept for the first time in two days.

The next morning Homma's intelligence officer, Lieutenant Colonel Hikaru Haba, and an interpreter entered Wainwright's quarters while the general was dressing. "I am here to discuss the details of your surrender," said Haba.

Wainwright was convinced that the Japanese would massacre the men on Corregidor unless all his commanders in the field also surrendered immediately. The man who commanded the greatest number, General Sharp, would have to be convinced first. A messenger had to be sent to Mindanao with an explanatory letter. For this important and dangerous mission Wainwright decided to use his operations officer, Colonel Jesse Traywick. He sent for Traywick and told him to deliver the following letter personally to Sharp:

To put a stop to further useless sacrifice of human life on the fortified islands, yesterday I tendered to Lieutenant General Homma, the surrender of the four harbor forts in Manila Bay. General Homma declined to accept my surrender unless it in-

cluded the forces under your command. It became apparent that
the garrisons of these said forts would be eventually destroyed by
aerial and artillery bombardment and by infantry supported by
tanks, which have overwhelmed Corregidor.

After leaving General Homma with no agreement between us I
decided to accept in the name of humanity his proposal and
tendered at midnight, night 6-7 May 1942, to the senior Japanese
officer on Corregidor, the formal surrender of all American and
Philippine Army troops in the Philippine Islands. You will therefore be guided accordingly, and *will* repeat *will* surrender all
troops under your command both in the Visayan Islands and
Mindanao to the proper Japanese officer. This decision on my
part, you will realize, was forced upon me by means beyond my
control.

Colonel Jesse T. Traywick, Jr., G.S.C., my assistant chief of
staff, G-3, who will deliver this to you, is fully empowered to act
for me. You are hereby ordered by me as the senior American
Army officer of the Philippine Islands to scrupulously carry out
the provisions of this letter, as well as such additional instructions as this staff officer may give you in my name.

You will repeat the complete text of this letter, and of such instructions as Colonel Traywick may give you, by radio to General MacArthur. However, let me emphasize that there must be
on your part no thought of disregarding these instructions. Failure to fully and honestly carry them out can have only the most
disastrous results.

By now Japanese were also occupying the other three
Manila Bay islands: Forts Hughes, Drum and Frank. At
nearby Hughes, ex-Navyman Cecil Browne and his mates
were sitting tensely in rows. A Japanese major was walking
up and down in front of them. He was furious. Some American or Filipino had stolen a can of food. The prisoners all
knew the culprit was an American officer but no one spoke.

"Imperial Japanese food has been stolen," stormed the
major. "Someone will have to account for it and be executed
or you will all suffer."

There was silence. When the guilty American officer made
no move, a small, thin sailor stepped forward and said, "I
stole it."

To everyone's amazement the Japanese major beamed.
"You are like the brave Japanese soldier." He unsheathed
his sword dramatically and tapped the puny American gob
on the shoulder. Then he called to one of his men, who returned with a six-pound can of corned beef. The major presented it ceremoniously to the seaman.

At 5:00 that afternoon, Wainwright and five of his staff
officers were led by Colonel Haba out of Malinta Tunnel's west

entrance. Once again the general passed groups of his men. They looked hot, weary and hungry. All rose; some stood at attention and saluted; others took off their hats and held them against their chests. Wainwright, eyes welling with tears, raised his hand to his worn sun helmet.

But as the little party headed for the dock, a scrawl on one of the wrecked buildings indicated that Americans had surrendered everything but their sense of humor. It read: CORREGIDOR STILL STANDS! UNDER NEW MANAGEMENT.

Far to the south, in Australia, MacArthur was solemnly penciling on a pad:

Corregidor needs no comment from me. It has sounded its own story at the mouth of its guns. It has scrolled its own epitaph on enemy tablets. But through the bloody haze of its last reverberating shots, I shall always see a vision of grim, gaunt, ghastly men, still unafraid.

2 Wainwright and his five officers were taken by assault boat to Lamao on Bataan. Here they waited for two hours, then ate rice and bony fish, their first food for two days. While another hour dragged on Wainwright reiterated his instructions to Colonel Traywick.

"Jesse, I'm giving you complete authority to handle this situation." Mindanao, he said, was his chief worry. Sharp must be made to comply with the surrender orders with absolutely no delay. In addition to the letter of instructions was another which Traywick was to use only in case Sharp refused to obey. It was a note permitting Traywick to place the Mindanao commander under arrest.

The general was completely broken up. His final words were, "Jesse, I'm depending on you to carry out these orders."

It was dark when the group headed north in a car. They followed the route of the Death March to Balanga, Orani and San Fernando. Then they turned southeast, arriving in the completely forsaken streets of Manila just before 11:00 P.M. The car drove up to radio station KZRH, where the party was met by Lieutenant Hisamichi Kano of the Propaganda Corps. Kano, who had been schooled in New York and New Jersey, greeted the general affably and gave the Americans some fruit.

Wainwright went over the prepared speech he was soon to broadcast. It was in stilted English and when Kano saw

Wainwright was having trouble reading it, he said, "General, I can straighten it out for you."

The young Japanese officer took the statement into his office, rewording it in more colloquial English.

At 11:43 P.M. Wainwright sat down at a small round bamboo table in front of a microphone. In the monitor room was Kano, ready to switch off the general if he varied the script.

Wainwright spoke every word as written, in a voice husky with suppressed emotion:

This is Lieutenant General J. M. Wainwright. Message for General William F. Sharp, commanding the Mindanao and Visayan Forces. Repeat for General Sharp, commanding the Mindanao and Visayan Forces. Anyone receiving this message please notify General Sharp at once. The message: By virtue of the authority vested in me by the President of the United States, I, as Commanding General of the United States Forces in the Philippine Islands, hereby resume direct command of Major General Sharp, Commander of the Visayan-Mindanao Forces and of all troops under his command. (Repeat message.)

I now give a direct order to William Sharp. I repeat, those receiving it please notify General Sharp at once. Subject: Surrender! To Major General William F. Sharp, Jr., commanding the Visayan and Mindanao Forces. The message: To fully stop the further useless sacrifice of human life on the fortified islands, yesterday I tendered to Lieutenant General Homma, the commander in chief of the Imperial Japanese Forces in the Philippines, the surrender of the four harbor defense forts of Manila Bay. General Homma declined to accept my surrender unless it included the forces under your command. It became apparent that the garrisons of these forces would be eventually destroyed by aerial and artillery bombardment and by infantry supported by tanks, which have overwhelmed Corregidor. After leaving General Homma, with no agreement between us, I've decided to accept, in the name of humanity, his proposal, and tendered at midnight of 6-7 May, 1942, to the Senior Japanese officer on Corregidor, a total surrender of all American and Filipino Army troops in the Philippine Islands. You will therefore be guided accordingly and will, I repeat, *will,* surrender all troops under your command to the proper Japanese officer.

This proceeding on my part, you will realize, was forced upon me by means entirely beyond my control. Colonel Jesse T. Traywick, Jr., General Staff Corps, my assistant chief of staff (G-3), who will deliver this letter to you personally is truly empowered to act for me. You are hereby ordered by me as a senior American Army officer in the Philippine Islands to scrupulously carry out the provisions of this letter as well as such additional instructions as this staff officer will give you. You will repeat the complete text of this letter and such other instructions as Colonel Traywick will give you by radio to General MacArthur. However, let me emphasize that there must be on your part no thought of disregarding these instructions. Failure to fully and honestly carry them out can have only the most disastrous results.

Wainwright, his voice growing even more choked, now broadcast instructions to Colonels Horan and Makar in north Luzon. After adding other explicit instructions to Sharp, Wainwright said:

The Japanese Army and Navy will not cease their operations until they recognize the faithfulness of execution of these orders. These orders must be carried out faithfully and accurately, otherwise the Imperial Japanese Army and Navy will continue their operations. If and when such faithfulness of execution is recognized, the commander in chief of the Japanese forces in the Philippine Islands will order that all firing be ceased.

The general coughed and was momentarily speechless. Then he said:

Taking all circumstances into consideration, and . . .

There was another long pause. Then the announcer, Marcela Victor Young, broke in with a blunt announcement and signed off. It was 12:20 A.M., May 8.

The ordeal over, Kano invited the emotionally drained Wainwright and the accompanying officers into his office. He poured them drinks from a hoarded bottle of Scotch while the Americans tried to comfort their stricken commander.

The speech was heard by many Americans and Filipinos on Mindanao. Those who didn't know Wainwright personally insisted it was a fake. Friends recognized his voice, even though it was huskier than usual. They felt he was broadcasting under duress.

General Sharp was in a quandary. That morning he'd received a radio from Wainwright relinquishing command of the Visayans and Mindanao. Later he'd received this message from Melbourne:

WAINWRIGHT HAS SURRENDERED. FROM NOW ON COMMUNICATE ON ALL MATTERS DIRECT WITH ME. HAVE YOU COMMUNICATED WITH CHYNOWETH?

MACARTHUR.

Sharp radioed MacArthur the gist of the Wainwright

broadcast, asking for further instructions. His problems were complicated by the deteriorating military situation in his vast command. The islands of Panay and Cebu were occupied. His own headquarters, transferred from Del Monte to Malaybalay, 40 miles farther inland, were now being threatened. On April 29 a strong Japanese detachment had landed at Cotabato and, against spirited but useless resistance, had driven north past Lake Lanao. Another detachment had landed in Cagayan and Bugo and was driving down the Sayre Highway. Advance units had already reached the Del Monte airfields and threatened to break through the last roadblocks in front of Malaybalay.

Sharp's escape route to the south was also cut off. Some of the invaders landing at Cotabato had driven east to Pikit, the southern terminus of the Sayre Highway. There they were being joined by other Japanese coming from the southeast coast of Mindanao.

When MacArthur received Sharp's message, he radioed Washington: I PLACE NO CREDENCE IN THE ALLEGED BROADCAST BY WAINWRIGHT. He was extremely annoyed. The chaotic surrender situation would never have occurred if Washington had let him retain control of the Philippines. If Wainwright had not been given over-all command, the Japanese would have been forced to accept surrender of the four fortified islands in Manila Bay.

After careful thought and much rewriting, MacArthur and his staff composed a radiogram they felt would be a guide to Sharp. At 4:45 A.M. it was sent.

> ORDERS EMANATING FROM GENERAL WAINWRIGHT HAVE NO VALIDITY. IF POSSIBLE SEPARATE YOUR FORCE INTO SMALL ELEMENTS AND INITIATE GUERRILLA OPERATIONS. YOU, OF COURSE, HAVE FULL AUTHORITY TO MAKE ANY DECISION THAT IMMEDIATE EMERGENCY MAY DEMAND. KEEP IN COMMUNICATION WITH ME AS MUCH AS POSSIBLE. YOU ARE A GALLANT AND RESOURCEFUL COMMANDER AND I AM PROUD OF WHAT YOU HAVE DONE.

When Sharp got this message, he felt his course of action was by no means clarified. Though he now had complete authority to act on his own judgment and had been relieved of responsibility to Wainwright, he could not ignore the latent threat of the Manila broadcast. On the brink of military disaster himself he decided to delay his final decision until he talked to Wainwright's emissary, Colonel Traywick, who reportedly had left Manila the morning after the broadcast.

In the meantime, he sent messages to his island commanders releasing them from his command. He also told his own officers that surrender was imminent; they could escape into the mountains and fight as guerrillas if they wished.

Sergeant Frank Trammell, formerly a bomber radioman and now Sharp's chief radio repairman, was getting ready to leave with a group planning to hide out in the rugged mountains of east Mindanao. Before leaving he radioed a last message to his wife, Norma, in Escondido, California.

PLEASE DON'T WORRY IT IS ALWAYS DARKEST BEFORE THE DAWN LOVE FRANKLIN TRAMMELL

Then Trammell and the others headed southeast over the grassy plains.

Jesse Traywick was already on Mindanao, having arrived by plane the day before with Colonel Haba. After the two were driven to Cagayan, the headquarters of Major General Saburo Kawamura, commander of the detachment attacking south down the Sayre Highway, Traywick had suggested he simply be driven along this highway to Sharp's headquarters.

Kawamura had a different plan. Hundreds of letters were written by hand, signed by Traywick, and dropped by plane on the afternoon of May 9.

To COMMANDING OFFICER OF THE FRONT LINE:

I, having a very important message from Lieutenant General J. M. Wainwright, must deliver it personally to Major General William F. Sharp.

When any one who receives this letter, he should raise a white flag visible to the Japanese Army and stop firing and the Japanese Army will do the same.

When both sides stop firing, you send a U.S.A. officer to the front line with a white flag. I will meet him.

In order to deliver my message to General SHARP as soon as possible you should be prepared to furnish a guide and a car for me.

JESSE T. TRAYWICK, JR.,
COLONEL. G. S. C.
UNITED STATES ARMY

May 9, 1942

Traywick protested in vain that this procedure was unrealistic and had little chance of success. At dusk a Japanese officer drove him south toward Del Monte on the Sayre Highway. Finally they dismounted and walked toward the Japanese front lines. Traywick was given a small map, a canteen of water and pointed southeast. The Japanese officer told him American trucks were 60 kilometers ahead.

Traywick insisted it was a ridiculous mission, but argument was useless. The American headed down a jungle trail in the pitch dark. He forded a river and climbed a steep ravine. Within an hour the trail ended and he pushed into dense undergrowth. He waded and swam across several small rivers and climbed more ravines until, at 2:00 A.M., May 10, he came to a nipa hut. He shouted. There was no answer. He walked into an empty house, lay down on a cot and tried to sleep. Just as he was dozing off a kitten jumped on the bed, curling up by his neck.

The two slept until dawn. When Traywick awoke he discovered he was in hilly, jungle country with mountains to the west. He started south and soon saw a Japanese machine-gun nest. He shouted. Five Japanese soldiers turned, looked at him in astonishment as he advanced with a piece of white sheet on a stick.

The weary, tattered colonel was driven back to Cagayan. This time he insisted on going up the Sayre Highway.

"You can't go far," said Kawamura through an interpreter. "The bridges are blown."

"I'll go as far as I can, then walk."

Accompanied by Colonel Haba, Traywick was again driven toward Del Monte. When they came to a blown bridge, the two men crossed on foot and continued down the Sayre Highway. It was a hot trip. Once they rested near three Japanese bodies. After they rose to leave, Traywick faced the dead soldiers and saluted. Colonel Haba bowed and patted the American approvingly on the shoulder.

Finally, that afternoon, they reached the American lines and were driven to Malaybalay. As he approached the building housing Sharp's headquarters, Traywick rehearsed what he would say. If none of his arguments worked he would have to arrest the general.

He walked up to the tall, thin Sharp, handing him the letter of instructions. To Traywick's surprise, Sharp made no protests but readily agreed to go forward and surrender to Kawamura. First he sent radiograms to his island commanders:

AS I HAVE NOT YET SURRENDERED, THE INSTRUCTIONS GIVEN YOU YESTERDAY RELEASING YOU FROM MY COM-

MAND ARE WITHDRAWN. I RESUME COMMAND AND DIRECT
YOU TO CEASE ALL OPERATIONS AGAINST THE JAPANESE
ARMY AT ONCE. YOU WILL RAISE A WHITE FLAG AND
AWAIT THE ARRIVAL OF MY STAFF OFFICER WHO WILL
MAKE THE TERMS OF THE NEGOTIATIONS FOR SURRENDER
OF THE FORCES UNDER YOU. THIS IS IMPERATIVE AND
MUST BE CARRIED OUT IN ORDER TO SAVE FURTHER
BLOODSHED. ACKNOWLEDGE.

SHARP COMMANDING

At 7:15 P.M. he sent another message, this one to Mac-
Arthur:

I HAVE SEEN WAINWRIGHT'S STAFF OFFICER AND HAVE
WITHDRAWN MY ORDER RELEASING COMMANDERS ON
OTHER ISLANDS AND DIRECTED SURRENDER. DIRE NECESSI-
TY ALONE HAS PROMPTED THIS ACTION.

Men all over Mindanao began to surrender. Others were
heading for the hills. Corporal Durward Brooks, former radio
combat operator of the 28th Bombardment Squadron, was
with a group of nine escapees. They had tried to get their
lieutenant to join them but his answer was, "I couldn't live
in the mountains. I'm from Boston."

In Washington, General Marshall was reading a message
from MacArthur:

I HAVE JUST RECEIVED WORD FROM MAJOR GENERAL
SHARP THAT GENERAL WAINWRIGHT IN TWO BROADCASTS
ON THE NIGHT OF THE 7/8 ANNOUNCED HE WAS RE-
ASSUMING COMMAND OF ALL FORCES IN THE PHILIPPINES
AND DIRECTED THEIR SURRENDER GIVING IN DETAIL THE
METHOD OF ACCOMPLISHMENT. I BELIEVE WAINWRIGHT
HAS TEMPORARILY BECOME UNBALANCED AND HIS CONDI-
TION RENDERS HIM SUSCEPTIBLE OF ENEMY USE.

3 John Horan didn't hear Wainwright's broadcast. Since the fall of Bataan, when he was promoted to
full colonel and given authority by Wainwright to change
his Casual Regiment to an official one, Horan and his staff
had kept on the move, going from village to village in the
wild mountains north of Baguio.

On May 10 he telephoned his regimental headquarters
in the Batang Buhay Gold Mine to tell Captain R. H.

Brown that since there could be no more effective fighting until after the rainy season, he and his staff were going to hide out in the Kalinga area for several months. Brown told him of the emotional Wainwright broadcast, demanding that he and Colonel Nakar, who was operating similar guerrilla detachments to the north, surrender immediately.

Horan was amazed, seeing no reason at all to surrender. Most of his ammunition was gone but he had safely dispersed his Bontoc fighters to their homes. He and his staff knew they would be safe with the faithful Kalinga tribe, and he was confident MacArthur would return as soon as the rains stopped.

Horan debated with himself four days. He knew he had the nucleus of a powerful guerrilla force. Already his men had become proficient in blowing up bridges, hijacking Japanese supplies and conducting deadly hit-and-run raids. His Bontocs made excellent guerrillas and several officers showed promise of developing into reliable leaders. One, Walter Cushing, a half-Mexican, half-Irish civilian mining engineer, was already a legend in the mountains, his sudden raids keeping the Japanese constantly terrorized. With storybook daring he even raided warehouses, carting away scores of cases of ammunition through enemy lines.

But Horan kept thinking about Wainwright's orders to put a stop to the further useless sacrifice of human lives. This meant, he guessed, that the men of Corregidor were being held as hostages.

After the third successive sleepless night, Horan decided, on the morning of May 14, to hike up the mountain to Lubuagan and surrender. He was consoled by the thought that the Japanese were getting very little except a few American officers. A month before he had made Cushing second in command, and told him, "In case I'm captured or surrender, ignore any orders I might give to surrender. You will carry on."

   4   Surrender in the Visayan Islands was even more complicated. Most of the commanders of the various islands heard the Wainwright broadcast, yet felt it was made under duress or was an enemy trick. The situation was further complicated by the strained relations between Sharp and many of his island commanders. Some of these younger men thought the general was too old to command fighting troops. They also felt he was unrealistic in his dealings with Filipinos and enlisted men. On an inspection trip early that

year Sharp had reportedly asked a Filipino, "Whose corporal are you?" The man, who knew little English, was confused. "You are not your company commander's corporal," continued Sharp. "Not your battalion commander's corporal; not your regimental or even division commander's corporal. You are *my* corporal." From that day on the corporal refused to obey his sergeant, his captain or even his colonel, telling them he was only supposed to take orders from General Sharp. Soon the entire regiment was out of control.

When Colonel Albert Christie, commander of Panay Island, and an exceptionally forceful and blunt man, received Sharp's radiogram instructing him to surrender, he promptly replied that he didn't see "even one small reason" why he should surrender just because "some other unit has gone to hell or some Corregidor shell-shocked terms" had been made. He questioned Sharp's authority to order his surrender, adding:

TO SATISFY ME I MUST HAVE MACARTHUR'S OKAY: OTHERWISE IT MAY BE TREASON.

The next day, May 11, Sharp again ordered Christie to surrender at once, assuring him that MacArthur had been informed of his actions and that Lieutenant Colonel Allen Thayer was flying to Panay with instructions. He warned:

YOUR FAILURE TO COMPLY WILL PRODUCE DISASTROUS RESULTS.

Christie, whose immediate commander was General Chynoweth on Cebu, still refused to obey. Months previously Chynoweth had made definite plans for guerrilla resistance in just such a case. Panay was geographically suited for guerrilla operations; its forces were fairly well trained and though short of weapons and ammunition, had sufficient food supplies. Christie replied:

YOUR RADIO SURRENDER OF MY FORCES SOUNDS TOTALLY UNNECESSARY. I STRONGLY URGE YOU TO HAVE THE APPROVAL OF THE WAR DEPARTMENT THROUGH MACARTHUR. I AM CONSULTING MY IMMEDIATE COMMANDER, GENERAL CHYNOWETH. IN THIS DELICATE SITUATION PLEASE DO NOT ISSUE ME ANY PEREMPTORY ORDERS THAT WILL EMBARRASS OR GET US INTO MUTUAL CONFLICT. RATHER DO I FEEL A FREE HAND IN CARRYING OUT MY MISSION UNINFLUENCED BY ANY HYSTERIA INHERENT IN

LOCAL ACTION. NO ARMY SURRENDERS PORTIONS STILL
FREE, INTACT, AND HAVING A GOOD CHANCE OF HELP-
ING THE GENERAL MISSION. MAKE ME INDEPENDENT.
DO NOT PUT ME ON THE SACRIFICE BLOCK.

The exasperated Sharp didn't answer this strong message.
He had already sent Colonel Thayer with a letter of instructions and a personal letter. These, he felt, would convince the stubborn colonel.

On that same day MacArthur, extremely distressed by
the unhappy situation, radioed Marshall the details of
Sharp's surrender. He concluded:

I HAVE HAD NO WORD FROM GENERAL CHYNOWETH
SINCE APRIL 12. I NOW HAVE NO MEANS OF COMMU-
NICATION WITH THE PHILIPPINES.

What happened in the Visayans was out of his hands.

Brigadier General Bradford Chynoweth was hiding with
his staff, a few hundred Filipino soldiers and about sixty
Navy officers and civilians in the dense mountainous forests
north of Cebu City. When he learned about Wainwright's
broadcast, he held a council of war with his chief of staff.
They concluded the order was not binding since it was
obviously issued under duress.

He decided to carry on, writing messages to Christie on
Panay, Colonel Roger Hilsman on Negros and Colonel Theodore Cornell on Leyte. But on May 12 his trusted adviser,
Dr. Emilio Osmeña, son of the vice-president, told him
the Filipino troops were so demoralized they were leaving
for their homes.

Because of this Chynoweth decided to take his staff to
Leyte and then Panay, making that island headquarters for
Visayan guerrilla operations. While completing plans for
the dangerous trip the next day a Christie message to Sharp
was heard faintly on the radio:

WHERE IS GENERAL CHYNOWETH? TELL HIM TO COME
BACK OVER HERE AND COMMAND US.

Chynoweth was cheered to hear the blunt, buoyant words
of his subordinate. A few minutes later a message from
Sharp came over the radio in the clear again ordering everyone in the Visayans to surrender. Chynoweth by now was
suspicious of anything coming from Mindanao and he

told his message center to accept no more radios from Sharp. Just then a courier arrived from Negros Island with a message from Colonel Hilsman. It stated that Sharp's order to surrender was authentic and that Sharp was sending a staff officer to negotiate the surrender of Chynoweth's forces.

Chynoweth now was utterly confused. He realized that Sharp was still in contact with General MacArthur and apparently MacArthur had approved the surrender. Even so Chynoweth hesitated, deciding to wait until the evening radio broadcast. Perhaps then MacArthur himself would clarify the situation.

That evening Chynoweth's aide, young Tom Powell, dejectedly returned from the radio. "The only word over KGEI," he said, "was a statement of General MacArthur that all contact with the Philippines was now cut off."

This sounded final, thought Chynoweth. MacArthur had crossed them off his book. The next few hours were torture. It was agony to determine what to do. He had gone through all the Army schools up to the War College, but had never been taught how, when, or when not to surrender.

He ordered all his scattered people to gather at the White Horse Inn in Sudlon Forest. Then he sent a message to the Japanese in Cebu City that he was expecting a staff officer from Sharp. He and Osmeña talked most of the night. The vice-president's son was in a difficult position. "You can leave us and return quietly to your home," said Chynoweth, "or you can go with us if we have to surrender." Osmeña was afraid the Japanese would force him to take an administrative job in the occupied government. "Someone will have to continue government," said the general. "They're your people. It would be better for you to do it than someone else."

"But I'm afraid the Japanese will ask me to do things inimical to the American forces. I won't do that."

The next morning they walked to the White Horse Inn. There they met Captain Gray, the emissary from Mindanao, who had written orders from Sharp and Wainwright. The Japanese, said Gray, were holding American troops on Corregidor, ready to turn their guns on them in case the surrender didn't go through.

Chynoweth gathered his men and told them he was surrendering. Any who wished could hide out in the hills. The following morning, May 16, the general led the sad march from White Horse Inn. With him were Dr. Osmeña, several staff officers, a few naval officers and fifty Filipinos. A day later, Japanese came up the road from Cebu

City to meet them and accept the surrender. Japanese newsmen took pictures while several movie cameramen recorded the scene.

The chief administrative officer of Japanese forces on Cebu, Colonel Kawakami, a tall, dark, somber man, came forward. Chynoweth was too overcome with emotion to say a word. Kawakami turned to Colonel Irvine Scudder, the general's chief of staff, and negotiations began.

Chynoweth, tongue-tied and miserable, did nothing as his staff officers carried on the necessary business. Then the prisoners were put in cars and taken to the large white administration building in Cebu City. But first they were toured around the burned buildings and docks of the city.

"Don't you think it was a terrible thing to destroy a city and cut off the water supply?" asked Kawakami through a stern-faced interpreter.

"I regret the horrors of war, too," said Chynoweth. "But I don't consider that we were the ones to initiate these horrors."

Kawakami said the auxiliary pumping machinery in the water line had been put out of action and the key was missing. Where was it?

"I cannot give you any information to help any of your activities," replied the general.

Kawakami turned to Scudder. The colonel told him where to find the key but refused to answer other questions. The courteous Japanese commander now told Chynoweth he was putting him in a separate house as a hostage. "You will be given an armband and the freedom of the city if you promise not to escape."

"If I ever see any chance of escaping, I will do so," said Chynoweth belligerently. Just then a radio in a nearby room burst out with "The Stars and Stripes Forever." It was too much for the general. Again he was so choked he couldn't talk.

"I know just how you feel," said Kawakami. He ordered tea.

Christie was still unconvinced. The day after Chynoweth's surrender he radioed Sharp asking what MacArthur's final answer had been. By now Sharp had lost all patience and replied curtly:

NO FURTHER COMMENTS FROM YOU ARE DESIRED. ACKNOWLEDGE THIS MESSAGE AND STATE ACTIONS TAKEN AT ONCE.

That same day, May 18, Sharp's emissary, Colonel Thayer, finally landed on Panay Island. "Wainwright's surrender of Corregidor," he told the recalcitrant Christie, "is conditional on the surrender of all forces in the Philippines."

Christie was now confronted with the same problem faced by Horan and Chynoweth. Was holding Panay Island worth the lives of all the Corregidor prisoners? He reluctantly agreed to surrender.

5 These were days of gnawing worry to Wainwright as he tensely waited in Manila. He couldn't understand why some of his commanders were taking so long to surrender. Didn't they know they were endangering the lives of thousands of comrades by their delays?

His conqueror, General Homma, was not in a triumphant mood. Even though he finally had won the Philippines, he knew he was in disfavor with the High Command. General Count Hisaichi Terauchi, commander of the Southern Army, had recently inspected the Philippines and had been very unhappy with Homma's lenient treatment of Filipino civilians. Homma admitted he had ordered his troops not to regard the Filipinos as enemies, to respect their customs and traditions and religion. His men had been forbidden to burn, pillage or rape. He also confessed he had prevented a pamphlet describing the exploitation of the Philippines by the Americans from being distributed.

"We must face the facts," he said. "The Americans never exploited the Philippines. It is wrong to make such false statements. They administered a very benevolent supervision over the Philippines. Japan should make better and more enlightened supervision."

Terauchi also criticized the general for not occupying Malacañan, the presidential palace.

"Even the United States didn't occupy Malacañan," protested Homma. "It would not be proper for the Japanese to take it over."

"You are much too lenient," said Terauchi sternly. He advised his subordinate to discontinue his soft methods.

Homma knew his military career was in danger, but it was not in his nature to change his methods. He still believed the best way to win the Filipino people was not through beatings but with enlightened leadership. He went ahead with plans for the immediate release of all Filipino prisoners.

In the meantime he ordered a victory parade through the streets of Manila. As his conquering army passed in review, thousands of Filipinos stood silently on the sidewalks. With undisguised resentment they watched Vargas, Laurel, Aquino and other members of the new "Quisling" government march by carrying little Japanese flags. Then came a Filipino band. As it approached Homma's reviewing stand, it suddenly began playing a stirring march. For the first time the onlookers broke into enthusiastic cheers.

The band was playing, "The Stars and Stripes Forever."

Not long after this, Homma was relieved of his command and forced to retire in semi-disgrace because of his persistent leniency. Four years later he would be tried and executed as a war criminal by the man he defeated, MacArthur.

1 When the Netherlands Indies collapsed after the Battle of Java Sea, many Japanese naval leaders, led by Yamamoto, felt the first goals of conquest had been far too modest. Japan should push her destiny to its limit. The Army planners disagreed, insisting that Japan should now consolidate her successes and proceed cautiously.

It was a difference in strategic concept. The Army General Staff agreed that neutralization operations in certain areas were practical, providing they were on a small scale. Japan, they argued, had captured immensely rich resources. These should be held and developed. From now on, the enemy should be forced to do the attacking. Naturally it would mean a prolonged war, but this was the general plan agreed on before the war started. Hasty improvisations could only lead to catastrophe.

The Navy believed systematic operations should be started against Australia, Hawaii and India. These would naturally result in great naval battles. And, as at the Battle of Java Sea, the enemy would be destroyed. In proof, they asked their critics to look at the record. Instead of the anticipated 25 per cent naval losses a mere 25,000 tons had been sunk in conquering an empire. The biggest warship lost had been a destroyer. The Navy persisted in pressing for immediate action. Being on the defensive was disadvantageous. The enemy should be kept on the defensive. The next conquest should be Australia, which was obviously being built up as a springboard for the counterattack.

Colonel Takushiro Hattori, Tojo's former secretary and now Army chief of operations, opposed this venture. Australia was twice the area of China with a population of only 7,000,000. Its land communications were poor. The Australians would defend their homeland tenaciously. Such an invasion, he told Captain Sadatoshi Tomioka, his opposite number in the Navy, would require the main body of the Combined Fleet and twelve infantry divisions. The shipping for the Army alone would run to 1,500,000 tons.

If it went through, he said, the Army would have to strip its defenses against the USSR in Manchuria and cut down drastically on the China front. "Total national power must be concentrated in the prosecution of a protracted war. It is vital at this point to develop resilience in national power and war potential under a sound plan."

When Tomioka insisted, Hattori picked up a cup. "The tea in this cup," he said, "represents our strength." He dumped it on the floor. "You see, it only goes so far. If the plan is approved I will resign."

General Sugiyama, chief of the Army General Staff, backed up Hattori. On March 4 a provisional compromise was reached. Three days later at a liaison conference a policy of future war guidance was adopted. The Australian scheme was dropped, but the Army agreed to extend its gains in less ambitious projects such as an amphibious operation on Port Moresby, a town only 400 miles north of Australia, on the southern coast of New Guinea, the second largest island in the world. Also approved by Hattori, after a staff study, was the conquest of three islands off the northeast coast of Australia: Samoa, Fiji and New Caledonia. This, he agreed, was a practical move for it would cut the lifeline between Australia and the United States.

Hattori didn't know it, but Admiral Yamamoto was pressing for a much more ambitious invasion: Midway and the Aleutians. This plan was being hotly disputed within the Navy itself. How could it be supplied, argued the Imperial General Headquarters Navy Section, even if won? How could an American counterattack be driven off?

Yamamoto refused to budge. Unlike many Japanese militarists he was well aware of the immense potential of American industry. "We can carry through for one year, some way," he said, "but after that I don't know." He insisted Japan's only possible chance of success was to lure the U.S. Pacific Fleet into the open and destroy it. And it had to be done before the great balance of naval power presently enjoyed by Japan was whittled down.

If the position of commander-in-chief of Combined Fleet had been selected by votes, Isoroku Yamamoto would have been the heavy choice among naval officers. Young officers admired him because he was a strong leader. Unlike many other Japanese admirals, brought up in the British tradition of gentlemanliness, he commanded his fleet with an iron hand. He was a fighting leader.

He was an expert poker and bridge player, following the instinctive hunches of a born gambler. He ran the fleet with the same bold, imaginative daring. Fliers swore by him because he was one of the few older officers who believed in aviation. In 1915, when he was young and unknown, an American writer had asked him what he considered the war vessel of the future. "The most important ship of the future," he promptly answered, "will be a ship to carry airplanes."

Under pressure the Navy Section finally bowed to the insistent Yamamoto and a directive to invade Midway and the Aleutians was issued on April 16. Yet it was far from a complete victory for Yamamoto. No date was set. The admiral begged for immediate action; time was running out. The Navy Section refused to be rushed. On April 18 a bolt from the blue, the Doolittle raid, gave Yamamoto the ammunition he needed.

Recalling the panic that seized the inhabitants when a Russian naval force suddenly appeared near Tokyo Bay during the Russo-Japanese War, he insisted the Midway invasion be executed immediately. Unless Midway was captured promptly, he argued, air and sea patrols in front of the homeland would have to be heavily strengthened. Even so it would be impossible to defend Tokyo from future attacks.

The deadline for invasion, he said, would have to be June 7. A few days' delay would mean a month's postponement, since his carrier air groups needed pre-dawn moonlight for night action. Even the most violent opponents of the plan now had to admit the threat from the east was more immediate than that from Australia. All opposition had vanished because of Doolittle. The Naval General Staff readily agreed to postpone the Fiji-Samoa invasion and attack Midway on June 7.

When the Midway project was submitted to the Army, Colonel Hattori was led to believe it was strictly a measure to defend the homeland. Since the occupation of the Aleutians would cut the line between America and Russia, he advised General Sugiyama to approve the Yamamoto plan.

2 While Yamamoto's Combined Fleet enthusiastically threw itself into preparation for the great Midway operation, the Port Moresby invasion started as scheduled. On May 3 Vice Admiral Shigeyoshi Inouye's Fourth Fleet seized Tulagi, a small island 25 miles north of Guadalcanal. The next day the Port Moresby Invasion Force left the northern New Britain port of Rabaul in 14 transports escorted by 1 light cruiser and 6 destroyers and covered by the light carrier *Shoho*, 4 heavy cruisers and 1 destroyer.

The Japanese still didn't have the slightest suspicion that their "Purple" Code had been broken months before by William Friedman and a team of U.S. army cryptanalysts. Consequently they didn't know that Admiral Chester Nimitz, who had replaced Kimmel at Pearl Harbor, was aware of their proposed invasion of Port Moresby. In fact, Nimitz, knowing the Japanese operations would start on May 3, had already assembled a naval force consisting of 2 carriers, 6 heavy cruisers, 2 light cruisers and 11 destroyers in the Coral Sea off northeast Australia under Rear Admiral Frank Jack Fletcher.

When Fletcher learned of the Tulagi landing he immediately launched an air attack from his flagship, the carrier *Yorktown*. In three strikes 99 planes hit Tulagi. Though the fliers reported they had sunk 2 destroyers, a freighter and 4 gunboats, and severely damaged other warships, they had done relatively little damage.

This attack gave the Japanese their first warning of the presence of an American task force. Vice Admiral Takeo Takagi, then some distance to the north with his Carrier Striking Force, immediately rushed south to engage the enemy with his 2 heavy carriers, *Zuikaku* and *Shokaku*, 2 heavy cruisers and 6 destroyers.

The arrival of Takagi in the Coral Sea gave Admiral Inouye an appreciable superiority over Fletcher: an extra light carrier, 2 destroyers and 7 submarines. In addition, close by was the group supporting the invasion transports: 2 light cruisers, a seaplane carrier and 3 gunboats.

Fletcher was well aware he was outnumbered and outgunned but when he learned from intelligence reports that the Port Moresby Invasion Force would probably round the eastern tip of New Guinea on May 7, he was determined to stop it. For the first time since Pearl Harbor, the U.S. Navy was steaming forth with capital ships to try and check the Japanese tide of conquest. Two of the four carriers in the Pacific Fleet were being put on the line. If these two great ships were sunk, as the *Prince of Wales* and *Repulse* had been in the last previous attempts to stop a Japanese convoy, victory in the Pacific could well be postponed indefinitely.

From intelligence reports Fletcher learned that the Port Moresby Invasion Force had already left Rabaul and would probably round the eastern tip of New Guinea on May 7. It was his job to stop them. Since they were probably protected by three enemy carriers and several heavy cruisers, he knew he had to employ his weaker forces cautiously.

On the morning of May 7, the day after Wainwright's

surrender, a Japanese search plane discovered the oiler *Neosho* and destroyer *Sims* and reported excitedly it had found an American carrier and cruiser. Soon high-level bombers struck in two waves. Then 36 dive bombers joined the attack. The *Sims* sank soon after noon. The *Neosho,* mortally wounded, was helplessly adrift.

In the meantime, Fletcher's task force was still unobserved. That morning he had ordered the support group under British Rear Admiral J. G. Crace to push ahead and attack the Port Moresby Invasion Force while he lagged behind to carry on an air duel with the Japanese carriers.

At 11:00 A.M., while the Japanese carrier planes were concentrating on the *Sims* and *Neosho,* 93 planes from the *Yorktown* and *Lexington* found the light carrier *Shoho* and began an aggressive bomb and torpedo attack. About 160 miles away comrades of the attackers strained to hear this action at their battle stations, but the voices of the pilots were almost inaudible because of static. Suddenly the voice of Lieutenant Commander Robert Dixon, leader of a scout bomber squadron, came in strong and clear: "Scratch one flat-top! Dixon to carrier. Scratch one flat-top!"

The *Shoho* went down at 11:36 A.M. For the first time in the five-month-long Pacific war, a Japanese ship larger than a destroyer had been sunk.

By this time Admiral Inouye had become so concerned he ordered his transports to turn back and wait until the seas had been cleared of Americans. That afternoon visibility decreased and squalls limited aerial observation. By midnight the two great naval forces had lost contact with each other.

Fletcher was determined to find the enemy again and attack his carriers. At 6:25 the next morning 16 search planes were launched from the *Lexington.* For almost two hours there was no news. Then at 8:15 A.M. a radio report came from Lieutenant J. G. Smith. He had sighted the Japanese striking force. Thirteen minutes later he radioed:

TWO CARRIERS, FOUR HEAVY CRUISERS, MANY DESTROYERS, STEERING 120 DEGREES, 20 KNOTS. THEIR POSITION 175 MILES, ROUGHLY NORTHEAST.

Fletcher immediately ordered both his carriers to launch air strikes. At 10:57 A.M. 39 planes from the *Yorktown* sighted the carriers *Zuikaku* and *Shokaku,* heavily screened by heavy cruisers and destroyers. Lieutenant Commander Joe Taylor, Torpedo Squadron 5, led the first American attack on a large carrier. Though all torpedoes missed or failed to explode, two bombs hit the *Shokaku,* starting several furious fires.

Less than an hour later 24 planes from *Lexington* found the same targets. They did little damage, scoring only one bomb hit on the already burning *Shokaku.*

At the same time, 70 planes from the two Japanese carriers were hitting *Lexington* and *Yorktown.* An 800-pound bomb pierced the flight deck of *Yorktown,* penetrating to the fourth deck, but fires were skilfully brought under control. *Lexington* was not so lucky. Two torpedoes ripped into her port side, while two small bombs hit the main deck forward and the smokestack structure.

The first battle in history between aircraft carriers was over by noon. It was also the first naval engagement in which opposing ships had never seen each other or exchanged shots. At that moment it looked like a clear-cut victory for Fletcher. He had sunk a light carrier, a destroyer and three small vessels, while losing only a destroyer and an oiler. Then that afternoon two explosions rocked the wounded *Lexington,* setting off raging fires. More and more explosions followed but the battle to save the "Lady Lex" continued all through the afternoon in spite of heavy casualties. Though everyone, including about 600 men on their first cruise, knew the ship's own ammunition stores might go off any moment, no one faltered. There was no panic.

The fight was hopeless. At 5:07 P.M. Rear Admiral Aubrey Fitch, commander of the carrier group, called down from his bridge to the *Lexington*'s skipper, Captain F. C. Sherman, "Well, Ted, let's get the men off."

Rafts were thrown overboard. The men neatly lined up their shoes on the flight deck and calmly began going over the sides. It was all as orderly as a drill. One group even raided the ship's service store for ice cream while waiting in line.

One of the last to leave the deck was Lieutenant Noel Gaylor, a fighter pilot. That afternoon he had knocked down 4 Zeros in a single flight to become the Navy's leading air ace with 8 victories. He dove 50 feet into the sea and swam for several minutes. Then he suddenly turned and soon was climbing up a rope to the *Lexington*'s deck.

"What did you come back for?" asked a friend.

"Oh, I got a bit lonely out there. I didn't know any of those guys. When are you fellows goin' to come?"

After everyone was off the ship—not a man was drowned and even Captain Sherman's dog, Wags, was saved—Admiral

Fletcher ordered the destroyer *Phelps* to sink the smoldering wreck. At about 8:00 P.M. four torpedoes drove into the carrier's starboard side. She shuddered and steam rose in great clouds.

On a nearby cruiser, newsman Stanley Johnston watched the big ship settle rapidly. She stayed upright until waves folded over her.

"There she goes," said an officer of the *Lexington* standing next to Johnston. "She didn't turn over. She is going down with her head up. Dear old *Lex*. A lady to the last."

With the sinking of the *Lexington*, the Coral Sea battle became a tactical victory for the Japanese. The strategic victory went to Fletcher. Just before dusk Admiral Inouye had definitely postponed the Port Moresby invasion and recalled the transports. Fletcher's primary mission had been accomplished. For the first time in the war a Japanese invasion had been turned aside.

When Yamamoto learned of the postponement he was furious. At midnight he ordered the cautious Inouye to continue the pursuit of Fletcher and destroy his "remnants." The unharmed *Zuikaku* and her escorts obediently turned southeast at 2:00 A.M., May 9, but it was too late. Fletcher had vanished.

The battle caused a sensation all over the world. The New York *Times* on May 9 announced in headlines:

JAPANESE REPULSED IN GREAT PACIFIC BATTLE, WITH 17 TO 22 OF THEIR SHIPS SUNK OR CRIPPLED; ENEMY IN FLIGHT, PURSUED BY ALLIED WARSHIPS

There was jubilation and immense relief in Australia. The Australians felt the battle fought just off their northeast coast had saved their country. Americans in Sydney and Brisbane were treated as heroes. Nothing was too good for the Yanks.

The Japanese claims were just as wild, announcing they had sunk 2 battleships and 2 carriers. On May 9 the headlines of Japan's leading newspaper, *Asahi Shimbun*, read:

DREAM OF COUNTERATTACK ON JAPAN LOST IN CORAL SEA ONLY 3 CARRIERS LEFT; SIGN OF FALL OF UNITED STATES

There was also jubilation in Germany. Hitler said, "After this new defeat the United States warships will hardly dare to face the Japanese Fleet again, since any United States warship which accepts action with the Japanese naval forces is as good as lost."

Imperial Headquarters firmly believed their Navy had

scored a tremendous victory. They were positive the *Lexington* and *Yorktown* had been sunk, leaving only two or three American carriers in the entire Pacific. Their optimism wasn't dimmed when *Zuikaku* and *Shokaku* steamed into port a few days later and it was learned both would have to be scratched from the Midway operation. *Shokaku* would take a month to repair and *Zuikaku* had lost too many planes and pilots.

By now even the former critics of the Midway plan were no longer worried. Japan was striking with the greatest sea force ever assembled: more than 200 ships, including 11 battleships, 8 carriers, 22 cruisers, 65 destroyers, 21 submarines and about 700 planes.

The seizure of Midway and the Aleutians was only of secondary importance. Yamamoto's main objective was to lure the remnants of Nimitz's fleet into the open where it could be completely destroyed. His plan was simple. On June 3 the Northern Force would raid the Aleutians. In addition to destroying enemy installations, this would protect Yamamoto's northern flank and momentarily draw attention away from the Midway area. The next day his most powerful unit, the 1st Carrier Striking Force of Admiral Nagumo, would launch a pre-invasion air strike on Midway, wiping out enemy planes. The landing itself would come on June 6.

This was the bait in the trap. Obviously Nimitz would react since Midway was so important and steam out of Pearl Harbor to do battle, never suspecting a force outnumbering him two or three to one was waiting in ambush. It would be a slaughter.

Unfortunately for Yamamoto, his plan was based on a fallacy, surprise. As at Coral Sea, decoded Japanese messages had already warned American naval leaders of the coming operation. This intercepted information, however, was spotty. The Japanese messages only referred to the invasion point as "AF." Washington thought "AF" stood for the island of Oahu. Nimitz disagreed. He was sure it meant Midway.

The admiral visited Midway and asked its commander what additional equipment and men were needed to stop a large scale amphibious attack. When he returned to Hawaii he sent back every plane he could spare: 16 Marine dive bombers, 7 Wildcat fighters, 30 Navy patrol flying boats, 18 Flying Fortresses and 4 B-26's. He also ordered additional anti-aircraft batteries installed, the garrison brought up to 2000, and three submarine patrol arcs set up. He did this knowing that if he was wrong, he might lose the entire fleet. He also knew it was a risk that had to be taken.

In the middle of May, Nimitz ordered Fletcher to leave the South Pacific area and return to Hawaii as fast as possible. The carriers *Hornet* and *Enterprise* were also recalled.

Since there was still doubt as to the invasion point, Commander Joseph J. Rochefort of Nimitz's Combat Intelligence staff suggested Midway be ordered to send a fake, uncoded message complaining of the breakdown of its distillation plant. Nimitz agreed and the decoy message was sent.

Two days later the cryptanalysts in Pearl Harbor's topsecret "Black Chamber" intercepted a Japanese dispatch: AF was low on fresh water. At last Nimitz knew for certain that he'd been right. Midway was Yamamoto's target.

Even with this information Nimitz realized he was still the underdog. His fleet would be greatly outnumbered. He had only two carriers ready for action. The third, the badly damaged *Yorktown*, was limping toward Pearl Harbor from its battle in the Coral Sea and wouldn't arrive until May 27.

He knew Yamamoto's main purpose was to lure him into a fight, yet even against these tremendous odds he had to take the challenge.

       3   Yamamoto's great plan moved into gear on May 26 when Rear Admiral Kakuji Kakuta's Second Carrier Striking Force sailed out of Ominato harbor at noon and headed east toward the Aleutians. His planes were to attack Dutch Harbor on June 3.

The following day the muscle of the Midway invasion, Vice Admiral Chuichi Nagumo's First Carrier Striking Force, left Hashirajima with 21 ships, including 2 heavy carriers and 2 light carriers. On this force depended ultimate success. Nagumo was fresh from his triumphs at Pearl Harbor and the Indian Ocean. Always noted for his fire and dynamism, some of his more perceptive junior officers were noticing that his once vigorous fighting spirit was gone. He had aged perceptibly.

Nagumo no longer took the initiative. This particularly worried his operations officer, Commander Minoru Genda, probably the most highly thought of and brilliant of the rising officers. It was he who had perfected the technique for the shallow-running torpedo attack at Pearl Harbor and had conceived the basic idea for the Midway operation. Lately Genda's plans were being approved by Nagumo almost without consideration. It worried Genda to find these plans coming out as formal orders, completely unchanged. He was self-confident, but not so self-confident he didn't realize anyone can make mistakes.

The following day Vice Admiral Moshiro Hosogaya, commander of the Northern Force, set sail with the rest of the Aleutian ships. And that same evening, far to the south, the fleet of transports carrying the 5000 troops scheduled to land on Midway embarked with its strong escort from the island of Saipan.

A few hours later, on the morning of May 29, the last two units left: first the 16 warships of the Midway Invasion Force under Vice Admiral Nobutake Kondo and finally the 32 warships of the Main Force.

From Yamamoto down to the last seaman there was complete confidence that the most decisive victory in naval warfare would soon be scored by the Emperor's Combined Fleet.

To stop Yamamoto, Admiral Nimitz had only 8 cruisers, 15 destroyers and 3 carriers. And one of these carriers, *Yorktown*, was so badly damaged some experts estimated it would take about three months to repair. Nimitz called in his two commanders, Rear Admirals Frank Jack Fletcher and Raymond Spruance, a last-minute substitute for Halsey, who was suffering from a skin disease. Nimitz told them what to expect, detailing almost exactly Yamamoto's actual plans. Their orders were to "inflict maximum damage on enemy by employing strong attrition tactics." In other words, they were to strike again and again from the air. Then Nimitz gave each commander a special Letter of Instruction:

In carrying out the task assigned . . . you will be governed by the principle of calculated risk, which you shall interpret to mean the avoidance of exposure of your force to attack by superior enemy forces without good prospect of inflicting, as a result of such exposure, greater damage on the enemy.

Two days before Yamamoto's last force left Japan, Spruance sailed out of Pearl Harbor with the carriers *Enterprise, Hornet,* 6 cruisers and 9 destroyers. Two days later, Fletcher steamed out with the *Yorktown*, 2 cruisers and 6 destroyers. Because of the remarkable efforts of more than 1400 workmen the damaged carrier had been patched up in two days.

In spite of bad weather, the transports carrying the Midway invaders were only 1000 miles west of their goal by May 31. In fact, they were advancing too fast.

Yamamoto's own 32 ships, the Main Force, were behind schedule, their fueling operations delayed by heavy seas and poor visibility. Yamamoto was not in a happy mood. In addition to stomach trouble, he had recently learned that Operation K, a plan to send two flying boats over Hawaii for reconnaissance, had bogged down. Now he wouldn't know what strength Nimitz had in Pearl Harbor.

He received another disappointment on June 1 when submarines failed to reach their positions on the cordon lines supposed to be laid northwest and west of Hawaii. They were two days behind schedule and the admiral was pushing toward Midway almost completely in the dark about Nimitz's strength or intentions. That same day a disturbing scrap of news came from Lieutenant Commander Yahachi Tanabe of the submarine I-168, who reported intensive flying patrols from Midway. The island seemed to be on a strict alert; many construction cranes were visible, indicating an expansion of defenses.

Six hundred miles ahead of Yamamoto, Admiral Nagumo knew even less than his superior. Since there was radio silence, he had no idea Midway was already alerted. His Striking Force, unaided by radar, was shrouded in a mist so thick that ships could see only the dim, unearthly outlines of their closest neighbors.

The following day, June 2, was even worse. Nagumo and his officers stared anxiously from the bridge of *Akagi*. They were completely blanketed in heavy fog. It was as if they were alone. Another problem was worrying the admiral. The entire Midway plan had been hastily drawn up and pushed through without ironing out certain inconsistencies. One of these was the double tactical mission he had been given. His planes were to attack Midway on June 4 as a preparation for the landing two days later. His other mission was to contact and destroy Nimitz's fleet. How could he do both? The second mission required freedom of movement and secrecy. If he hit Midway, mobility and secrecy were gone.

He decided the time had come to settle the matter of priority and gathered his staff. Captain Oishi, his senior officer, spoke first. "The Combined Fleet operation order gives first priority to the destruction of enemy forces. Cooperation with the landing operation is secondary. But if we do not neutralize the Midway-based air forces as planned, our landing operations two days later will be strongly opposed and the entire invasion schedule will be upset."

"But where is the enemy fleet?" asked Nagumo.

Oishi admitted nobody knew, then said, "Even if they are already aware of our movements and have sortied to meet us, they cannot be far out from base at this moment and certainly can't be near us. I think, therefore, that the first thing for us to do is to carry out the scheduled air strike on Midway."

The others agreed.

The next morning, June 3, planes from Admiral Kakuta's carriers bombed Dutch Harbor in the Aleutians. Little damage was done. The raid's main purpose, to divert Nimitz's attention to the north, also failed since the American admiral had long since known where the main attack was going to fall.

At 9:00 that same morning Ensign Jack Reid, flying a Catalina on patrol from Midway, suddenly saw what looked like a mass of miniature ships in a backyard pool about 30 miles ahead.

"Do you see what I do?" he asked his copilot.

"You're damned right I do!"

Dodging behind clouds, Reid followed the ships, finally reporting at 11:00 A.M. that 11 ships less than 700 miles from Midway were heading east at 19 knots. It was, he thought, the main Japanese fleet.

Reid had seen only the invasion transports. They, in turn, had spotted Reid. This information was relayed to Yamamoto. Late that afternoon he received an even more alarming message: at 4:24 P.M. nine Flying Fortresses, apparently based on Midway, had bombed the Midway-bound transports but scored no hits.

The complete confidence of the day before deserted the bridge of Yamamoto's flagship *Yamato*. No one had ever imagined the transports would be discovered before Nagumo's air strike on Midway.

That evening Fletcher and Spruance, 300 miles east-northeast of Midway, were about 400 miles east of the position where Nagumo was planning to launch his planes the next morning for the strike on the island. When Fletcher, in overall command of the two forces, had finally learned that Japanese ships had been sighted he correctly guessed they were only transports and their escorts, not, as reported by Ensign Reid, the main Japanese fleet. Figuring the enemy carriers would approach Midway from the northwest, he turned his ships to the southwest at 7:50 P.M. He wanted to be about 200 miles north of Midway. From here he could launch his planes against Nagumo's carriers the next day.

The Americans, from admirals to seamen, knew a great and decisive engagement was approaching. The day before, Spruance, by visual signal, had told his men:

An attack for the purpose of capturing Midway is expected.

The attacking force may be composed of all combatant types including four or five carriers, transports and train vessels. If presence of Task Forces 16 and 17 remains unknown to enemy, we should be able to make surprise flank attacks on enemy carriers from position northeast of Midway. Further operations will be based on results of these attacks, damage inflicted by Midway forces, and information of enemy movements. The successful conclusion of the operation now commencing will be of great value to our country. Should carriers become separated during attacks by enemy aircraft, they will endeavor to remain within visual touch.

That night there was a feeling of tension and excitement in the wardrooms and mess halls. Rumors spread that the Japanese code had been broken and a trap was being set for the Midway invaders. The first big victory, long hoped for by every Navy man, could come the next day.

At 2:45 A.M., June 4, the loudspeakers of Nagumo's flagship, *Akagi*, blared. Air crews tumbled out of bunks to the deafening roar of warming motors. The noise woke Commander Genda, Nagumo's young operations officer. He hurried from the sick bay, where he had been confined, to the bridge, his eyes feverish. "I am very sorry, sir, to have been absent so long," he told Nagumo.

The admiral put an arm around his shoulder. "How are you feeling?"

"I have a slight temperature but am feeling much better now."

Everyone on the bridge was buoyed by the sight of Genda. Still uninformed by Yamamoto that the invasion transports had already been sighted by the Americans, Genda ordered launching preparations for the first wave. The four carriers were now only 240 miles northwest of Midway and steaming full into the wind.

At 4:30 A.M. the wind gauge on *Akagi* indicated the required velocity and Nagumo said, "Commence launching." A Zero fighter sped down the flight deck and, as the crew shouted enthusiastically, waving hands and caps, took off into the black sky. Eight Zeros followed, then 18 dive bombers.

About two miles to port, *Hiryu* was launching. The illuminated decks of *Kaga* and *Soryu* were also being cleared of planes. In fifteen minutes a total of 108 were in the air and forming. A moment later they circled and those on the ships below could see neatly grouped red and blue lights heading toward Midway Island.

At the same time, reconnaissance planes were being catapulted from the battleship *Haruna*. Half an hour later, delayed by catapult trouble and balky engines, the rest of the search planes left the heavy cruisers *Tone* and *Chikuma*.

Genda watched them go with some misgivings. They were bound on a one-phase search. He knew it should have been two-phase but he was short of aircraft and wanted to throw as many into the Midway attack as possible. The flight deck of the *Akagi* was now empty and strangely silent, but just before the sun rose at 5:00 A.M. the loudspeaker blared, "Prepare second attack wave!"

Instantly the uproar began again as bells clanged and the planes of this wave were brought up by elevator and rolled into place. All 18 of the *Akagi* planes carried torpedoes, as did the 18 of *Kaga*. The other two, the light carriers *Hiryu* and *Soryu*, were filling their decks with dive bombers. Thus Nagumo was ready, even if enemy ships should unexpectedly appear. Excitement and expectation swept the Striking Force.

Fifteen Flying Fortresses, commanded by Lieutenant Colonel Walter Sweeney, had already taken off from Midway before dawn with orders to attack the Japanese transports heading for the island.

Catalina search planes had also left Midway, looking for the enemy's Striking Force. At 5:25 A.M. one of these planes, PBY-5, approached Nagumo's force. A moment later Lieutenant Howard Ady and his copilot, Lieutenant William Chase, were staring in awe at a mass of ships ahead of them. It was hard for Ady to believe what he saw. He said later it was "like watching a curtain rise on the Biggest Show on Earth."

ENEMY CARRIERS, Ady radioed Midway. Then the big plane dodged behind clouds, circled and approached the Striking Force from the rear.

Enterprise intercepted this message at 5:34 A.M. Eleven minutes later came another:

MANY ENEMY PLANES HEADING MIDWAY BEARING 320°, DISTANT 150.

Then at 6:03 A.M. those aboard the *Enterprise* heard Ady's third report:

TWO CARRIERS AND BATTLESHIPS BEARING 320°, DISTANT 180, COURSE 135°, SPEED 25.

This information was relayed to Admiral Fletcher on the

Yorktown. Though he realized this was the Japanese Striking Force, Fletcher decided not to attack until his own search planes returned and there was more explicit information. He radioed Spruance:

> PROCEED SOUTHWESTERLY AND ATTACK ENEMY CARRIERS WHEN DEFINITELY LOCATED. I WILL FOLLOW AS SOON AS PLANES RECOVERED.

Two hundred miles to the west, air-raid sirens were shrieking on Midway. Radar had picked up the approaching 108 attackers from Nagumo's carriers. Planes of all types were scrambling. Bombers and search planes scattered. Fighters sped to the northwest to intercept the Japanese. Six Avenger torpedo planes and four Army Marauders, also carrying torpedoes, headed toward the enemy carriers.

Marine fighters sighted the first Japanese bombers 30 miles out of Midway, coming in at 13,000 feet in a rigid V formation with Zero fighters above. The Marines climbed to 17,000 feet and dove on the horde of attackers. There was a savage battle but the Americans, outnumbered two to one, had no chance in their antique Brewster Buffaloes and outclassed Wildcats.

The Japanese bombers continued unopposed to their target. Climbing to 14,000 feet, they began releasing their bombs at 6:30 A.M. A few minutes later "Val" dive bombers swept in through heavy anti-aircraft fire, blasting buildings, the powerhouse on Eastern Island, oil tanks on Sand Island and the seaplane hangar.

It was over in twenty minutes. In the greatest Marine air loss of the entire war, 15 of the 25 fighter pilots had died. The 10 survivors were acrimonious. One, Captain Philip White, later said, "It is my belief that any commander who orders pilots out for combat in an F2A (Buffalo) should consider the pilot as lost before leaving the ground."

The damage to Midway itself was not critical. Though many buildings were burning and the gasoline system was damaged, few men had been killed and the main purpose of the attack had failed. Midway was still in the airplane business. Five minutes after the attack, at 6:55 A.M., 16 U.S. Marine dive bombers took off and headed for Nagumo's carriers.

The Japanese raiders were returning with mixed feelings. They figured they had shot down 42 planes while losing only 5, but their leader, Lieutenant Joichi Tomonaga, realizing he had not knocked out Midway's air force, radioed Nagumo at 7:00 A.M.:

THERE IS NEED FOR A SECOND ATTACK.

By the time this message reached Nagumo his flagship, *Akagi*, was in a state of alarm. The PBY of Ady and Chase had been seen. Fighters had gone after the persistent Catalina but it kept hiding in the clouds.

Five minutes after Tomonaga's message from Midway was received, a bugle sounded Air Raid. Everyone on *Akagi*'s bridge peered anxiously to the south. Though there were fairly heavy clouds at 6000 feet, the sky was clearing. It was going to be a beautiful day. Then a screening destroyer suddenly hoisted a flag signal: ENEMY PLANES IN SIGHT.

The 4 Army Marauders and 6 Avengers which had left Midway just after the attack on the island were coming in for their own raid.

Those on the bridge of *Akagi* saw 4 planes, apparently torpedo bombers, approach from 20 degrees to port. Japanese fighters swooped down, shooting down 3. The other fled to the east. A moment later a lookout shouted, "Six medium land-based planes approaching, 20 degrees to starboard! On the horizon!"

Destroyers and cruisers fired. Then the battleship *Kirishima* opened up with her main batteries. The 6 planes—4 Marauders and 2 Avengers—kept coming in spite of the wall of fire. Now *Akagi*'s guns fired and 3 Zeros dove on the stubborn Americans.

Within a minute 3 attackers were in flames. The other 3 kept boring in, finally dropping their torpedoes and swinging sharply to the right. Two escaped but the lead plane skimmed over the *Akagi*, nearly grazing the bridge, then suddenly burst into flames and tumbled into the sea.

The *Akagi* abruptly swerved and the torpedoes churned by harmlessly. This narrow escape convinced Nagumo that a second attack on Midway should be made. He ordered those planes of the second wave carrying torpedoes for attack on ships to de-arm and reload with bombs. Since *Hiryu* and *Soryu* carried only dive bombers for this wave, they had nothing to do but wait, but there was frantic action on *Akagi* and *Kaga*. The torpedo planes on the flight decks had to be lowered to their hangars one by one for the arduous job of removing torpedoes and rearming with bombs.

The tension on the bridge of *Akagi* finally abated. Then at about 7:40 A.M. Nagumo was handed a message from one of the tardy search planes from the cruiser *Tone*;

TEN SHIPS, APPARENTLY ENEMY, SIGHTED. BEARING 010°, DISTANT 240 MILES FROM MIDWAY. COURSE 150°, SPEED MORE THAN 20 KNOTS. TIME 0728.

The enemy surface force wasn't supposed to arrive for two days. The American position was quickly plotted. Only 200 miles away! At 7:47 A.M. Nagumo curtly radioed the *Tone* plane:

ASCERTAIN SHIP TYPES AND MAINTAIN CONTACT.

The rearming of the planes with bombs was instantly stopped since torpedoes were considered more effective against ships. Before the *Tone* search plane could answer Nagumo's impatient message, enemy planes were sighted.

These were the 16 Marine dive bombers from Midway. At 7:55 A.M. the flight commander, Major Lofton Henderson, ordered his planes to make a glide-bombing attack since his inexperienced pilots knew little about dive-bombing. All headed straight for *Hiryu*.

Zeros quickly pounced on the Marines, knocking down 8. The others gallantly kept on course. When their bombs finally dropped *Hiryu* was enveloped in smoke and splashes. Finally the smoke cleared and those on *Akagi* saw to their relief that the *Hiryu* was still steaming ahead, completely untouched.

By this time an identification finally came from the *Tone* search plane: ENEMY SHIPS ARE FIVE CRUISERS AND FIVE DE-STROYERS. There was great relief. Without carriers the enemy was of no immediate danger. There was no time for con-gratulations. Fifteen American land-based heavy bombers were over *Hiryu* and *Soryu*. From 20,000 feet the big bomb-ers dropped their loads. Great geysers shot up on all sides of the two carriers. Again no damage was done.

The bombers were the 15 Flying Fortresses which had left Midway before dawn to attack the invasion transports. They had been diverted en route and sent against these richer targets. As they started home unharmed they reported 4 hits.

A few minutes later another message came from the *Tone* search plane:

ENEMY FORCE ACCOMPANIED BY WHAT APPEARS TO BE AIRCRAFT CARRIER BRINGING UP THE REAR.

Some on *Akagi* doubted there was a carrier. If so why hadn't they already been attacked? At worst, what was there to fear? The three harmless attacks from Midway had proved the enemy level of attack efficiency was very low. Just then a screening destroyer signaled that more enemy planes had been spotted. The destroyer fired several rounds, then quickly stopped in embarrassment. The planes were Japanese, the first of the 108 raiders returning from the Midway strike.

At that moment, 8:30 A.M., the *Tone* search plane reported two additional ships in the enemy force, probably cruisers. Nagumo now realized by the size of the force that it must contain at least one carrier. Genda agreed and recommended that an immediate attack be made on these ships. Since many planes had not yet been rearmed with torpedoes, Nagumo was in a quandary. Should those torpedo planes presently armed with 800-kilogram bombs be sent off at once with the 36 dive bombers of the two light carriers *Hiryu* and *Soryu*?

Genda agreed that, under the circumstances, bombs had to be used; they could still do heavy damage. What worried him was the absence of fighter protection. All the Zeros of the second wave had been sent aloft to intercept the attackers from Midway.

While this discussion was going on, Nagumo received a message from Rear Admiral Tamon Yamaguchi, commander of the two light carriers and a possible eventual successor to Yamamoto.

CONSIDER IT ADVISABLE TO LAUNCH ATTACK FORCE IMMEDIATELY.

Nagumo hesitated and finally turned to Genda in perplexity. The young commander had a new worry. He was anxiously watching the hordes of planes returning from Midway hover above their carriers. Many were obviously down to their last few gallons of gas. Several were smoking from hits. The fighters were also low on fuel after their successful defense against the three American attacks. They would have to accompany the attackers as cover or the whole operation might fail. Even if they had enough gas to reach the American force and protect the bombers, it was a certainty not a one would have enough to get home safely.

Genda pondered. Almost every one of the bomber and fighter pilots was a personal friend. He turned to Nagumo. "I believe all our aircraft should first land and refuel. Then we can launch the attack."

Taking his advice, Nagumo ordered the decks cleared so the waiting planes could land. One by one the planes on *Akagi*'s deck were lowered to their hangar. When there was enough space on the flight deck the tired Midway attackers began landing. By 8:55 A.M. although recovery of the Midway planes was still incomplete, Nagumo impatiently ordered by blinker:

AFTER COMPLETING RECOVERY OPERATIONS, FORCE WILL TEMPORARILY HEAD NORTHWARD. WE PLAN TO CONTACT AND DESTROY ENEMY TASK FORCE.

It wasn't until 9:18 A.M. that the last planes landed. Then Nagumo raised speed to 30 knots and turned sharply to the east-northeast, away from Midway. In the meantime, the 4 carriers had been feverishly rearming and refueling for attack. In addition to fighter escort, 36 dive bombers and 54 torpedo bombers would be thrown at the U.S. Pacific Fleet. Excitement increased. The big victory was approaching.

At 6:07 A.M. Fletcher had ordered Spruance to attack the enemy carriers as soon as they were definitely located. At first, Spruance planned to make his strikes at 9:00 A.M. when he'd be approximately 100 miles from his targets. When reports from Midway told of the heavy Japanese attack on that island Captain Miles Browning, the chief of staff Spruance had inherited from Halsey, vigorously pressed for an earlier attack. Browning, a temperamental but extremely perceptive man, pointed out that this might well catch the Japanese carriers while refueling their aircraft.

No two commanders could have been more different than Halsey and the man who had replaced him. Spruance, already known in the Navy as a "brain," was quiet, studious and thoughtful. He always projected himself into the future and was aggressive only when he thought it well worth the risk.

Halsey, like his army counterpart, George Patton, knew the value of publicity. Spruance, like Courtney Hodges, had a distaste for the public eye and did not enjoy being interviewed by correspondents. Consequently, little was known of him. Even to most of those on the *Enterprise* Spruance was enigmatic. He would pace the deck of his ship for several hours each day for exercise. In his cabin he would study charts covering areas of operations posted on the bulkhead.

To Spruance the Midway operation had resolved itself along these clear-cut lines: the Japanese had to be prevented from capturing Midway; since the enemy was probably much stronger, the Americans must retain the element of surprise and not be surprised; therefore, the Japanese carriers had to be hit at the earliest possible moment with everything available.

Spruance's first important decision was to take Browning's advice. His second was just as important: he ordered every operational plane, except patrol craft, to make the attack. At 7:02 A.M. they began leaving the two carriers: 60 dive bombers, 20 fighters and 29 torpedo planes. They would have barely enough fuel to return home, if lucky. Spruance had taken the chance Nagumo feared to.

Planes from the third American carrier, *Yorktown*, didn't start leaving until 8:38 A.M. By 9:06 A.M. 12 dive bombers, 6 fighters and 17 torpedo planes had left the deck of Fletcher's flagship and were winging toward Nagumo's Striking Force.

It was twelve minutes later that Nagumo made his abrupt turn to the north-northeast, away from Midway. Nagumo did this because he feared another air strike from Midway. He didn't realize, of course, that this sharp turn to the left was also turning the Striking Force away from the 144 American carrier planes now trying to find it.

A few minutes later *Hornet*'s 35 dive bombers and 10 fighters reached the point where they were supposed to intercept the Japanese carriers. The leader of these planes, Commander Stanhope Ring, saw only clouds to his right—Nagumo was behind them. Ring concluded that the Japanese had raised their speed and continued on toward Midway. And so he turned southeast, away from the enemy carriers.

Three groups of lumbering American torpedo planes were heading almost directly for Nagumo. The first to reach the Striking Force were the 15 unescorted torpedo planes from *Hornet*. They had not followed Ring toward Midway since their leader, Lieutenant Commander John Waldron, had a hunch the Japanese would do exactly what they had done.

Waldron was a seamy-faced, square-jawed man from South Dakota. One of his great-grandparents had been a Sioux Indian. His men looked like a band of Mexican revolutionaries, each wearing a .45 pistol under the left shoulder, another at the hip and a hunting knife.

The night before Waldron had written his wife, Adelaide:

I believe that we will be in battle very soon—I wish we were there today. But as we are up to the very eve of serious business, I wish to record to you that I am feeling fine. My own morale is excellent and from my continued observance of the squadron —their morale is excellent also. You may rest assured that I will go in with the expectation of coming back in good shape. If I do not come back—well, you and the little girls can know that

this squadron struck for the highest objective in naval warfare—
"to sink the enemy."

. . . . I love you and the children very dearly and I long to
be with you. But I could not be happy ashore at this time. My
place is here with the fight. . . .

Then he wrote another letter to his men:

. . . . My greatest hope is that we encounter a favorable tactical situation, but if we don't, and the worst comes to the worst,
I want each of us to do his utmost to destroy our enemies. If
there is only one plane left to make a final run in, I want that
man to go in and get a hit. May God be with all of us. Good
luck, happy landings and give 'em hell.

Below him to the right eight miles away lay the enemy carriers in a box-like formation. It was obvious they had seen
the glint of sunlight on the wings of Torpedo Squadron 8 for
all ships were zigzagging to avoid attack.

Anti-aircraft fire reached out from the ships screening the
four carriers. Then about 30 Zeros streaked toward the unprotected torpedo planes. Waldron waggled his wings, signal-
ing his men to follow, and headed forward at full speed.
Soon a plane plunged into the water.

"Was that a Zero?" Waldron asked his radioman in the
rear seat.

It was American. Moments later a second torpedo plane
went down. "Let's go back and help him, sir," Radioman
Robert Huntington suggested to his pilot, Ensign George Gay.

"To hell with that. We've got a job to do."

A third and fourth American plane pinwheeled into the
sea. Yet not one of the survivors wavered from his course,
continuing through the wall of anti-aircraft fire, even though
it was now apparent that chance of survival was almost impossible. The much faster Zeros were swooping down like
hawks on chickens.

Soon half of Torpedo Squadron 8 was dead. Still Waldron
bored in, followed by his gallant remnants. The barrage from
the ships became even heavier. The air was filled with acrid
black smoke.

Suddenly Gay saw his leader's plane burst into flames.
Waldron stood up and tried in vain to get out of the flaming
cockpit as it crashed into the waves.

Gay saw another comrade spin into the water and disappear. It reminded him of a day long ago when he was throwing orange peels from a speedboat. There were only two other
planes left: one to the left, one ahead and just below the nose

of his own plane. Gay lowered his plane's nose. There was nothing ahead. He looked to the left. Nothing. He was the only one left. He remembered Waldron's letter, the instructions for the last plane "to go in and get a hit."

He heard his radioman say, "Mr. Gay, I'm hit!"

"You hurt bad? Can you move?" When there was no answer Gay turned. Huntington's head hung limp. Gay felt a sharp jab in his upper left arm. There was a hole in his jacket sleeve. Shifting the stick to his left hand, he ripped the sleeve and pressed a bullet from the wound. When he tried to put it in his pocket as a souvenir, the safety belt held it shut. He put the bullet in his mouth.

He was approaching a carrier. It turned to starboard. Gay also swung to the right and pressed the button to release the white-nosed "pickle" under the belly of his plane. Nothing happened. Holding the stick between his knees, he pulled the emergency lever with his right hand and the torpedo dropped.

Less than half a mile from the carrier now, he executed a flip-over, skimming 10 feet over the big ship's bow. As he climbed and tried to turn back, several Zeros dove. His left rudder pedal was hit and he crashed into the water about 400 yards beyond the carrier.

As his plane sank he ripped open the hood and popped out. When he got to the surface he grabbed a black seat cushion and held it over his head. Two Japanese cruisers steamed past. Then a destroyer came so close he could see white-clad sailors pointing at him. It sped past without firing.

At that moment the 14 torpedo planes from *Enterprise* sighted the enemy carriers. Their leader, Lieutenant Commander Eugene Lindsey, circled, hoping to make a beam attack on *Kaga*. He, like Waldron, was also without fighter protection. With the same dedicated courage of Waldron's fliers, Lindsey's men ignored Zeros and anti-aircraft fire and hurtled directly at the Japanese carrier. The first ones didn't have a chance; in minutes Lindsey's plane and 9 others spun into the sea. This time 4 Americans broke through the barrage. They released their torpedoes but the carriers dodged them.

While the Japanese were recovering from these close calls, *Yorktown's* torpedo squadron, under Lieutenant Commander Lance Massey, appeared. Before it reached the carriers its 6 fighter escorts were swamped by Japanese interceptors. Like the other 2 squadrons, VT-3 bored in relentlessly, regardless of the consequences, just skimming the waves. Massey and 6 mates were shot down before they reached their target, *Hiryu*.

Five of his planes broke through and dropped torpedoes but only 2 planes survived.

The 5 torpedoes plowed toward the desperately dodging *Hiryu*. All missed. On *Akagi*, Nagumo and his officers were limp with relief. Though the attacks had completely failed and 35 of the 41 torpedo planes had been shot down, the dauntless courage of the American pilots had kept the issue in doubt to the end. It had been a thrilling drama to watch but the sudden silence was welcome.

The Americans had thrown their heaviest punches at Nagumo. Ten torpedo planes, 27 dive bombers and 15 Flying Fortresses from Midway and 41 torpedo planes from the *Enterprise, Yorktown* and *Hornet* had failed to score a single hit.

Now only the carrier dive bombers were left. If they failed, it could mean the end of the Pacific Fleet. The 35 dive bombers of *Hornet,* under Commander Ring, were already eliminated. The 17 dive bombers from the *Yorktown*, under Lieutenant Commander Maxwell F. Leslie, were to the southeast. If Leslie pursued his present course, he, like Ring, would miss the Japanese carriers, passing to their south.

The 37 dive bombers of the *Enterprise*, led by Lieutenant Commander Clarence McClusky, had taken off more than an hour before Leslie. When Nagumo made his abrupt turn to the left, McClusky, like Ring, had missed him, but when he continued and still could find nothing, McClusky decided to turn to the north.

At 9:55 A.M. he sighted the white trail of a Japanese destroyer, the *Arashi*, speeding northeast. Correctly guessing that *Arashi* was heading toward Nagumo's Striking Force, McClusky also turned. A moment later he heard an excited voice shouting over his radio telephone, "Attack! Attack!"

It was Captain Miles Browning, Spruance's chief of staff. It wasn't until a moment before that the *Enterprise* had learned Nagumo's carriers had been definitely located.

"Wilco," replied McClusky. "As soon as I find the bastards." He continued northeast for twenty minutes but nothing was in sight. His fuel was running low and in a minute he would have to give up the search and set course for home. It was 10:20 A.M.

At that same moment all of *Akagi*'s planes were on the flight deck, their engines warming up. The bombers of the other three carriers were also in position, neatly lined up.

"Launch when ready," ordered Nagumo. The carrier turned into the wind. Genda and the others on *Akagi*'s bridge felt much easier. In five minutes their planes would be in the air and winging toward the enemy carriers.

1 Just before Genda gave the order to launch, Lieutenant Commander Leslie, leader of the 17 *Yorktown* dive bombers, sighted smoke smudges on the horizon to his right. He signaled his squadron to turn to the northwest. For a few minutes the sea was blanketed by clouds. Then suddenly there was an opening and Leslie saw two Japanese carriers about 20,000 feet below.

One was relatively small, the *Soryu*; the other large. Since all the Japanese fighter planes had been drawn down to stop the three torpedo attacks, and hadn't yet regained altitude, Leslie had plenty of time to make his choice. Waldron and the others had not sacrificed their lives in vain. Leslie signaled his men by patting his head, then, with the bright morning sun at his back, pushed over in a steep dive on the bigger ship. It was probably the *Kaga*.

Leslie's own 1000-pound bomb had unfortunately been dumped by accident an hour earlier, but he led his men toward the target at a 70-degree angle. He could see dozens of planes ready for take-off as he aimed at a large red sun painted on the yellow flight deck.

Leslie began firing his machine guns at 10,000 feet. When they jammed at 4000 feet, he pulled up into a climb. Behind him, Lieutenant Paul "Lefty" Holmberg continued to dive. At 2500 feet, with the red sun directly in his sights, Holmberg pushed the bomb-release button, then instantly pulled back the emergency lever to make sure.

At that moment, McClusky's 37 dive bombers suddenly appeared from the southwest. Just as they were about to set course for home, they saw hundreds of square miles of ocean covered by carriers, battleships, cruisers and destroyers.

In addition to his own squadron, McClusky commanded those of Lieutenants Wilmer Earl Gallaher and Dick Best. McClusky saw two carriers turning into the wind to launch their planes. He ordered Best to attack the smaller one, the *Soryu*, while he and Gallaher took the other. By mistake three of Best's planes followed Gallaher and McClusky as they dove on the 27,000-ton *Akagi*.

Gallaher sighted on the flaming Rising Sun at the forward edge of the flight deck. From the day he saw the *Arizona* lying at her berth in Pearl Harbor, smoldering and smashed, he had dreamed of making a dive-bombing attack on a Japanese carrier. There was little anti-aircraft fire and no fighter resistance as he swept low. At about 1800 feet he released his bomb, then pulled up into a steep climb and kicked his plane around so he could watch the progress of the bomb. For months he had warned his pilots never to do this since it made the plane a sitting duck for anti-aircraft fire, but he was so sure his bomb was going to hit he couldn't resist the temptation. A moment later he saw it explode in the middle of the planes parked on the after part of *Akagi*'s flight deck. It was a moment of exultation. He thought, "*Arizona*, I remember you!"

A minute after Genda's order to launch had been signaled to the *Kaga* those on the bridge saw black dive bombers screaming out of the sun at them. This was Leslie's squadron. The first few bombs missed, then four struck in rapid succession, hitting the forward, middle and after sections of the flight deck. *Kaga* was soon raging with uncontrollable fires. She was obviously doomed.

The *Akagi* was also ablaze from several direct hits by the planes of McClusky and Gallaher. A huge hole had been blasted out of its flight deck. The amidship elevator was twisted like molten glass. Planes were standing rakishly, tails up, shooting out tongues of fire and black smoke. Flames jumped from plane to plane. Soon their torpedoes began to explode, driving away those trying to control the fire. The blazes spread to fuel and munition reserves carelessly stacked on deck. These exploded, tearing out great chunks of the ship and shaking the bridge.

In minutes the hangar area was in flames. As the fire spread toward the bridge, Rear Admiral Ryunosuke Kusaka, Nagumo's chief of staff, begged his chief to transfer his flag immediately to the light cruiser *Nagara*.

Nagumo, stricken by the sudden disaster, seemed dazed. "Sir," continued Kusaka, "most of our ships are intact. You must command them."

The admiral refused to budge from the bridge. The skipper of the ship, Captain Taijiro Aoki, also entreated him. "Admiral, I will take care of the ship. Please, we all implore you, shift your flag to *Nagara* and resume command of the Force."

When he still refused, Kusaka ordered several officers to

drag him by the hand. While the admiral was being half-pulled, half-persuaded, the flag secretary, Lieutenant Commander Nishibayashi, reported that all passages below were afire. Almost choked by clouds of smoke, Nagumo said good-bye to Captain Aoki and then, boosted by Nishibayashi, climbed out the bridge window and clambered down a rope to the deck.

The light carrier *Soryu*, Best's target, was also in flames. At 10:25 A.M. a bomb had dropped through its flight deck, exploding in the hangar. Second and third hits straddled the amidship elevator, blowing the deck to shreds. Fires spread, quickly reaching gasoline tanks and munition storage rooms. By 10:30 A.M. the 688-foot-long carrier was a fiery hell. Explosions rocked the ship, the main engines stopped. *Soryu* was soon helpless, its steering system out, its fire mains in shambles. By 10:45 A.M., seeing only a mass of flame, Captain Ryusaku Yanagimoto shouted, "Abandon ship!"

But he refused to leave his bridge. A Navy wrestling champion, Chief Petty Officer Abe, was picked to save the captain in spite of himself. Abe climbed up to the bridge through the black smoke. There he saw Captain Yanagimoto holding a sword and staring forward with resolution.

"Captain," said Abe, "I have come on behalf of all your men to take you to safety. They are waiting for you." The captain acted as if he hadn't heard. "Please come with me to the destroyer, sir." Abe approached the captain, hands outstretched.

Yanagimoto turned. His grim determination stopped Abe. The sailor, tears in his eyes, sadly turned around. As he started toward the deck he could hear Yanagimoto calmly singing "Kimigayo," the national anthem.

In a few minutes 54 American pilots had completely wrecked 3 carriers and turned the tide of the Pacific war. Out of Nagumo's 4 carriers, only *Hiryu* was left. It was up to the aggressive Admiral Yamaguchi, once a student at Princeton, to carry on the duel with the U.S. Pacific Fleet. He gave immediate orders to strike back. At 10:45 A.M. 6 Zero fighters and 18 dive bombers took off, led by Lieutenant Michio Kobayashi. The planes headed in the general direction of the American carriers at 13,000 feet. Soon Kobayashi spotted groups of American dive bombers apparently returning to their mother ship. He signaled his pilots to lay behind. They would follow the homing planes to their roost.

This was Fletcher's flagship, *Yorktown*, the scarred veteran of Coral Sea.

Just before noon, as Leslie's dive bombers, fresh from their great victory over *Kaga*, were preparing to land, *Enterprise*'s radar indicated 30 to 40 enemy planes about 40 miles to the west-southwest. Leslie's dive bombers were waved off and a combat patrol sent off to intercept the approaching raiders.

"The attack is coming in, sir," warned Admiral Fletcher's aide.

The admiral looked up from the chart he was studying. "Well, I've got on my tin hat. I can't do anything else now." He returned to his work.

The Wildcats threw themselves so fiercely at Kobayashi's formation that only 8 Japanese dive bombers broke through. These raced toward the dodging *Yorktown*. Two were quickly shot down by anti-aircraft fire, but 6 dropped their bombs.

The recently repaired *Yorktown* was hit 3 times. The first struck the flight deck, setting fires below. The sprinkler system and water curtains put out the blazes almost instantly, then a second bomb exploding in the smokestack started other fires and knocked out two boilers. The final bomb only ignited a rag-storage compartment.

By 12:20 P.M., with 5 of the ship's 6 boiler fires out, *Yorktown* was at a standstill; but damage control parties worked so fast that the big ship was steaming at 18 knots by 1:40 P.M. As she was refueling her fighter planes, warning came of new raiders only 40 miles away.

Twelve Wildcats sped out to do battle. They ran into more planes from Yamaguchi's *Hiryu*: 10 torpedo planes and 6 fighters. The Zeros tied up the Wildcats while the 10 torpedo planes raced, unhindered, toward the *Yorktown*. At 2:32 P.M. they split up and began to make runs from various directions.

Though 5 raiders were shot down, 4 torpedoes were dropped. The sluggish *Yorktown* dodged 2, but 2 others tore into the damaged carrier. With rudder jammed and all power connections severed the big ship listed 17 degrees. When the list increased Captain Elliott Buchmaster was afraid his ship was going to capsize at any minute and just before 3:00 P.M. ordered, "Abandon ship."

There were still 2 American carriers intact, Admiral Spruance's *Enterprise* and *Hornet*. At 3:30 P.M. Spruance ordered dive bombers to make their second strike of the day. Since McClusky had been wounded in the arm on his trip home from the morning attack, Lieutenant Gallaher commanded the group. The 24 dive bombers took off without a single fighter and headed toward *Hiryu*. Spruance then informed Fletcher, who had transferred his flag to the heavy cruiser, *Astoria*, what he had done and asked:

DO YOU HAVE ANY INSTRUCTIONS FOR ME?

Since Spruance had 2 carriers and he had none, Fletcher decided to let his subordinate have a free hand. He replied:

NONE. WILL CONFORM TO YOUR MOVEMENTS.

The first word of the great battle had come to Yamamoto at 10:50 that morning when the Main Force was about 700 miles northwest of Midway. The radio message was wordlessly handed to the admiral by the chief signal officer, Commander Yushiro Wada:

FIRES RAGING ABOARD KAGA, SORYU, AND AKAGI RESULTING FROM ATTACKS BY ENEMY CARRIERS AND LAND-BASED PLANES. WE PLAN TO HAVE HIRYU ENGAGE ENEMY CARRIERS. WE ARE TEMPORARILY WITHDRAWING TO THE NORTH TO ASSEMBLE OUR FORCES.

Yamamoto couldn't believe such an immense disaster had struck so suddenly. Unable to speak, he groaned. Finally he said, "Is Genda all right?"

The stern-faced commander soon got control of himself. He knew there was only one hope: to gather all his forces and crush the Pacific Fleet by sheer power. He ordered Admiral Kondo to detach part of his powerful force to cover the invasion transports in their temporary retreat to the northwest. The remainder plus Kakuta's Second Carrier Striking Force, far north near the Aleutians, were to join Nagumo's depleted force as soon as possible. His own Main Force, spearheaded by the battleships *Yamato*, *Mutsu* and *Nagato*, also steamed full speed toward the battle area. It was a potent force. The 63,700-ton flagship, *Yamato*, was the world's mightiest warship. Her main battery of giant 18.11-inch guns alone could hurtle a broadside of 13 tons of steel.

With this force Yamamoto still thought he could destroy the U.S. Fleet and seize Midway.

This optimism was not felt on board *Nagara*, Admiral Nagumo's new flagship. The admiral and his staff were still depressed by the morning's catastrophe. His operations officer, Commander Genda, was already analyzing the reasons, coming to the objective conclusion that he had made two mistakes. First, he should have sent out a two-phase search early that morning; second, and more important, he should have launched the strike on the American carriers immediately without waiting for the Midway planes to land. He had been thinking as a pilot, not a commander; he had been influenced by fear of condemning friends to death. The man who was destined to become Japan's postwar chief of the Air Self-Defense Force had learned there is no friendship in battle.

Not far away on the carrier *Hiryu*, all planes had returned from the second *Yorktown* attack by 4:30 P.M. From pilots' reports Admiral Yamaguchi believed his 2 strikes had hit different targets and that 2 American carriers had been destroyed. Just before 5:00 P.M. he ordered his men to prepare for another strike. The airmen still on General Quarters were relieved and served sweet rice balls. As they began eating, Yamaguchi ordered a fast plane to search out the enemy's "last" carrier. The search plane was rolled into position at 5:03 P.M. Just then a lookout yelled, "Enemy dive bombers!"

Everyone on the bridge looked to the southwest and saw a terrifying sight. Lieutenant Gallaher's 24 dive bombers were darting out of the sinking sun. As Gallaher's planes screeched in a steep dive, several Zero fighters swooped down, picking off one American. The others continued hurtling toward the *Hiryu*. Gallaher was sure he had the carrier cold. Then it made a sudden sharp turn in the opposite direction. Gallaher pulled out of his dive sharply in an attempt to throw his bomb at the dodging ship but it fell 50 feet astern. Those behind Gallaher had more time and soon four bombs exploded in rapid succession near the bridge. Fires quickly spread from plane to plane.

"Look at that bastard burn!" said Gallaher over his radio. Every carrier in Nagumo's Striking Force was ablaze and sinking. A large percentage of Japan's best fliers were dead—and irreplaceable.

Gallaher himself was in trouble. He had injured his back in the abrupt pull-up and by the time he brought his group back to the *Enterprise*, he was in such pain he couldn't reach down to lower the hook designed to catch in one of the retarding wires stretched across the carrier's flight deck. He turned over the lead to his number 2 wing man and circled while the others landed.

He knew he couldn't land aboard without the hook. If he ditched in the water he was afraid he wouldn't be able to get out of the plane. He forced himself to put down the hook, almost passing out from pain. He approached the *Enterprise* as slowly as possible. Suddenly there was an explosion of pain as the hook caught and his plane jerked to a stop. He taxied into his parking spot. He was lifted tenderly out of the cockpit. It was the end of the battle for Gallaher.

With *Yorktown* out of action, Nimitz put command of future American attacks completely in Spruance's hands. Although Spruance knew heavy damage had been dealt Nagumo, he wasn't sure how badly the 4 Japanese carriers had been hit. By evening he had intercepted a message from 12 Flying Fortresses which had bombed, and missed, the blazing *Hiryu* about an hour after Gallaher's strike. They reported Zeros in the area. These were homeless *Hiryu* planes fighting until their tanks ran dry but Spruance had to consider the possibility of a fifth carrier.

He remembered Nimitz's "calculated risk" instructions. Was he justified in risking a night encounter with possibly superior forces, knowing the Japanese were superior to Americans at this kind of action? If he were the skipper of this possible fifth Japanese carrier what would he do? He certainly wouldn't continue on the same course. He'd probably go west.

Spruance decided not to risk a night action, figuring that this was probably what the Japanese high command was hoping he would do. Instead he slowed Task Force 16 to 15 knots to conserve fuel and headed back east. Later, since he wanted to be in air-supporting distance of Midway in case the Japanese decided to push their attack on that island, he would reverse his course.

It was now dark, the vast sea battleground a flaming graveyard. The *Soryu* tilted. Watching from destroyers were her survivors. At 7:13 P.M. the carrier dove out of sight. With her went 718 corpses and one live man, Captain Yanagimoto.

About 40 miles to the south another burning hulk was being torn by two great explosions. This was *Kaga*, and a few minutes later she and 800 of her crew were swallowed up.

While the water above the vanished *Soryu* was still bubbling, Yamamoto was sending out a message to all his scattered forces designed to bolster sagging morale:

(1) THE ENEMY FLEET HAS BEEN PRACTICALLY DE-
STROYED AND IS RETIRING EASTWARD.

(2) COMBINED FLEET UNITS IN THE VICINITY ARE
PREPARING TO PURSUE THE REMNANTS OF THE ENEMY
FORCE AND, AT THE SAME TIME, TO OCCUPY MIDWAY.

(3) THE MAIN BODY WILL REACH CBJ ° 08'N, 175 °
45'E AT 0300 ON THE 5TH. COURSE, 090 °; SPEED, 20
KNOTS.

(4) THE CARRIER STRIKING FORCE, INVASION FORCE

(LESS CRUISER DIVISION 7), AND SUBMARINE FORCE WILL
IMMEDIATELY CONTACT AND ATTACK THE ENEMY.

Yamamoto and his staff still had not lost hope of crushing
the Pacific Fleet, their main objective, but even the most
eager of his officers was dismayed when a message from the
shaken Nagumo arrived at 9:30 P.M.:

> TOTAL ENEMY STRENGTH IS 5 CARRIERS, 6 HEAVY
> CRUISERS, AND 15 DESTROYERS. THEY ARE STEAMING
> WESTWARD. WE ARE RETIRING TO THE NORTHWEST ES-
> CORTING HIRYU. SPEED, 18 KNOTS.

When this inaccurate message was read Rear Admiral
Matone Ugaki, the chief of staff, said with disgusted gloom,
"The Nagumo Force has no stomach for a night engagement."

As time passed it was obvious that the Americans were not
steaming west but doing just what Yamamoto had prayed
they wouldn't do—backing away from a night action. By
midnight all hope that Spruance's surviving carriers could be
lured into an engagement was gone.

Now Yamamoto's staff began considering the most desperate and impractical schemes and Captain Kameto Kuro-
shima, senior Fleet operations officer, even drew up a tentative
plan to shell Midway with all battleships.

"The stupidity of engaging such shore installations with a
surface force ought to be clear to you," was Admiral Ugaki's
answer to this wild proposal. "The battleships would be sunk
by air and submarine attacks before they moved in close
enough to use their guns." He suggested they postpone another
air strike until the Second Carrier Striking Force from the
Aleutians joined them. "But even if that proves impossible
and we must accept defeat in this operation, we will not have
lost the war. There are still 8 carriers in the Fleet. So we
should not lose heart. In battle, as in chess, it is the fool who
lets himself be led into a reckless move through desperation."

Some of the officers were willing to gamble anything to
save face. "How can we apologize to His Majesty for this
defeat?" asked one.

Yamamoto, silent until now, had made up his mind. He
said sharply, "Leave that to me. I am the only one who must
apologize to His Majesty." Fifteen minutes after midnight he
ordered Kondo and Nagumo to turn west and join the Main
Force.

A few hours later he faced another problem new to the
Japanese Navy. The *Akagi*, its fires long out of control, had to

be scuttled. Its skipper, Captain Aoki, had already requested permission to sink her and then lashed himself to the carrier's anchor. Yamamoto reluctantly approved and soon 4 destroyers were sending torpedoes into the great ship.

The last carrier, *Hiryu*, was also reaching the end of its career. Dead in the water, its engine rooms were raging with uncontrollable fires. The former Princeton student, the indomitable Yamaguchi, finally gave up hope and ordered all men topside at 2:30 A.M., June 5. Then he solemnly addressed the 800 survivors. "As commanding officer of this carrier division I am fully and solely responsible for the loss of *Hiryu* and *Soryu*. I shall remain on board to the end. I command all of you to leave the ship and continue your loyal service to His Majesty, the Emperor."

Though his staff pleaded, he would not let them stay on board with him. They all drank a silent toast in water. The admiral said he had no farewell messages and gave his senior staff officer, Commander Ito, his black deck cap as a memento. He took from Ito a length of cloth. Everyone knew he would use it to lash himself to the bridge.

Captain Tomeo Kaku made a last appeal to Yamaguchi to leave the ship. The admiral only smiled and shook his head, but didn't protest when the skipper took his place beside him on the bridge.

Before dawn of June 5 misfortune continued to dog Yamamoto. The heavy cruisers, *Mogami* and *Mikuma*, collided. Not long after dawn a Midway-based Catalina sighted the 2 lagging ships and 6 Marine dive bombers and 6 Vindicators took off from Midway. They followed an oil slick and at 8:05 A.M. attacked the 2 cruisers. Anti-aircraft was so heavy and accurate that not a bomb went home but Captain Richard Fleming purposely dove his burning plane into one of *Mikuma*'s after turrets.

That afternoon Ensign Gay, the only survivor of Waldron's torpedo squadron, was picked up by a Catalina. When a doctor asked how he had treated his wounds Gay replied, "Soaked 'em in salt water for ten hours."

The next day, June 6, action resumed almost as soon as the sun rose on a cloudless sky. *Enterprise* search planes sighted the two slow-moving cruisers which had helped sink *Perth* and *Houston*. Spruance launched three attacks, finally sinking *Mikuma*. Though *Mogami* was smashed by six bombs, damage control parties saved the badly wounded ship and she limped safely to the west.

In the meantime the Japanese were also striking. At about

11:00 A.M. Lieutenant Commander Yahachi Tanabe was standing on the bridge of his submarine I-168, searching the sea. Suddenly he saw a dot on the sea. He decided to approach on the surface and investigate. The speck grew larger. When he was six miles away a thrill went through him. It was the *Yorktown*! He'd received a message that it was drifting, listing to port, and he should find and destroy it. Though his boat was in poor condition with chlorine gas seeping from the damaged bow torpedo room, he decided to attack. He submerged and approached.

Through his periscope he could see about 7 destroyers darting around the big ship. He dove, passing under the carrier, then reversed and took another look. Now, though he heard many sounds on sonar, he could see no destroyers—only the *Yorktown* looming up like some huge, prehistoric monster. He slowly maneuvered into position.

At 1:30 P.M. he was ready. From a depth of 57 feet he cautiously approached the carrier. When he was 1300 yards away he launched 2 torpedoes. Three seconds later he fired 2 more. Without waiting, he dove to 100 feet. Suddenly everyone on the submarine felt three tremendous jars. The crew shouted, "Banzai!" They were wild with excitement. They had scored 3 hits.

"Shut up," shouted Tanabe. The slightest noise inside a submarine could be picked up. A sailor brought him cider.

One of Tanabe's torpedoes had hit the destroyer *Hammann*. She broke in two, sinking within four minutes. The other two hits were on the *Yorktown*. Her death was lingering. Hours later some of her crew were still hopelessly trapped in submerged compartments. An officer finally made contact by phone with one of these compartments. "Do you know what kind of a fix you're in?" he asked.

A voice from under the sea answered, "Sure, but we've got a hell of a good acey-deucey game down here. One thing though, when you scuttle her, aim the torpedoes right where we are. We want it to be quick."

Before she could be scuttled the *Yorktown* rolled over on her port side and, just after dawn the next day, sank with all battle flags flying. As she slid out of sight, men on nearby destroyers stood by at attention with hats off.

An hour and a half after Tanabe launched his torpedoes, Yamamoto was still desperately trying to salvage victory. At 3:00 P.M. he ordered all ships:

COMBINED FLEET UNITS OPERATING IN THIS AREA WILL

CATCH AND DESTROY THE ENEMY TASK FORCE WITHIN AT-
TACK RANGE OF AIR FORCES BASED ON WAKE ISLAND.

It was a useless gesture. The wily Spruance, the happiest
choice as a replacement for Halsey that Nimitz could have
made, refused to be lured into a battle in which he would be
heavily outgunned. Yamamoto realized this the next morning, June 7, and dejectedly headed back toward Japan.

One of the greatest sea battles in history was over. It had
been won by a unique combination of Japanese mistakes, a
broken code, brilliant command decisions, and the courageous determination of men like Waldron, Gay, Leslie, Mc-
Clusky and Gallaher.

The Japanese Navy had been dealt an unexpected defeat
and with one stroke America had seized control of the Pacific Ocean. Though some criticized him for being premature,
Admiral Nimitz was essentially right when he said in his
communiqué of June 6:

> Pearl Harbor has now been partially avenged. Vengeance will
> not be complete until Japanese sea power is reduced to impotence.
> We have made substantial progress in that direction. Perhaps we
> will be forgiven if we claim that we are about midway to that ob-
> jective.

2   Coupled with the repulse of the Port Moresby
invasion in the Coral Sea, the Midway triumph gave Australians their first real sense of security.

The victory put the spotlight on the Pacific. The period of
withdrawal and holding in this area was over. For the first
time since Pearl Harbor the Allies were in a position to attack.

MacArthur, insisting that the tide had turned, pressed his
demands for an all-out surprise attack on Rabaul. Now he
had two fresh American divisions, the 32nd and the 41st, as
well as the battle-tested Australian 7th. He was impatient to
start on the road back to the Philippines.

In the Philippines many were preparing for his return.
Spontaneously, hundreds of leaders—Americans, Filipinos,
civilian and military—were forming guerrilla bands. Others
were already organizing intricate spy rings.

High in the Zambales Mountains, not far from Clark Field,
two American civilians, William Fassoth and his twin brother,

Martin, had set up an elaborate rescue camp for many American escapees of the Death March. Here came Sergeants Ray Hunt and Frank Bernacki. Here also came Major Russel Volckmann, Captain Donald Blackburn and more than 200 other American officers and men, half-dead from starvation and disease.

The Fassoths, sugar planters since 1913, had only one purpose: to bring their gaunt, sick charges back to health. But most of the Americans were not merely interested in hiding in the mountains until MacArthur returned. Men like Hunt, Volckmann and Blackburn were already making plans to form groups, steal arms from the Japanese and start their own private wars.

To the north, in the mountains near Baguio, two groups had been operating for months. One was commanded by a Filipino, Lieutenant Colonel Guillermo Z. Nakar. The other, originally organized by Colonel John Horan, was now led by the former miner, Walter Cushing. Striking like lightning, the redoubtable and volatile Cushing was the man most wanted by the Japanese in Luzon.

Far to the south in the island of Cebu his brother, Jim, also an ex-miner as well as ex-boxer, was building his own legend as the most capable and daring of the many leaders in the Visayan Islands. Nearby Panay was being well organized by General Chynoweth's former operations officer, Macario Peralta, Jr. And farther south, in Mindanao, hundreds of Filipinos and Americans were beginning to form a guerrilla army of formidable proportions that would soon be led by one of General Casey's engineers, Colonel Wendell Fertig. One of the most effective of these groups was the band of fierce Moros under Major Salipala Pendatun, formerly a Moro lawyer.

Civilians were also busy undermining the uneasy regime of General Homma. Dr. Romeo Atienza, medical director of the Philippine Red Cross, was risking his life daily to smuggle medicine, food and messages to the starving, disease-ridden prisoners of Camp O'Donnell. Here 370 Americans and Filipinos were dying every day. The tragic toll would have been much higher but for Atienza, his wife and their helpers.

Atienza's principal support came from a group of men and women organized by a remarkable woman, Mrs. John Utinsky, wife of one of the prisoners. Using such *noms de guerre* as "Miss U" (Mrs. Utinsky), Dr. A (Atienza), Morning Glory (Father Loler), High Pockets (Mrs. Claire Phillips), Fahny (Fanny Greenwell) and Sparky (Ramon Amusategui), this improvised organization brought life and hope to men who thought they had been abandoned and forgotten.

The islands were far from conquered. All over the Philippines men and women and even children were plotting against the Japanese, working and waiting for the coming of the man they knew would keep his word: MacArthur.

3   In Japan the real facts of the Battle of Midway were hidden by Imperial Headquarters from leading officials as well as the public. Survivors of sunken ships were kept isolated and the battle was being celebrated as one of the empire's greatest victories. On June 11 the *Asahi Shimbun* carried this announcement from Imperial Headquarters:

MIDWAY DETERMINES PACIFIC WAR SITUATION

As a result of the Battle of Midway, the United States has lost almost all her carriers and Japan has secured supreme power in the Pacific. Our suicide method of letting the enemy slice our flesh while we cleave them in two brought us success in this great sea battle of carrier against carrier. . . .

This well-fought battle helps eliminate our anxiety in the future. The situation of the Pacific War was indeed determined in this one battle.

To celebrate the great triumph enthusiastic citizens of Tokyo staged a flag procession and a lantern parade.

There was one Japanese who was not celebrating. This was Ensign Kazuo Sakamaki, the only survivor of the submarine attack on Pearl Harbor, now in a POW camp in Tennessee. (His midget submarine was being toured around the United States to spur the War Bond drive.) From the day Sakamaki had entered the Japanese Naval Academy every moment had been devoted to strict conditioning of mind and body, preventing him from understanding any human being except other fanatic servants of the Emperor.

But his few months of captivity had done a curious thing. In spite of himself he had gradually come to admire and respect Americans. This realization had come like a hammer blow against the heart of his whole past. The entire history and culture of Japan out of which he had been born had abruptly collapsed. It had been, he realized, the rebirth of reason.

What he read about Midway in American newspapers, he believed. After the countless factories he had seen on his recent trip down the Mississippi from Camp McCoy, Wisconsin, he knew the United States was just starting to fight. He was sure that Midway was the beginning of the end of Japan' hope of conquest.

It was. Midway was more than victory. Like a boxer who has swung wildly with an all-out punch and missed, Japan was wide open, vulnerable. By now the "Arsenal of Democracy" was in full production. No longer would Allied pilot have to fight the Zero with obsolete planes. No longer would Japanese tanks have to be stopped with gasoline-filled Coca Cola bottles, grenades or rifles.

The first six months of the war in the Pacific had been fought by poorly trained, ill-equipped and, in many cases ineptly led soldiers and sailors. These men had been flung into battle without knowing the true nature of their enemies They had been forced to fight with bullets, fuel and food strictly budgeted. That they were forced into a series of disastrous retreats and humiliating surrenders was no fault of theirs. It is true they often fought to no avail; but not in shame.

Nor did their military leaders deserve the calumny many critics were already heaping on them. The essential blame for the disasters of these six months should not have been laid on Kimmel, Short, MacArthur, Percival, Wavell or Helfrich; even less on the political leaders, Roosevelt and Churchill, who had been begging for arms long before battle came. The entire peoples of America and Great Britain were responsible for the scandalous state of unpreparedness in the Far East.

After the Battle of Midway the crisis was over in the Pacific. The war here, however, would not turn into a simple parade of easy victories. The Allies would have to dig out a deeply entrenched and tenacious enemy in a series of costly battles of extermination. With Nimitz and MacArthur sharing command, the new-won Japanese empire would shrink island by island: Guadalcanal, New Georgia, Bougainville, New Britain, New Guinea, the Philippines, Tinian, Saipan, Iwo Jima. And finally in 1945 the Allies would produce the atom bomb.

When Sakamaki learned of Hiroshima and Nagasaki he was overwhelmed—and repentant. "We fought and lost," he told himself. "We cannot blame others. We cannot complain. It is all our fault. It was we who were weak, inadequate and ignorant. We must rebuild our country with our own hands in silence. That is the only way we can pay our debts."

The past must not be forgotten, or even forgiven—only understood.

Acknowledgments

To gather material for this book it was necessary to travel more than 75,000 miles and visit eight countries. The majority of the almost 800 people interviewed do not appear in the book, but the accounts of such people were invaluable. Without knowing their stories, a full understanding of the events would sometimes have been impossible.

For example, I spent many hours in half a dozen interviews with Colonel William L. Osborne. He fought with the 51st Infantry on Bataan, then escaped in a small boat with Lieutenant Mabini Fontanilla across Manila Bay. After being hidden for months by Fontanilla and other Filipinos, Osborne and Captain Damon Gause sailed a small boat to Australia. Theirs was the first personal information MacArthur's intelligence officers had from the Philippines since the surrender of Corregidor. Yet, because of space limitations, not a line of Osborne's saga appears in this book. Air General Shu-ming "Tiger" Wang, Claire Chennault's intelligence officer, told how the Flying Tigers were often alerted promptly by three captured Japanese disguised as Chinese radio operators whenever enemy raiders approached. It is a fascinating inside story, never even revealed to Chennault himself, but had to be cut from the final draft.

Libraries contributed greatly to the book: the Historical Archives in Alexandria, Virginia; the library of the Office of the Chief of Military History, Department of the Army, Washington, D.C.; the Library of Congress; the library of the Naval History Division, Washington, D.C.; the Air University Library at Maxwell Air Force Base; the Main Branch of the New York Public Library; the U.S. Army Infantry School Library at Fort Benning, Georgia (Miss Ruth Wesley); the Diet Library, Tokyo; and the Red Bank, N.J., Public Library.

Numerous agencies, organizations and individuals made this book possible. To list them all would be impossible but here are a few:

Washington, D.C.: Major General William Quinn, Brigadier General Chester Clifton, Colonel Sidney Williams, Lieutenant Colonel John Chesebro and Major R. F. Prentiss of the Office, Chief of Information, U.S. Army; Major James F. Sunderman and Alice Martin, Magazine and Book Branch of the U.S. Air Force; Major Ben Fern and Edith Midgette, Office of News Services, Department of Defense; Commander Russell L. Bufkins, Magazine and Book Branch, U.S. Navy; Rear Admiral E. M. Eller, Director, Naval History Division; Judge Israel Wice; Lieutenant Colonel and Mrs. Herbert Trattner; General Carlos Romulo; and Roger Pineau.

Philippines: President Carlos P. Garcia; Secretary of National Defense Alejo Santos; Lieutenant General Manuel Cabal, Chief of Staff, Armed Forces of the Philippines; Major General Pelagio A. Cruz, Vice Chief of Staff, Armed Forces of the Philippines; Brigadier General Isogami Campo, Chief of the Philippine Constabulary; Brigadier General Pedro Molina, Commanding General, Philippine Air Force; Commodore Jose Francisco, Philippine Navy; Brigadier General Tirso Fajardo, Commanding General, Philippine Army; Lieutenant Colonel Wilfredo Encarnacion, Constabulary Commander of Iloilo; Major José Reyna, SEATO; Lieutenant Hanover D. Gloria, PIO, Camp Crame; Lieutenant Fernando Edralin, Philippine Navy; Lieutenant Aurelio Repato, PAF Historical Officer; Major Samuel Quiwa, Camp Olivas, Luzon; Lieutenant Colonel Leo Gaffney, JUSMAG; Dr. W. T. T. Ward, Historian, 405th Fighter Wing, Clark Field; H. J. H. C. Hildreth, Shell Company of the Philippines.

Hong Kong: Forrest Edwards and Roy Essayan, AP; Leo Landau of Jimmy's Kitchen; Joe Lowe; Irving Hoffman.

Taiwan: Dr. Sampson Shen, Yu Wei, and Robert C. H. Liao of the Government Information Office; Lieutenant General P. C. Yu, Vice-Chief of General Staff; Spencer Mousa, AP; Major Kenneth Weber and Technical Sergeant C. W. Curry, MAAG; H. S. "Newsreel" Wong.

Japan: Lieutenant General Robert W. Burns, Commander, United States Forces in Japan; Colonel Ray Vandiver, Captain Ben Scarpero, Isaac Taira and Dr. Kazutaka Watanabe of the Office of Information Service, Fifth Air Force; CM Sergeant Thomas Rhone, Master Gunnery Sergeant Alan Sydow, Master Sergeant Art Hicks, A2C Stewart Diamond, Toki Koizumi (the grandson of Lafcadio Hearn) and Miss Yasuko Hoshiba of the Press Liaison Office at the Sanno Hotel; Sol Sanders, *McGraw-Hill World News*; Igor Oganesoff, *Wall Street Journal*; Count Ian Mutsu; Captain Sanematsu; Captain Tsunoda; Colonel Takushiro Hattori; Captain Susumu Nishiura, Chief of War History Office, Defense Agency; General Moriya Wada, Army Staff Office; General Takeo

Imai; Tokiji Matsumura; Dr. Keigo Okonogi; Mrs. Saburo Kurusu; and Mrs. Masaharu Homma.

Hawaii: General Emmett O'Donnell, Jr., Commander in Chief, Pacific Air Force; Colonel C. B. Whitehead and Major Alfred J. Lynn of Cincpacaf; Commander Herbert Gimpel, Anne Kelly and the many others at Fourteenth Naval District who were so cooperative; Rear Admiral Ernest Holtzworth.

Guam: Lieutenant Commander George York and Francisco Q. Cruz.

Wake: The anonymous Air Force captain who lent me his truck for a day to explore the atoll.

Others include Colonel Laurence H. Macauley and Dr. Albert Simpson of the Air University; Dr. Robert F. Futrell, Air Force Historian, Pacific; Colonel James Chesnutt, Presidio, San Francisco; Mr. and Mrs. Malcolm Champlin, Oakland, California; Florence Clark and Janet Ludwick of Los Angeles; Mr. and Mrs. Lawrence Dugan, Philadelphia; Charles Dornbusch, New York Public Library; Audrey Sinclair, London, England; Mr. and Mrs. Pete Upton, Lubbock, Texas; Colonel Ray O'Day, Seattle, Washington; Franklin Trammell, of the American Guerrillas of Mindanao, San Diego, California; Dr. Louis Morton, Dartmouth College; Stephan de Voogd, Netherlands Information Service, New York; and Paul R. Richter, of the American Ex-Prisoners of War, San Antonio, Texas.

I would like also to thank my typists, Edith Lentz and Helen Toland, my chief interpreter and translator, Toshiko Toland, and John Jamieson and Professor Fred Stocking for their encouragement and advice. Finally, this book could not have been written without my editor, Robert Loomis, who gave me the basic idea, and my agent, Rogers Terrill.

The main sources for each chapter are listed later with explanatory details. Those books which proved of great value in numerous chapters, and will not be listed again, are: *The Fall of the Philippines* by Dr. Louis Morton; *The Rising Sun in the Pacific* by Samuel Eliot Morison; *Battle Report: Pearl Harbor to Coral Sea* by Walter Karig and others; *The Japanese Thrust* by Lionel Wigmore; *Grand Alliance* and *Hinge of Fate* by Winston Churchill; *They Fought with What They Had* by Walter D. Edmonds; *General Wainwright's Story* by Jonathan Wainwright; *The Good Fight* by Manuel Quezon; and *MacArthur and the War Against Japan* by Frazier Hunt.

Dr. Morton's book, a rare combination of scholarship and readability, was indispensable.

Japanese documentary material came from a group of histories written by Japanese Army and Navy officers at the direction of the Intelligence Officer, U.S. Far East Command; the collection of the Allied Translator and Interpreter Section; numerous monographs prepared by the Japanese Research Division of the Military History Section, U.S. General Headquarters, Far East; and the 30 volumes of testimony of Homma's trial. More important were the 123 interviews with Japanese war veterans and civilians. Many of these were arranged by Captain Susumu Nishiura, Chief of the War History Office, Japanese Defense Agency. Conferences of experts and participants were held on every campaign. Captain Nishiura and Captain Tsunoda were present at all these as advisers and Captain Sanematsu acted as interpreter. Without the full cooperation of all these men many revealing stories of the war would still be untold. Captain Nishiura's office is presently working on an authoritative history of the war, a ten-year project. When finished it should be a major contribution to war history.

PROLOGUE

This was based primarily on interviews with Colonel Takushiro Hattori, former private secretary to Prime Minister Tojo; Mrs. Saburo Kurusu, widow of the Special Envoy; Admiral Kichisaburo Nomura; and the following books: *On Active Service in Peace and War* by Henry L. Stimson and McGeorge Bundy; *Back Door to War* by Charles Tansill; *Kishi and Japan* by Dan Kurzman; *The Cause of Japan* by Shigenori Togo; *Chief of Staff: Prewar Plans and Preparations* by Mark Watson; *Japan Fights for Asia* by John Goette; *The Road to Pearl Harbor* by Herbert Feis; and *Political Strategy Prior to Outbreak of War* by Rear Admiral Sadatoshi Tomioka.

CHAPTER 1

Of the many interviewed on these fateful hours the most important were: Admirals Nomura, W. W. Smith, Harold Stark, C. C. Bloch, Colonel Hattori, Captain Nishiura, Sergeant Frank Trammell, Brigadier Generals Paul Putnam and James P. S. Devereux, Sergeant Lorenzo Alvarado, and Kazuo Sakamaki. The information concerning the lone Japanese Navy spy in Hawaii, Takeo Yoshikawa, came from Lieutenant Colonel Norman Stanford, USMC, Naval Attaché at the U.S. Embassy in Tokyo. An article on Yoshikawa by Stanford appeared in the December, 1960, issue of *U.S. Naval Institute Proceedings*. Further information came from a series of articles by Yoshikawa himself in the Mainichi *Daily News*. He is now living on Shikoku Island and manages a gas station near Matsuyama. George Elliott's story of the radar contact came directly from him, his testimony at the Pearl Harbor investigation and an interview in the Red Bank, N.J. *Register*, Dec. 7, 1959, by Art Kamin. Information concerning the visit of Admiral Phillips to the Philippines came from Rear Admiral W. G. Lalor and Vice Admiral F. A. Rockwell. The reactions of President Roosevelt to the message brought on the eve of Pearl Harbor are based on Kramer's testimony and Robert E. Sherwood's *Roosevelt and Hopkins*.

Books include: *On Active Service in Peace and War* by Stimson and Bundy; *The Lost War* by Masuo Kato; *Day of Infamy* by Walter Lord; the 40 volumes of the U.S. Congressional investigation; *Admiral Kimmel's Story* by Admiral Husband Kimmel; *What Happened at Pearl Harbor?* edited by Hans Louis Trefousse; *The Final Secret of Pearl Harbor* by Rear Admiral Robert Theobald; *Admiral Halsey's Story* by William Halsey; *The Cause of Japan* by Togo; *This Is Pearl* by Walter Millis; and *Sunk* by Mochitsura Hashimoto.

CHAPTER 2

Those interviewed included Robert Overstreet, Ordnanceman 3rd Class Donald Briggs, Admirals Bloch and Smith, 1st Class Metalsmith Lawrence Chappell, Yeoman C. O. Lines, Rear Admiral Ernest Holtzworth, Major General Richard Carmichael, Colonel William Welch, Ensign Wilbert Cain, Admiral Chester Nimitz, Sergeant Jesse Gaines and Dr. Wang Shih-chieh. To familiarize myself with the scene I flew over Oahu several times, following the routes of the invasion planes. In addition to touring Pearl Harbor, I was taken by destroyer through the harbor mouth to the scene of Lieutenant Outerbridge's experiences.

CHAPTER 3

Because of its controversial nature 85 people were interviewed on the Clark Field attack. A few of these were: Colonel William Morse, Brigadier General Joseph Moore, Stella Setzer, Major Douglas Logan, Major Durward Brooks, Colonel Tom Dooley, Major Glenn Cave, Colonel Fred Roberts, Commander Kenichi Tanaka and Colonel Allison Ind, author of *Bataan: The Judgment Seat.*

As at Oahu, I traced the attacks at Clark and Iba by air.

The most helpful printed material came from Walter Edmond's extensively researched book, a monograph compiled at the Air University, *Problems of Historiography: Pacific Theatre, Initiation of Air Hostilities in the Philippines, 8 December, 1941,* and *The Brereton Diaries* by Lewis Brereton.

The Japanese historians helped solve to my satisfaction the disputed time element, providing times of departure and attack from Imperial Navy after-action reports. A probable solution to the disagreement about the number of planes to raid Iba and Clark came when the Japanese revealed, for the first time, the embarrassing attack on their own Army planes returning from the Philippines.

Those who have read Wainwright's book may wonder why the phrase, "I was more afraid of you than the bombs," is deleted from Tom Dooley's reply to the general's question: "You didn't drive past Clark during this bombing, did you?" When Colonel Dooley checked the portions about himself he wrote, "General Wainwright told that story many times and I think believed it himself but I was never afraid of him or his reactions. He was a fine man and soldier and I cannot recall any time during our five or six years association that he said an unkind word to me, so no fear of him could have developed. The old man told the story and liked it so he continued it."

CHAPTER 4

Yates McDaniel, now with AP in Washington, D.C., provided the anecdote concerning Vice-Admiral Sir Geoffrey Layton. Other information came from Cecil Brown's book, *From Suez to Singapore;* "Operations in the Far East" by Air Chief Marshal Sir Robert Brooke-Popham; *The Royal Australian Navy* by G. Herman Gill; "Loss of H. M. Ships *Prince of Wales* and *Repulse*" by Vice-Admiral Sir Geoffrey Layton.

CHAPTER 5

Interviewed: Juan Perez, Colonel Ind, Captain Masamichi Fujita, Lieutenant Haruki Iki, Cecil Browne, Admiral Rockwell, Carl Mydans, Robert Taylor (now a brigadier general and deputy chaplain of the Air Force), Jess Villamor, Malcolm Champlin. Champlin, a lawyer in Oakland, has written an unpublished book of his wartime experiences, "One Man's Story." Jess Villamor, who lives in Washington, D.C., is presently writing a book of his adventures. Three useful books detailing different aspects of the sinking of the two great British warships were *Samurai* by Saburo Sakai with Martin Caidin and Fred Saito, H.M.S. *Electra* by Lieutenant Commander T. J. Cain as told to A. V. Sellwood and *Main Fleet to Singapore* by Russell Greenfeld. Captain George McMillin checked the material on Guam.

CHAPTER 6

Admiral Nimitz told how he first learned he was to relieve Kimmel. The incredible story of "The Battle of Lingayen Gulf" came directly from Carl Mydans. Admiral Frank Jack Fletcher himself revealed why he did not relieve Wake Island. The Hong Kong sections are based on accounts given by 43 interviewees, including Tony Weller, Malcolm Swan, Sonny Capell, Bill Stoker, T. J. Cruz, General John Price, Francis Kendall, Dr. L. T. Ride, Alex Dinnen and Douglas Hunt. Leo Landau drove me all over the hilly island, pointing out the various battlefields. Transportation for a tour of the New Territories was provided by Joe Lowe. Other information came from *The Hong Kong Volunteer Defence Corps in The Battle For Hong Kong*, *A Tear for the Dragon* by John Stericker, "Operations in Hong Kong" by Major-General C. M. Maltby and *Japanese Land Operations*.

The scene between Eisenhower and Marshall came from the former's *Crusade in Europe*. Important background information was provided by *Strategic Planning for Coalition Warfare* by Maurice Matlow and Edwin Snell, *United States Submarine Operations in World War II* by Theodore Roscoe, and *Samurai* by Sakai and Caidin.

CHAPTER 7

The Wake Island story is based on interviews with Lieutenant Colonels Clarence McKinstry and Arthur Poindexter, Brigadier Generals Putnam and Devereux, Sergeant Dave Rush, Captain Iwao Kawai and Commander Giichi Kikuchi. Books used were: Devereux's *The Story of Wake Island*, *History of Marine Corps Aviation in World War II* by Robert Sherrod, and *The Defense of Wake* (Marine Corps monograph).

I have known for several years of the claims of Rear Admiral Winfield Scott Cunningham, the Island commander, that he was in sole command and made the decisions at Wake. His book, *Wake Island Commander*, written with Lydel Sims, presents many facts unknown to the general public, but the main fact cannot be altered. Devereux commanded the fighting troops and the fighting decisions were his. While it is true that Cunningham was technically in command of all the service personnel, he was a naval aviator, untrained in land warfare. It was agreed, quite logically, before hostilities that Devereux would coordinate the fighting efforts of the atoll.

For those who revisit old battlefields Wake Island is one of the most evocative. The ruined gun emplacements, the foxholes, the shell cases are still strewn over this coral island. Walking along the deserted beach between Peacock Point and Camp One at night, one can almost see the remodeled Japanese destroyers stealthily heading for shore while the surf booms.

CHAPTER 8

I first listened to the Tony Aquino story at an artificial lake on his huge sugar plantation in the shadow of Mt. Arayat on a sweltering New Year's Eve. This story, among others, was lost when one of my bags was stolen in Hong Kong, but Mr. Aquino obligingly wrote it out in 48 pages.

Former President Osmeña was interviewed in his beautiful home on the island of Cebu. It was time at last, he said, that the world knew the hidden truth of the so-called collaborators. Now that the other principals—Quezon and Laurel—were dead, he felt he could break his promise not to reveal the facts of the important meeting on December 24.

Others who gave valuable firsthand information were Colonel John Horan, Admiral Rockwell, Carlos Romulo, author of *I Saw the Fall of The Philippines,* Colonel William Morse and Captain Hattie Brantley.

Arch Gunnison's book, *So Sorry, No Peace,* was helpful here and in subsequent chapters on Manila. The Roosevelt-Churchill anecdote came from Sherwood's *Roosevelt and Hopkins.*

CHAPTER 9

See Chapter 6 for Hong Kong sources.

Major General Albert Jones gave the information about his participation in the Philippine battles in two long interviews at the Presidio, San Francisco.

CHAPTER 10

The story of the Calumpit bridges came from Generals Jones, Weaver and Casey and Colonel Harry Skerry, whose voluminous papers give a detailed picture of engineer activities in Luzon. Among others interviewed were General Emmett O'Donnell, now Commander in Chief, Pacific Air Forces; President Osmeña, Colonel Allen Stowell, Sergeant Frank Trammell and Corporal Durward Brooks. The story of the looting in Manila came from Carl Mydans and Gunnison's *So Sorry, No Peace.*

CHAPTER 11

The Layac Bridge account is based primarily on information from Colonel Skerry and Colonel Ray O'Day. O'Day's diary, written in prison camp, provided a fund of detail on the entire Philippine campaign.

Two of the most important Japanese contributors begin their stories in this chapter. Colonel Takeo Imai granted permission to use all material in his long article in the *Sunday Nippon*, No. 44, "Tragedy of Fukuyama Regiment: Was It Imperial Headquarters Mistake?" The two lengthy interviews with Lieutenant General Akira Nara in the Sanno Hotel were invaluable. All the information about Colonel Takechi (now deceased) and most of the personal data have never before been revealed, not even to Imperial Headquarters. Other major interviewees were Major Ernest Brown, who now sells cars in San Antonio, General Jones and Colonel Frederick Ward.

CHAPTER 12

Some of the most valuable new information in this and following chapters came from General Clifford Bluemel. Others who contributed greatly were Colonel Rigoberto Atienza, author of an unpublished book, "Retreat to Samat"; Captain John D. Bulkeley (now Commanding Officer, Clarksville Base, Clarksville, Tennessee); Hisamichi Kano; General Sadamu Sanagi; and Major General K. L. Berry (Adjutant General for the State of Texas).

I traveled the entire length of the Abucay Line on Bataan by truck and foot. The long trench, reminiscent of World War I, is still there. Several farmers have built their nipa shacks directly over it.

Accompanying me by foot up the rugged slopes of Mt. Natib were a dozen men of the Philippine Constabulary, armed with rifles, pistols and sub-machine guns. We followed the foxhole line until it disappeared, then continued up the dense slope, which was often steeper than 45 degrees. It seems incredible that Colonel Takechi and his men could have scaled such heights with equipment and mountain guns. Six months after leaving Bataan I learned from my host, Lieutenant Colonel Wilfredo Encarnacion, then Philippine Constabulary Chief of Iloilo, why such a large armed guard had been necessary. Mt. Natib was the hiding place of die-hard Huks, Communist outlaws, and Colonel Encarnacion wrote that he and his men had just captured Linda Bie, the *nom de guerre* of Silvestre Liwanag, Number 3 Huk chief.

The excerpt from Lee's poem "Abucay Withdrawal" came from his book, *Nothing but Praise*. The poems were buried in Luzon before Lieutenant Lee was transferred to Formosa and were recovered only after the war. The talented young man met a tragic death, killed like so many others by an American bomb that sank his prison ship en route to Formosa.

Documentary aids to the Bataan battles included *Armor on Luzon,* The Armored School, Fort Knox, Kentucky, and monographs written at the Fort Benning Infantry School by Major Charles C. Underwood, Major Kary C. Emerson, Major Donald G. Thompson, Major John I. Pray, Major Everett V. Mead, Major Eugene B. Conrad, Major Henry J. Pierce, Major Louis Besbeck, Major John E. Olson, Major Ernest L. Brown, Captain Harry J. Stempin, Major William E. Webb, Major William R. Nealson, Major Brice J. Martin, Major Beverly N. Skardon, and 1st Lieutenant Sheldon H. Mendelson.

CHAPTER 13

Information for the Battle of the Pockets came from Colonel Glen Townsend, author of two unpublished manuscripts, "Defense of the Philippines" and "Documents Pertaining to the War in the Philippines"; Colonel Adrianus van Oosten, author of the monograph, "Operations of the 1st Battalion, 45th Infantry (Philippine Scouts) in the Battle of the Tuol Pocket"; Major Archie McMasters, author of "Memoirs of the Tuol Pocket"; General Berry, General Jones, and Colonel Saburo Watanabe.

It took two days to find the Tuol River and the Pockets. Today the valley between the two extinct volcanoes is nothing like the dense jungle area of the war. Great banana plantations now extend south of the cobblestone road across Bataan. The battle blasted off almost every tree. Even so, the hills and streams are so numerous that guides who had fought in the Pocket battle couldn't recognize the slaughter-ground. On the second day of the search, we finally found the nest of foxholes that Colonel Yoshioka's men had dug in the Big Pocket. Nearby was a pleasant stream, the Tuol River. Some of our party drank from it, but I remembered the bodies clogging the tiny river.

Material on the Points came from Captain Ray Hunt, Jr., author of an unpublished book on his Philippine adventures; *The Dyess Story* by William Dyess; *They Were Expendable* by W. L. White; Colonel Saburo Watanabe; and Colonel Cecil Sanders, author of the monograph, "The Operations of the 57th Infantry (Philippine Scouts) at Anyasan and Silaiim Points."

Since the former road from Mariveles up the west coast is now impassable after about 10 miles, I was flown up and down the coast several times at low level in a small observation plane to see the formidable terrain the Battle of the Points was fought over.

The story of Homma's conference came from Colonel Tatsuo Haki, General Moriya Wada, Lieutenant General Monjiro Akiyama, the unpublished Homma diary, and documents used in the defense of General Homma at his trial. Eijiro Namikawa and Lieutenant General Eiichi Tatsumi gave valuable material concerning General Homma.

The scene between Roosevelt and MacArthur is based on *The Untold Story of Douglas MacArthur* by Frazier Hunt. The Quezon scenes came from his own book, as well as *The Good Fight, Mac-*

Arthur 1941-1951 by Major General Charles Willoughby and John Chamberlain, and from interviews with President Osmeña and Tony Aquino.

CHAPTER 14

This chapter is based mainly on more than a dozen interviews with Yates McDaniel in the Pentagon. Details of the Yamashita-Percival meeting came from General Ichiji Sugita, presently Chief of Staff, Ground Self-Defense Force of Japan and from Ronald McKie (author of *The Heroes,* the suspenseful story of the two Singapore raids), who corresponded at length with the widow of Colonel Wild. Other information came from Newsreel Wong, the Rt. Reverend John Leonard Wilson, now Bishop of Birmingham, and these books and documents: *Suez to Singapore* by Cecil Brown, *Fortress* by Kenneth Attiwell, *Singapore Is Silent* by George Weller, "Operations of Malaya Campaign, from 8th December, 1941, to 15th February, 1942" by Lieutenant-General A. E. Percival; and *Why Singapore Fell* by H. G. Bennett. *The Royal Australian Navy* by G. Herman Gill was useful in this and the next three chapters.

CHAPTER 15

Admiral Conrad E. L. Helfrich gave many of the details for this and the following two chapters. For a complete picture of the battle for the Netherlands East Indies, the two volumes of the Admiral's *Memoirs* must be read. These contain a detailed and accurate picture of the complicated situation. Unfortunately they are in Dutch and probably were not studied carefully, if at all, by some American authors in their accounts of these contentious days.

Readers of Samuel Eliot Morison's extremely readable *Rising Sun in the Pacific* may wonder why the score of U.S. destroyers in Makassar Strait is recorded here as three, instead of four, transports. Japanese survivors of this American raid revealed that one of the transports, the *Tsuruga Maru,* was sunk by a Dutch submarine four hours before the American action.

CHAPTER 16

For the Battle of Java Sea 89 men of four nationalities were interviewed. Chief among these were: Captain H. S. Hamlin, Jr., author of "The *Houston*'s Last Battles" in the May 1946 issue of *Shipmates;* Midshipman Hachiro Kimura; Commander P. O. L. Owen; Commander Yasumi Toyama; Vice Admiral Thomas Binford; Captain William Giles, Jr., author of "War Log of the U.S.S. *John D. Edwards*"; Rear Admiral Edward Parker, now Chief Defense Atomic Support Agency; Captain Joseph Dalton; and Yeoman 3rd Class John Harrell. The book by Commander Cain, *H.M.S. Electra,* was helpful as was the lengthy report by

Rear Admiral Henry E. Eccles, commander of the *John Edwards,* entitled, "The Java Sea Battle."

CHAPTER 17

For the savage engagements following the Java Sea debacle main interviewees were Captain Robert Fulton, Lieutenant Commander Tsujimoto and Senior Lieutenant George Cooper. Rear Admiral Welford Blinn provided documentary information on the sinkings of *Exeter* and *Pope.*

Much of the data on U.S. air activities in Java came from a long statement compiled by Lieutenant Colonel William A. Sheppard and Major Edwin Gilmore.

The story of the sinking of the four Japanese transports in Bantam Bay was told by Commander Shukichi Toshikawa, the man detailed to apologize to General Imamura for his unceremonious immersion. For details of the heroic last hours of the *Perth* I am indebted to Ronald McKie for permitting use of material from his book, *Proud Echo.*

CHAPTER 18

The story of the Mt. Samat attack plan, based on interviews with Colonel Hattori and Captain Nishiura, is another first-told tale. The famous MacArthur PT escape from Corregidor was told by Brigadier General Morhouse, now Air Surgeon of Fifth Air Force, Captain Bulkeley, Colonel Frederick Ward, Admiral Rockwell and General Casey. Useful also were *They Were Expendable* by W. L. White and *MacArthur, His Rendezvous With History* by Courtney Whitney.

The date of leaving Corregidor, March 11, is not a typographical error, although MacArthur's official report and even *Fall of the Philippines* give the date as March 12. This error has been passed down from book to book. Admiral Rockwell and Captain Bulkeley both confirm the March 11 date from their records. Colonel Morse, who met the boats in Mindanao, asserts the arrival was on March 13, not March 14. For details of the flight from Del Monte to Australia 32 people were interviewed including Colonel Morse, Colonel Ind, Captain Monay and Major General Carmichael. Although one man insisted he helped load a refrigerator and a mattress full of gold pesos on the MacArthur plane, the 31 others insisted categorically that General MacArthur and his family took no more than the usual 35 pounds of luggage apiece.

Captain Bulkeley was helpful in correcting important details of certain stories that have gained general credence. He also added a comment on General MacArthur that deserves quotation. "MacArthur was really a man without any fear. He never flinched and was inflexible in his purpose to get to Australia and continue the war against the Nips. A truly inspirational man in all respects and professionally competent in that he let the competent commander run his show if he was good and fired him if he was bad. Also a man of great loyalty and appreciation afterwards."

CHAPTER 19

Based on information from General Bluemel, Jones and Nara, Colonel Atienza, Colonel Tom Dooley, Captain Matt Dobrinic and Captain Hattie Brantley. Official histories of the divisions involved and *I Served on Bataan* by Juanita Redmond were also useful.

CHAPTER 20

Material concerning the last hours of Bataan came from more than 100 men and women. Among them were: General Romulo, Imai, Nara, Jones and Bluemel, Sergeants Frank Bernacki and James Madden, Tony Aquino, and Lieutenants Dan Jopling and Lucy Wilson, who is now Mrs. Jopling.

Details of the surrender were based on testimony of General King, General Funk and Colonel Collier at the Homma trial. Japanese officers testifying for General Homma also gave many details of the events of April 9.

CHAPTER 21

I walked over much of the 55-mile route of the Death March in the hottest part of the day. Along the way Bataan citizens, many of whom had witnessed the tragic parade, were interviewed. More than 100 survivors contributed to this chapter. They include: Colonel O'Day, General Jack Schwartz (now Commandant of Letterman General Hospital), Tony Aquino, Generals Jones, Bluemel, Stevens and Berry, Colonels Aldridge, Browne, O'Connor, Revak and Stowell, Sergeants Grow, Cape, Graef, James, Franklin, Bernacki, Hunt and Duran and Corporal Castleberry. The documents for defense of the Homma trial, Homma's papers and *The Dyess Story* by William Dyess were helpful. Particularly revealing was the thesis written by Stanley Lawrence Falk for his Masters Degree at Georgetown University, 23 May, 1952, entitled, "Bataan Death March."

CHAPTER 22

Information on the Doolittle raid came from General Doolittle, Aviation Chief Machinists Mate Respess, Captain Toshikazu Ohmae and several books, including *Thirty Seconds Over Tokyo* by Ted Lawson. The Bradford story was told by "Jitter Bill" himself, one of the most remarkable fliers in aviation history. Colonel Arthur Fischer, who brought the cinchona seed to the U.S., was also interviewed. His story alone deserves a chapter.

The last days of Corregidor came from Private Ralph Houston, Rear Admiral Dempsey, Colonel Dalness, Lucy Wilson and the article by Colonel William C. Braly, "Corregidor—A Name, A Symbol, A Tradition," in the *Coast Artillery Journal*, July-August, 1947.

I flew over Corregidor several times, finally landing at Kindley Field on the tail of the polliwog. The grass on the old strip was about three feet high and we learned it was the first landing in many years. I spent some time in Malinta Tunnel, exploring the important laterals. The island itself is still a gold mine for scrap collectors. A company of Philippine marines attempts to keep pirates from stealing the great shells which remain in abundance.

CHAPTER 23

The surrender details came from Corporal Irving Strobing, Captain Melvyn McCoy, Colonel Jesse Traywick, Colonel Tom Dooley and the Homma defense papers. Also helpful was the book by newsman Uno, *Corregidor: Isle of Delusion*. Printed during the war, its objectivity is remarkable.

I visited the Castillo home in Cabcaben. The son of the former owner showed me the remains—a few concrete posts. A breeze was blowing in from Manila Bay. Corregidor, only a few miles away, was distinct in every detail. It must have looked the same that day in May almost 20 years ago, except that no columns of smoke were rising from the rock island.

Wainwright's radio speech on the night of May 6-7 over KZRH was taken from a transcript of the short-wave broadcast by the Foreign Broadcast Intelligence Service of the F.C.C. Certain unintelligible words were deciphered by studying a copy of the original draft of Wainwright's speech.

The details of Colonel Traywick's bizarre and historic trip to Mindanao were told by Traywick in San Antonio, where he now lives. This is the first time they have been published. Much of the material concerning the north Luzon area came from a long unpublished account written by Colonel Horan, "The First Five Months of Guerrilla Warfare in Northern Luzon." This too appears for the first time. Additional new material came from General Chynoweth. In addition to a long interview, the general granted permission to use material from his unpublished book "Strange Surrenders."

John H. Skeen, Jr., now a lawyer in Baltimore, was appointed chief counsel for the defense at Homma's trial by authority of General MacArthur; Skeen had only been admitted to the bar in 1941, a year before entering the Army. He was allowed 15 days to prepare the defense, whereas preparation for the prosecution had been going on for some months and apparently had accumulated a great amount of evidence.

Skeen said the trial was not conducted according to recognized legal procedures. Hearsay testimony and affidavits were accepted in evidence with no opportunity for cross-examination of deponents.

He still feels it was wrong for Homma to be tried by authority of a man he had defeated on the field of battle and by whose authority both defense and prosecution personnel were appointed and any appeal would be reviewed. "It was a highly irregular trial, conducted in an atmosphere that left no doubt as to what the ultimate outcome was to be."

This opinion was not his alone. The others on the defense staff signed a letter to General Homma stating they felt he had been unfairly convicted. Equally concerned were two Associate Justices of the U.S. Supreme Court, Wiley Rutledge and Frank Murphy.

"This nation's very honor, as well as its hopes for the future, is at stake," write Murphy. "Either we conduct such a trial as this in the noble spirit and atmosphere of our Constitution or we abandon all pretense to justice, let the ages slip away and descend to the level of revengeful blood purges. . . . A nation must not perish, because in the natural frenzy of the aftermath of war, it abandoned the central theme of the dignity of the human personality and due process of law." While Homma was waiting for sentence he wrote his wife, Fujiko, on January 25, 1946:

To My Wife,

I have already written what I wanted and said almost all I wanted to say. There's no longer anything I want to leave in this world. No, there's a lot. But there's nothing I can do about it being the way I am now. Japan will recover unexpectedly soon. I believe in five years Japan will start a positive step forward.

I'm not afraid of a death sentence. I'm prepared for it. I think I'll be able to face execution with little thought but just thinking the time has finally come. When I was in Omori Prison an army doctor told me it was a painless way to die to be shot to death. It is only that I feel I haven't expressed my thanks enough to my wife. In the twenty years of our married life we've had many differences of opinion and even violent quarrels. Those quarrels have now become sweet memories. You are a righteous person. Unusually righteous, and therefore, you are fearless and strong. You would speak far more irritating words than you meant with your sharp tongue. This used to start our fights. However, in my mind I had absolute confidence in you. In many ways you have offset shortcomings of my character and assisted me in the right sense.

Now as I am about to part from you, I particularly see your good qualities, and I have completely forgotten any defects. I have no worry about leaving the children in your hands because I know you will raise them to be right and strong. I also have no doubt that you will take good care of my mother in Sado after I die. My mother will die a peaceful death attended by you and her grandchildren.

Twenty years feels short but it is long. I am content that we have lived a happy life together.

If there is what is called the other world, we'll be married again there. I'll go first and wait for you there but you mustn't hurry. Live as long as you can for the children and do things I haven't been able to for me. You will see our grandchildren or great-grandchildren and tell me all about them when we meet again in the other world.

Thank you very much for everything.

The last words from Homma came in a letter to his children just before execution:

I don't know if this letter will reach you. But I'm writing because they gave me the paper. I had never thought "a death sentence," "execution by shooting," etc. had any connection with our life, but they have now become the reality before my eyes. Of the 15 condemned prisoners here, only I and Sub-Lieutenant Okuda who is in a cell next to mine are to be shot, the rest will all be hanged. General Yamashita and three others were already executed several days ago. I consider myself luckier to be at least shot to death with the honor of a military man. Your mother as well as all our friends have done their best for my sake. There's nothing more to do but to leave it to fate. [All of you mustn't forget why and because of whom* your father was executed by such severe punishment.] ** There are six men here who have been sentenced for life. It will be better to be shot to death like dying an honorable death on the battlefield than spending a disgraceful life in such a cage the rest of one's life. Don't lose courage, children! Don't give in to temptation! Walk straight on the road of justice. The spirit of your father will long watch over you. Your father will be pleased if you will make your way in the right direction rather than bring flowers to his grave. Do not miss the right course. This is my very last letter.

My address: Three-*jo* (mat) room fenced all
around with wire, about 30 miles
southeast of Manila

CHAPTER 24

The story of Japanese operational planning after the Battle of Java Sea came mainly from Colonel Hattori. American planning for the Battles of Coral Sea and Midway was told by Admirals Nimitz, Spruance and Fletcher. The story of two of the mistakes that lost the Midway battle came from General Genda. He spoke of himself and what he should have done as a third person, with complete objectivity. Mrs. John Waldron checked her husband's story and gave permission to quote his last letter to her. Also helpful were: *Queen of the Flat-Tops* by Stanley Johnston; *Climax at Midway* by Thaddeus Tuleja; the articles, "Never A Battle Like Midway," by J. Bryan, III, from the *Saturday Evening Post*, March 26, 1949, and "Torpedo Squadron 8," *Life* magazine, August 31, 1942; *History of Marine Corps Aviation in World War II* by

* MacArthur

** The bracketed lines were censored. Later a friend sent the censored portions to Mrs. Homma.

Robert Sherrod; and a report by Admiral Soemu Toyoda. Much Japanese material came from the authoritative book, *Midway*, by Mitsuo Fuchida and Masatake Okumiya, edited by Clarke Kawakami and Roger Pineau.

CHAPTER 25

Earl Gallaher gave the details of his two strikes. His personal story has never been told before. Other firsthand information came from the three American admirals responsible for the great victory and Commander Tanabe, who sank the *Yorktown*. The identities and positions of the four Japanese carriers, long disputed, are based on Japanese information and the ingenious reasoning of Thaddeus Tuleja in his book on the battle.

For the section on Philippine guerrillas and underground workers, 64 men and women including Representative Pendatun, Jess Villamor, Wendell Fertig, Dr. Atienza, Fanny Greenwell, William Fossoth, Jr., Frank Bernacki, Lacsamana (brother of the Baluga king), Jim Cushing, Senator Peralta, Salvador Abcede, Colonel Ind, Julian Manansala and Colonel Marking were interviewed. Contrary to the opinion of many American observers who have spent their time almost wholly in the Manila area, today most Filipinos have a deep affection for America. They remember the deadly struggle, the agony of hunger and defeat they shared with us. Anti-American stories to the contrary, the Philippines remain a bridge to the continent of tomorrow, Asia.